Let There Be Light

Social and economic history of science and technology has emerged as a major theme of interdisciplinary research in South Asian history since the late 1990s. This book contributes to the field by exploring the correlation between technological knowledge and industrial performance with a focus on electricity, an emerging technology during 1880 and 1945. The arrival of electricity necessitated the introduction of new institutional facilities and with the growth of technological systems, the culture of entrepreneurship grew – there was demand for trained manpower to handle machines and need for better educational facilities. Taking a broad view of the subject, the narrative is built around the historical experiences of the local Bengali-speaking population in colonial Bengal.

While recent research on science and technology under the colonial rule tends to focus on elite actors – both European and Indian – it is important to identify people, mostly Indians, who excelled in the field of technology, without prior academic training in engineering or science. This monograph brings back focus on the hitherto unexplored vernacular sources and emphasizes that the history of technology in India is basically a history of India, the history of its people, and not simply a history of the Indian techno–scientific tradition as proposed by the literature emerging from the West. Adopting the social constructionist model, it presents an amalgamation of archival and Indian language source materials to delineate the diverse nature of the appropriation of technological ideas into Indian culture.

Suvobrata Sarkar teaches at the Department of History, Rabindra Bharati University, Kolkata, India. His research looks at the social history of technology in colonial India. He was nominated an International Scholar of the Society for the History of Technology for a two-year term, 2016–2017. He is also the recipient of the Maurice Daumas Prize 2019 awarded by the International Committee for the History of Technology.

Let There Be Light

Engineering, Entrepreneurship and Electricity in Colonial Bengal, 1880–1945

Suvobrata Sarkar

CAMBRIDGE
UNIVERSITY PRESS

CAMBRIDGE
UNIVERSITY PRESS

University Printing House, Cambridge CB2 8BS, United Kingdom

One Liberty Plaza, 20th Floor, New York, NY 10006, USA

477 Williamstown Road, Port Melbourne, vic 3207, Australia

314 to 321, 3rd Floor, Plot No.3, Splendor Forum, Jasola District Centre, New Delhi 110025, India

79 Anson Road, #06–04/06, Singapore 079906

Cambridge University Press is part of the University of Cambridge.

It furthers the University's mission by disseminating knowledge in the pursuit of education, learning and research at the highest international levels of excellence.

www.cambridge.org
Information on this title: www.cambridge.org/9781108835985

First published 2020

Printed in India by Thomson Press India Ltd.

A catalogue record for this publication is available from the British Library

ISBN 978-1-108-83598-5 Hardback

Contents

List of Figures vi

Preface vii

Acknowledgements ix

List of Abbreviations xiii

Introduction 1

1 Technical Knowledge and Its Institutes 29

2 Entrepreneurship, Industry, and Technology 78

3 Electrification: The Shaping of a Technology 115

4 Domesticating Electricity 153

5 Assimilation of Technological Ideas 190

Conclusion 244

Bibliography 259

Index 284

Figures

1.1	*Shibpur College Patrika* (1902)	42
1.2	*Journal of the College of Engineering & Technology* (1938)	60
2.1	Howrah–Sheakhalla Light Railway, a dream project of Rajendra Nath Mookerjee	89
2.2	Manufacture of soap at Panihati, BCPW	103
3.1	Laying the underground cables of the CESC (1920s)	118
4.1	An article on X-ray by Dhirendra Nath Bandopadhyay	162
4.2	Dey, Sil & Co. – the pioneering Bengali entrepreneurs in the electrical industry	166
4.3	Bengal Electric Lamp Works, popularly known as Bengal Lamp	171
4.4	Dr B. N. Dey, who prepared an economical electricity generation and supply scheme	179
5.1	Jogesh Chandra Ray, Lecturer of Science, Ravenshaw College	209
5.2	A limerick on the 'Engineer' published in the *Bharatbarsha* (1917)	213
5.3	*Mahajanbandhu*, a monthly periodical of the early twentieth century	216
5.4	An article on the Tata hydro-electric scheme by Chandra Sekhar Sarkar, *Bharatbarsha* (1919)	218
5.5	*Bijoli*, an illustrated Bengali monthly dealing with electricity and things electrical	220

Preface

LET THERE BE LIGHT is a sacred phrase: It is found in Genesis 1: 3 of the Torah. There it is mentioned, in the beginning God created the heavens and the earth. The earth was formless, and darkness prevailed all around. Then God said, 'Let there be Light', and there was light. God saw that light was good and thus separated it from the darkness. God called the light 'day', and the darkness 'night'. However, now in modern times, after sunset, another day emerges – night, with its electric lights, is sometimes brighter than the day! Just imagine what would have been our state of existence without electricity. Modern industry could not exist without it. The transformation of science into economic goods is not new. There have been many instances of scientific ideas transforming into industrial practice since the advent of the Industrial Revolution, the classic example being the electrical industry.[1] What is new is the magnification of this process, including the shortening of the time span between invention and application, and the increased reliance of entrepreneurs on knowledge manufactured in academic institutions.

The significance of the history of technology is realized when technology is understood not simply as an artefact or technique, but as part of the history of a culture and of the social and intellectual development of human civilization. There was a close connection between commercial interests, technological changes, and government policy in India from the early years of British rule. Western technologies are significant, Roy Macleod and Deepak Kumar emphasize, not only as 'tools', but also as forms of knowledge, occasionally mentioned as technical education in the colonial archives.[2] From an artefact to a modern machine, a certain amount of knowledge must be embedded in it. The use of the term 'techno-science' in this book is to explain the application of scientific knowledge (both pure and applied) for technological solutions, sometimes loosely used in the literature as 'engineering sciences'.[3] Several new technologies came to India as colonial baggage. However, Indians were not mere spectators; on numerous occasions they manipulated and contributed to the domestication of modern technologies. The journals, periodicals, and monographs written in Indian languages represented these incidents. The Bengali 'middle-class material' is essential to understand the problems of cultural and linguistic translation inevitable in the formation of a distinct Indian modernity in a non-European context.[4] Thus, the use of specific historical material from middle-class Bengali context is primarily methodological and crucial to trace the psychological dimension of traditional societies' response to new technologies of knowledge.

Recently we have witnessed a great deal of interest and discussion in academic as well as non-academic circles on the problem of how to make India technologically independent – the official slogan is 'Make in India'. Along with other social scientists, historians, especially those engaged with the study of science, technology, and society at large, have also felt the urge to contribute to the current discussion. While a student of history is seldom able to prescribe remedies for the present, one may draw the attention of policy-makers by explaining to them the initiatives already taken by our forefathers in this regard and the possibilities that lay therein. The interface of technology, industry, and public policy presents a demanding and important area of study. This book explores how this interface evolved in the context of colonial Bengal. It brings out the role of both better-known and less-known individuals in the process and the impact this interface had on society at large.

Notes

1. Henry Etzkowitz, Andrew Webster, and Peter Healey, 'Introduction', in *Capitalizing Knowledge*, ed. Henry Etzkowitz, Andrew Webster, and Peter Healey (Albany: State University of New York Press, 1998), 2.
2. Roy Macleod and Deepak Kumar, 'Introduction', in *Technology and the Raj*, ed. Roy Macleod and Deepak Kumar (New Delhi: Sage, 1995), 15.
3. This term delineates the application of mathematical and physical sciences and the principles of engineering analysis to professional and creative work for the construction of structures, machines, equipment, or processes. Daniel Edward Alexander, 'The development of engineering education in the United States', unpublished PhD Thesis, Washington State University, 1977, 1.
4. Dipesh Chakrabarty, *Provincializing Europe* (Princeton and Oxford: Princeton University Press, 2000), 20.

Acknowledgements

This book is a revised version of a doctoral thesis at the Zakir Husain Centre for Educational Studies (ZHCES), Jawaharlal Nehru University (JNU), New Delhi, and while writing it I have received endless help and support besides incurring several academic debts. The largest component of this debt is due to Professor Deepak Kumar, whose intellectual stamp on this book is so clear that it can hardly escape detection. His *Science and the Raj* (2nd Edition, 2006) had been the inspiration which first attracted me to the history of science and technology in colonial India. I am a beneficiary of his style of academic training, which combines rigorous archival research with total intellectual freedom. Professor Kumar has extended me such total support, both emotional and material, that I can unhesitatingly say that without his help the course of my life would have been very different.

To Professor Smritikumar Sarkar, I am indebted for conversations about the history of technology in colonial Bengal and generous advice on many other details that go into the making of a book. Special thanks are due to Professor Suranjan Das, who has read through an earlier version of this argument and has always offered valuable words of encouragement. Stimulating discussions with Professor Ranjan Chakrabarti provided me with invaluable insights. I am also grateful to Professor Ross Bassett, Professor Arun Bandopadhyay, Professor Sujata Mukherjee, and Professor Raj Sekhar Basu for their valuable suggestions and help in developing the theme for the book. Many thanks to Dr Prakash Kumar for his constant encouragement and consistent confidence in the project. Professor Tirthankar Roy was generous with his time and advice.

I must acknowledge my debts to Professor Suchibrata Sen, Professor Chhanda Chatterjee, Professor Sandip Basu Sarbadhikary, Professor Bipasha Raha, Professor Syed Ejaz Hussain, Dr Sangeeta Dasgupta, Dr Arpita Sen, Dr Shouvik Mukhopadhyay, and Dr Subhayu Chattopadhyay at Visva-Bharati and Professor Dhruv Raina at Jawaharlal Nehru University. From all of them, I have learnt much which I have used here.

At Rabindra Bharati University I found amazingly supportive colleagues who created a fertile environment for the development of my ideas. I thank Professor Hitendra

Kumar Patel, Professor Anuradha Kayal, Professor Ashis Kumar Das, Professor Susnata Das, Dr Ajanta Biswas, and Mr Sk Ali Abbas Mamud for their enthusiasm about my work. Professor Nirmalya Narayan Chakraborty and Dr Sahara Ahmed offered thought-provoking conversations and enthusiastic support. Initial ideas for this project were nurtured at the University of Burdwan where I was fortunate to work with Professor Arabinda Samanta, Professor Achintya Kumar Dutta, Dr Sudit Krishna Kumar, Dr Malabika Ray, Dr Aparajita Dhar, Dr Binata Sarkar, Dr Rajarshi Chakrabarty, and Professor Syed Tanveer Nasreen.

I am also indebted to Professor Chittabrata Palit, Professor Arnab Rai Choudhuri, Professor Mahua Sarkar, Professor Sutapa Chatterjee Sarkar, Professor Samir Kumar Saha, Professor S Irfan Habib, Professor Rup Kumar Barman, Dr Madhumita Mazumdar, Dr John Mathew, Dr Jayanta Bhattacharya, Dr B Eswara Rao, Dr John Bosco Lourdusamy, Mr Dhrub Kumar Singh, Dr Madhumita Saha, Dr Y Srinivasa Rao, Dr Sambit Mallick, Dr Radha Gayathri, Dr Aparajith Ramnath, and late Professor Srilata Chatterjee for showing a keen interest in my work and for constant encouragement. Dr Neelam Kumar had been extremely encouraging about this project and had patiently provided me with much-needed support.

Sections of the research had been presented at seminars in the Annual Meeting of the Society for the History of Technology (SHOT), National University of Singapore; Bern University, Switzerland; Indian National Science Academy (INSA), New Delhi; Indian Institute of Technology (IIT) Madras and Guwahati; Bankura University, West Bengal; and Itihas Academy Dhaka, Bangladesh. The opportunity that the organizers provided to share ideas and the comments of fellow participants are gratefully acknowledged. Special thanks are due to Dr David N Lucsko, Dr George Wilkenfeld, Dr Christiane Berth, and Dr Yovanna Pineda.

My research would not have been possible without the generous financial support provided by various institutions. Initially, it was funded by the University Grants Commission (UGC) – as the Rajiv Gandhi National Fellowship (RJNF) which enabled me to complete my Ph.D. thesis. A timely grant from the Charles Wallace (India) Trust and the Indian Council of Historical Research's (ICHR) Foreign Travel Grant enabled me to do some follow-up research. I would especially like to thank Mr Richard Alford, Secretary, Charles Wallace (India) Trust, and Dr Antonia Moon, Lead Curator, India Office Records, British Library, for their guidance and help.

I take this opportunity to thank the librarians and staff of West Bengal State Archives, National Library, Bangiya Sahitya Parishad Library, Centre for Studies in Social Sciences Calcutta, Jadavpur University Library, West Bengal State Secretariat Library, Ramakrishna Mission Institute of Culture Library, Rabindra Bharati University

Library at Kolkata; Burdwan University Library, Bardhaman; Indian Institute of Engineering, Science & Technology Library, Sibpur; National Archives of India, Nehru Memorial Museum & Library, Jawaharlal Nehru University Main Library and ZHCES Seminar Library in New Delhi; Institution of Engineering & Technology Archives, and the British Library in London; and Centre of South Asian Studies Archive, University of Cambridge, Cambridge.

Endless thanks to my editor, Qudsiya Ahmed, and the entire team at Cambridge University Press, especially Sohini Ghosh and Aniruddha De, for their interest, patience, and support. They oversaw the transition of the draft manuscript into a book. I am grateful to my anonymous readers for their insights and incisive suggestions.

An earlier version of chapter 4 had originally been published in *The Indian Economic and Social History Review*, Vol. 52, No. 3 Copyright 2015 © The Indian Economic and Social History Association. Similarly, parts of chapter 3 had been originally published in *Studies in History*, Vol. 34, No. 1 Copyright © 2018 Jawaharlal Nehru University, New Delhi (All rights reserved. Reproduced with the permission of the copyright holders and the publishers, SAGE Publications India Pvt. Ltd, New Delhi).

Jyoti Arora's friendship sustained me through some of the toughest times in my life. My debt to her is immense. In Rashmi Sharma I have found the firmest and the most dependable friend. Ajeet Thakur has been more than a brother! Shilpi Rajpal and Abhik Mukherjee's intellectual support, warmth, and help has made my research and work very stimulating.

I remain in debt to Ma, Babi, Masi, and Bhai. Their love and ready willingness to support all my endeavours sustain me. It will be a matter of great regret that my father-in-law was not able to see this book. He kept full faith in me when I was struggling as a cub-researcher. Chordibhai was a source of support and good food. Duggu has regularly reminded me that there is more to life than my study-desk and computer.

Finally, 'some' component of my debt is owed to Sneha, my fellow-traveller, as well! She has been with me constantly through all the highs and lows, the excitement and the depression that a long project like this inevitably entails. This book is as much hers as it is mine.

Abbreviations

AICTE	All India Council for Technical Education
BCPW	Bengal Chemical & Pharmaceutical Works Limited
BELW	Bengal Electric Lamps Works
BISCO	Bengal Iron & Steel Company
BL	British Library
BNC	Bengal National College
BNCCI	Bengal National Chamber of Commerce & Industry
BP	British Pharmacopoeia
B.S.	Bangla San (Bengali Year)
BTI	Bengal Technical Institute
CESC	Calcutta Electric Supply Corporation Ltd
CET	College of Engineering & Technology
CIT	Calcutta Improvement Trust
CMG	*Calcutta Municipal Gazette*
CSAS	Centre of South Asian Studies
CTC	Calcutta Tramways Company
CWIT	Charles Wallace (India) Trust
DPI	Directorate of Public Instruction
GSI	Geological Survey of India
HESI	Hydro-Electric Survey of India
IACS	Indian Association for the Cultivation of Science
ICOHTEC	International Committee for the History of Technology
IEI	Institution of Engineers (India)
IET	Institution of Engineering and Technology
IIEST	Indian Institute of Engineering, Science and Technology, Sibpur
IISCO	Indian Iron and Steel Company
IIT	Indian Institute of Technology
IJHS	*Indian Journal of History of Science*
INSA	Indian National Science Academy

JNU	Jawaharlal Nehru University
MIT	Massachusetts Institute of Technology
MPI	Miscellaneous Public Improvement Branch
NAI	National Archives of India
NCE	National Council of Education
NPC	National Planning Committee
PWD	Public Works Department
SHOT	Society for the History of Technology
SCOT	Social Construction of Technology
SPTE	Society for the Promotion of Technical Education
STS	Science and Technology Studies
TISCO	Tata Iron and Steel Company Limited
WBSA	West Bengal State Archives
ZHCES	Zakir Husain Centre for Educational Studies

Introduction

> Perhaps, it is too early yet to judge of the results of a movement which began in right earnest not more than a decade ago. But I am constrained to sound a note of warning and to try to dispel an illusion, more, because of the share, however, humble, I have had in the Technical Education movement, and because, I confess, I have been under the illusion myself. The illusion is, that with the progress of technical education and with persistent endeavour, India will gradually become studded with factories after the manner of the flourishing countries of Europe owned and managed by Indians.
>
> —P. N. Bose, the noted geologist and science enthusiast, in 1916[1]

> Many consider an electrification is luxury even today. But this is not true. We know the electrification leads to rapid industrialization. The recent industrial growth of our country creates huge demand for continuous power supply. Use of the diesel engine is economical compared to the steam engine on several reasons. To fulfil the huge industrial demand, we need plenty of such engines for power supply without an interruption. How long we will depend on the foreign counties for supply of these engines? Or shall we try to manufacture such engines in our country itself?
>
> —Jatindranath Basu, Professor at the Bengal Technical Institute (1928)[2]

Recent scholarship has recognized well the significance of technology in understanding the history of modern India. During the second half of the twentieth century, the 'colonial world' became a prominent research focus for historians, and the history of modern technology is written in the backdrop of the empire. The history of technology on the subcontinent thus framed narrates a general story about the character of empire and the other forces that shaped this history up until independence in 1947. But today historians of technology share an interest in the history of knowledge,[3] the relation between the global and the local, and the role played by experts and know-how. As Karel Davids rightly observes, 'software' has become as crucial as 'hardware' for technology's storytellers; information techniques are as important as instruments and machines.[4]

Today, most industrialized states in the world attempt to secure the most effective utilization of their respective knowledge base. Creating science-based industries from academic research is a common theme of industrial policy, which is constructed based on a new relationship between universities and industry, involving transfer of technology as well as access to trained personnel. Transfer of knowledge to industry was theoretically available through the literature.

But in practice, industry needed relationships with academic engineers to translate this knowledge to the functional level. During the twentieth century, the need to produce highly trained engineers to meet the demands of industry became a subject of serious concern in India. Very different solutions to the problem appeared from different quarters, and these duly engaged the attention of the government, business circles, and intellectuals.

The need for a historical consciousness for the rejuvenation of the techno-scientific base of India is widely recognized today. The relevance of the study of modern Indian history in this respect arises from the fact that the pattern of technological development (or underdevelopment?) of post-independence India depends, to a considerable extent, upon its inherited structure of techno-science from the British Raj. Here historians have essentially tried to show how the task of providing advanced technical instruction in various institutions was proposed in several very diverse political, economic, and social contexts. They have examined these diverse variables which they saw as crucial in fashioning not just the course of educational development but also that of industry.

Thus, both education and industry appear as the products of the same multifaceted social, cultural, and economic background that accelerate the techno-scientific advancement of any country.[5] Already, between the mid-nineteenth century and the Second World War, the industrialized and industrializing countries of Europe and America had made some provision, often of an elaborate kind, for the preparation of their engineers. What was new during this period was the emergence of institutions and courses that aimed specifically to prepare technical employees for work at manufacturing industries. Western techno-scientific discourse occupied an extremely important place in the colonization of India. It is well known that Western technology and ideas influenced various technological projects in the colony, including education.[6] This study is basically on the education of engineers as it had evolved and developed in the late years of the Raj, and the interface it had with entrepreneurship and industry in Bengal. The twentieth century was to be the age of electricity. The transition from technical education to electrical engineering is well documented, and care has also been taken to situate it within the larger social, political, and economic context vis-à-vis an emerging Indian modernity. This study hopes to investigate, in addition, the governmental and popular concern about technology which shaped the electrification of Calcutta – the second city of the empire – and the perceptions and responses (thoughts and practices) of the politicians, bureaucrats, engineers, and residents that helped in shaping the electrification process.

The Historiographical Foundation of Technology

We might well question the value of studying the history of technology. As Reinhard Rurup claims, 'Technology is a basic element in historical process; without the history of technology one cannot grasp the history of modern socioeconomic structures and dynamics.'[7] Hence the need to integrate the history of technology into general history. What then are or should be the common talking points of the history of technology? Before we suggest how this question might be answered, let us glance through some of the answers which have already, in effect, been given. Cardwell says that the modern interest in the history of technology, in the context of Britain, shows itself in at least four different ways. In the first place, there is the enthusiasm for industrial archaeology, which was truly unique, and these should be preserved for prosperity. Second, there are the efforts of the general historians and of the economic historians. They have written several illuminating studies of the ways in which technology has contributed to the general progress of society and to the growth of wealth. Third, there are 'antiquarians' who take specific objects, or families of objects, and study them to the exclusion of all else. Cardwell has added another complementary approach – it is possible to envisage a history of technology which is closely related to the history of science and to the history of ideas generally. Technology so regarded is not to be thought of as a 'dependent variable', drawing its concepts from science; rather, it is an equal partner enriching the human civilization.[8]

It is interesting to see how a historiographical account regarding the relation between techno-science and the British Empire can be considered as a model. Prakash Kumar identifies two parallel tracks for the study of science and technology in South Asian history – the colonial science (technology) and the social history of science (technology) in colonial South Asia. The first league of scholars, while analysing broader questions of colonialism and modernity, explores the transfer and movement of knowledge, science, and technology as tools of empire, and the nature of engagement between Western and native knowledge systems. Second, the social study of science and technology in South Asian historiography has emerged from the traditions of exploring knowledge as a social form – the different interpretations of knowledge, the flexibility of the local society, and the place of native traditions have left their permanent imprint within this scholarship. With the passage of time, both underwent significant changes: Historians of colonial science rectified their earlier simplistic assumptions that modern knowledge was of Western roots and that it gradually diffused to the rest of the world. Instead, they started focusing on the local development of techno-science in the colony.

The British Raj was unable to completely dislocate the traditional knowledge base. Thus, for a better understanding of the emerging Indian modernity, the historians of South Asia started arguing for an exploration of the collisions and contestations between European and Indian knowledge forms in a local context.[9]

In terms of recent scholarship, which has gathered momentum since the 1990s, much interpretive analysis is to be found in works emanating from other historical sub-disciplines – economic history, cultural history, environmental history, medical history, and, most prominently, history of science – which have brought their own agenda to the discussions on technology. History of science in India has a particularly seminal role in identifying and investigating technology-related issues. But as early as the 1950s, the question of who is best suited to tell the story of technological change has been debated in Western academia.[10] With the foundation of the Society for the History of Technology (SHOT) in America (1958), history of technology received recognition as a distinct sub-discipline.

To understand this history of technology several approaches are evident in the literature, approaches to solve the 'black box' equations of technology. Within the orthodox history of technology, the internalist approach focuses on endogenous technological development. As opposed to decoding the internal logic of the development of technology, the external approach is attentive to the cultural context and not just the technological design. The contextualist approach attempts to integrate two characteristics: the design of technology and its historical ambience.[11] These approaches have been applied, according to John M. Staudenmaier, to four key problems in the history of technology: technological creativity, the science–technology relationship, the American system of manufactures, and electricity. Of late, two additional items have appeared on the agenda of the history of technology. The first is the inclusion of workers and technicians into the narrative of technology and, second, an agenda of rectification visible in the absence of non-Western technology and related ideological perspectives.[12] The literature on the history of technology has lately grown in both volume and complexity.

David Arnold identifies three main approaches since the mid-1960s: The first approach, equating technology with 'industrial technology' as developed in Europe and North America, saw the establishment of modern technology in the non-European world as primarily a legacy of colonial intervention. Conceived and created in the West, such technologies were diffused to the rest of the world almost entirely 'through European agency and without significant local input'. The second approach points out that numerous Asian societies had long and noteworthy histories of technology of their own, some of which not only preceded, but even contributed to those Europe is commended for. But these were somehow superseded by colonialism and international capitalism. The third approach, categorized as 'postcolonial' by Arnold, looks temporarily beyond the colonial moment to its consequences and draws its 'interpretive inspiration from the contemporary movement of postcolonial criticism'.[13] James Secord rightly observes that historians of science and technology of whatever school are unanimous about the 'circulatory property of knowledge'.[14]

From Diffusion to Circulation: Concepts and Contours

Historical studies of science and technology outside the West have focused mainly on bringing to light the contributions of non-Western cultures to the ocean of modern knowledge on the one hand, and on the diffusion and response to modern science and technology on the other. The most influential statement of the diffusionist model of Western science was made by George Basalla in 1967, and though it now appears passé and one-dimensional, it is still worth summarizing as the basis for much of the ongoing discussion of the history of science. Basalla presented a three-phase linear evolutionary framework to explain the spread of Western science (and technology) to extra-European territories.[15] The idea of diffusion inspired other studies as well throughout the 1980s. These scholars see modern science and technology as the hegemonic 'master narrative' of Western power, a discursive creation through which the rest of the world was gradually conquered.[16]

But perhaps Basalla's later work is more relevant so far as the history of technology is concerned. For him, continuity exists between artefacts and they are not unique but rather related to what has been made before. Such continuity, he argues, has been disguised by the 'myth of the heroic inventive genius, by nationalistic pride, by the patent system', and by the tendency to link technological change with social, scientific, and economic revolutions. Technological knowledge has often been transferred from one culture to another and thus ushered in technological diffusion.[17] But can this be applied to a colonial situation?

Thus, Basalla's thesis has been more critically engaged with three major themes: the non-West as a scientific (technological) tabula rasa, diffusionism, and colonial scientific policy. His critiques have brought forth the discriminatory character of science and technology in the colony and have argued that 'diffusion' hinders the normal reception and appropriation of the receiving society at the time of techno-scientific transfers. For example, if one takes a long-term view, patterns of technological diffusion have clearly not been from Europe alone. Historically, technologies have travelled in several different directions, and not simply outwards from Europe. Arnold Pacey has developed the concept of what he calls 'technological dialogue'. It was the inventive exchange of different technologies that took place between different regions of Asia.[18] According to Roy Macleod and Deepak Kumar, the history of technology is no longer the story solely of machines. Technologies do not operate in a vacuum – they have a specific socio-economic and cultural context. Technology and society exist in an 'intricately interwoven' relationship. Technology, whether as tool or form of knowledge, is not value-free; it always manifests political qualities. In colonial conditions, it naturally acquired the contours of the colonial power, both commercial and administrative.[19] The idea of science and technology having a European centre and a periphery created a confusing understanding of the relations of techno-scientific knowledge and locale. Ian Darbyshire has shown that the building of the railways in India was not a case of transfer of European technology in an 'undiluted form'; instead, 'a new syncretic Indian approach' developed and was used throughout the construction process. Here 'syncretism' means a method that combined the Indian and Western experiences in way-levelling, plate-laying, tunnelling, bridge-building, and so forth.[20]

The colonies were themselves significant sites of technological innovation – this might be through direct borrowing and adaptation from indigenous practices and local knowledge. S. Irfan Habib and Dhruv Raina think that 'the standard tale of assimilation of modern science as a Western cultural import was inadequate and missed out the multifarious nature of exchange between modern science and so-called traditional knowledge forms'.[21] Some technologies developed first in the colonies for reasons that had much to do with the local environment and social conditions or economic and political circumstances, and then were brought to Europe. The expansion of colonial power and the production of techno-scientific knowledge were symbiotically related and, in the process, India served as an arena for the construction of a large-scale scientific research system. Zaheer Baber explores the immanent connection between instruction on science and technology in India and the emergence of the colonial capitalist state.[22] This required that the colonial state be innovative in the founding of formal technical institutions. Because until the end of the nineteenth century, England had no formal institutions imparting technical education, and engineers received their training as apprentices, the engineering schools established in colonial India served as models for replication in England and the colonial encounter contributed to the development of technical education in Britain.[23]

The mobility and spread of techno-scientific knowledge beyond their site of origin has become another major focus of the recent scholarship. It has been convincingly shown that scientific and technological knowledge and practices are neither characteristically universal nor forcibly imposed on others. Rather, they disseminate only through complex processes of accommodation and negotiation. Kapil Raj argues that the term 'circulation' serves as a strong counterpoint to the Eurocentric concept of 'diffusion'. This can even replace binaries like metropolitan science/colonial science or centre/periphery, which all imply a producer and an end user.[24] The circulatory perspective allows one to see techno-scientific knowledge as being co-produced through the encounter and interaction between heterogeneous specialist communities of diverse origins.

Zooming in on the Local

Contending with historical developments of global dimension requires us to consult the complexities of local settings and the exchanges they housed. David Chambers and Richard Gillespie introduced the 'locality approach' which focuses on the local dimensions. Their intention is to highlight the local intellectuals and socio-economic interests in the 'colonial world' that stood to gain or lose by the introduction of modern techno-science.[25] They use the terms 'local' and 'locality' flexibly to indicate 'places' in which science is accomplished. A locality may be a region, country, city, or even a single institution, combining social, cultural, political, and economic factors. How does one articulate the place of knowledge or the locality of science (technology)?

Until recently, a scientific locality was defined simply by nominating a local frame of reference within which one may examine the role of knowledge construction and inculcation. The history of colonial science is arguably little more than the gradual connection of the locality into the global scientific communications network, which historically was based in and controlled by the metropolitan centre. But this network is more than a science system, more than just an information exchange. As Warwick Anderson suggests, it is also instrumental to social control, commodity transaction, exploitation, and appropriation: 'The recognition that even the most formally structured technical knowledge may be implicated in colonial accumulation and acquisition is long overdue.'[26] In the whole gamut of literature, the indigenous knowledge systems take almost the centre stage. The locality approach allows the voice of the colonized and subjugated cultures to be heard in their own terms. Perhaps the local/global debate will not end here, but the local will be reinforced and the opportunity of mutual exchange and contribution will be increased.

The advocates of the 'locality approach' believe that as modern techno-science is rooted in the social, cultural, and intellectual context that produced it, the best way to write a balanced history of science and technology in South Asia is to unearth the local knowledge traditions that went through several reformulations with the introduction of European science. Concepts like colony and empire are basically the products of a moment in history. By adopting this approach, we can avoid another great divide, for example, historians of science writing about metropole and historians of colonial science writing about peripheries separately.

Claudio Canaparo, while discussing the histories of empires in relation with the transmission of techno-scientific knowledge, considers empire as a 'substitute notion', which is relevant only if placed in its 'geo-epistemological' context. This approach tries to establish a link between spatial location (geography) and conceptual evolution (knowledge), and to see how each location develops a specific way of conceiving knowledge.[27] With this approach one can tackle the question of knowledge generation and transmission more accurately while making it more intertwined with a local space rather than with a global-imperial conception.

Techno-scientific Knowledge and Indian Modernity: *Technomodernity*

The transmission of techno-scientific knowledge between Europe and Asia has been dominating the literature for the last couple of years. The complication of the transmission process, which comprises the contexts of diffusion and reception, the centre–periphery relationship, the cross-cultural interactions, and many other fascinating questions, continues to capture the attention of scholars. Recent advances in the history of science and technology have demonstrated a new sensitivity to the non-Western contributions towards the emergence of contemporary global technomodernities. As Lissa Roberts argues, it is essential to capture the ways in which local exchanges and global circulation concurrently shaped scientific and technological developments and integrated them with the broader political, economic, and cultural developments in history. Thus, one can appreciate the role played by science and technology in shaping modernity.[28]

David Arnold also prefers to deal with science and technology in colonial India in terms of modernity. Such knowledge was closely associated with both colonial and indigenous concepts of what created the modern world; as Arnold continues, 'it gave shape and authority to the understanding of modernity'.[29] Gyan Prakash also argues in a somewhat similar line. He argues that the Indian imagination of the nation (a hybridized concept) was not a mere imitation of colonial modernity, but rather 'actualized India as a culturally rooted moral community with a rational will to industrialize and achieve technological mastery'. It was the nation's coming into being in 'modernity'.[30] These questions of middle-class identity formation and its role in framing local modernities also raise fundamental questions about the nature of modernity itself. This apparently did not mean everyone was equally modern or perceived as such by either themselves or their contemporaries. Religion, caste, gender, urbanity, education, and so on, made Bengali modernity partial and selective.[31] Dipesh Chakrabarty talks about two 'conceptual gifts of nineteenth-century Europe', concepts integral to the idea of modernity, 'historicism', and 'the very idea of political'.[32] European thought is both indispensable and inadequate in understanding the arrival of modernity in countries outside the Western capitalist democracies. Chakrabarty admits that the evolution of modernity in India is different from its evolution in Europe.[33] The traditional knowledge that Indians inherited played a significant role in the formation of Indian modernity, in addition to the role played by Western knowledge.

The Bengali Ayurvedic modernity is identified as a 'technomodernity' by Projit Mukherji because in the early twentieth century it was materialized around a series of small technological objects and instruments. These minor technologies gradually and fundamentally altered the way these practitioners of indigenous medicine imagined and understood the human body. These small-scale technologies often acquired new genealogies or pasts. It was part of the process of reframing their identities. Such new pasts, as identified by Mukherji, frequently sought to indigenize these technologies by finding local antecedents. These identities were sometimes unpredictable due to the heterogenous traditions of knowledge through which Ayurveda evolved. Thus, it was not simply a matter of recreating the identity of an object or a concept passing from one monolithic culture to another. 'It was rather', Mukherji argues, 'reimagining the possibilities of a technological object at the interface of myriad culture, intellectual, and practical traditions.'[34]

Contested Terrain: Technical Education, Engineering, and Industry

Historians of science and technology, with some exceptions, have paid little attention to the educational aspects to the transmission of modern science. The history of technical education in India during the period 1880–1945 is of special significance since it is marked by a growing interest in techno-scientific education; it witnessed the maturity of several institutions at various levels, and was characterized by intense debates on the scope, character, and relevance of such education in the Indian context. Technical knowledge and ideology can be actively redefined in the local setting by the recipient culture. The receiving society, far from being a dump or flat, 'subverts, contaminates, and reorganizes the ideology of science as introduced by Europe'.[35]

In this context, Madhumita Majumdar asks: how did the political image of Indian science evolve and take shape vis-à-vis Indian participation in professional scientific practice at the close of the nineteenth century? She argues that the emerging profession of modern science and the cultural politics of middle-class nationalism in colonial India were ideologically distinct; however, the pedagogic role of science was propagated in the nationalist political discourse. Majumdar makes a plea for a serious engagement with science's links with the shifting imperatives of cultural nationalism which is evident in the representation of scientists as nationalist icons.[36] Dhruv Raina states that the history of science has inadequately addressed the concept of localization of science since it is separated from the history of education. On the contrary, the history of education has searched for the pre-history of educational innovations in England: resulting as an encounter between oriental and occidental knowledge practices in India. Raina also talks about the connection between localization and globalization of science. He emphasizes on the dynamics of the flow of knowledge and its adaptation to different institutional contexts.[37] Thus, the recent historiography has questioned the diffusion of knowledge as a key element of the interaction between Britain and her colonies like India. Instead, Raina claims, the notion of 'appropriation' is a more coherent and fruitful analytical instrument.

Raina later argues that the analytical tools of the history of science, namely the transmission, circulation, and reception of scientific ideas and cognitive movements, are equivalent with the history of education's interest in the transmission of theories and the inculcation of methods and disciplines in communities and generations of students in schools and colleges.[38] Similarly, Jahnavi Phalkey traces the academic roots of India's nuclear research to universities and laboratories. An Indian community of physicists was convinced to build within the country the facilities and capabilities required for international standards in nuclear physics research. Phalkey shows that the choice of creating 'a centralized top-class research facility' in nuclear research (both time and resource intensive) was substituted by continuous support for broad-ranging physics education and research in Indian universities in the twentieth century, which yielded an interesting result.[39]

Engineers were at the centre of numerous discussions between the state, commercial bodies, and other social actors in post-independence India. One R. C. Goel commented at the first Indian Engineering Congress, Calcutta (1987), '... technological innovation for new engineering educational policy should be aimed to broaden the imagination and enhance the ability of our scientists, engineers and planners and prepare the country for the fast changes taking place in the outside world.'[40] The literature on the trajectory of engineers in India remains highly underdeveloped and it is only recently that a research field has begun to emerge. W. H. G. Armytage described the subcontinent as the 'Indian laboratory' and claimed that the challenging environment of India sharpened the technological acumen of British engineers.[41]

In his study of the engineering profession (in the three key sectors: public works, railways, and private industry) in early twentieth-century India, Aparajith Ramnath finds science and technology not simply as a harbinger of modernity or as a knowledge system, but also as a force to serve certain fundamental administrative and economic functions. Until the nineteenth century, the profession was dominated by British engineers, mostly civil, employed in the various government departments. Later, the profession was diversified to include mechanical and electrical engineers engaged in large-scale industry. In the beginning, the colonial engineers defined the working culture, and were very apprehensive about the quality of Indian engineering education and the maintenance of working standards. As India's status in the empire was negotiated and renegotiated in the early twentieth century, the fate of Indian engineers also started changing accordingly. The increasing proportion of 'native' engineers during this time was the result of the evolution of the economic and political relationship between Britain and India (Indianization). Citing examples of Indian bureaucrats in the central and provincial services, technical personnel attached with the Tata Iron and Steel Company Limited (TISCO), and the formation of the Institution of Engineers (India), Ramnath questions the viability of using terminologies like 'colonialism' and 'nationalism'.[42]

Deepak Kumar emphasizes the importance of dialogues and conversations (adoption and adaptation) at the time of knowledge production and dissemination. As transmission is no longer seen as originating from a powerful centre, we need to think beyond: It is a much more complex process. It could be socio-cultural as well as politico-economic. Changes are not always forced or persuaded from above or outside; these can come from within and on their own. Kumar talks about the disparity apparent in the techno-scientific policies for development both in the government circle and the nationalist camp; each imagined and formulated their own road map for material development of India in the first half of the twentieth century.[43] Here perhaps Ross Bassett's thesis on the importance of international, extra-imperial networks in the development of techno-scientific knowledge is worth a mention. He identifies a group of Indians who studied at the Massachusetts Institute of Technology (MIT) with the sponsorship of the princely states. These MIT-trained engineers, after their return to India, became successful entrepreneurs, and their 'technological identity' was shaped during their interaction with America.[44] One can identify such tendencies in the context of early twentieth-century Bengal too, when students visited Germany and the United States in large numbers to study technology, completely bypassing Britain.

The New History of Technology

David Arnold and Erich Dewald claim technology's social fashioning is a more difficult concept to employ in an Asian colonial context than in relation to the far more autonomous European and North American industrial societies. These were not designed and manufactured locally, but in the West. The social construction of these technologies in a colonial or semi-colonial setting perhaps takes a different form. How various technologies were locally accepted or rejected depended on significant 'local emendation and reinvention to match the local cultural norms and social usages'.[45] There has been a growing interest in small-scale, 'everyday technologies', from the sewing machine to the wristwatch, radio, typewriter, bicycle, and so on, along with the 'big technologies' such as steamships, railways, telegraphs, hydro-electric projects, and so on, in writing the history of technology. Colonial regimes were unable to monopolize or were disinclined to control the 'everyday technologies', and, according to Arnold, these technologies passed with relative ease into the work regimes, social life, and cultural aspirations of the colonized and postcolonial populations.[46]

It was not possible to avoid the entire regime of modern technologies that came to India as colonial baggage. Irrespective of their size, they created a permanent imprint on the psyche of the colonized. As recently shown by Smritikumar Sarkar, the bioscope, petromax light, gramophone, along with the conventional technologies such as the railways, telegraph, steamer, and new roads and bridges, could be 'development rolling out of the metropolis to the periphery'. Not only did it end the physical and cultural isolation of the village, but it also carried new tastes and demands to the interior. Along with the connectivity of space, Sarkar argues, technology also enhanced 'communion of minds'.[47] The recent emphasis on 'everyday technologies' does not mean that big technologies should not be researched or reworked. Sarkar demonstrates that it is possible to write a history of technology in South Asia that does not discriminate between 'big' and 'small' technologies, and in which the voices of the colonial regime are analysed alongside that of ordinary Indians – the peasantry, artisans, and so on.

Taking an uncritical view of history as providing the context for a technology, David Edgerton problematizes the fact that the very 'context' also should be an object of analysis. Then one should try to find out 'the nature of technology and its relations to wider culture'. Writing 'post-contextual' histories of technology, Edgerton implies, can advance our understanding of history itself.[48] It is more important to find out about how science and technology travel, not whether they belong to one culture or another. As Asif A. Siddiqi has recently articulated, the patterns of local transactions are very important, 'that were understood as – or in some cases, gave rise to – global meanings and/or universalist claims, whether grounded in geography, time or communities'.[49] A different milieu, culture, tradition, and existing indigenous knowledge systems provided the context in which the gradual spread of Western knowledge occurred, followed by its adaptation and articulation through various reformulations.[50] Another lacuna is the undue focus on elite actors – both European and Indian. While admitting that elite actors were important for outlining the standard trope of Indian science and technology, the recent works try to unearth the personalities (practices), forgotten by the state as well as their fellow countrymen, who (which) significantly contributed to the knowledge production system of India.[51]

While analysing technological modernity, these scholars try not to overlook the impact of colonialism. Instead they ask what impact colonialism had in the incorporation of South Asia into global networks of technology and the dissemination of various technologies – networks that stretched far beyond the limits of equation between the metropolis and the periphery. They also identify the achievement of these technologies in the context of South Asia, which can be found more in the vernacular publications than in the repositories of the state. The aim of the book is to locate such sources written in Bengali to understand the appropriation of modern technological knowledge in Bengal. But this is not to be a comprehensive survey of what Bengali thinkers were writing. It seeks to do a very limited job: to point the reader in the direction of some major issues that surfaced in contemporary Bengali journals and periodicals on technological themes.

Locating Electricity in South Asian History: Interactive Expansion of Utilities, Academia, and Industry

In the summer of 1896, two brothers met in London – Narendra Nath Datta, then already famous as Swami Vivekananda, and his younger brother, Mahendra Nath. The latter had gone there to study law. However, Narendra Nath insisted that he learn electrical engineering in New York, which, according to him, was the centre of excellence then. The saint was obsessed with electricity, especially after his visit to America just prior to the London trip: 'America is full of electricity.' He wanted his fellow countrymen to learn the intricacies of electricity in America and on their return spread the knowledge of this technological marvel back home. He strongly believed in the developmental aspects of electricity.[52] Electricity was not a new subject in the nineteenth century, but it was then that electricity was to receive its greatest theoretical extension and, in the form of the telegraph, become an indispensable part of social life. It was with the introduction of the electric telegraph in India, as in Britain, that the profession of electrical engineering came into existence.[53] Yet it was only at the end of the century, with the development of electric light and electric power, that its full practical capacities were beginning to be realized.

Interests in the interdisciplinary studies of technology have expanded in the last twenty years, raising new questions in response to contemporary developments. Some studies have looked at the ways in which foreign technology was adopted and adapted in Asia. Others have looked at how techno-scientific knowledge from Asia has travelled across the globe. Here one technology is surprisingly missing, at least in the South Asian context – electricity. Western academia has long traditions of study of the history of electricity and the power industry from the days of the magnum opus *Networks of Power* (1983). Comparing the American and European scenarios, Thomas Hughes illustrates that electrification follows a pattern from invention to development, innovation, transfer, growth, competition, consolidation, and rationalization. Each stage involves different people and institutions.[54] Hughes focusses on Western industrialized societies, which are not typical to most of the world. Electrification was not a natural activity (it came as colonial baggage) in India and took shape in a different way from its development in the West. The relationship between electricity and society in the backdrop of colonialism was somehow absent in the literature until recently in South Asia.

Electrification was a science-based high technology that demanded educated technicians and scientists as well as enormous amounts of capital and industrial capability. According to Jonathan Coopersmith, electricity does little that cannot be done by other technologies and energy sources. In its modest applications, he argues, electricity replaced those sources, but 'in its more advanced and developed forms, conceived within a broader systematic context, electricity could radically transform a workplace, an industry, and even a nation'.[55] Around 1900, in many countries of the world, manufacturers tended to replace mechanical with electrical systems to run their prime movers, and shortly thereafter, started purchasing power from the utilities. Domestic and public use took off after the utilities consolidated themselves. These were significant transitions, and each one saw the state and private enterprises sometimes collaborating, sometimes quarrelling over pricing, production and distribution, and increased research for efficiency, and the last phase saw a sporadic increase in consumption and acceptance. How did the political, economic, and social factors shape the development of electrification in South Asia?

In a slightly different context, Nazia Hussain argues that the city is a complex phenomenon and that no aspect of it should properly be studied in isolation. She relates two variables, the growth of population and the pattern of water and electricity supply provisions in Dacca in the early decades of the twentieth century, to understand the process of urbanization. Unlike other South Asian cities, the two important civic amenities, water supply and electricity, came to Dacca as royal patronage. The *nawabs* of Dacca were instrumental in providing the services, initially free of cost. The Dacca Municipality bore the cost of maintenance. Hussain claims that means and influence, rather than need, played a significant role in selecting the areas for water supply and electrification. Technical hitches, too, were an important catalyst here.[56]

For Y. Srinivasa Rao, electricity was urban centric initially: with the expansion of electricity, the boundaries of the urban area also expanded; urban growth, in turn, created a greater demand for electric power. Madras initially lagged behind Bombay and Calcutta in the development of electricity largely because of industrial underdevelopment. Thus, a basic requirement for electrification was power-demand. In the case of the Madras Presidency, Rao narrates, the officials had to create the demand by introducing new industrial and agricultural ventures, which, in turn, provided the power-demand essential for the big power generation stations to sustain their viability. Apart from a genuine suspicion of the colonial state's economic agenda, contextual reasons such as unsuitability of the technology and economic condition also influenced the local acceptance of and resistance to electricity.[57] The context determines the choice of technology, but a social constructivist approach may not suffice. Rao opines that in the Indian conditions one should look at the societal circumstances too.

Rao talks about a new corporate construction culture which coincided with the construction of huge power generation stations. Using electricity as a prism, he analyses the problems of introduction and transfer of new technologies. Since the beginning of the twentieth century, both Indian and foreign engineers perceived electricity as rejuvenating to the economy. Realizing the vital role of electricity in rural industrial and agricultural transformations, local electrical engineers strongly advocated for rural electrification in Madras.[58] But the colonies were technology utilization centres, not centres of technology production. Rao concludes that the technological community in India developed as 'assemblers of system' rather than as 'system builders'. They were 'administrative engineers', rather than 'entrepreneur engineers', and could not do much for the technological independence of their country.

The rise of New Delhi as a planned capital and a model of the power of centralized institutions to produce synchronized technological change engaged the colonial bureaucracy and nationalist Indians over time. Leo Coleman explores how, at an important moment in Indian history, the electrification process was shaped by the stately rituals, political thought, and legal struggles. Debates among officials, constitutional proprieties, and actions at law and in government are significant to his account of electrification: how did the processes of electrification and, subsequently, shifting patterns of regulation and distribution of electric power in the capital city of India focus governmental and popular concern on technology?[59]

Electrification in colonial India was enmeshed in empire-wide networks of capital and law. The nationalist Indians fought for freedom from the clutches of colonial economic control, while also seeking to create substantially a new basis for 'interdependence and modern interconnection' through the regulation of basic infrastructures and industries like electric power. In the twenty-first century, Delhi experiments with electricity privatization that intervenes in an urban grid and institutes global ideas of good governance (in the form of new meters and upgraded connections). Coleman claims that although his examples are drawn from a 'single urban and national history' of technological change, regulation, and reform, together they can address wider historical and anthropological debates like 'technology and freedom, state power and citizenship, inclusion and participation'.[60] The colonial electrical infrastructures had been built without much Indian expertise or participation. Coleman identifies this as an explanation of the present deplorable state of the electricity sector and a lesson for the future. For successful cultural integration of a technology, participation of the users (knowledge about the technology) in the system is essential. Swami Vivekananda, as we have seen in the beginning of our discussion on electricity, advocated this long ago, without much success.

On 19 May 2015, the following editorial appeared in the *Economic Times*, under the headline 'Politics the Villain in India's Power Sector':

> In an interview to this newspaper, coal and power minister Piyush Goyal claimed that the government will supply electricity 24×7 to all Indians within five years. India has enough coal, technical ability and capacity to generate electricity, but the minister's noble goal remains out of reach. The real cause of failure to deliver power lies in politics, at the level of state, district and municipality. Goyal believes pumping more money into power transmission – the heavy-load lines that carry electricity around India – will solve half the problem; the other half will be solved by auctioning coal blocks for captive power and metal producers.[61]

Thus, every consecutive government has its own remedy to improve the power sector of India. But even after 71 years of independence, the world's largest democracy is still fighting to supply electricity round the clock. Forget about the villages, even India's smart metro-cities are not completely self-sufficient in this regard – power cuts ('load-shedding' in colloquial usage) are very much present in the urban Indian vocabulary. Electricity is a 'day-dream' for many villages in this country. India witnessed several powerful leaders from Nehru to Modi, and produced thousands of technocrats during this period, but her power-puzzle remains unsolved. What is the reason for such uneven development?

The new history of technology focuses often upon the management of various technological projects rather than earlier heroic inventions (Thomas Edison or the Ford Motor Company).[62] In early twentieth-century Calcutta, the electrification of the city, its industrial application, and transportation narrative all stand out as the biggest engagement for the politicians and technologists – both Europeans and Indians. Over the past century, from early electrification to contemporary privatization, struggles over technological changes and the form of urban society have defined key moments in the history of the country. Leo Coleman argues that the contemporary Indian thinkers' analysis of India's place in the wider history of industrial change during the twentieth century can be understood as their pronouncement of the relation between energy and progress.[63] This is also an attempt to know the 'unknown history' of electrification in colonial Calcutta and to explore the interaction between electricity, as a new technology, with education, industry, and society at large.

Social Construction of Technology (SCOT), Archive, and the Vernacularization of Modernity

Sabyasachi Bhattacharya argues that in the 1920s there began a redefinition of Bengal's identity. It involved, first, a reconsideration of the concept of nationalism and then the evolution of a new 'Bengali patriotism'.[64] But there was another trend which augmented this process – this was the appropriation of modern techno-scientific knowledge vis-à-vis the evolution of the (Indian) ideas of modernity. Techno-scientific development was often seen as the yardstick through which a nation endorsed its claim of modernization and progress. The techno-scientific ideas and their terminologies entered so deep into the political and cultural lexicon of the country that no political or social reformer could afford to ignore them.[65] What was the correlation between technological development and the citizen's perceived sense of patriotism and belonging to the nation?

It would not be wrong to assume that the study is primarily empirical in nature. Social construction of technology (SCOT) serves as a theoretical framework for the study. How does technological change both shape and is shaped by social change? Such an approach is possible only through the application of micro-analysis of historical data that considers local patterns, needs, and logic, putting social change on the same platform as technological change. Very recently, Hyungsub Choi has identified a fundamental mismatch between the history of technology in the global periphery (modern Korea, for example) and the mainstream methodology in the history of technology – SCOT. He raises an important question: Can imported technologies be socially constructed?[66] We need to keep in mind that there were no fundamentally 'Indian technologies' in the true sense of the term; these technologies mostly came as colonial baggage and happened to circulate through the Indian subcontinent, shaping Indian society and taking specific forms adapted to local conditions.

What is the possible way out then? Earlier Ruth Schwartz Cowan introduced the theory of consumption: rather than highlighting the inventors and designers of new technologies, she started talking about the consumers of the technologies to study how the network of production and consumption of technology may look when viewed from the 'inside out'.[67] More recently, another group of scholars, instead of focusing on the big technologies (railways, bridge-building, hydro-power, and so on), have attempted to trace the spread of small-scale mundane technologies (bicycles, sewing machines, gramophones, and so on) into South and South-East Asia during the early twentieth century. Their intention is to explore the adoption and adaptation of technologies as they were integrated into

Asian societies, while ignoring the difference of technological designs, if any.[68] Hyungsub Choi, however, tackles the problem of imported technology in the global periphery – where the inception of technological design rarely takes place – somewhat differently. Utilizing the vast literature in the Korean language on the theme, Choi identifies two possible strategies: (*a*) without analysing the detailed content and design of scientific knowledge and technological artefacts, concentrate on institutional development of techno-scientific knowledge and (*b*) pay attention to the technologists and engineers in telling the story of modern technology in the periphery. The concept of 'locality' is also used distinctively in the context of Korea; 'localizing' means, according to Choi, not reforming the machine to suit local needs but substituting imported parts with ones manufactured locally.[69] Thus, the story of the technologists and engineers are significant here. The Asian engineers and technologists were not innovators in the true sense of the term, but they were 'maintainers' of those imported machines.[70]

The endeavour has been to sketch a convincing picture of late nineteenth- and early twentieth-century Bengal – tease out the attainment of the Indian elites in modern techno-science and the public perception of the same, explore the cautious yet firm approach towards nation-building and the role of modern technology therein, identify the much-needed educational and industrial linkages – through the prism of the official archival records and a wide variety of Bengali-language sources. The private papers of the British engineers who lived and worked in India during the period also provide important information on various technological issues.

Most of the scholarly work on the history of science and technology in colonial India has been based on English-language sources. But the use of vernacular source materials is important for our purpose as it brings out the role and attitude of the Indian population in the process of appropriation of modern technical knowledge and hence the need was felt to go beyond the available source materials of the English language alone. Among the primary sources, the contemporary tracts, books, and journals are very important. During the second half of the nineteenth century, numerous pamphlets, articles, and tracts were written in Indian languages, especially in Bengali. These are truly fascinating and give us a glimpse of the local response on several issues.

About the Book

Though this book deals with Bengal, its analysis applies to the history of other parts of the erstwhile British Empire. This is not because the historically specific experience of Bengal is being presented here as typical of the larger part of the Indian subcontinent. Rather, since Bengal had two significant engineering colleges (one government and another nationalist) and produced several trained engineers who often took up employment beyond the geographical limits of the province – a few technologists-turned-entrepreneurs excelled in their respective fields and often influenced the ideas of the ordinary Indians – and since Calcutta was the second city of the empire, Bengal served as a model to the rest of India regarding electrification and, therefore, can be a reference point for similar studies in other parts of the country.

The time frame within which this book operates stretches roughly from 1880 to 1945. The logic of taking 1880 as the entry point lies in the fact that the *Report of the Famine Commission* that year perhaps for the first time categorically identified the lack of provision for technical education as responsible for the stunted industrial growth and many other plights of the country.[71] From then onwards, various education commissions and numerous government reports talked about it, but with little effect.[72] In the realm of technical education, the major thrust of the colonial education system was on civil engineering alone. After 1880, other branches of engineering like mechanical, electrical, mining, and so on, were gradually introduced as courses of study which brought forth interesting results. By then the Indian intelligentsia also sharpened their criticism of the scheme of technical education provided by the government. The contemporary Bengali press was very vocal and asked for better facilities and training in technical education.[73] When their demand remained unheeded, the erudite Bengali elites came up with their alternative model. They established an engineering college that proved beneficial for the industrialization of the country. Another relevant point is that the 1880s onwards several Bengali entrepreneurs – mostly medium and small in character – emerged and successfully exploited modern technological knowledge in their business ventures. The examples of Hemendramohan Bose (H. Bose & Co.), Kishori Mohan Bagchi (P. M. Bagchi & Co.), Surendra Mohan Basu (Bengal Waterproofs Works, or Duckback), Suren Roy and Kiran Roy (Bengal Lamp),[74] and, above all, Sir Rajendra Nath Mookerjee (Martin & Co.) and Prafulla Chandra Ray (Bengal Chemical & Pharmaceutical Works Ltd) proved that there was no dearth of entrepreneurial abilities among the Bengali community. The study focuses on the changes in technological education and research within the wider industrial and business scenario of Bengal in the latter half of the Raj.

Chapter 1 traces the institutional history of modern technical knowledge in Bengal considering the chronicles of the Bengal Engineering College, Sibpur, and the College of Engineering and Technology, Jadavpur. How did the Bengali intellectuals, who were beginning to construct their alternative educational system by the early years of the twentieth century, conceptualize modern technology? Did the modernization project and the promotion of technological knowledge through the systematic design of engineering curriculum bring about a change in the existing industrial scenario? There is an abundance of literature on the history of industrialization in India. This has engaged the attention of scholars for long and even today has a huge audience. It has been generally recognized that the colonial government consciously and deliberately adopted policies that had deleterious effects on the economy and industry of the subject country.

Chapter 2 reminds the readers that along with such an exploitation paradigm, there are a few issues that need to be investigated in the interest of a more comprehensive understanding of the theme. The attitude adopted by the Indian promoters of industry for the selection of technology for their industrial ventures is one of such issues. Were they self-sufficient in the realm of production technologies or were they borrowers of such technologies from the West? Can one locate Bengali entrepreneurship in the engineering industry? Comparing the career of the two entrepreneurs with training in techno-science, Sir Rajendra Nath Mookerjee, the doyen of Indian engineering, and Dr Prafulla Chandra Ray, a great chemist and science enthusiast, the chapter studies the perceptions and responses of the Bengali entrepreneurs towards modern technology and their role in transforming the industrial life of Bengal.

Percy Dunsheath, the former president of the Institution of Electrical Engineers and the International Electro-technical Commission, rightly observed that no single force dominated human civilization so completely as electricity. While documenting the history of electrical engineering, he remarked that it was not easy to identify one single example from this branch to symbolize the civilizing influence of electrical engineering. As electricity became essential for the industry dealing in power and light, and also the major motive force of several other industries, there arose a need for technically competent manpower in electricity and others capable of managing the business end: 'The ideal would have been men who were equipped for both aspects of the industry.'[75] This book also explores several techno-socio-political aspects of the early years of electrification in colonial Calcutta. It emphasizes the importance of local technical, topographical, and other forms of knowledge for understanding the dynamics of electrification. Situating the analysis in a general colonial context of electrification, it shows that the British did not enjoy ultimate control over the development of the electrification process; the local context, consumers, and maintainers had significant influence, thereby complicating the hypothesis of electrification as a 'tool of empire'.

Chapter 3 is an attempt to understand how electric light and power facilities were established and managed in colonial Calcutta, and how they subsequently grew and changed. While there is a formidable literature on the origins of electrification in many specific areas of the world, and on the electrical manufacturing companies that formed the technological base of the industry, very few have studied the role of foreign electric companies in the lighting up and providing of electric motive power in a colonial set-up. Technological change was a critical part of the story, as was the stance of the colonial government and the role of technologists. The credentials of the Bengali entrepreneurs and intellectuals in the field of electricity, which Chapter 4 tries to explore, offers an interesting example of the Indian response to the new knowledge. Could the electrification of Calcutta create new conditions? What impact did it have on the socio-economic conditions of the city? The *bhadralok* leadership acted as a pressure group and several times manipulated the direction of electrification. The Bengali electrical engineering community gradually oriented themselves towards ideas of industrial development based on Indian realities. A few trained electrical engineers entered the business sector and became very successful. High-level technological innovations like hydro-electricity were also exploited by the Bengali entrepreneurs. When various electrical appliances such as electric lights and fans, tramcars, electric-lift, X-rays, and so on, were introduced in Calcutta, these technologies were only beginning to be adopted on a global scale. This chapter also explores how the colonial society negotiated the wide range of transformations shaped by electricity. While recognizing that many fundamental principles of electricity were learned from Europe, this chapter emphasizes the role of local participation in the development of this technology, along with Indian appropriation in the early twentieth-century Bengal.

The study ends with the Sarkar Committee report. In February 1946, the interim report of the Sarkar Committee appeared with a provocative opening statement: 'The existing facilities for higher technical education in India are inadequate, both in quantity and quality, to satisfy India's post-war needs for high grade technologists.'[76] The committee recommended the establishment of technological institutes based on the Massachusetts Institute of Technology in the four regions (north, south, east, and west) of the country. According to them, 'a right relationship between the public, industry and education' was very important for the growth of India. So, they felt that the proposed institutions should be located within easy reach of the large industrial areas of the country. This resulted in the setting up of the first Indian Institute of Technology (IIT) at Kharagpur in the modern-day state of West Bengal in 1950.[77]

Chapter 5 explores the imagination(s) of the *bhadralok* community regarding technological knowledge and industrialization to make the future India self-reliant. There was the urge to comprehend the modern knowledge and tools that the colonizers had brought, and to assimilate them. Indian intellectuals had become aware of the role of techno-scientific knowledge in transforming the economy. There was certainly no dearth of persons who could pinpoint the pros and cons of the official policy. At the same time, they provided their alternative models. How did the Indian nationalists situate modern technology in their broader agenda of 'nation building'? Apart from the elite response, one needs to examine the different sections of society for a better understanding of the topic. The bulk of the literature dealing with twentieth-century Indian techno-science is constituted of celebratory biographies of the greatest Indian scientists and technocrats. A few case studies of the self-made Indian engineers show that not only the British government but also contemporary elite society was equally responsible for underestimating the unknown 'Vishwakarmas', craftsmen with a high degree of engineering skills, in favour of Western-educated engineers and scientists. Can we call them justifiably the 'subaltern technologists'?

At a theoretical level, any study on the history of science and technology relates to the everlasting debate concerning issues like the nature of Indian modernity in social science academia and beyond. This study is also no exception. The questions of appropriation of modern technical knowledge and the beginning of the engineering curriculum and its industrial linkages in the colonial Indian context must be read in that light, and it certainly brings forth the issues of modernity. Today everybody will readily admit the importance of technological knowledge in the making of a successful entrepreneur. Entrepreneurs are held responsible for the economic development of the modern state by introducing and implementing innovative ideas, among which technological innovation, perhaps, stands high on the agenda. While the new buzzword of the twenty-first century is 'technological knowledge and business innovation', as a student of history one may like to go back to the past to study what our forefathers thought about engineering knowledge, entrepreneurship, electrical energy, and industry. David E. Nye warns technology's storytellers to be aware of the complexities of narrative while drafting their stories. Business historians may write a history based on the testimonials of the manager of some factory, while labour historians always try to recreate the worker's experience. For an engineer's perspective, Nye suggests, we need to integrate both. Beyond the factory, the public perception may be entirely different from the above three.[78] As technologies are embedded in these stories, a part of our job is to remain conscious about not missing or undermining any such perspective.

Notes

1 P. N. Bose, *The Illusions of New India* (Calcutta: W. Newman & Co., 1916), 103–5.

2 *Arthik Unnoti* 3, no. 3, Aswar 1335 Bengali Sambat (B.S.) (1928): 221.

3 Knowledge may be described as the basis of the capability to undertake a task in the production process. Dev Nathan and Abhishek Kumar, 'Knowledge, Education and Labour Practices in India', *Economic and Political Weekly* 51, no. 36 (September 2016): 37.

4 Karel Davids, 'Connecting and Globalizing History of Science, History of Technology, and Economic History', *Isis* 106, no. 4 (December 2015): 835.

5 Robert Fox and Anna Guagnini (eds), 'Introduction', *Education, Technology and Industrial Performance in Europe* (Cambridge: Cambridge University Press, 1993), 5.

6 Roy Macleod and Deepak Kumar (eds), 'Introduction', *Technology and the Raj* (New Delhi: Sage, 1995), 11–21. See in the same volume: Arun Kumar, 'Colonial Requirements and Engineering Education: The Public Works Department, 1847–1947', 216–32.

7 Reinhard Rurup, 'Historians and Modern Technology: Reflections on the Development and Current Problems of the History of Technology', *Technology and Culture* 15, no. 2 (April 1974): 192.

8 D. S. L. Cardwell, *Technology, Science and History* (London: Heinemann, 1972), viii–xi.

9 Prakash Kumar, *Indigo Plantations and Science in Colonial India* (New Delhi: Cambridge University Press, 2012), 9–13.

10 Thomas P. Hughes, 'Emerging Themes in the History of Technology', *Technology and Culture* 20, no. 4 (October 1979): 697–711.

11 Dhruv Raina, 'Situating the History of Technology in a Philosophical Triptych: Contours of Future Research', International Centre for Theoretical Physics, Internal Report, IC/93/88 (May 1993), 3.

12 John M. Staudenmaier, 'Recent Trends in the History of Technology', *American Historical Review* 95, no. 3 (June 1990): 715–25.

13 David Arnold, 'Europe, Technology and Colonialism in the 20th Century', *History and Technology* 21, no. 1 (March 2005): 86–7.

14 James A. Secord, 'Knowledge in Transit', *Isis* 95, no. 4 (December 2004): 655.

15 During Phase I, the non-scientific society provides a source for European science; Phase II is termed colonial science; and Phase III completes the process of transplantation with a struggle to achieve an independent scientific tradition or culture. George Basalla, 'The Spread of Western Science', *Science* 156, no. 37 (May 1967): 611–22.

16 Daniel R. Headrick, *The Tools of Empire* (New York: Oxford University Press, 1981). Also see Michael Adas, *Machines as the Measure of Men* (Ithaca: Cornell University Press, 1989).

17 George Basalla, *The Evolution of Technology* (Cambridge: Cambridge University Press, 1988), 208–9.

18 India played a major role in textiles and in the propagation of crop plants. Arnold Pacey, *Technology in World Civilization* (Cambridge and Massachusetts: The MIT Press, 1990), 15.

19 Macleod and Kumar, 'Introduction', *Technology and the Raj*, 20.

20 Ian Darbyshire, 'The Building of India's Railways: The Application of Western Technology in the Colonial Periphery 1850–1920', in *Technology and the Raj*, ed. Roy Macleod and Deepak Kumar (New Delhi: Sage, 1995), 202.

21 S. Irfan Habib and Dhruv Raina (eds), 'Introduction', *Social History of Science in Colonial India* (New Delhi: Oxford University Press, 2007), xxiii.

22 Zaheer Baber, *The Science of Empire* (Delhi: Oxford University Press, 1998), 205–6.

23 Russel Dionne and Roy Macleod, 'Science and Policy in British India, 1858–1914: Perspectives on a Persisting Belief', *Proceedings of the Sixth European Conference on Modern South Asian Studies* (CNRS, Paris, 1979): 55–68.

24 Kapil Raj, 'Beyond Postcolonialism and Postpositivism: Circulation and the Global History of Science', *Isis* 104, no. 2 (June 2013): 344. Earlier, he described South Asia as a 'Contact Zone': It was a site to produce certified knowledge due to the intercultural encounter between South Asian and European intellectual and material practices that took place here. Kapil Raj, *Relocating Modern Science* (Delhi and Ranikhet: Permanent Black, 2006), 11.

25 David Chambers and Richard Gillespie, 'Locality in the History of Science: Colonial Science, Techno-science, and Indigenous Knowledge', *Osiris*, 2nd Series 15 (2000): 221–40.

26 Warwick Anderson, 'Where Every Prospect Pleases and Only Man Is Vile: Laboratory Medicine as Colonial Discourse', *Critical Inquiry* 18, no. 3 (Spring: 1992): 509.

27 Claudio Canaparo, 'Science and Empire: The Geo-Epistemic Location of Knowledge', in *History and Philosophy of Science and Technology*, Vol. 4, ed. Pablo Lorenzano, Hans-Jörg Rheinberger, Eduardo Ortiz, and Carlos Delfino Galles (Oxford: EOLSS and UNESCO, 2010), 25.

28 Lissa Roberts, 'Situating Science in Global History: Local Exchanges and Networks of Circulation', *Itinerario* 33, no. 1 (March 2009): 25.

29 David Arnold, *The New Cambridge History of India: Science, Technology and Medicine in Colonial India* (Cambridge: Cambridge University Press, 2000), 15–18.

30 Gyan Prakash, *Another Reason: Science and the Imagination of Modern India* (New Delhi: Oxford University Press, 2000), 159–200.

31 Dipesh Chakrabarty, 'The Muddle of Modernity', *American Historical Review* 116, no. 3 (June 2011): 663–75. See also Sanjay Joshi (ed.), *The Middle Class in Colonial India* (New Delhi: Oxford University Press, 2010).

32 Dipesh Chakrabarty, *Provincializing Europe* (Princeton and Oxford: Princeton University Press, 2000), 6.

33 Ibid., 15–21.

34 Projit Bihari Mukherji, *Doctoring Traditions: Ayurveda, Small Technologies, and Braided Sciences* (Chicago and London: The University of Chicago Press, 2016), 11–20. For Mukherji, modernization is a complex process of braiding. The creative braiding of ideas, objects, and practices resulted in a series of body imageries or 'Physiograms' that Ayurveda practitioners came to rely on by the early twentieth century. The term 'technomodernity' has been borrowed from Mukherji.

35 Dhruv Raina and S. Irfan Habib, *Domesticating Modern Science* (New Delhi: Tulika, 2004), 83–4.

36 Madhumita Majumdar, 'Science and the Nationalist Agenda in Bengal – 1904–1947', unpublished PhD thesis, University of Calcutta, 2004, 2–3.

37 Dhruv Raina, 'Travelling Both Ways: The Adaptation of Disciplines, Scientific Textbooks and Institutions', in *Science between Europe and Asia*, ed. Feza Gunergun and Dhruv Raina (Dordrecht and Heidelberg: Springer, 2011), 173–6.

38 Raina, while tracing the disciplinary history of science, comments, '… the history of science over the course of nineteenth century could as well as subsumed within the history of higher education.' Dhruv Raina, *Needham's Indian Network* (New Delhi: Yoda Press, 2015), 2.

39 Jahnavi Phalkey, *Atomic State* (Ranikhet: Permanent Black, 2013), 1–9.

40 R. C. Goel, 'Engineering Education for Technological Innovation', *Mapping Technovation through Multi-Goal Synthesis* (Calcutta: First Indian Engineering Congress, 1987), 4. Goel was Professor of Electrical Engineering at the Madan Mohan Malaviya Engineering College, Gorakhpur.

41 W. H. G. Armytage, *A Social History of Engineering* (Cambridge and Massachusetts: The MIT Press, 1961), 167.

42 Aparajith Ramnath, *The Birth of an Indian Profession* (New Delhi: Oxford University Press, 2017), 223–33.

43 Deepak Kumar, 'New Knowledge and New India: Lessons from the Colonial Past', in *Education in Colonial India: Historical Insights*, ed. Deepak Kumar, Joseph Bara, Nandita Khadria, and Ch. Radha Gayathri (New Delhi: Manohar, 2013), 45–61.

44 Ross Bassett, *The Technological Indian* (Cambridge, Massachusetts, and London: Harvard University Press, 2016).

45 David Arnold and Eric Dewald, 'Everyday Technology in South and Southeast Asia: An Introduction', *Modern Asian Studies* 46, no. 1 (2012): 1–17.

46 David Arnold, *Everyday Technology* (Chicago and London: University of Chicago Press, 2013). See also David Arnold and Eric Dewald, 'Cycles of Empowerment? The Bicycle and Everyday Technology in Colonial India and Vietnam', *Comparative Studies in Society and History* 53, no. 4 (2011): 971–96.

47 As the age-old social organization of occupations disappeared due to technological intervention, psychological intimacy among the villagers increased across the limits

of caste, kin, and community. Smritikumar Sarkar, *Technology and Rural Change in Eastern India* (New Delhi: Oxford University Press, 2014), 303–5.

48 David Edgerton, 'Innovation, Technology and History: What Is the Historiography of Technology About?' *Technology and Culture* 51, no. 3 (July 2010): 680–97.

49 Asif A. Siddiqi, 'Introduction: Technology in the South Asian Imaginary', *History and Technology* 31, no. 4 (2015): 341–49.

50 One of the primary means of reformulation and dissemination of such knowledge were the journals and periodicals written in Indian languages. Pradip Kumar Bose, 'Introduction: Health, Science and Society in 19th Century Bengal', in *Health and Society in Bengal*, ed. Pradip Kumar Bose (New Delhi: Sage, 2006), 9–15.

51 David Hardiman and Projit Bihari Mukherji (eds), *Medical Marginality in South Asia* (London and New York: Routledge, 2012).

52 However, Mahendra Nath refused to study electrical engineering in America; he was already in love with the literature at the British Museum, London. Mahendra Nath Datta, *Londone Swami Bibekananda*, Vol. 2 (Kolkata: The Mahendra Publishing Committee, 2013, 7th edn), 42–5.

53 J. D. Bernal, *Science in History* (London: Watts, 1957, 2nd edn), 389.

54 Thomas P. Hughes, *Networks of Power* (Baltimore and London: John Hopkins University Press, 1983).

55 Jonathan Coopersmith, *The Electrification of Russia* (Ithaca and London: Cornell University Press, 1992), 4.

56 Nazia Hussain, 'The City of Dacca, 1921–1947: Society, Water and Electricity', in *The City in South Asia*, ed. Kenneth Ballhatchet and John Harrison (London and Dublin: Curzon Press, 1980), 197–223.

57 Y. Srinivasa Rao, 'Electrification of Madras Presidency', unpublished PhD thesis, IIT Madras, 2007, 11.

58 Ibid., 194–255.

59 Leo Coleman, *Electrification as Political Rituals in New Delhi* (New Delhi: Speaking Tiger, 2017).

60 Ibid., 4.

61 *Economic Times*, 19 May 2015, 12.

62 Thomas P. Hughes, *Rescuing Prometheus* (New York: Vintage Books, 1998), 3.

63 Coleman, *Electrification as Political Rituals*, 21.

64 In the 1920s, the vernacularization of the language of politics, increasing focus on Bengali language and culture, strengthening of regional patriotism, and continuous negotiations between regionalism and Indian nationalism were some of the identifiers of a new 'Bengali patriotism'. Sabyasachi Bhattacharya, *The Defining Moments in Bengal 1920–1947* (New Delhi: Oxford University Press, 2014), 1–41.

65 Deepak Kumar, *Science and the Raj* (New Delhi: Oxford University Press, 2006, 2nd edn), 240.

66 Hyungsub Choi, 'The Social Construction of Imported Technologies: Reflections on the Social History of Technology in Modern Korea', *Technology and Culture* 58, no. 4 (October 2017): 905–20.

67 Ruth Schwartz Cowan, 'The Consumption Junction: A Proposal for Research Strategies in the Sociology of Technology', in *The Social Construction of Technological Systems*, ed. Wiebe E Bijker, Thomas P. Hughes and Trevor J. Pinch (Cambridge, MA: MIT Press, 1987): 261–80.

68 Arnold, *Everyday Technology*; Nira Wickramasinghe, *Metallic Modern: Everyday Machines in Colonial Sri Lanka* (Oxford: Berghahn Books, 2014).

69 Choi, 'The Social Construction of Imported Technologies', 911–17.

70 For Choi, they were closer to *tinkerers*, 'who tweaked in the margins of imported technologies, sometimes taking them apart and putting them together in novel arrangements'. To put it differently, they were the tinkered version of the maintainer-engineers: '… those individuals whose work keeps ordinary existence going rather than introducing novel things.' Ibid., 917.

71 *Report of the Indian Famine Commission* (London: George Edward Eyre and William Spottiswoode, 1880), 163.

72 S. N. Sen, 'Technological Education in India: 1884–1914', in *Technological Education – Technological Style*, ed. Melvin Kranzberg (San Francisco: San Francisco Press, 1986), 91–9.

73 Suvobrata Sarkar, *The Quest for Technical Knowledge* (New Delhi: Manohar, 2012), 97–144.

74 Amit Bhattacharya, *Business, Politics and Technology* (Kolkata: Readers Service, 2005).

75 Percy Dunsheath, *A History of Electrical Engineering* (London: Faber and Faber, 1962), 342.

76 *Development of Technical Institutions in India: Interim Report of Sarkar Committee* (Simla: Government of India Press, 1946), 2.

77 Subsequently, four other IITs were also established in Bombay (1958), Kanpur (1959), Madras (1960), and Delhi (1961). From the beginning, the IITs have been committed to a unique system of educational excellence and their single-minded pursuit of technological innovation. See Saroj Bangaru, 'Debates on Technical Education: A Prelude to the Foundation of the Indian Institutes of Technology', MPhil dissertation, Jawaharlal Nehru University, New Delhi, 2004.

78 David E. Nye, 'How Does One Do the History of Technology?' Plenary Lecture, SHOT, Dearborn, Michigan, 6 November 2014, 1–9.

1

Technical Knowledge and Its Institutions

I may be privileged to say a word on the microscopes turned out of your workshops. I tested them and found them in design and execution as good as anything I have used manufactured by British and German makers. The increase of pupils and the extension of the Research Laboratory of the National Medical College of India in the departments of Physiology and Bacteriology have made it incumbent on us to add to the microscopes and other instruments. We were thinking of indenting these from Germany but what I saw last night has inspired me with the hope that we might be able to satisfy our wants nearer home. Your boys have inaugurated a new era in the production of scientific instruments in India and I see no reason why we should not be a self-sufficing nation even in regard to these delicate instruments.

—Dr S. K. Mallik, M.D., C.M. (Edin.), Dean of the National Medical College, Calcutta, to Satish Chandra Mukherjee, Principal of the Bengal National College (1909)[1]

Presiding over the annual prize-giving of the Bengal Engineering College at Shibpur, Howrah, yesterday afternoon, the Hon. Khan Bahadur M. Azizul Haque, Minister of Education, said that India's resources had not yet been fully trapped, and it would be the task of student engineers of to-day to realize those untapped resources for the good and betterment of this country. The Hon. Minister pointed out that though in the past former students of the college had done excellent work in later life, modern India would make even greater demands than had been made in the past.

— 'Great Demand for Engineers: Minister's Speech', annual prize-giving at Shibpur College (1936)[2]

Institutional history is an emerging field within the broader – and yet nascent – field of the history of technology. This chapter elucidates the history of Bengal Engineering College, Sibpur, and the College of Engineering and Technology, Jadavpur. A brief account of the history of the two higher educational institutions will illustrate the complexity of the issues involved in the progress of technical education during the period 1880–1945. The importance of these two institutions will be easily granted, because until the first decade of twentieth century, the Bengal Engineering College was one of the four government-sponsored colleges that were imparting advanced engineering training (the other three being Thomason Engineering College in Roorkee, Madras Engineering College, and the College of

Science in Poona); and the upsurge of political, intellectual, and cultural activity associated with the Swadeshi Movement in Bengal found its educational expression in the formation of the College of Engineering and Technology, Jadavpur, which became an institute of advanced technical education in the 1920s. Back home in England, close to the end of the nineteenth century, there were no formal institutions for imparting technical education or producing engineers.[3] Inspired by a college in Glasgow, a civil engineering college was established at Roorkee, India, in 1847, while the Imperial College, London, was founded in 1879. The shortfall of textbooks and teaching materials for engineering schools in England was initially met by the periodically revised lecture notes, examples, drawings, and college manuals circulated amongst students at Roorkee. These materials codified Indian engineering practices as well and were 'hailed as the most complete and satisfactory work on the subject in the English language'.[4]

As India emerged from decades of anti-colonial struggle, Dhruv Raina and S. Irfan Habib opine, her paths to modernization revealed a variety of political and cultural features. The modern structures of knowledge generation, such as the university and scientific institutions, that had appeared in Europe came to occupy a central place in the developmental projects of India, although these institutions carried the very cultural characteristics of their location.[5] But the evolution of engineering education somehow followed a different path. Modernization through techno-science and industrialization were the crucial ingredients of the developmental projects. All this had been preceded by a vociferous demand for techno-scientific education. The modernization was not to be achieved at the cost of peasants and artisans. A recent study shows how the significance of artisans and technicians was brought into focus in the early twentieth century.[6] At the same time, the demand for heavy industries was ably advocated and pushed by Indian interlocutors. All that was needed was a fine blend in the engineering curricula which could cater to both the future technologists and artisans.

What were the technical, economic, and institutional factors that allowed modern technology, first, to be adopted in India, then to be widely applied in the country while rapid technological development was proceeding in the West? The growth and development of technical education in India cannot be studied in isolation from colonial policies relating to technical and general education. These policies were conditioned by the policies of colonial expansion and the consolidation of British rule in India.[7] What stimulus did the British colonial administration give to education, research, and the adoption of modern technological practices? Contrary to the repeated claims by the British that the educated class of India showed no interest in technical or scientific instruction, there is much evidence of a considerable stirring of indigenous activity in the second half of the nineteenth century,[8] despite the equally evident lack of techno-scientific employment opportunities offered by the Raj.[9] The beginning of the twentieth century witnessed a growing interest in technical and technological education, the establishment of a number of institutions at various levels, and was characterized by intense debates on the scope, character, and relevance of such education in the Indian context. What vision did the Bengali intellectuals have of 'modern' techno-scientific institutions? What new strategies did they think of?

Technological Education: Debate, Policy, and Practice

The Indian Famine Commission of 1880 recognized, perhaps for the first time, that apart from the economic advantages that were to be expected from the expansion of industry, it offered the promise of progress in other directions – scientific, social, and so on. The Education Commission of 1882 was struck by the complete neglect of the useful and practical studies that were calculated to help students establish themselves in life. The growing unemployment among the university-educated middle class was by now clearly visible in the uneven humanities-oriented educational programmes against which the public reaction was increasingly louder, aided by the example of a successful movement in western Europe, America, and Japan in favour of technological education.[10] In consequence, the Commission (1882) for the first time introduced a technical bias in the educational apparatus by its concept of bifurcation of studies at the stage of the entrance examination, a concept that started a new debate on the whole question of technical and technological education. The government circulated a new resolution on the importance of bifurcation of studies in 1884 to all provincial governments,[11] and shortly thereafter arranged for a full report on the state of technical education in the country. This was done by A. P. MacDonnell, Home Secretary, in July 1886, after examining the condition of technical education in the various provinces and the steps taken by each local government for the improvement of practical and industrial training. About engineering, MacDonnell pointed out:

> The facilities afforded for University training in Engineering appear, as far as mere teaching goes, to be as extensive and complete as the circumstances of the time require. The Colleges at Calcutta, Madras, Poona, and Roorkee are well-equipped, and the theory of Engineering is all well taught as perhaps in England. The defects seem to lie in the too theoretical nature of the teaching, in the complete isolation of these

> colleges, and in the want of facilities for practical instruction.... The workshops at Sibpur and Poona do much towards making the instruction in these colleges of a practical character.[12]

E. W. Collin investigated in 1890 the principal arts and industries of Bengal and in his report recommended the training of mechanical engineers in the workshops connected with the state railways, the institution of improved industrial schools and the encouragement of industrial classes, and the stimulation of native industries by the purchase of materials for public works in India, among others. But Collin ruled out the question of any large schemes for technical education claiming that the native industries were scattered and that it would be much easier to send students to Europe to study the improvements which had been made in the system of manufacture.[13]

In the beginning of the twentieth century, expressions like 'technical' and 'technological' education were used in the same sense despite subtle differences.[14] The period also witnessed the formation of several state technical scholarships for the encouragement of Indian students in the higher branches of technical studies. These would enable students to receive a higher level of technical education and thus, in turn, qualify them to contribute to the improvement of the existing industries as well as the development of new industries.[15] Sir E. C. Buck, Secretary to the Government of India, was aware of the ripples in the minds of the local erudite class regarding promotion of technical education of the higher class, and so he recommended the constitution of a special enquiry committee in India, and, if necessary, in Europe, 'to advise what if any, technological instructions for specialized training are required in the country, and to frame a working-plan which should be carried into effect when men and means are forthcoming'.[16] The terms 'technological education' and 'technological institutes' were used in connection with the plans of technical education. The purpose of such an institute would be to provide scientific and technical instruction of an advanced character. Thus, Francis Spring, Under Secretary to the Government of Bengal in the Public Works Department (PWD), talked of technological education in the advanced sense and recognized the desirability of establishing a Central Technological Institute, of which the necessary elements already existed in the scientific departments of the Presidency College, the Bengal Engineering College at Sibpur, and the Calcutta Medical College.[17]

Throughout the second half of the nineteenth century, Western-educated Bengalis were raising the demand for a full-fledged techno-scientific research system, a demand that was not accepted by the imperial administration until

1904, when the Indian Universities Act was passed that permitted post-graduate teaching and research in the humanities and the sciences.[18] What impact did it have on contemporary engineering education? Taking stock of the much-diversified system of instruction, length of the courses, and nomenclature adopted by the various engineering colleges, the Act asked for uniformity in the system and stated that further provision was needed for instruction in mining and electrical engineering.[19] These recommendations were hotly debated in the official circle. Spring was of the opinion that excellence in engineering depended chiefly upon racial and personal qualifications of the candidate, and next upon the quality of teaching in the colleges, and these had better be dissociated from the universities altogether. He further recommended that 'the universities should leave on one side practical engineering, and should only test the men's knowledge of scientific principles, while the college authorities should test practical ability'.[20] H. W. Orange, another official, thought that a technical institution should either be independent, like a higher polytechnic, and should grant its own degrees, or that it should be an organic part of a teaching university, instances of which were the Massachusetts Institute of Technology at Boston and the German polytechnics. He ridiculed the idea of an institution for master's in civil engineering, considering that in the previous 50 years no candidate had ever attained a master's degree in Calcutta. At that time there were three engineering degrees, namely the licentiate, the bachelor's, and the master's.[21] One R. Nathan remarked:

> It is doubtful whether the universities have done, much to foster or improve the study of engineering. The main object of the four engineering colleges is to give a practical training to candidates for the engineering and subordinates grades of the PWD.... This must be always borne in mind and no arrangements should be introduced which will in any way interfere with the recruitment of the PWD.[22]

Major E. Atkinson, Principal of the Thomason College, Roorkee, while underlining the three essential qualifications of an engineer, stated the importance of specialization, and thought that it was necessary to recognize the different branches of engineering with an appropriate training for each and it was desirable that the degree should indicate the special branch in which the graduate was trained – civil, electrical, mechanical, or mining.[23] As regards uniformity, Atkinson opined that a great deal could be done towards standardizing syllabus, distribution of marks, standard of proficiency, and nomenclature without unduly interfering with the responsibility of individual colleges to regulate their policy, which would be decided by local requirements. To the advancement of technical or technological education there were, of course, no objections on the grounds of policy. But although the significance of the progress in this direction was long recognized, little was achieved for many years. Four engineering colleges had been in existence for long and had been successful in training civil engineers, but these students mainly entered government employment and did little to foster the industries of the country.

J. G. Cumming, the officiating Commissioner of the Presidency Division, in his much celebrated report advised, among others, the following:

> (1) improvement of technical instruction through a larger expenditure on central institutions, (2) subsidizing by the government of the associations for industrial or scientific education of Indians, (3) by giving of greater encouragement to district exhibitions of industries and industrial arts, (4) through increased dissemination among the public of information on industrial matters.[24]

During the same time, G. N. Gupta prepared another report for Eastern Bengal and Assam which for the first time suggested the creation of a new department of industries, the creation of a central technological institute, the opening of factories, instead of schools, with apprentice classes for imparting education regarding the manufacturing process, and the idea of direct state assistance for 'pioneering' new industries and by rendering pecuniary assistance to individuals willing to engage in any profitable industry.[25]

Very few of the recommendations of these reports were translated into practice. An indirect contribution of the Government of Bengal during this period was the publication of annual monographs to facilitate private individuals interested in the industry to benefit by its study. These monographs were written by qualified Indian and British officers based on reports submitted to them by various district and sub-divisional authorities and on personal tours and research.[26] These monographs were of special interest as these were written to cover almost all the minute details of the subject under study. Thus, for example, in the case of iron and steel works, it studied the extent of the industry, the methods of production, the raw materials used, condition of labour and wages, and the prospect of the industry. Here the writer also brought to the notice of prospective investors the benefit of the modern iron and steel industry in place of the primitive methods practised by the village blacksmiths.[27] However, it would have been much more effective had these monographs been written in Bengali rather than English, which was unintelligible to the large majority of the people. Moreover, these reports were hardly available in the *mofussil* area outside Calcutta.

Riding the wave of nationalism that marked the first decade of the twentieth century, enthusiasm for industrial advance became general among the educated Indians. The Indian Industrial Conference, which began in 1905, gave a forum to the leaders of this movement and they trenchantly criticized the official policy of confining technical education to the improvement of the work of carpenters, smiths, and other handicraftsmen, pointing out that Bengal already had enough skilled artisans. What the province needed were modern engineers. The main goal of technical education was thus the establishment of new, large-scale industries that would produce goods that were then imported. R. C. Dutt (1848–1909), in his presidential address at the first Indian Industrial Conference, stated that a shift in emphasis from cottage crafts to urban industries was inevitable and asked for modern industrial training.[28] The tone was perhaps set by Dewan Bahadur K. Krishnaswami Rao:

> If India is to regain her lost place in her industries, she must learn to use steam, gaseous or electric power much more extensively than at present. Hand machines, however good they may be, will not meet the demand of the country for manufactured articles; and make us independent of imported goods. The use of steam, gas, and electricity require a thorough knowledge of mechanism, theoretical and practical, and of the scientific processes used in America, Europe and Japan in manufactures. It is a matter of deep regret that India is not yet blessed with an institution, in which required scientific and technical knowledge and training could be obtained to enable us to work our industries on advanced lines without foreign aid.[29]

This statement is important since it recognized the importance of science-based manufacturing industries with indigenous capital in national economic regeneration and the role of technological education in preparing the skilled workforce appropriate for such industrialization. But it was the statement of a well-meaning individual interested in technical and technological education; it did not reflect government policy. The establishment of indigenous manufacturing industries and industrialization in general ran counter to the interests of industries established in Britain and the overseas trading and business communities the government was pledged to support.[30] Although the recommendations of various committees and individual officials were valuable in the context of technical education in general, technical education at the advanced level made little progress apart from the occasional lip service from the government.

Academic Engineering: The Search for a 'Suitable Boy'

The term 'academic engineering' is used to describe the teaching of engineering within a university or college of higher education; it differentiates an institutional teaching framework from the broader assimilation of engineering working practices by the method of apprenticeship or pupillage. The growth of academic engineering, both in terms of student numbers and the variety of courses, profoundly influenced the structure of what we might call 'practical engineering',[31] the status of engineering as a profession searching for recognition within society, and the corporate relationship between the administrators, engineers, and places of higher education. The emerging discipline of academic engineering in the late nineteenth and early twentieth centuries was by no means uniform and unvarying across the range of institutions of higher education. One might wonder why a college of engineering was opened at Roorkee (1847) at a time when Britain itself did not provide academic training to engineers except for military purposes. While in France the state had always played a key role in engineering, British engineering arose from below and the pioneers of industry there were working men trained by apprenticeship and self-taught in industrial science.[32] It was only in the last quarter of the nineteenth century that engineering education became a part of the university curriculum. Engineering education gradually moved away from the hands-on lab-oriented arts and practices of the old 'apprenticeship' approach to emphasize the fundamentals of technology. In other words, engineering education in western Europe and the United States had increasingly emphasized the conceptual, theoretical, and mathematical aspects of engineering.[33] This development is partly because the major engineering institutes there had become increasingly research oriented. The rise of research as an integral part of an engineering institute's agenda meant that the universities began affecting the direction of industry. This easy movement between academia and industry gave rise to a new technological culture.

This sub-section will highlight some of the relevant issues of academic engineering and its industrial linkages in the context of the Bengal Engineering College, Sibpur. The year 1880 was a major milestone in the history of the college, as in that year the college was restored to its former status of independent existence after an uneventful 14 years (1865–1879) under the administrative control of the Presidency College. The workshops of the PWD at Sibpur were attached to the college for the practical training of the students. At the instance of the Government of Bengal, the University of Calcutta revised its regulations further in order to enable a candidate to obtain a License in Engineering or the degree of Bachelor's in Engineering in either of the two branches: civil engineering and mechanical engineering.[34]

Though the college was founded for training civil as well as mechanical engineers, in actual practice, however, no proper arrangement was made for imparting training in higher mechanical engineering of the standard of the degree course. In November 1884, a Parsee student, Sarabji Shavaksha, applied for permission to take up the mechanical engineering course. He also expressed that the reason behind his joining the Sibpur college was to pursue this branch of engineering, as he could easily have learned civil engineering in Bombay. At this the principal communicated his inability to teach the mechanical engineering course 'up to the university standard' to the higher authority and proposed that 'a properly qualified European should be appointed, upon whom would devolve the duties of superintending both Engineer and Apprentice students whilst engaged in the shops'.[35] Ultimately, it was decided in July 1885 to appoint E. F. Mondy, Professor of Physical Science, as also Professor of Mechanical Engineering. It was further decided that this arrangement would be applicable only when a class of at least six students had been formed for the study of mechanical engineering. No class, however, could be formed.

Here the attitude of the British Raj towards the technological calibre of their subject people is significant. The Superintendent of the Workshops, Sibpur Engineering College, was apprehensive as he found that a great many of the native students considered manual labour distasteful and endeavoured to avoid it. To stop such a tendency, he introduced rigorous rules for annual examinations that he hoped would 'convert the idlers into earnest workers'.[36] Such a negative attitude remained throughout the colonial rule about the techno-scientific proficiency of Indians. Of course, there were loopholes in the system and were pointed out by several educationists and bureaucrats. In one such instance, Sir Alexander Pedler, Professor of Chemistry at the Presidency College and later appointed as the Director of Public Instruction, Bengal, remarked, '... the present constitution of the Engineering College, and the course of studies pursued in it, require to be thoroughly overhauled. There is no doubt that the College is, for some reason or other, not attractive to students....'[37] His recommendation to the students was to look for the private fields of employment where the modern, practical, and adaptable worker alone was valued.

Sibpur workshops, as has been mentioned earlier, were under the control of the PWD and run on a commercial basis. The college could not, therefore, utilize the workshops solely for instructive purposes. When the advice of F. J. E. Spring, Engineer-in-Chief of the East Coast Railway and a member of the Board of Visitors of the College, was sought, he submitted a memorandum on the subject in January 1893:

> It must be ever borne in mind that the problem with which we are dealing, when treating of Sibpur College matters, is not one which solely concerns the well-being of the College itself, but that it is a problem which is intimately bound up with the entire technical education pyramid of which, in Bengal, Sibpur is, of rather ought to be, the top stone.... Now when I pass for the handing over the shops to the College authorities, I do so far two principal reasons; because I am convinced from a careful study both at home and out there of the now fairly well understood subject of technical education that until the shops shall have become strictly and solely educational and no longer commercial shops, they will fail in efficiency for educational purposes.[38]

In May 1894, the government sanctioned the transfer of a part of the workshops to the Education Department and placed a grant of 50,000 rupees at the disposal of the principal of the Sibpur college to erect new workshops for it. The workshops were finally transferred to the Education Department in April 1897.[39] An important decision aimed at promoting the study of engineering as a career was taken in September 1891, and all appointments in the Upper Subordinate Grade of the PWD of the Government of Bengal were reserved for being filled by the graduates of the college.[40] By this time, E. W. Collin, under the direction of the Government of India, drew up a report on the arts and industries of Bengal, which contained certain comments and suggestions in regard to the Sibpur college.[41] The establishment of a special class for the training of mining assistants was one of them. The Directorate of Public Instruction, Bengal, also suggested that an alternative course for mining engineers should be introduced into the university curriculum. It was decided accordingly that successful candidates would receive a 'diploma of qualification as Mining Engineers issued by the Principal of the Sibpur College and countersigned by the Superintendent of Mine'.[42] Subsequent things, however, shaped slowly. The proposal took another 14 years to see the light of day. On the recommendation of a committee set up by the government in 1903 to consider the question of providing facilities for the training of qualified managers and assistant managers for the mines in India, a Mining Department for the college was sanctioned in 1905. Another committee under the chairmanship of the Commissioner of the Burdwan Division was appointed for finalizing the curriculum of mining instruction with reference to the practical training of the students. The mining classes were opened in February 1906.[43]

In April 1893, the then principal of the Bengal Engineering College, Sibpur, J. S. Slater, wrote to the Director of Public Instruction about the 'liberal loan' from the Messrs Martin & Company, a Calcutta-based engineering firm, of certain electric machines with a view to beginning electrical engineering at the college. The principal stated that this would enable him to demonstrate to the students various electrical equipment which were hitherto unavailable to him due to high costs. As this branch of engineering was in an underdeveloped state because of the unavailability of trained manpower, efforts were made to install a small electric lighting plant at the college and train interested students in electrical engineering.[44] Thus, a full practical course in electrical engineering was introduced at the Bengal Engineering College in 1895 and in the same year the proposal for a complete electric lighting installation was initiated.[45] The early installation work was supervised by Dr P. Bruhl, Professor of Physics of the college, and helped by some senior students of the Apprentice Department. Three students who had gone through the new electrical course completed their studies in 1898–99, and the Directorate of Public Instruction (DPI) in Bengal reported that 'all obtained well-paid appointments at once'.[46]

Research activities in the college started as far back as 1901 when one Upendranath Kar was awarded an Elliot Research Scholarship of 100 rupees, tenable for one year, for conducting investigations in the region of electricity and magnetism with special reference to electrical engineering in the college laboratory.[47] There was, however, no proper arrangement for any sustained research until the 1950s. In 1902, the post of Professor of Mechanical and Electrical Engineering was created.[48] As a measure of developing the workshops, the principal sent up a proposal for the introduction of electric-power drive into the shops. The substitution of the old steam-power drive by the modern electric drive was necessary from the point of view of training, as the major shops of those days, namely the Calcutta Tramways Company, the Cauvery Falls in Madras, the railway workshops at Jamalpur, Lillooah, Khragpur, and so on, had already decided to install electric drives. The proposal was accepted in 1902 and the new electric-power plant was inaugurated in March 1904 by Sir Andrew Fraser, the then Lieutenant Governor of Bengal.[49]

During these twenty years (1880–1900) of its existence, the Bengal Engineering College, Sibpur, produced several efficient engineers. To name a few who graduated in the late 1890s and made their mark, mention may be made of Surendra Kumar

Basu, who cleared Bachelor of Civil Engineering (B.C.E.) in 1880 after the college opened at Sibpur. The degree of B.C.E. was replaced by B.E. (Bachelor's in Engineering) in the year 1885. Basu was the famous author of the popular textbook *Building Materials and Construction*. Aannada Prosad Sarkar (1883) rose to the position of the first Indian Chief Engineer (Irrigation), Government of Bengal. Anukul Chandra Mitra (1887) became famous as a practical engineer of great skill. He oversaw the construction of the Victoria Memorial. Girish Chandra Das (B.E. in 1891) became the Chief Engineer of the Light Railways under Messer Martin & Co. He was also the Engineer-in-Charge of the construction of the High Court at Calcutta. Another engineer, Amar Nath Das (1895), joined the Indian Service of Engineers. Later, he rose to the position of Chief Engineer of Bengal. Another distinguished student of the period was Benimadhab Mitra (B.E. in 1900), who made his mark as an authority on road construction.[50] But the combination of engineering and entrepreneurship was extremely rare in those days. The only notable exception was Sir Rajendra Nath Mookerjee (1854–1936).

In the year 1902, the students of the college started publishing a monthly journal in Bengali, the *Shibpur College Patrika*. Their intention was noble:

> Can we improve the existing state of our agriculture and industry with the help of science? To learn the basic scientific principles, we need a command over the English language. But one feels comfortable in his own mother tongue while learning a complex subject like science. Alas we don't have such comfort. Hence only the English-educated have the entry-pass to the wonder world of science. Thus, the mass, without the English-skill, miss the chance to get the flavour of modern science. Unfortunately, our artisan class, the flag-bearer of our industry, belongs to this section. The transmission of techno-scientific ideas, in simple Bengali, among them is the main purpose behind our humble effort....[51]

This journal published a wide variety of popular articles on science and technology and the contributors were mainly students of the college. In one such instance, the author narrated the marvels of electricity:

> The main gossip of today's Calcutta is the electric tramways! This modern mode of transport is not horse-driven or human-driven, not even steam-driven – but electricity is the prime mover for tramcars. One becomes perplexed while considering the vast range of activity of this

> new technology! In every aspect of our life electricity is now an obedient servant to mankind. Electric-stove for modern cooking (as substitute of fire), electric-fan during the hot summer season, and electric-lamp for illumination in the night – everywhere is electricity. To run the machines of a factory, electricity plays the pivotal role by producing hundreds and thousands of horse-power. If one wants to talk with a friend mile away from him, the remedy is telephone – another offshoot of electricity. One cannot think without electricity in modern times.[52]

On another occasion, the journal observed:

> To man the Public Works Department, Municipalities and District Boards, the college was first established at Sibpur. So, the general conception about the college is that its main intention is to train the engineers, overseers, and sub-overseers. To some extent it is true as the favourite destination above 80% of the alumni of the college to these departments and bodies. It does not imply that the college only entertains the job-seekers. The choice for government job, over entrepreneurship, among the youths is not the result of the instructions of this college. It is the common tendency and result of the overall national degradation of our society. The college courses are ideal for the potential entrepreneurs and industrialists. But unfortunately, those who come here for training in engineering, come only when they failed in general education and with an intention for quick employment. So mostly they are job-seekers, not would-be entrepreneurs and industrialists.
>
> The demand for Mechanical Engineering has been increasing speedily. The reason behind this is that our educated-folk become aware of the benefit of entrepreneurship and industry. Compared to other engineering colleges of India, Sibpur provides a thorough training in engineering and the courses are also of advanced character. Manufacture of engineers for the Public Works Department is not its main goal – but, the students of this college have every potentiality to become a successful engineer-entrepreneur.[53]

This venture, however, did not last long, and with the departure of the editors (Atul Chandra Bagchi and Upendranath Kar) from the college, the publication was discontinued in 1908.

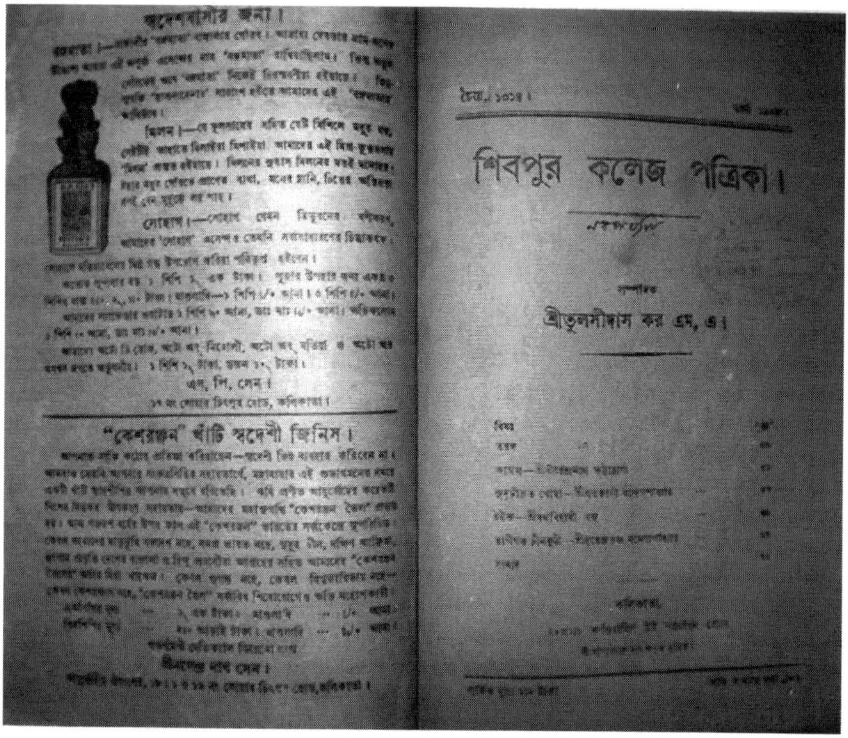

Figure 1.1 *Shibpur College Patrika* **(1902)**
Courtesy: Bangiya Sahitya Parishad Library, Kolkata.

A scheme to impart training in industrial chemistry at the Sibpur college was worked out and submitted to the government, saying 'instruction should be given in the scientific principles underlying the chief industries of the country, and the facilities should be afforded for research work', in 1907. It was practically a post-graduate scheme for students with science degrees, except those who had passed the intermediate examination in engineering. It also proposed to offer admission of occasional students with a practical knowledge of some industry and wanted to study the theory underlying that industry. According to the proposal, the course of instruction was divided into two: (*a*) technological chemistry and (*b*) dyeing and chemistry of dyeing.[54] Although the Bengal government was optimistic, the Secretary of State was sceptical about the demand for men with such advanced training in India and asked the Bengal government to justify its proposal.[55]

The Government of Bengal tried hard to convince the Secretary of State that the objective of the proposed courses was to train men for direct employment in the different cotton mills, engineering firms, and manganese concerns, or 'who will at least be in a position to proceed to a further course of practical work in actual manufacturing concerns such as is necessary to make them experts in their respective subjects'. Several Indians also thought that such an advanced level of training was not the call of the time and instead suggested confining it to the artisan level.[56] But this time a determined Bengal government argued:

> Applications are also received occasionally by the Principal of the Civil Engineering College for chemists for iron works, engineering firms and manganese concerns. Such applications have to be refused owing to the absence of any properly qualified men, since the chemistry hitherto taught at Sibpur and the other Bengal colleges has not been such a nature as to fit students to take up analytical work of a special kind. The new classes, however, will be able to turn out men suitable for such appointments.... Indians with an enthusiasm for the commercial development of the country on Indian lines are founding and will no doubt continue to found business of their own in preference to seeking employment with European firms; and as the dyeing industry, unlike cotton industry, is one which can be profitably conducted in small factories, and with a moderate capital, it may confidently be anticipated that in the immediate future private enterprise will provide a large field of employment for students who have taken the course of dyeing under proposed scheme.[57]

Finally, sanction was given for an experimental period of three years with a clause that the continuance of the classes would depend upon the practical results obtained. The inauguration of the classes originally fixed for November 1909 had to be postponed by a year as Rajendra Nath Sen, who had been selected for the post of Professor, was pursuing his training at the University of Leeds. In the meanwhile, steps were taken to equip a laboratory and to purchase a large stock of chemicals and apparatus. Sen was eventually appointed for three years as Professor of Tutorial Chemistry at the college and the classes were started in January 1911.[58] Although the number of students declined in the subsequent years, a few of them were successfully employed in various industries and started their own businesses.[59] The Government of India felt that the paucity of students might be to some extent due to public ignorance and hence suggested to the local government the desirability of advertising with a view to attracting students not only from Bengal but also from other parts of India.[60]

As discussed earlier, in the early twentieth century an important step in the form of a State Technical Scholarship was taken for the Indian students to pursue technological studies in Europe or the United States for the betterment of Indian industry. It was decided to exclude engineering from the scope of such scholarship and the mining industry, in the case of Bengal, was found to be the most favourable field.[61] The Government of India declared: 'There is an urgent demand in this province (Bengal) for persons who had some training in mining; and a scheme for utilizing the Sibpur Engineering College as a centre where such instruction should be imparted....'[62] Accordingly, it was decided to send a few selected persons to Europe for a special training course in mining. The Government of India encouraged the local governments to consult the leading commercial firms, both European and Indian, in the task of selecting scholars. But the European firms were generally hostile to the scheme. They were apprehensive about the idea of 'natives of India trained in business methods and capable of competing with them on their own ground in the capture of the European markets'. The Government of India believed that a sound commercial education, on the lines of Manchester and Birmingham Universities, would benefit the emerging Indian entrepreneurship to compete in various modern business ventures. The scheme of the State Technical Scholarships would be beneficial to the prospective Indian students of engineering as it enabled them to proceed to various foreign countries for advanced technological training.[63]

In 1909, the Bengal government recommended 'two outstanding students', Girindra Nath Dutt and Jitendra Nath Das Gupta, for the State Technical Scholarships in the field of mechanical engineering. But the Government of India rejected both the proposals claiming that engineering was 'expressly excluded from the scope of technical scholarship' and asked for alternative proposals.[64] At this, the Bengal government recommended one Manmatha Nath Baysack in the field of textile chemistry and the proposal was readily accepted. But this did not go without debate. Finally, in the very next year the Government of India announced:

> ... electrical and mechanical engineering should be considered as falling within the scope of the technical scholarship scheme, as the instruction available in these subjects in this country is far less advanced than the procurable in civil engineering, while the demand for qualified electrical and mechanical engineers to take charge of factories and works is steadily on the increase.[65]

In those days, electrical engineering mainly dealt with electrical power generation, transmission, and utilization. With the multiplication of the number of electrical power houses, and with the increase in its industrial usage, the demand for men trained in the use of electrical machinery and acquainted with the fundamentals of this technology began to grow and the contemporary engineering colleges started upgrading their facilities for this branch of engineering.

Bengal Engineering College was not an exception.[66] The training in electrical engineering in the early twentieth century was confined almost entirely to the apprentice (or subordinate) stage at the Sibpur college. Students in this branch first had to undergo the ordinary four years' course for PWD overseer students, and then specialize in electrical work for some 15 months. In the first four years, they spent much time in the various mechanical workshops and took such subjects as steam engine and applied mechanics. Thus, a huge time was devoted to civil engineering and other subjects of little subsequent use to them in later life.[67] Mechanical engineering was not a favourite destination of these students as the course was not meant to train electrical men. W. H. Everett, the then Acting Superintendent of Industries, Bengal, was all praise for the plant:

> In the running of plant the students get an excellent training, both with direct and alternating machinery, including testing of engines and boilers. They have to keep a regular log daily, and work out the costs for each month. I know of no college in England where such a full training is given in actual running, the plant being in actual use for power and light and about 12 hours daily. The students also get much experience in wiring; and several 1 ½ H.P. motors have been made by them. They go through a simple course of electrical testing, as well as lectures and class work.[68]

When the college was steadily developing into an institution of high standard in Sibpur, it was suddenly decided to shift it to another site on the ground of unhealthiness of the place. Meanwhile, the advisability of creating a technical institute in Calcutta itself was brought to the notice of the government from various quarters.[69] The creation of a Technical Institute of Calcutta was advocated on the grounds that in all European countries in which technical education had reached a considerable degree of development, such education had been almost entirely confined to industrial centres.[70] The proposal of abolishing the Bengal Engineering College at Sibpur aroused considerable opposition in Calcutta. One Surendra Nath Roy moved a resolution in the Bengal Legislative Council in February 1914 to the 'effect that the proposal to abolish the Sibpur Engineering College be dropped'.[71] Finally, in 1918, the Government of Bengal decided to retain the Bengal Engineering College at its original site, Sibpur.

In the meanwhile, the Government of India had deputed E. H. Atkinson and Tom S. Dawson to enquire into the state of technical education in the country with special reference to its industrial applicability. They visited various industrial concerns, both private and government owned, and prepared a huge report.[72] The general assumption of the employers (that is, various industrial firms) in Bengal, as mentioned in their report, was that the educated Bengalis were averse to manual labour as a regular employment even after their training in a technical institute. Their other major observations include:

> There is at present no demand with a university training in mechanical and electrical engineering ... the university type of education unfits a Bengali for practical work, and although an engineering graduate would have a more complete scientific education he would be far behind the technically-trained student in practical ability and less valuable to an employer.[73]

Instead, they suggested training as an apprenticeship on a living wage, working with hands, and observing factory hours and rules. Such training would enable the Bengali job-seekers to convince the employers of their employability as there was a huge opportunity for those with practical knowledge in mechanical and electrical engineering.

Despite the hindrances created by the proposal to shift the Sibpur college, B. Heaton, the then principal of the college, proposed a three-year Overseer Course in the mechanical and electrical branch. The Director of Public Instruction, Bengal, was also in favour of creation of a professorship in mechanical engineering who would confine his attention to electrical engineering with the addition of the electrical portion of physics.[74] In January 1914, the Government of Bengal sanctioned the proposal.[75] In the session of 1912–13, the Electrical Engineering Department was separated from the Mechanical Engineering Department. The Mechanical Engineering Department received great impetus in 1914 when the newly appointed Professor C. A. King put forward a scheme for the development of the department by improving the courses of studies and all sections of the laboratories, including prime movers and workshops, by procuring some essential equipment from abroad and also by preparing a large number of small equipment and models in the college workshops.[76] During the period of uncertainty as to the future of the college, only some minor projects were taken up. A motor mechanic class was opened in 1907 and abolished in 1910. A class to train selected telegraphers was also opened in 1909. A dyeing class was opened in 1910 and abolished in 1916 as it failed to attract students.[77]

Technology, Education, and Imperialism between the World Wars

A change in the official attitude was around the corner as priorities were shifting from agriculture to industry, and hence to technical education. The First World War (1914) exposed India's industrial backwardness and her dependence on other countries for a variety of commodities like machines, prime movers, and, most importantly, technical skill. Being an important source of war related manpower and material, technical education and the subsequent industrialization became prominent features of the colonial policy formation.[78] The most significant outcome of this change in attitude was the appointment of the Indian Industrial Commission (1916) which was constituted to study the question of India's industrialization and explore the possibility of state participation in it. It was in this connection that the commission directed its attention to the various aspects of techno-science, including education, research, and development.[79] Its findings revealed several lacunas in the existing state of technological development and the government approach to that. In order to remove these drawbacks, the commission emphasized the necessity for closer coordination amongst technologists, government departments, universities and institutes, and industry. It wanted to relate technical education and research to the actual industrial needs of the country.[80] However, the changes suggested in the report were never translated into practice. In fact, the recommendations suffered from inherent contradictions. The needs and interests of the foreign masters and their subject people were mismatched. So, the recommendations were bound to be doomed.

The Indian Industrial Commission discussed the engineering curricula, method of teaching, and so on, and recommended substantial changes. The commission visited the Sibpur college in 1916–17. The then principal, B. Heaton, although dissatisfied with the Bengali character in terms of technological proficiency, was optimistic: '… a Bengali student, whose tendency is more towards philosophy and the abstract ideas found in law, we must take every possible means to bring his mind from the clouds, from thoughts of the abstract to the practice of the concrete.'[81] His proposal was to retain the Thomason College, Roorkee, for higher civil engineering course and convert the other three (Sibpur, Madras, and Pune) into 'mechanical and electrical engineering colleges and into mining colleges where facilities could be offered for advanced courses of a university type'.[82]

In pursuance of the policy recommended by the Industrial Commission, the mechanical and electrical engineering classes of the college were developed independently of the University of Calcutta and it was intended that the university would in due course recognize these courses for awarding degrees in mechanical and electrical engineering. It was thought that the ideal method of training mechanical engineers was to combine workshop practice and technical instruction as closely as possible.[83] Since the mechanical and electrical engineering and mining classes were separated from the civil overseer classes four years ago (1914), the students who applied for these two branches had increased enormously. The Bengal government sought to raise the strength of the faculty by appointing 'an Assistant Professor of Mechanical Engineering and a first-class Mechanical Draughtsman'.[84] This time the local government had a valid reason as it wrote: 'A further important consideration is that the classes in Mechanical and Electrical Engineering and Mining are rapidly increasing both in importance and popularity. There is an ever-increasing demand for well-trained Mechanical Engineering for the development of the industries....'[85] Both the proposals were sanctioned in 1919. The principal of the Sibpur college selected Purna Chandra Ganguli, a B.Sc. from Glasgow and Professor of Mechanical Engineering at the Bengal Technical Institute, for the post of Assistant Professor 'on probation for six months'. Ganguli was selected because of his nine years' teaching experience as incharge of the Mechanical Engineering Department and his familiarity with and understanding of Bengali students and local conditions.[86]

One of the major reforms undertaken during the period was to reorganize the various departments of the college, which was suggested by the Mookerjee Committee. This committee, under the chairmanship of Sir Rajendra Nath Mookerjee, was formed in February 1919 to coordinate the Apprenticeship Training Scheme of the Eastern Bengal Railway Workshops at Kanchrapara with the mechanical engineering classes of this college.[87] The committee recommended that the lower classes in the Mechanical Engineering Department of the college should be given up and instead a Technical School at Kanchrapara should be established. The Sibpur college should be utilized for the final training of the mechanical engineers after they had completed the full course of apprenticeship at Kanchrapara or other large workshops in Bengal. In accordance with these recommendations, the Board of Control for Apprenticeship Training was created in 1921.[88] The improved courses received government sanction the next year and with this reform the college was mainly concerned with the training of persons to occupy a higher position in the engineering industries of the country.

During the deputation of W. H. Everett, Professor of Mechanical and Electrical Engineering, B. C. Gupta had overseen the Electrical Engineering Department and Power Installation. One Jitendra Nath Chakravarti was appointed in the department as a demonstrator to the special class for training subordinate telegraphists of the Government of India. It was said that both were acclaimed for their teaching efficiency.[89] The Indian School of Mines at Dhanbad was built by one of the ex-students of the college, Anath Bandhu Bhattacharya, under Messrs Martin & Co. in 1926. So, the admission of students to the mining classes was stopped and mining was finally closed at the Bengal Engineering College in 1929.[90] To utilize the space vacated by the Mining Department, it was proposed that a course of instruction in advanced metallurgy might be introduced, but without effect.

The next important event in the history of the college was the introduction of the degree course in mechanical engineering, and the first batch of mechanical engineering graduates, six in number, passed the degree examination of the University of Calcutta in 1932.[91] There was some impact of the Great Depression on the development of the college. It was due to financial stringency that the degree course in electrical engineering could not be introduced along with mechanical engineering. It was only in 1935 that the degree course in electrical engineering came into existence.[92] The degree course in metallurgy was introduced in 1939–40.[93] Dr A. H. Pandya, a renowned engineer of international repute, took over as principal of the Bengal Engineering College in 1939 and he was the first Indian principal of the college.

During the First World War, the testing laboratory of the college was utilized for the testing of war materials. During the Second World War, many technicians for the munitions factories, armed services, and the technical wing of the Air Force were trained in the college workshops, which served as a combined centre under a special technical training scheme. The Second World War impacted on the college adversely, as the entire energy and attention of the college was diverted towards producing war technicians. Temporary barracks and classrooms were built in 1940, and training commenced the next year. During this entire academic year, no admissions were made to the first-year class in order to make room for the technicians![94] It did not take long to realize the massive potentialities of techno-science for the successful conduct of a modern war. As the war raged, it once again badly exposed India's technical and industrial backwardness and her dependence on others for a large variety of goods and commodities irrespective of wartime requirements.[95]

The Bengal government constituted a committee under the chairmanship of F. Rahman in 1943 to enquire, amongst other things, the prevailing state of technical and industrial education in Bengal and also to suggest a comprehensive scheme to serve the needs of the prospective industries of Bengal.[96] In regard to the

Bengal Engineering College, it was pointed out by the committee that the workshops and laboratory arrangements at the college were inadequate, and for successful training in higher engineering these defects should be removed. The committee further observed that apart from the degree courses in civil, mechanical, electrical, and metallurgical engineering, which were already in existence, arrangements for starting new courses, such as ship-building, aeronautics, and so on, should also be made, and that this college should impart training in higher engineering only, leaving the diploma and apprenticeship courses to the Calcutta Technical School.[97]

Soon after the outbreak of the Second World War, various committees had been constituted to meet the war's different, especially technical, requirements in India, and along with it came the realization of the magnitude of the task of reconstruction.[98] But for India, with divergent interests of the rulers and the ruled, the post-war reconstruction was rendered more difficult. The importance of applied science and technology and the necessary manpower for the fulfilment of the task were, however, keenly felt. Meanwhile, industries in the country were expanding and their needs as well as the needs of the government for higher technical personnel to meet various increasing activities became urgent. In its report on the post-war educational development of the country, the Central Advisory Board of Education remarked, 'In view of the recent expansion of industry and the likelihood of further development after the war it is necessary to plan immediately a comprehensive system of technical education at all stages.' It also emphasized:

> … the necessity for ensuring that in the University technological departments ample facilities are provided for research directed towards the solution of practical industrial problems and that the need for testing the results of laboratory experiments on a commercial scale is not overlooked. It is not less important that technological degree courses generally should be made more practical than they are at present and that the students should spend a considerable part of their time throughout the course, and not merely at the end of it in works and factories.[99]

The Bengal Engineering College, which was one of the few institutions for producing higher engineering personnel, had to keep pace with these expanding activities. A Committee for the Development of Higher Engineering and Technical Education in Bengal was accordingly formed in 1945 under the chairmanship of the DPI.[100] The committee submitted its reports in two parts, one containing the 'Immediate Plan' and the other a 'Five Year Plan'. While submitting its report under the 'Immediate Plan', the committee confined its recommendations to higher engineering training and the training of supervisory personnel, and aimed at increasing the number of qualified engineers and supervisors in the more important and immediately necessary branches of engineering, improving their quality and standard and also providing facilities for advanced instruction and research.[101] In the opinion of the committee, these improvements were urgently needed in the light of post-war expansion. The government accepted these recommendations and the University of Calcutta, after consulting the Faculty of Engineering and the Board of Studies in Engineering, framed new curricula and revised the regulations relating to degree examination in various branches of engineering in 1946.

The college was so far generating its own electricity. To meet the increased load, the electric supply system of the institution was remodelled and the supply of energy in bulk at 6,000 volts was arranged from the Calcutta Electric Supply Corporation (CESC) from December 1946.[102] The objective of the 'Five Year Plan' prepared by the Development Committee was the ultimate conversion of the Bengal Engineering College into a modern and well-equipped institution comparable to the best institutions of the world, with a greater range of degree courses and facilities for post-graduate and research work. But the scheme saw the light of the day almost 10 years later, after independence.[103] The collective adoption of the 'Immediate Plan' and the 'Five-Year Plan' recommended by the committee was with a view to fostering close cooperation and collaboration between industry and the college.

Technical Education: A National Want

The first two decades of the twentieth century were to prove significant for science and technology in India, in terms of its institutional manifestation. The prevalence of unemployment among the Bengali *bhadralok* and the partition of Bengal (1905), which shattered the Bengali selfhood, strengthened the already raging nationalist movement. Sumit Sarkar has identified a four-fold classification of trends in Bengal's Swadeshi Movement: moderate mendicancy, passive resistance, aggressive resistance, and constructive *swadeshi*.[104] While aggressive resistance required political mobilization of the people and was characterized by armed revolt and acts of terrorism, those committed to constructive *swadeshi* shifted the focus of the debate to technical education and the onset of industrialization. What role did techno-scientific knowledge, and its institutional manifestations through engineering education, play in transforming Indian society within the larger project of industrialization? The nationalist stand on techno-science in Bengal can be understood by studying the National Council of Education (NCE) and its progeny, the College of Engineering and Technology, Jadavpur.

In a recent study, Sambit Mallick discusses the 'democratization' of scientific knowledge through the building of institutions in the nineteenth-century Indian context. By this term, he refers to the way democratic norms, institutions, and practices evolve, and are disseminated both within and across national and cultural boundaries.[105] The historical analysis of a few higher educational institutions, Mallick argues, indicates that the democratization of techno-scientific knowledge, and the creation of equal opportunities, in terms of evaluation and application of knowledge, and so on, in the colonial period began to occur not because of the colonial government but in spite of it. The Indian intelligentsia realized the significance of modern techno-science for the material and cultural transformation of the country and attempted to democratize science and technology in their own way by establishing institutions. In 1876, an Indian doctor, Mahendra Lal Sircar, founded the Indian Association for the Cultivation of Science (IACS) in response to a pressing demand from educated Indians that the university must cease to be merely an examining body. The IACS sought to combine the character, scope, and objectives of the Royal Institution of London and the British Association for the Advancement of Science, with an objective to create a scientific research system outside the state-system.[106] The association flourished in the wake of the emerging nationalist struggle, and the greater the reluctance displayed by the imperial administration in terms of scientific research, the greater was the determination on the part of the incipient techno-scientific community to strengthen their independent efforts.

The lead given by the IACS in the nationalist pursuit of science was carried forward by the Dawn Society, founded by Satish Chandra Mukherjee in 1902. Before that, he launched the *Dawn* magazine in 1897 to propagate his ideas of national education. The *Dawn* was widely circulated in educated households as a journal of high standard and repute. These landmarks highlight important conceptual shifts in the contemporary thinking on science, technical education, and industrialization.[107] Satish Chandra criticized the syllabus of the University of Calcutta as 'all too-academic, all-too literary, unscientific and un-industrial'.[108] The Dawn Society had a definite syllabus in science and technology. It had the four-fold objective of retrieving the worthy elements of traditional science, absorbing the benefits of modern science, disseminating science to the masses, and offering market-oriented technical education. The Dawn Society served as a vital link between the IACS and the future NCE, which founded the Bengal Technical Institute and finally the College of Engineering and Technology (CET).

The Bengal partition caused dismay among the educated Bengalis and they decided on a political movement of boycott, *swadeshi*, and national education. The programme involved national education for *swadeshi* industrialization, by which it meant a curriculum of science and technology for national reconstruction. The Dawn Society had already started such a course. This was merged within the activities of the NCE, which was founded in 1906 by the contemporary intellectual cream of Bengal. It attempted to extend the research character of the IACS into the domain of pedagogy of techno-scientific education: namely founding an educational system on 'national lines' and under 'national control'.[109] Since the NCE was heavily loaded with personalities committed to the programme of cultural nationalism,[110] its commitment to science and technology also being a cultural one, some of them went on to found the Society for the Promotion of Technical Education (SPTE) in 1906. The SPTE went on to set up the Bengal Technical Institute (BTI), while the NCE established the Bengal National College (BNC) the same year. Thus, the council institutionally planted the seeds of literary, scientific, and technical education in Bengal along national lines.

Techno-scientific education was a precondition for industrial growth, and the technical institutes were visualized as directly providing skilled workmen who would become the agents of technological progress. The task was to initiate an 'industrial regeneration of India' and this had to be undertaken by educating the 'Indian artificer' in the skills of modern science and technology.[111] The proposed modernization of the industrial system required a new educational philosophy that was different from the traditional apprenticeship system. The new pedagogy of the industrial era displaced the site of technical training from the workshop or the factory to a workshop-cum-educational classroom, for the new system sought to be 'instructional' and not 'commercial'.[112] The Dawn Society visualized an Indian path of industrialization and the objective of technical education was to make artisans self-supporting. In the debate on technical education, the development of the country along industrial lines effectively meant 'a simultaneous double process' where the worker was replaced by the machine, and where huge industrial organizations were promoted through organized finance and management. To protect the artisan and industrial worker from the evils of 'Western industrialism', the nationalists worked out three strategies: (*a*) provision of a modern technical education, so that the artisan had the technical skills to compete in a modern technical environment, (*b*) provision of a general education, so that the artisan had a feel for the market situation and commercial organization, and (*c*) provision of capital, to free the artisan from the clutches of the vintage structure.[113]

But a shift of emphasis was inevitable, as the essence of the modern industrial system was its ability to produce commercial goods on a gigantic scale through the agency of machinery. The 'fabric' of the modern industrial West was supported by the 'two great pillars' of concentrated capital and up-to-date machinery, the latter being a product of the skills developed in techno-science. The disjunction between machine-based industry and the 'artistic hand industry' was 'affected by the application of steam and electricity on a stupendous scale to machinery'.[114] To man those modern industries, the infrastructure for advanced technical training was necessary along with the artisans, and this transition was heavily dependent upon the growth of academic engineering.

What must be recognized is that, in class terms, the members of the two bodies, NCE and SPTE, were one, committed to the same political programme of nationalism. Further, some of them were on the governing councils of both bodies. Despite that, they had divergent perceptions of scientific and technical education, and of the modalities of industrial development and social transformation. Benoy Kumar Sarkar (1887–1949), the great promoter of national education, described the difference in the attitudes of the two bodies as *Kulturkampf*, or cultural war.[115] He described his three stages of technical education as 'mistrification, industrialization and factorification', which were all visible in the institutional history of the NCE and the CET. This illustrates the transition from technique to technology – when 'science' blended with it, it got elevated into technology for industrialization. The split among the Bengali intelligentsia, two scholars have recently argued, was predominantly over the place of science and technology in a 'liberal education', and what a technical education suited to the Indian environment involved.[116] Both the bodies were convinced of the need for techno-scientific education to produce manpower and skills that were necessary for the task of nation-building and economic transformation; but despite their common agenda, the strategies they adopted for accomplishing this goal separated them.

From the membership of the executive council of the BNC, it is difficult to comprehend who provided the inputs for the educational reconstruction necessary for the promotion of industrialization and economic modernization of Bengal. The council wanted to function as a full-fledged university and had the ambition of imparting literary, scientific, as well as technical education from the primary to the post-graduate level.[117] But it had no representatives from industry or business organizations. While the technical intent of the BNC was to provide technical manpower for the emerging industry, the nationalist intent is inferable from the curriculum of the college. Teachers were recruited to teach subjects considered necessary for a liberal education at a British university; in addition, there were faculties of Sanskrit and Indian philosophy, Arabic, Bengali, Hindi, Marathi, Pali, Persian, and Urdu.[118] The introduction of Indian cultural history into the curriculum can be termed as a pedagogic departure from the state educational system, which only glorified the history of the West. In such a gloomy technical atmosphere, the Foreman Instructor of the college, Nagendra Nath Rakshit, was an ideal example of Bengali attainment in the field of technology. Benoy Sarkar opined that 'he may be regarded as the first Bengali teacher of Bengali youths in a modern college of technology'.[119] In 1908, the Technical Department was remodelled and the service rendered by the Manufacturing Section of the college was duly recognized by the local erudite Bengali elites and entrepreneurs.[120] The college course of the Technical Department was divided into three parts: (*a*) agriculture including forestry, (*b*) manufacture including mining, and (*c*) commerce and *zemindary* management. The advanced technical courses of study were still under consideration of the committee. One Phanibhusan Biswas, mechanical engineer from the Bengal Engineering College, Sibpur, joined the BNC and was entrusted to teach carpentry and machine drawing.[121]

The quality of the produce of the Manufacturing Section was able to draw the admiring notice of many European specialists like Paul Bruhl, professor at the Bengal Engineering College, Sibpur.[122] The articles, implements, and apparatus manufactured in the laboratories and workshops of the Scientific and Technical Department were occasionally placed for exhibition – public spectacles of technological development. In January 1908, one such exhibition was held and the event captured the attention of the city very well.[123] The second exhibition, held the next year, was an overall success. Numerous articles, implements, and apparatus turned out during the year 1908 in the workshops and laboratories of the BNC and several other institutions affiliated to the NCE in various districts of Bengal were placed for exhibition.[124] W. H. Everett, Professor of Electrical and Mechanical Engineering, Government Engineering College at Sibpur, was all praise for the institution and observed: 'I did not notice much, if any, soldering work on exhibition, a little practice at this subject is very useful; some simple joints of electric wires could be included, with insulation also....'[125]

Benoy Kumar Sarkar lamented that in the Swadeshi period (1905–10), real entrepreneurs and businessmen were rarely found among the Bengalis. There was none who could become an ideologue of *swadeshi* industrialization. There were leaders in the political and cultural fields, but there was a void in the economic field, as there were no experts who could guide the youth in business enterprises by setting up factories or machinery.[126] He considered economic recovery the main goal and wanted to orient the minds of the educated towards the *swadeshi* enterprise. This position is echoed in the first report (and perhaps only!) of the SPTE, published in 1908, where it states:

> Our attention is first directed to the great industrial awakening that has of late taken place in the country. Everywhere the signs of this new industrial spirit have manifested themselves. Our eyes have been opened to the vast natural resources of the country lying practically underdeveloped. The success of Europeans in the field of industrial enterprise has also been an object-lesson to us and has stimulated our energies.[127]

The dearth of higher technical institutions in the country was a major concern for the intelligentsia. Students had to visit foreign universities for the requisite training and only a limited number could avail such opportunities. The founders of the SPTE, in addition to Tarak Nath Palit, Nilratan Sarkar, Rajendranath Mukherjee, and Bhupendranath Basu, felt that since a literary and scientific education was already provided for under the existing system, the society's efforts should be directed exclusively towards technical education. The institutional differentiation between the NCE and the SPTE, according to Raina and Habib, is more in terms of the differing conceptions of pedagogy than the personality clashes between individuals.[128]

Among the twenty executive members of the SPTE, most belonged to the legal profession and very few from the scientific community and the business class. Surat Datta, Gopal Sen, and Jatin Das-Gupta joined this institute as members of the faculty after their training at different engineering schools in Berlin and Leeds. The Bengali *bhadralok* were determined to overcome their caste taboos and started soiling their hands under the tutelage of the artisans. Thus, according to Benoy Kumar Sarkar, the deplorable economic condition of the middle class alarmed the members of the society and that was apparent from the programme of the SPTE.[129]

The curriculum of the BTI was divided into primary, intermediate, and secondary branches of technical education. The primary branch was meant to produce skilled artisans, and the secondary branch was to prepare students as competent prospectors, foremen, industrial chemists, and assistant engineers. The higher-level course offered training in subjects like mechanical, electrical, and chemical engineering, geology, and chemistry. The compulsory papers in the mechanical and electrical courses were higher mathematics and physics, along with training in machine-drawing and pattern-making. There was something for school-dropouts as well – the intermediate branch prepared them to be skilled operatives, assistants to foremen, engine drivers, fitters, and mechanical draughtsmen. The course included mechanical and electrical fitting, dyeing, electroplating, lithography, soap-making, and tanning.[130] The burgeoning industrial environment of the province influenced the choice of the subjects. In the first decade of the twentieth century itself, the BTI had attained the potential to become a perfect engineering college producing efficient engineers as well as entrepreneurs.

The BNC charged their counterparts at the BTI as materialistic, unpatriotic, anti-national, and Western-minded. The cultural guardians of Bengal of the time were behind such charges and so the technocrats tried to set up their position on a more secure footing. They claimed that the battle was one between 'mistrification' or 'technocratization' and culture.[131] The NCE, however, rejected this technology–culture divide, and claimed that by combining the literary, scientific, and technical education with national glory, all-round nationalism, and mistrification, they were in fact contributing to the war against Western domination.

Finally, both sides called it quits. Despite the conflict, the two bodies amalgamated into one institution under the NCE on 25 May 1910. The long-standing dispute ended, and the council declared its intention to establish and maintain a central educational institution for imparting general and technical education in all its phases.[132] The most notable incident of the period was a grant (30,000 rupees) received from Radha Kumud Mukherjee and Benoy Kumar Sarkar that enabled the council to constitute seven technical scholarships for advanced training in the United States. By taking this opportunity, one Hem Chandra Das Gupta went to Yale University to study mechanical engineering.[133] In 1911, the secondary programme of the BTI was extended to cover a period of four years. The City and Guilds of London Institute recognized the BTI and exempted students of electrical and mechanical engineering of the BTI from appearing at the preliminary examination of the institute.[134]

However, the crisis continued. Because of low salary, many of its reputed teachers left the institution. The crisis aggravated in 1912 when Taraknath Palit and the Maharaja of Cooch Behar decided to withdraw their money from the BTI and transfer it to the University of Calcutta. The university, under the vice-chancellorship of Sir Asutosh Mookerjee (1906–14, 1921–23), pursued a curriculum that had the approval of Palit and others. Their decision to transfer grants helped Sir Mookerjee to initiate post-graduate teaching and research at the University of Calcutta. The BTI could not attract enough students to its courses during these years.[135]

The BNC also found it difficult to attract students to a training programme where both cultural education on national lines and techno-scientific education were imparted. Although initially the NCE scored a triumph over its rival, the SPTE, over the question of ideology, the institution that eventually survived was the BTI – according to Benoy Kumar Sarkar – the institution of alleged materialism or bread-butter (*dal-bhat*) philosophy.[136] By 1916–17, the BNC found itself with empty benches and eventually ceased to exist.

Towards Engineering Education and Industrialization

The BTI students of the second decade of the twentieth century constituted practically the first batch of young men looking for careers in mechanical, electrical, chemical, and allied industries after a systematic technological training. By this time, industrialists with a nationalist persuasion started recruiting students from the BTI.[137] The higher technical department consisted of (*a*) mechanical engineering, (*b*) electrical engineering, and (*c*) industrial chemistry. In fact, the first generation of mechanical and electrical engineers in Bengal were BTI scholars. By 1918, the managing committee of the BTI itself was radically transformed. Of its 19 members, only 9 were 'non-industrial, non-engineering, non-business' people.[138] It was decided to buy land in the suburbs for its new campus, encourage students for self-employment, and grant scholarships for research, among other things.[139] The engineering students of the institute went on to found industries or become managers and proprietors in them; to that extent, the nationalist programme progressed as scheduled. One of the important steps during this time was to employ foreign-educated Indian students as teachers of the BTI. In this context, the expression *knowledgeable-internationalism*, coined by Kris Manjapra, is important. According to him, intellectual *swadeshi*, the effort to create new nationalist institutions to channel the techno-scientific creativity of the people, was not rooted in local vistas alone, but in interchange with foreign institutions and habits in mind. Thus, intellectual *swadeshi* developed within an international horizon.[140] The nation's productiveness was augmented through an intellectual connection with the world beyond the British Empire, *swadeshi* knowledgeable-internationalists internationalists insisted. In the case of the BTI, the protagonists had both awareness of the progress of the engineering sciences and first-hand experience in founding industry. These individuals realized that the new industries, based on the developments in the exact sciences, such as synthetic organic chemistry, electricity, and so on, as disciplines necessitated different kinds of specialization and training. The needs of new technical skills and knowledge specializations were met by sending scholars on foreign study tours.

In 1921, it was decided to expand the scope of studies in engineering. A Syllabus Revision Committee was formed with Dr P. C. Ray as chairman. The syllabus of industrial chemistry was thoroughly revised. The new curriculum included chemical engineering, besides mechanical and electrical.[141] The next year, in view of the difficulty of securing competent teachers, especially in the Mechanical and Electrical Engineering Departments, it was decided to send four students to Germany for higher training with a contract of service on their return.[142] Under the scheme, in 1923, three scholars were sent to Germany for higher training under the contract with the council.[143] The advantage of such a scheme started showing soon. The Electrical Engineering Department was strengthened by the appointment of Suren Roy, master's from Harvard. He was the first scholar with an electrical engineering degree to be appointed by the NCE.[144] Hira Lal Roy, after receiving the degree of 'Doctor-Ingenieur' from the Technische Hochschule of Berlin, took charge of the newly reformed Chemical Engineering Department in 1925. The same year, the City and Guilds of London Institute Examination allowed students of the BTI to enter for the Grade II Examination in both electrical and mechanical engineering without appearing for the Grade I Examination.[145] The second generation of the BTI students, who came to be referred to as the Jadavpur engineers and technologists, turned out to be the pioneers of a new techno-scientific spirit and tradition. The industrial experience of Banesvar Dass, another alumnus, was varied. After graduating from Illinois (USA), he spent eight years in several American firms in the capacity of Chemical Engineer. He spent two years in Germany also and was the Director of an American export–import firm in the chemical department, which used to supply German chemicals to the US Navy. His researches, particularly in hydrogenation and the oil industry, were extensively utilized by several indigenous business concerns.[146] A versatile genius, Banesvar Dass became an asset to the institute.

By 1925, the power house, mechanical laboratory, chemical and physical laboratories, workshops, and so on, were constructed which were of immense importance for the smooth functioning of a technical institute. The council set up its own installation of electric lighting. The faculties of the Electrical Engineering Department, with the help of their students, successfully installed the power utility system at the Jadavpur campus.[147] The Calcutta Corporation sanctioned a yearly recurring grant of 30,000 rupees to the BTI for the theoretical training of the Corporation Workshop apprentices and for training them in various industrial subjects like 'oil industry, tar distillation, sugar manufacturing, soap making, etc.' The *Annual Report* of the NCE for the year 1927 proudly announced: 'University of Edinburgh has of its own accord granted recognition to the Technical Institute under section 4 (2) of the ordinance controlling degrees in Engineering and under section 6 (2) of the ordinance controlling degrees in Mining.'[148] The Mechanical and Electrical Engineering Departments of the BTI were placed under the supervision of H. C. Das Gupta (graduate from Michigan) and S. K. Roy (master's from Harvard) respecively – both alumni of the BTI. The engineering aspirants preferred electrical engineering over mechanical. A. T. Weston, Director of Industries, Bengal, who paid a visit to the BTI in 1927, was satisfied with the overall progress of the institute towards advanced training in technology.[149] Being an institute of a nationalist character, such recognition from the bureaucracy is significant.

Figure 1.2 *Journal of the College of Engineering & Technology* **(1938)**
Courtesy: Rare Division, Jadavpur University Library.

It was now felt that the BTI should be renamed the College of Engineering and Technology (CET), as a parallel institution to the Bengal Engineering College, Sibpur. A college magazine, the *Journal of the College of Engineering & Technology*, started in the year 1928.[150] It was the result of a cooperative endeavour between the faculty members and students of the institute. The journal was not a mere students' magazine or a mouthpiece of the college for news and views. It provided a glimpse of the techno-scientific and industrial world view of the Indian technocrats. One Satyabrata Majumdar, a third-year student of mechanical engineering, lucidly explained the inner mechanism of television (1936).[151] Mention may also be made of another interesting article titled 'What Is Electricity?' by Nirmal K. Sengupta, a final-year student of electrical engineering. The following is an excerpt from his learned article:

> Now as to the different eras of thought about the nature of electricity; in the first of these eras, beginning probably with the earliest observations in the middle of the sixteenth century, electricity was regarded as a soul or spirit; the second era may be said to have been opened by Carden in 1551 and closed by Maxwell in 1865, during which electricity was regarded as a material fluid of one or two kinds; in the third era electricity with its various manifestations was regarded as some kind of another disturbance of a continuous nature; the fourth era is that which is still with us. It may be called the atomic or quantum period, in which it is noteworthy that but little attention, has been paid to the ultimate nature of electricity and a great deal to its structure. Of course knowledge of the structure is likely to give some useful hint in future as to the nature of electricity.[152]

The techno-scientific milieu, both at home and abroad, for the Jadavpur engineers of the third decade (1930–9) was overall quite encouraging. The atmosphere of the educational institutions for engineering and technology could not be more favourable.[153] External stimulus was therefore plentiful – talks of an impending war had been instrumental in intensifying the urges for engineering and scientific education.

The demand for the electrical, mechanical, and chemical engineering among the Bengali intelligentsia was steadily on the increase. The CET authorities were also in the mood for expansion in the context of 'rapid development in ideas about the standard and scope of Technical Education'.[154] Accordingly, the courses were reframed: the Engineering Department with a five-year course in (*a*) mechanical, (*b*) electrical, and (*c*) chemical engineering; the Junior Technical Department with a three-year course in mechanical and electrical engineering, and the Survey and Draftsmanship Department with a two-year course.[155]

Like the Bengal Engineering College, Sibpur, the facilities for research work at the CET were practically nil. In those days, research in engineering was very expensive and required vastly superior equipment. The authorities, however, thought such work was only possible 'where post-graduate classes are held and teachers are saddled with less routine teaching work and there is sufficient money at disposal'.[156] The techno-industrial boom of the Second World War was reflected at the Jadavpur college as the authorities of the college decided to strengthen the Mechanical, Electrical, and Chemical Engineering Departments with additional apparatus and appliances. To meet the demands of the time, they also intended to introduce mining engineering, communication and automobile engineering, and sugar and film technologies in the existing curriculum of the college.[157] In the prevailing war-scenario, the government was compelled to change its attitude towards the CET, a nationalist institution. To meet the huge demand for technical manpower, at first the Defense Department recognized the chemical engineering graduates of the college and next the Director General of Posts and Telegraphs allowed the mechanical and electrical diploma-holders to be recruited to the grades of (*a*) Engineering Supervisors and (*b*) Assistant Foreman, Examiners, Instrument Testers.[158] A direct contribution of the Jadavpur college to the war effort was the provision of training to war-technicians for military and civilian industries. A special department was instituted in April 1941 with 16 electrician trainees. Courses for training of blacksmiths, fitters, turners, and carpenters were introduced. The trainees were directly selected by the National Service Labour Tribunal, Government of India. Most of the tools and machines were supplied by the government and the college received 7 rupees per month from the government as training expenses for each trainee.[159] The war ecology thus enriched the college in the larger project of 'mistrification' and 'technocratization'. A Manufacturing Department was opened at the college to utilize the workshops on a profitable basis without, however, weakening its efficiency for teaching purposes. It was considered that such an undertaking would benefit the students by giving them a practical demonstration of the commercial side of the workshop while increasing the avenues of income of the college.[160] For giving practical training to the students there were different workshops such as the machine shop, fitter's shop, pattern shop, foundry, and smithy. The machine shop was fully equipped with several types of modern machines. The electrical engineering laboratory consisted of different types of modern electrical machines and instruments for demonstrating the application of the general rules and principles of electrical engineering. There was also a moderately equipped laboratory for communication engineering, where various experiments on radio, telegraphy, and telephony were carried out. In the electrical workshop, facilities were provided for repairing, designing, and building electrical generators and motors, and so on.[161]

Triguna Sen, a doctorate from Munich, joined the Mechanical Engineering Department in 1943 and was subsequently appointed as the special officer to develop the resources of the Jadavpur college.[162] The Executive and Managing Committees of the NCE were considerably 'fortified' with the inclusion of contemporary engineers and industrialists. Of the 29 members of the Managing Committee for 1945, only Charu Biswas (justice) and Satyananda Bose (advocate) were of non-technical background. All the rest were engineers, employed either academically as professors or in industry and commerce. This change in the professional character of the members of the governing bodies, according to Benoy Kumar Sarkar, was an index to the sociocultural transformation of the Bengali people. The leadership of Bengal was passing, to some extent, into the hands of engineers, technologists, and industrialists.[163]

The Jadavpur college produced thousands of engineers and chemists of diverse denominations during its career in the first half of the twentieth century. They were being utilized far and wide throughout India in positions of technical, industrial, and commercial importance. A considerable part of the technical and industrial activities of the Indian population was being manned by the mechanical, electrical, and chemical engineers of Jadavpur as founders, proprietors, managing directors as well as technicians.[164]

At the end of our period of discussion, the course in electrical engineering at Jadavpur provided training in the fundamental subjects of the science of electrical engineering with applications in the broad fields of design, construction, operation, and maintenance of electrical machinery, electric supply schemes, illumination, electric railways, communications, and other branches. The theoretical work ran parallel with an elaborate course in the laboratories, which were provided with apparatus adapted to the needs of undergraduate study. Here the 'S. Ghosh Memorial Scholarship' was awarded annually for practical training in the subject abroad to a deserving 'Bengali Hindu' candidate who passed the final examination.[165] The course in Mechanical Engineering was planned to provide a sufficient foundation of basic science applied to engineering methods and techniques, to prepare the graduate to enter the industries dealing with heat, power, materials, and machinery, and to take charge of design, operation, maintenance, management of factories, workshops, power house, waterworks, and so on.

In the year 1945, the Massachusetts Institute of Technology (Boston), the University of Michigan, the Carnegie Institute of Technology (Pittsburgh), and Cornell University (Ithaca, New York) recognized the graduates of the Jadavpur college as qualified enough to join their post-graduate classes. The same year, the Imperial College of Science and Technology, London, accepted a graduate student of Jadavpur for post-graduate studies in chemical engineering. Thus, within 40 years of its glorious journey, the NCE and its progeny, the CET, Jadavpur, was one of the recruiting grounds of 'big business' for engineers, foremen, workshop managers, technicians, researchers, and proprietors – top to bottom of any industrial concern. The chemistry behind the success of this institution was brilliantly captured by Benoy Kumar Sarkar, one of the celebrated teachers of the NCE:

> My *sutra* (formula) in the pedagogies of technocracy and mechanism runs to the effect that not every *mistri* or technician can or will become an engineer. But, on the other hand, nobody can become an engineer who has not been a *mistri*. The daily handling of tools, implements and machineries belongs to the *mistri*'s routine work. This routine of daily tool-handling is the fundamental schooling for the engineer.[166]

Conclusion

We commenced this discussion with a reference to the transmission of knowledge in colonial South Asia. This was followed by a discussion on the shaping of the institutionalization of technical knowledge first by colonialism, and subsequently by national resistance to colonial rule. The industrialization programme was underway in the minds of those shaping the future of India's technical institutions. The mood of the nationalist uprising was such that these efforts in the institutional pedagogy were driven by the urgency of achieving economic self-reliance. The evolution of engineering education was complicated not just by the diverse motivations of colonial bureaucrats and technologists, but was also deeply influenced by the Indian men of science and technology. The Bengal Engineering College, Sibpur, sandwiched between its colonial connection and nationalist antagonism, fulfilled for long the demand for technical manpower in eastern India. However, the new urban intelligentsia was dissatisfied with the elementary character of the state-run technical education system and pleaded for advanced training in technology. This plea gradually turned into a search for alternatives to the colonial policy of governing technical institutions. The idea of having a system of higher technical education under a national management and on national lines was spreading.

The alternative crystallized as the National Council of Education (NCE) and its progeny, the College of Engineering and Technology (CET), Jadavpur.

The Bengal Engineering College, compared to other three government engineering colleges, maintained a practical character of teaching from the beginning which, in turn, provided better industrial orientation to the students. But colonial constraints compelled this college to adopt a 'go-slow' policy in the field of advanced technology, especially in mechanical and electrical engineering. Although it produced a large cadre of civil engineers, in the fields of mechanical and electrical sciences its performance was meagre. The result was as expected; among the alumni of Sibpur, with the rare exception of Sir R. N. Mookerjee, very few turned to business. In the fields of mechanical, electrical, or mining engineering, with rudimentary training, the students were mostly eligible for lower-level technical jobs. Entrepreneurship was not part of the vocabulary of the Sibpur students.

Unlike the predominant historiography which highlights the 'centre–periphery' relationship and the influence of the PWD and the military on engineering education, this chapter elucidates several positive points – in the case of the Sibpur college and its struggle to transcend the barrier imposed by colonialism. On several occasions, British bureaucrats acclaimed the superior quality of teaching, apparatus, and workshop facilities at the college, which was sometimes better or at least equal to their 'home' condition. Many demanded the upgradation of training and courses, but without success. Almost all the latest engineering sciences – mechanical, electrical, mining, industrial chemistry, and so on – were introduced immediately after their introduction in western Europe, but on a limited scale. Sibpur was unable to always attract the best brains of Bengal. This is evident from the testimony of the principal of the college in front of the members of Indian Industrial Commission (1916–18) and from the writings of the contemporary students (1907). The favourite destination of the Bengali youth was the legal profession, followed by medicine. On the eve of the Swadeshi and the national education movement, the situation was somewhat different. The Bengali educated class identified technological training and the subsequent industrialization as the final solution of their problems.

Convinced of the need of the time, the Indian luminaries, however, were sceptical of the Western model of industrialization, and for long argued for the need for alternative models better suited to the industrial climate of the country. However, within this group a section with technical background discarded those alternative models and pressed for the implementation of heavy industrialization, albeit under national control. The CET became a tough competitor of the Sibpur engineering college for the variety of its advanced engineering courses. The stakeholders of the NCE created a nationalist tradition from the generation of Surendra Kumar Roy and Hiralal Roy to Banesvar Dass and Triguna Sen. Its alumni went on to become the architects of modern industrial India. Many established *swadeshi* industries, and others manned such concerns at various capacities. Thus, science, technology, and nationalism went hand-in-hand in creating a concrete base for industrialization and a pool of indigenous manpower to sustain it. However, Sir P. C. Ray, President of the NCE in the 1930s and early 1940s, had a different vision:

> The Universities and Technical Schools of Bengal are producing their graduates or diploma-holders in any number. The teaching profession is already overcrowded and we are now confronted with the very serious problem of finding suitable careers and outlets for these young men. The lesson is obvious. A university-man sometimes does very well when appointed to a ready-made or going concern. But it is the self-made man with business instincts, struggling hard against adverse circumstances, who, as a rule, founds the business; who is known as the 'Entrepreneur'.[167]

Notes

1 *NCE Annual Report, 1909–10* (Calcutta: NCE, Bengal, not dated), Appendix H, ii.

2 *The Statesman*, 24 May 1936, 7.

3 Penny Summerfield and Eric Evans (eds), 'Introduction', *Technical Education and the State since 1850* (Manchester: Manchester University Press, 1990), 1–17.

4 K. V. Mital, *History of the Thomason College of Engineering* (Roorkee: The University of Roorkee, 1986), 98.

5 Dhruv Raina and S. Irfan Habib, 'South and South-East Asia: Introduction', in *History of Humanity: Scientific and Cultural Development*, Vol. VII, *The Twentieth Century*, ed. Sarvepalli Gopal and Sergei Tikhvinsky (UNESCO: Routledge, 2008), 722.

6 Bidisha Dhar, 'Technical Education Discourse in India: State and the Artisans, 1880s–1914', *Studies in History* 33, no. 2 (August 2017): 213–33.

7 S. Ambirajan, 'Science and Technology Education in South India', in *Technology and the Raj*, ed. Roy Macleod and Deepak Kumar (New Delhi: Sage, 1995), 112.

8 Suvobrata Sarkar, *The Quest for Technical Knowledge* (New Delhi: Manohar, 2012), 124–44.

9 Deepak Kumar, 'Racial Discrimination and Science in Nineteenth Century India', *Indian Economic and Social History Review* 19, no. 1 (January 1982): 63–82.

10 *Education Gazette O Saptahik Bartabaho*, 25 January 1889, 37.

11 Government of India Resolution No. 10/399, dated 23rd October 1884, in K. D. Bhargava (ed.), *Selections from Educational Records of the Government of India*, Vol. IV (Delhi: NAI, 1968), 15.

12 Home, Education, A Proceedings, July 1886, No. 27, NAI.

13 E. W. Collin, *Report of the Existing Arts and Industries in Bengal* (Calcutta: Bengal Secretariat Press, 1890), 31.

14 *Resolution of the Simla Conference (1901) on Technical Education*, Home, Education, A Proceedings, November 1901, No. 57, NAI.

15 Home, Education, A Proceedings, October 1902, Nos 67–75, NAI.

16 E. C. Buck, *Report on Practical and Technical Education* (Calcutta: Government Printing, 1901), 27.

17 Francis Spring, *Technical Education in India* (Calcutta: W. Newman & Co., 1887), 3.

18 Dhruv Raina, 'Institutions and Knowledge: Framing the Translation of Science in Colonial South Asia', *Asiatische Studien Études Asiatiques* 65, no. 4 (2011): 945–68.

19 Home, Education, Deposit, Proceedings, October 1904, No. 20, NAI.

20 Home, Education, A Proceedings, August 1903, Nos 41–44, NAI.

21 Home, Education, Deposit, Proceedings, October 1904, No. 20, NAI.

22 Ibid.

23 Atkinson identified three essential qualifications for a successful engineer in India, namely engineering knowledge: theoretical and practical, physical qualities, and moral qualities. Ibid.

24 J. G. Cumming, *Review of the Industrial Position and Prospects in Bengal in 1908 with Special Reference to the Industrial Survey of 1890* (Calcutta: Office of the Superintendent Government Printing, 1908), 45–7.

25 G. N. Gupta, *A Survey of the Industries and Resources of Eastern Bengal and Assam for 1907–08* (Shillong: Government Printing, 1908), 112–17.

26 The monographs for the various years were as follows: brass and copperware (1893–4), pottery and glassware (1894–5), cotton fabrics (1896–7), woollen fabrics (1897–8), silk fabrics (1898–9), ivory carving (1899–1900), wood carving (1901–2), tanning and leatherwork (1902–3), gold and silverware (1903–4), stone carving (1904–5), carpet making (1905–6), iron work (1906–7), paper making (1907–8), and ware and tinsel industry (1908–9). The publication of annual monographs seems to have stopped after this period. A. Z. M. Iftikhar-ul-Awwal, *The Industrial Development of Bengal 1900–1939* (New Delhi: Vikas, 1982), 43.

27 E. R. Watson, *A Monograph on Iron and Steel Work in the Province of Bengal* (Calcutta: Government Publication, 1907), 53.

28 *The First Industrial Conference: Full Text of the Papers Held at and Submitted to the Industrial Conference Held at Benaras in December, 1905* (Benaras: Industrial Conference, 1905), 1–5.

29 Dewan Bahadur K. Krishnaswami Rao, 'Indian College of Technology', in *The First Industrial Conference*, 21.

30 Bipan Chandra, *The Rise and Growth of Economic Nationalism in India* (New Delhi: Anamika, 2004).

31 Ben Marsden, 'Engineering Science in Glasgow: Economy, Efficiency and Measurement as Prime Movers in the Differentiation of an Academic Discipline', *British Journal for the History of Science* 25, no. 3 (September 1992): 319–46.

32 Peter Lundgreen, 'Engineering Education in Europe and the USA, 1750–1930: The Rise to Dominance of School Culture and the Engineering Profession', *Annals of Science* 47, no. 1 (1990): 49–51.

33 Melvin Kranzberg, 'Broadening and Deepening U.S. Engineering Curricula', in *Technological Education – Technological Style*, ed. Melvin Kranzberg (San Francisco: San Francisco Press, 1986), 78.

34 Spring, *Technical Education*, 20.

35 S. F. Downing, the then principal of the college, stated, 'The subject laid down by the University authorities for the above examination, which, I with my present instructive staff, I am unable to teach, are as follows – (i) Mechanical Machine design, (ii) Design and workshop appliances, (iii) The Steam Engine (in its practical aspect).' Proceedings of the Government of Bengal, General, Education, No. 3709, July 1885, WBSA.

36 *General Report Public Instruction in Bengal, 1884–85* (Calcutta: Bengal Secretariat Press, 1885), 7.

37 *General Report Public Instruction in Bengal 1885–86* (Calcutta: Bengal Secretariat Press, 1886), 75.

38 'Sibpur Civil Engineering College and Its Connection with the Sibpur Workshops', Note by F. J. E. Spring, *General Report Public Instruction in Bengal, 1893–94* (Calcutta: Bengal Secretariat Press, 1894), 17.

39 *General Report Public Instruction in Bengal 1897–98* (Calcutta: Bengal Secretariat Press, 1898), 9.

40 *Bengal Engineering College Centenary Souvenir* (Calcutta: no pub., 1956), 29.

41 Collin, *Report of the Existing Arts and Industries*, 3–7.

42 Proceedings of the Government of Bengal, General, Education, File No. 1485, May 1892, WBSA.

43 Home, Education, A. Proceedings, August 1907, Nos 84–86, NAI.

44 The following electric machines were received by the Bengal Engineering College, Sibpur – Ferranti (120 Incandescent 16 C.P. lights), one dynamo motor, two brush lamps, one brush and eight light dynamos, one gramme excitor for the Ferranti dynamo. General, Education, File No. 4C/22 – 1 and 2, Nos 4–5, May 1893, WBSA.

45 PWD, Civil Works – Miscellaneous, April 1896, Nos 1–7, NAI.

46 *General Report Public Instruction in Bengal for 1898–99* (Calcutta: Bengal Secretariat Press, 1899), 115.

47 *Bengal Engineering College Centenary Souvenir*, 80.

48 Home, Education, A. Proceedings, October 1901, Nos 80–4, NAI.

49 *General Report on Public Instruction in Bengal for 1903–04* (Calcutta: Bengal Secretariat Press, 1904), 30.

50 *Bengal Engineering College Centenary Souvenir*, 26–35.

51 *Shibpur College Patrika* 2, no. 1 (January 1903): 4.

52 *Shibpur College Patrika* 1, no. 8 (August 1902): 231–2.

53 *Shibpur College Patrika* 1, no. 2 (Phalgun 1314 B.S. [1907]): 25–29.

54 The course in technological chemistry would include: (*a*) lectures and laboratory work in organic chemistry and applied chemistry and (*b*) theoretical and practical work in the following branches of mechanical and civil engineering, heat engines, principles of machine design, drawing of building and machines, and manual training, carpentry and fitting. Home, Education, A. Proceedings, November 1907, Nos 47–50, NAI.

55 Home, Education, A. Proceedings, March 1908, Nos 8–13.

56 Raja Peary Mohun Mukherjee, member of the Association for the Advancement of Scientific and Industrial Education for Indians, commented:

> A graduate who has gone through a three years' course of special study and obtained a diploma will, I am assured, except not less than Rs. 100 per mensem from his employer, and very few of the smaller industries on which the Government of Bengal lays so much stress can hope for a margin of profit after paying so much.

Home, Education, A. Proceedings, October 1908, Nos 110–11.

57 H. C. Streatfeild, Officiating Secretary to the Government of Bengal, wrote to his counterpart at the Government of India, Home Department (dated 1 July 1908). Ibid.

58 General, Education, File 4C/81 – 1, Nos 61–65, November 1913, WBSA.

59 The final examination was held for the first time in 1912 and two candidates out of three cleared it. One obtained employment at the Tata Iron & Steel Works while the other remained at the college for research work. One occasional student started a dye factory in Calcutta and became very successful, while another was employed at Dr K. C. Bose's technical lab. Ibid.

60 General, Education, File No. 4C/9 – 12, No. 253, July 1914, WBSA.

61 Home, Education, A. Proceedings, October 1903, Nos 14–18, NAI.

62 Home, Education, A. Proceedings, October 1904, Nos 91–124, NAI. Three students were selected for advanced training in mining at the University of Birmingham. A short introduction about the first three scholars who received the State Technical Scholarship: (*a*) S. C. De was trained at the Bihar School of Engineering and obtained

a Survey Standard Certificate. He served the Birbhum Coal Company and Nandi Coal Company in the capacity of Mining Surveyor. (*b*) Asoke Bose, son of the great geologist P. N. Bose, was studying geology at the Presidency College when he was selected for the scholarship. He had already received practical and theoretical training in mining at the West Baraboni Coal Company which belonged to his father. (*c*) P. K. Majumdar was the Manager at the estate of the Maharaja of Gidhour. In that capacity he established a mica mining industry there and thus gained a practical knowledge of mining. Ibid.

63 Home, Education, A. Proceedings, July 1907, Nos 134–43, NAI. Many times, these Indian students encountered difficulties in the foreign countries due to the lack of sufficient information. In 1907, the Secretary of State appointed a committee to enquire into the position of theses scholars in England. In one such instance, the committee helped one Gopal Bhaduri, who came to England to study electrical engineering without much information, to locate an ideal institution for this branch of engineering. Home, Education, A. Proceedings, October 1908, Nos 27–35, NAI.

64 Home, Education, A. Proceedings, June 1909, Nos 145–52, NAI.

65 Home, Education, A. Proceedings, October 1910, Nos 69–70, NAI.

66 The Bengal government sanctioned a contingent grant for the Electro-Technical Laboratory of the College in 1911 under the head 'Provision for additional teaching staff for Electrical Engineering Department'. General, Education, File No. 4C/37, Proceedings Nos 221–2, June 1911, WBSA.

67 *Report on Public Instruction in Bengal for 1910–11* (Calcutta: The Bengal Secretariat Book Depot, 1911) 35–7.

68 Ibid., 41.

69 J. G. Cumming, *Technical and Industrial Education in Bengal, 1888–1908* (Calcutta: Office of the Superintendent Government Printing, 1908), 31.

70 The following subjects were recommended to be included at the proposed Technical Institute: 'Mechanical and Electrical Engineering, in both the higher and lower grades; Civil Engineering, up to and including the Overseer grade in any case; Textile subjects, and Commercial subjects.' *Proceedings and Report of the Committee Approved to Advise on the Creation of a Technical Institute for Calcutta and Allied Subjects* (Calcutta: Bengal Secretariat Book Depot, 1912), 7.

71 *Calcutta University Commission Report 1917–19*, Vol. III (Calcutta: University of Calcutta, 1919), 94.

72 E. H. Atkinson and Tom S. Dawson, *Report on the Enquiry to Bring Technical Institutes into Closer Touch and More Practical relations with the Employers of Labour in India* (Calcutta: Superintendent Government Printing, 1912).

73 Ibid., 89–90.

74 General, Education, File No. 4C/59 – 1, Proceedings Nos 50–3, March 1913, WBSA.

75 General, Education, File No. 6E/19 – 1, Proceedings No. 61, January 1914, WBSA.

76 *Bengal Engineering College Centenary Souvenir*, 54.

77 *Report on Public Instruction in Bengal for 1915–16* (Calcutta: The Bengal Secretariat Book Depot, 1916), 19–23.

78 Jagdish N. Sinha, *Science, War and Imperialism* (Leiden & Boston: Brill, 2008), 27–9.

79 *Report of the Indian Industrial Commission* (Calcutta: Superintendent Government Printing, 1918), 109–10.

80 Ibid., 95.

81 Evidence of Mr B. Heaton, *Indian Industrial Commission, Minutes of Evidence 1916–17, Vol. II, Bengal & Central Provinces* (Calcutta: Superintendent Government Printing, 1918), 249–50.

82 Ibid., 253.

83 Government of Bengal, General, Education, File 4 – C/3 1-2, Nos 1–6, April 1918, WBSA.

84 Government of Bengal, General, Education, File No. 4-C-11 (1), Nos 11–15, June 1919, WBSA.

85 Government of Bengal, General, Education, File No. 4-C-11 (2), No. 16, June 1919, WBSA.

86 *Report on Public Instruction in Bengal for 1920–21* (Calcutta: Bengal Secretariat Press, 1922), 58.

87 *Report on the Bengal Engineering College for the Quinquennium 1917–18 to 1921–22* (Calcutta: Bengal Secretariat Book Depot, 1922), 6.

88 The Upper Subordinate Classes were abolished after long years of existence. The last link of the college with the PWD was severed, and no more students were sent up for the examinations under the Joint Technical Board after July 1922. The control of examinations in the improved mechanical and electrical engineering courses was transferred to the newly created Board of Control for Apprenticeship Training from March 1922. Now the various departments of the college were thus recognized: (*a*) Civil Engineering Classes, (*b*) Mechanical and Electrical Engineering Classes, and (*c*) Mining Classes. The latter two were formerly Apprentice Departments. Ibid., 7–9.

89 *Report on Public Instruction in Bengal for 1923–24* (Calcutta: Bengal Secretariat Press, 1924), 27.

90 Arun Kumar, 'Bengal Engineering College (Sibpur): A Study in Historical Perspective', in *Science and Environment*, ed. Chittabrata Palit and Arun Kumar (Delhi: B. R. Publishing Corporation, 2013), 17.

91 The successful candidates were Brojendra Chandra Bagchi, Satipati Bhattacharya, Kumudranjan Chaudhuri, Bijoygopal Dutt, Ahmed A. N. Kaliruddin, and Ambikacharan Mukhopadhyay. *Report on Public Instruction in Bengal for 1932–33* (Calcutta: Bengal Secretariat Press, 1933), 19.

92 The first batch of students appeared at the degree examination of the University of Calcutta in 1936. The successful degree holders were three in number: Ramendra Nath Bandopadhyay, Sibapada Chattopadhyay, and Md Mahibul Majid. *Report on Public Instruction in Bengal for 1937–38* (Calcutta: Bengal Secretariat Press, 1938), 34.

93 *Report on Public Instruction in Bengal for 1939–40* (Calcutta: Bengal Secretariat Press, 1940), 7.

94 *Bengal Engineering College, Calendar for 1940–41*, 14.

95 Jagdish N. Sinha, 'Science and Globalization: Indian Experience in the Second World War', *Indian Historical Review* 33, no. 2 (July 2006): 134–60.

96 *Bengal Engineering College Centenary Souvenir*, 40.

97 *Bulletin Bengal Engineering College: One Hundred Twenty Fifth Anniversary Issue* (Calcutta: no pub., 1981), 13.

98 N. Das, *Plans for a Better Bengal: Progress of Post-War Reconstruction Planning in Bengal from 1st January 1944 till 31st October 1944* (Alipore: Superintendent Government Press, 1944), 32–5.

99 *Post-War Educational Development in India: Report by the Central Advisory Board of Education* (Delhi: Manager of Publications, January 1944), 41–7.

100 *Report of the Committee for the Development of Higher Engineering and Technical Education in Bengal*, quoted in *Report of the Director of Public Instruction, Bengal, 1945–46* (Calcutta: Bengal Secretariat Press, 1946), 9.

101 Ibid., 10.

102 *Bengal Engineering College Centenary Souvenir*, 44.

103 The University of Calcutta approved the new regulation for the degree of Master of Engineering in civil, mechanical, electrical, and metallurgical engineering in 1953. The first batch of post-graduate students were admitted in the year 1956. During the same time, the doctorate programme was also introduced to enhance the research activities of the college. *Bulletin Bengal Engineering College*, 14.

104 *Swadeshi* means self-reliance. The concept gained popularity during the Swadeshi Movement (1905–8), the first attempt to mobilize the masses into the elite nationalism of early twentieth-century Bengal. Sumit Sarkar, *The Swadeshi Movement in Bengal* (Ranikhet: Permanent Black, New Edition, 2010).

105 Sambit Mallick, 'Democratizing Scientific Knowledge through Building Scientific Institutions in Nineteenth Century India: The Sociology of Science Perspectives', *Current Science* 90, no. 8 (April: 2006): 1138–45.

106 Pratik Chakrabarti, *Western Science in Modern India* (Ranikhet: Permanent Black, 2011, paperback edn), 150.

107 Dhruv Raina and S. Irfan Habib, *Domesticating Modern Science* (New Delhi: Tulika, 2004), 85.

108 *The Dawn* 1, no. 12 (February 1898): 334.

109 Haridas Mukherjee and Uma Mukherjee, *The Origins of the National Education Movement* (Calcutta: NCE, Bengal, Second Revised Edition, 2000), 38.

110 The group included the leading nationalist figures of the day: lawyers, some among whom were to become leaders in the Indian National Congress, and a few scientists and

doctors. Prominent among them were Satish Chandra Mukherjee, Brajendra Nath Seal, Girish Chandra Bose, Ramendra Sundar Trivedi, Tarak Nath Palit, Nil Ratan Sarkar, Subodh Chandra Mullick, Rashbehari Ghosh, Gooroodas Banerjee, Chittaranjan Das, Radha Gobinda Kar, and Rabindranath Tagore, among others. Amitabha Mukherjee, *Fifty Years of National Education*, (Calcutta: NCE, Bengal, 1992), 32–5.

111 G. Subramaniya Iyer, 'Our Artisans and Mechanics: Or Indian Arts and Crafts', *The Dawn* 7, no. 9 (April 1904): 245.

112 'The Indian System of Training Workmen for the Manual Industries', *The Dawn and Dawn Society's Magazine* 1, no. 2 (November 1904, New Series): 75.

113 *The Dawn and Dawn Society's Magazine* 7, no. 3 (March 1911, New Series): 5.

114 'India's *Industrial Revolution*: What It Means and Involves', *The Dawn and Dawn Society's Magazine* 7, no. 10 (October 1911, New Series): 37.

115 Benoy Kumar Sarkar, *Education for Industrialization* (Calcutta: Chuckervertty, Chatterjee & Co., 1946), 94.

116 Raina and Habib, *Domesticating Modern Science*, 124.

117 *The National Council of Education, Bengal, Calendar 1906–1908* (Calcutta: NCE, Bengal, 1908), 37.

118 Ibid.

119 Sarkar thus praised Rakshit:

> In those days we Bengali were unfamiliar with mechanical or electrical engineers. It is interesting to recall that myself, several years younger than Rakshit as I was, used to look upon him as a veritable 'technical genius', a machine-man, a lathe-expert, a person of extraordinary merit. Perhaps it is relevant in this connection to add that Rakshit has since then exhibited his *forte* in machines and engines by undertaking iron foundries and engineering works of substantial dimensions at Tatanagar and elsewhere. Rakshit is by all means a pioneer of Bengali industrialism, 'mistrification' and technocracy.

B. K. Sarkar, *Education for Industrialization*, 85.

120 The Annual Report of the NCE, 1908, quoted:

> This department supplied some scientific instruments to the Ripon College for which the Principal of that college gave a good certificate. Some delicate surgical instruments of Dr. Indu Madhab Mullick were also repaired to his satisfaction. This department also secured some orders for repairs to certain oil mill engines in Ultadingi and for chimney erection works in Sulkia and Calcutta. It also secured and carried out an order for the complete installation of a sugar factory at Baghbazar and also the erection of a pencil factory at Tallygunge.

NCE Annual Report, 1908 (Calcutta: NCE, Bengal, not dated), 22.

121 *The National Council of Education, Bengal, Calendar 1906–1908*, 78.

122 *NCE Annual Report, 1907* (Calcutta: Bowbazar Street, not dated), Appendix F, xxii.

123 Radhakumud Mukherjee, 'The Exhibition at the Bengal National College', *The Dawn and Dawn Society's Magazine* 4, no. 4 (February 1908, New Series): 96–98.

124 *The Dawn and Dawn Society's Magazine* 5, no. 4 (April 1909, New Series): 130–46.

125 *The Dawn and Dawn Society's Magazine* 5, no. 7 (July 1909, New Series): 249.

126 B. K. Sarkar, *Education for Industrialization*, vii.

127 Quoted in ibid., 91.

128 Raina and Habib, *Domesticating Modern Science*, 131.

129 B. K. Sarkar, *Education for Industrialization*, 87–92.

130 *Directory of Technical Institutions in India Including Agricultural, Industrial, Technical, Commercial and Science School and Colleges* (Allahabad: Standard Press, 1909), 104–5.

131 *National Council of Education, Bengal: A History and Homage* (Jadavpur: Jadavpur University, 1956), 64.

132 Chittabrata Palit, 'The National Council of Education and Its Progeny: The College of Engineering and Technology, 1906-47', in *Science and Modern India: An Institutional History, c. 1784–1947*, ed. Uma Das Gupta (New Delhi: Pearson Longman, 2011), 857.

133 Before leaving for America, these seven scholars entered into an agreement with the council to serve it for at least seven years on their return to the country. *NCE Annual Report, 1909–10* (Calcutta: NCE, Bengal, not dated), 6.

134 *NCE Annual Report, 1912* (Calcutta: NCE, Bengal, not dated), 19.

135 Jogendra Chandra Ghose observed:

> The difficulty is in securing students because there is little chance of employment in Government offices. This difficulty will always remain as long as there are not sufficient factories under Indian management. Under the present circumstances in order to make the Institution successful the various technical departments should be worked on commercial basis.

NCE Annual Report, 1909–10, Appendix H, p. ii.

136 B. K. Sarkar, *Education for Industrialization*, 99.

137 *NCE Annual Report, 1918* (Calcutta: NCE, Bengal, not dated), 36–8.

138 *The National Council of Education, Bengal*, 28–9.

139 Student enrolment at the BTI rapidly increased. It became necessary to find a new campus and, after a hectic search, a plot of 100 *bighas* was taken on lease at a rent of 210 rupees per year at Jadavpur for 99 years from the Calcutta Corporation. *NCE Annual Report, 1922* (Calcutta: NCE, Bengal, not dated), 8.

140 Kris Manjapra, 'Knowledgeable Internationalism and the Swadeshi Movement, 1903–1921', *Economic and Political Weekly* 47, no. 42 (October, 2012): 53–62.

141 *NCE Report, 1919–21* (Calcutta: NCE, Bengal, not dated), 11.

142 *NCE Annual Report, 1922*, 5–6.

143 *NCE Annual Report, 1923* (Jadavpur: NCE, Bengal, not dated), 13.

144 B. K. Sarkar, *Education for Industrialization*, 248.

145 *NCE, Annual Report, 1925* (Jadavpur: NCE, Bengal, not dated), 5.

146 B. K. Sarkar, *Education for Industrialization*, 228–29.

147 *NCE Annual Report, 1926* (Jadavpur: NEC, Bengal, not dated), 9.

148 *NCE Annual Report, 1927* (Jadavpur: NCE, Bengal, not dated), 9.

149 A. T. Weston remarked,

> I can only say that in its equipment, machinery, power plant, varieties of actual engine and boiler plant, the institution has more resources than were available to me when I took the Honours Engineering Degree Course at the University of Manchester (1900–04). I am satisfied that both as regards equipment and the qualification of its teaching staffs the institution….

NCE Annual Report, 1927, Appendix H, 27.

150 *NCE Annual Report, 1929* (Jadavpur: NCE, Bengal, not dated), 8.

151 The most amazing wonder of the present times which argues to go a long way towards the welfare of man is the recent invention of the phenomenon of television. Most of us have had the direct experience of working a radio or getting a radio receiver caters songs, orchestra, speeches, etc. to our satisfaction. The performances occur at a spot far away from the radio receiver the function of which is just to catch those things from the air and serve us the same. Likewise, television helps us to see before our eyes speakers, actors, etc. making their respective performances which they do at a great distance.

Satyabrata Majumdar, 'Television', *Journal of College of Engineering & Technology* 8, no. 1 (September 1936): 37.

152 Nirmal K. Sengupta, 'What Is Electricity', *Journal of the College of Engineering & Technology* 9, no. 2 (December 1937): 121.

153 Benoy Kumar Sarkar, *India's Advances in Industrialism* (Calcutta: N. M. Ray-Chowdhury & Co., 1936), 6.

154 *NCE Annual Report, 1932* (Jadavpur: NCE, Bengal, not dated), 11.

155 *NCE Annual Report, 1934* (Jadavpur: NCE, Bengal, not dated), 7.

The Electrical Engineering Department in the late 1930s consisted of the following main courses: Elements of Direct Current Engineering, Direct Current Machines, Direct Current Measuring Instruments, Principles of Alternating Current, Electrical Drawing, Alternating Current Machinery, Transmission & Distribution, Industrial Motors & their application, Telegraphy & Telephony, and Electrical Power Generation & Distribution. The Mechanical Engineering Department taught the following: Drawing, Description Geometry & Mechanical Drawing, Engineering Mechanics (Elementary & Higher), Applied Thermodynamics, Steam Engine & Boiler, Steam Turbine, Internal

Combustion Engine, Mechanism, Hydraulics, Hydraulic Machines & Water Power Engineering, Machine Drawing & Design. Some of the papers were in common for both the departments.

College of Engineering & Technology, Bengal, Session 1937–38 (Jadavpur: Superintendent, NCE, not dated), 41–7.

156 Satish Chandra Chakrabarty, Professor-in-Charge of Mathematics, was conducting research for long. J. N. Basu, Professor of Mechanical Engineering, claimed to have invented a new design of gas generators. *NCE Annual Report, 1939* (Jadavpur: NCE, Bengal, not dated), 10.

157 *NCE Annual Report, 1940* (Jadavpur: NCE, not dated), 11.

158 *NCE Annual Report, 1941* (Jadavpur: NCE, not dated), 5.

159 Ibid., 10.

160 *NCE Annual Report, 1942* (Jadavpur: NCE, not dated), 9.

161 *College of Engineering & Technology, Bengal, Prospectus Session 1941–42* (Jadavpur: Secretary, NCE, not dated), 6.

162 Dr Triguna Sen had substantial industrial exposure at the Bavarian Provincial Water-supply Works and the Munich Municipal Water and Canal Works in Germany, and the Electric Supply Company of Dibrugarh in the capacity of General Manager in India. Later on, he became principal of the CET. *NCE Annual Report, 1944* (Jadavpur: NCE, not dated), 8.

163 Sarkar, *Education for Industrialization*, 27–31.

164 In this context, it is worth mentioning a few of the alumni of the NCE who ushered in a new technological culture in the country. Banshidhar Pal (1910) became Chief Engineer of Lahore Electric Supply; Dhirendra Lal Banerjee (1912) became Assistant Engineer of the Tata Iron & Steel Co. Ltd; Hemendra Kumar Roy (1921) became Managing Director of the Bengal Electric Lamp Works Ltd; Phanindra Mohan Basu (1922) was the Superintendent Power House, Delhi Cantonment; Durlav Krishna Basu (1923) was the Manager and Resident Engineer, Kasuli Power House, Simla; Nalini Bhusan Bhattacharji (1925) was Engineer at the Tinnevelly Electric Supply Co., Tuticorin; Dhirendra Saha (1926) was the Chief Inspector of the Lighting Department, Calcutta Corporation; Sudhansu Chakrabarty (1927) was the Exchange Inspector of Bengal Telephone; Rajendra Lal Bose (1927) became the Manager-Engineer, Gauhati Electric Supply Co.; Benoyendra Banerjee (1928) was the Engineer-in-Charge, Pabna Electric Supply Co.; Sudhir Kumar Chakrabarty (1928) was employed at the U.P. Electric Supply Co. Ltd., Lucknow, as the Main Superintendent; Arun Chandra Bhar (1931) was the proprietor of Bengal Electric Co.; Subodh Chandra Ghosh (1931) was the proprietor of Gopal Hosiery, Dhakuria; Arabinda Bramhachari and Lalmohon Ghosh (1933) were Shift Engineers at the Garden Reach and Cossipore Power Stations, respectively, of the Calcutta Electric Supply Co. Ltd; Sachindra Prosad Saha (1933) was the proprietor of Bharat Battery; Pravat Kumar Roy (1936) was In-Charge of the

Machinery Department, Bata Shoe Co., Batanagar; Surhit Kumar Das Sarma (1942) became Electrical Superintendent, Central PWD, Jharsuguda, BNR; among others. See the relevant *NCE Annual Reports*.

165 *College of Engineering & Technology, Bengal, Prospectus Session 1944–45* (Jadavpur: Secretary, NCE, not dated), 44.

166 B. K. Sarkar, *Education for Industrialization*, 5.

167 P. C. Ray, *Life and Experiences of a Bengali Chemist*, Vol. I (Calcutta: Chuckerverty, Chatterjee & Co. Ltd, 1932), 355.

2

Entrepreneurship, Industry, and Technology

> Bengal is the poorer for the death, which took place yesterday at the age of only 52 of Mr. H. Bose, the well-known perfumer. Mr. Bose was a born businessman. He came from Eastern Bengal and studied both at University and Medical College at Calcutta. He did not graduate either in Arts on Medicine, but his Medical studies appear to have directed his attention to the subject of perfumes and here his business acumen enabled him to score a veritable triumph. But Mr. Bose's energies were too great to be confined to a single trade, and a few years ago he developed a large Gramophone Business, started a well-equipped printing press, and launched out into the motor trade. Most if not all these enterprises have been highly successful....
>
> —*The Statesman* commemorates the sudden demise of Hemendra Mohan Bose, popularly known as H. Bose, famous perfumer and mechanic (1916)[1]

> An important subject to which I should like to refer is the progress of science and industry in this country. Faced as we are with international conflicts of gigantic proportions, it does not require much imagination to see that the scientific and industrial development of a country is essential not only for its prosperity but also for its very existence. The industrial development of a country is, however, conditioned not only by research but also by the all-important questions of finance and national policy. In Germany, the intimate cooperation among the government, universities and the industrial organizations resulted in a very rapid development.... If the government, universities and industrial organizations are made to participate in a national policy of intensive industrialization, none can resist the early attainment of India's economic freedom.
>
> —Syama Prasad Mookerjee, eminent educationalist and politician, in his speech delivered at the Banaras Hindu University Convocation (1940)[2]

The collaboration between academic institutions, industry, and the state is vital to innovation and progress in a knowledge-based economy. Innovation, the reconfiguration of elements into a more productive combination, takes on a wider connotation in today's world. Earlier, a small section of specialists in industry and academia were interested in innovation, but recently the ideal configuration between academia, high technology, and business-firm formation has become a matter of public concern and debate. The current buzzword, triple helix, expands the scope of interaction between the three – university, industry, and government.[3] It focuses on the university as a source of entrepreneurship and technology as well as pioneering research. Entrepreneurship is an individual as well as collective initiative. The latter is typical of knowledge-based firms that require both technical and managerial expertise which is rarely available in a single person. Entrepreneurs may be professors, engineers, inventors, or businesspersons. Entrepreneurial training should be part of general education in an era of a knowledge-based innovation system in which universities, firms, and governments interact closely even as they maintain their primary roles and distinct identities.

Higher educational institutions and the state may also act as entrepreneurs, signifying that entrepreneurship is not limited to business alone. Entrepreneurship has also expanded in recent years as it can be taught to a diverse community. A rapid advance in entrepreneurial education in India, across the universities, from the engineering and business schools to the arts and sciences, demonstrates its significance to business innovation, industry, and economic growth. Innovation is the dominant ideology of our time, embraced by the economic and political elites. As the pursuit of innovation enthuses engineers, technological novelty takes centre stage. Andrew Russell and Lee Vinsel ask, what happens after innovation? According to them, the maintenance and repair of technologies that already exist and were innovated long ago have a huge impact on the everyday lives of people rather than technological innovations.[4] The maintainers are responsible for the proper functioning of technology. Their labour sometimes goes unappreciated due to our obsession with novelty. As most of the Indian engineers during the colonial times were maintainers, not innovators, in the true sense of the term, a shift of focus on maintenance provides opportunities to locate them and identify their perspectives appropriately. How did Bengali entrepreneurs and managers acquire the technological capacities, first, to operate the new technologies and, second, to do so at levels of efficiency enough to withstand the competition from the world's technological leader, Britain? What was the perception of Bengali entrepreneurs about modern technical knowledge?

Overall Trends in Industries

South Asian economic history, until recently, has debated the questions of deindustrialization, development, and underdevelopment as well as under-capitalization of the economy and society. One new dimension to this archive recently added includes new small-scale industries such as leatherworks, metalworks, woodworks, and so on, whose existence provides further information about the transformations and continuities in Indian crafts industries.[5] It is also important to consider the question of large-scale industry: industrialization provided the necessary impetus for the developments of the twentieth century. As the British were unsure about the consequences of uncontrolled technology transfer and subsequent increase in competition, they were reluctant to initiate the industrialization of the country. The process of diffusion of technologies received patronage only when the knowledge systems concerned were 'useful to the imperialists'.[6] Michael Mann argues, as a result, even the importation and introduction of steam engines were delayed for several decades. He identifies a disparity in the railway network: unlike the industrialized countries in Europe and the United States, in India barely any '"locomotive effect" dissipated out from the hub of the rail network influencing the surrounding industries'.[7]

After the financial debacle of 1846, Indian elites were not very confident about establishing industrial enterprises in Bengal. However, they again joined hands with British capital when the latter founded textile mills in Bombay and Calcutta during the 1870s. Within a short time, the number of jute mills along with looms increased almost six times in Calcutta. The jute industry was entirely owned by Europeans, which made the business environment of the city completely different from that of Bombay.[8] The intention of the Indian entrepreneurs was to replace the textiles imported from Britain with local products and to ultimately control the Indian market. The owners and managers of the cotton industry of Bombay were mostly Indians. Thus, the strategy of gradual substitution of foreign products was successful in the cotton industry, but not in the leather or the iron and steel industry. Rothermund identified two major obstacles that prevented the smooth industrialization of the subcontinent – lack of capital markets and a general deficiency of mechanization throughout.[9] The industrial belts in India were also unevenly distributed, in accordance with the geographical characteristics of the land. Bombay and Ahmedabad specialized in cotton processing, Calcutta dominated jute production, whereas Jamshedpur, from the beginning of twentieth century, excelled in iron and steel works. As no structural links connected these belts, Tomlinson argued, any beneficial 'synergistic effects' failed to materialize. On the eve of independence, the two textile production regions produced two-thirds of the entire output of British India, which Tomlinson cited as another indicator of the 'asymmetrical industrialization' establishing long-term disparities in the primary sector.[10]

Throughout the colonial era, Tirthankar Roy opines, two conditions prevailed: First, Indian large-scale industry continued to depend on the import of capital goods and manufactured items such as electrical apparatus, transport equipment, and heavy chemicals. Second, it continued to depend on highly paid foreign technicians. Although such dependency weakened gradually, its pace varied across key industries. The colonial state, Roy continues, neither encouraged industrialization nor blocked its development. The urban capitalists were free to pursue their trade, and many identified mechanized industry as a profitable avenue for investment.[11] The industrial sector's logistical inequalities enhanced the geographical variations and the numerous administrative directives. Thc British were reluctant to provide sufficient repairing facilities, including replacement materials. The undeveloped urban power supply remained a constant problem throughout, which compelled several industrial firms to produce their own electricity. On the contrary, Indian elites rarely thought of investing in machine-making and developing a curriculum to replace the foreign technicians with their own.[12] Indian entrepreneurs established the Victoria Jubilee Technological Institute (1888) in Bombay for advanced training in technology. Although Morris declared such initiative as exceptional and very unlikely for the rest of the country, where European experts largely dominated,[13] one can find a similar example of founding an institute for professional training in Calcutta. But the initiative here came from the educated strata, not from the business class of the society. A few educated Bengali elites with advanced training in techno-science invested in industry in the late nineteenth and early twentieth centuries. Some of them were also involved in the management of as well as teaching in the premier engineering and science colleges of the city.

Choice of Technology

Recently, economic historians, along with the historians of science and technology, have started exploring the approach of Indian industrialists towards technology during colonial times. The newly built cotton textile industry in western India was almost an exact replica of Manchester. According to Morris D. Morris, not only the technology (spinning and weaving machinery), but also the physical layout of the premises of the British and Indian mills resembled one another a lot.[14] The 'organizational and institutional environments' of India were responsible for such technological backwardness.[15] The Indian promoters of industry had neither knowledge nor experience in dealing with modern technology. Due to their mercantile origin, they restricted themselves to the financial aspects and hired British experts for managing their cotton mills. The British experts were mostly the agents of various British machine manufacturers and they had a natural bias towards foreign technology. In the early nineteenth century, Indian engineers were not readily available as there were very limited training opportunities in the country.

The early Indian cotton textile manufacturers continued to ignore various new technologies (ring technology, automatic power looms, and so on) due to their fascination with British-made machinery. China and Japan, on the other hand, were quick to adopt these technologies and, as a result, Indian textile firms faced tough competition from them within India. A significant attribute of a modern entrepreneur is personal knowledge of technology – as he is responsible for identifying appropriate technology for the enterprise. Due to the imperial connection, Dwijendra Tripathi notes, the Indian promoters of industry were unable to develop such essential technological inclinations.[16] As the leading industrial nation, Great Britain influenced and even dominated the technological choices in India.

Rajnarayan Chandavarkar argues that on closer examination a different picture of the development of the cotton textile industry begins to emerge. It was not so much the continuous application of new techniques which characterized the growth of the industry in India as much as the relentless improvization in relation to the use of old machinery, the manipulation of raw materials, and the exploitation of cheap labour. The increasing competitiveness of the new mills of Kanpur, Sholapur, and so on, was not based upon the use of machines that were newer and better than those used in Bombay and Ahmedabad but upon second-hand machinery that had sometimes already been scrapped by their older rivals.[17] Apart from cotton manufacture, another prominent industry of the first half of the twentieth century was steel production. The industry remained almost synonymous with the House of Tatas as the Tata Iron and Steel Company Ltd. (TISCO) at Jamshedpur was the only Indian concern in the field which was doing well at the time of independence. J. N. Tata, its founder, first explored the possibility of securing technical expertise from Great Britain. Having failed in his attempt, he turned to the United States, the largest single producer of steel in the world. Tata's other ventures, too, depended on imported technology, with no attempt to modify it or use it as the basis for developing indigenous 'know-how'. Of these, the hydro-electric system was for all practical purposes managed by an American syndicate between 1930 and 1951.[18] Generally, at the stage of the initial industrial surge, the tendency to import a range of consumer goods is replaced by successful import substitution, that is, by industrial production at home. During industrialization, the initial high level of importation of capital equipment and modern technology – paid for by the export of manufactured goods – gradually gives way to a rise in the internal production of such goods. But this structural change, led by the trading sector, depends upon economic sovereignty. Under the dominance of British colonial policy, Ian Inkster argues, India was in fact unable to instigate effective sovereignty of decision-making over economic matters.[19]

Finally, although the jute and cotton textile industries were the most important ones in the modern manufacturing sector, their contribution to the total national income or the growth of national income was insignificant in relation to the contribution made by the agricultural and small-industry sectors, and, more particularly, by exports of raw materials and food grains.[20] Industry types can be defined by three basic characteristics relating to: technology, organization, and government regulation. Large-scale industry used machinery and steam-powered technology. It was a relatively more capital-intensive sector in manufacturing. Tirthankar Roy argues that small-scale industry can be further divided based on a fourth characteristic, vintage.[21] Large-scale industry was a product of the Industrial Revolution, and its growth in India was partly a result of colonial India's economic relationship with Britain. For the majority of the small-scale industry firms, on the other hand, the products and technologies dated to the pre-colonial period. This set of enterprises can be referred to as the 'traditional' small-scale industry. There was, however, what Roy identifies as a few small-scale firms of modern origin. Compared to the large-scale industry, these were units of a smaller scale, which were usually unregulated and, when compared with the traditional industry, were usually of recent vintage, used machinery to a greater extent, and, on average, were of a higher scale.[22]

A big question mark in Indian industrial history concerns modern small-scale industry. Recently, scholars have started questioning the homogeneity of the Indian capitalist class and the promoters of this view argue that the Indian capitalist class can be divided into two sections – the big, on the one hand, and the small and middle, on the other. While the big bourgeoisie class was interested more in the importation of Western technology than in initiating indigenous research, the small and middle-class bourgeoisie sought to move in the opposite direction.[23] Although this dependency was also partly noticeable among the small- and middle-scale entrepreneurs, at least in the early twentieth century, with the passing of time they pursued a policy of self-reliance and sought to make innovations in technology in different branches of industry and thus to remove the reliance on foreign machinery as far as possible. One of the most important names in the field of the *swadeshi* machine-building industry is Alamohan Das, the founder-proprietor of the India Machinery Co. The company published the following advertisement: 'For the textile industry, the *India Cotton Loom* – Here indeed is great news, a mighty machine which will help India to achieve more triumphant glories in the field of her Textile Industry. *India Cotton Looms* are manufactured and designed by the country's greatest development in machinery research....'[24]

Many of the early promoters of Indian mills had been traders and moneylenders before entering the industry. Thus, the businesses were run by persons who had little personal insight into technical matters. However, even the entrepreneurs with technical competence did not demonstrate a willingness to promote technological innovation.[25] The technological vision of neither the established houses nor the technically qualified entrepreneurs went beyond import substitution. Technology development was their lowest priority. The story, however, was different for at least the small- and medium-sized entrepreneurs of Bengal.

Despite Bengal's traditional aversion to business, during the first two decades of the twentieth century several Bengali-owned small- and medium-sized firms were established. This was largely a result of the nationalistic *swadeshi* agitation that followed Curzon's partition of Bengal in 1905, but also a response to the slogans of economic nationalism emanating from the Bengali intellectuals from the late nineteenth century onwards. Enthused by science and the strident technocratic nationalism, they went into several advanced lines of manufacture.[26] The backgrounds of the big Indian industrialists and the small- and medium-sized Bengali entrepreneurs were somewhat different. Among the first to start chemical production in Bengal was Prafulla Chandra Ray, who had a PhD in chemistry from the University of Edinburgh and later taught the subject at the Presidency College, Calcutta. Suren Roy and Kiran Roy, proprietors of Bengal Lamp, were educated in Germany and later closely associated with the College of Engineering and Technology, Jadavpur. Their's was the pioneer electric bulb manufacturing company. Most of these firms specialized in relatively technologically intensive production lines that demanded constant upgrading, modernization, and diversification; in short, there was a requirement for an emphasis on research. Surendra Mohan Basu, the founder of the Bengal Waterproof Works, popularly known as Duckback, formulated a new process known as the 'Duckback Process' for the manufacture of waterproofs. He remarked,

> There are many categories of waterproof – Chemical Proofing, Tarpaulin or Canvas Proofing, Paper Proofing and Oil-cloth or Rubber-cloth. Tarpaulin was also previously manufactured in our country. But in the field of chemical proofing we are the pioneer. One can understand the feasibility of paper proofing if we look to the examples of Europe and America. Many

> products are vulnerable to air or water. To keep these products fresh for a long time, the only remedy is paper proofing. For example, take the Gillette blade – every piece of which is wrapped with a proofed-paper. The same is true for imported biscuits. We are successful at producing excellent quality proofed paper at our factory. Our products are cheaper than the imported foreign paper. But, unfortunately, people are not aware about its utility in our country. We manufacture the following products at our proofing section – raincoats, motor-hoods, hold-alls, and curtains.[27]

In the case of small- and medium-sized firms, master craftsmen often became entrepreneurs themselves. Since they were directly involved in the process of production, they had complete command over the process. The way the Indian big industrialists emerged and developed was basically different from the way small and medium entrepreneurs developed. This section differed from the former in terms of social origin, methods of primary accumulation, knowledge of the process of production and engagement in original research, dependence on foreign experts for the selection of sites for factories, building plans, machinery, and a variety of other ways. Each industry had its own somewhat unique history, shaped by its technology and the nature of its connection with the existing economic and social system. It is necessary to have some idea about these specific aspects, as well as about general tendencies. Considering two case studies, Sir Rajendra Nath Mookerjee and Dr P. C. Ray, the section that follows presents brief studies of two major industrial ventures managed and run by Bengali entrepreneurs.

Sir Rajendra Nath Mookerjee: The Doyen of Indian Engineering

Two sorts of Indians acquired Western technical culture: experts, as a result of their education and experience, and entrepreneurs, who purchased the expertise they needed. In the late nineteenth century, India had hundreds of working engineers and almost all of them were subordinates. The very few who rose beyond that level did so by leaving government service and rising to prominence either in private enterprise or in the service of the native states. The life and work of Sir Rajendra Nath Mookerjee (1854–1936) serves to illustrate this point.

Sir Rajendra Nath, the acknowledged leader of commerce and industry in Calcutta, was a self-made person who scaled the highest peaks of success as an engineer and in multifarious business enterprises. Starting from modest beginnings, he reached this position of eminence by sheer will-force and determination.

He was born in 1854 into a middle-class orthodox Brahmin family in Bhabla, a small village near Basirhat, not far from Calcutta. He lost his father at a very early age and had to depend on his relatives for his education. Ill-health and poverty greatly hampered his education.[28]

After passing the matriculation examination, Rajendra Nath joined the engineering class of the Presidency College. The Civil Engineering Department of the Presidency College was, at that time, simply a medium through which the Public Works Department (PWD) recruited its surveyors, overseers, and so on. The obvious result was that those who took up this line seldom looked beyond subordinate posts within the PWD. In those days, entrepreneurship in the field of engineering was rare. Rajendra Nath remained at the college for three years and developed a genuine and passionate liking for this branch of engineering. However, before he could take his diploma, he was forced to give up his studies on account of poor health.[29] At this stage, Rajendra Nath received a job offer as a surveyor, with an offer of good remuneration. The offer was made through a friend, who was then head clerk to the Chief Engineer of the Government of Bengal. After careful consideration, he decided to refuse the offer. Unlike his contemporaries, Mookerjee somehow retained an independent spirit; instead of entering government service, he struck out on his own as a private contractor.

Rajendra Nath developed immense curiosity in relation to engineering problems, especially in the field of civil engineering, and never lost an opportunity to carefully study big buildings and engineering schemes in Calcutta.[30] One day, as he was watching a bridge in the course of its construction, he found that the English engineer in charge had great difficulty in explaining to the workmen how an abutment wall was to be built, just before the spring of an arch, at the Alipore Zoological Garden, which had just been sanctioned and was being planned. He understood the situation instantly, and calling over the foreman, explained clearly to him in Bengali what was to be done. This brought him into contact with the English engineer, Bradford Leslie, and then the Chief Engineer of the Calcutta Corporation, who was later to become famous as the designer of the Hooghly Bridge. Leslie took Rajendra Nath round the Palta Waterworks, which was being extended at that time, and was so favourably impressed by his grasp of detail that he gave Rajendra the contract for the entire work.[31]

Then came the all-important question of capital. For an unknown Bengali businessman, with hardly any antecedents, it was impossible to arrange financial aid, even though he had the corporation's agreement in hand. One of his friends, Debendra Nath Sen, at that time a student at the Sanskrit College, lent him 1,000 rupees to begin his work. Fresh from his academic studies, Rajendra devoted his attention at first to an extensive use of the level and the theodolite – this was a natural choice because these were the instruments he could readily handle in an efficient manner.[32] The contract for the construction work at Palta was completed to the satisfaction of the Chief Engineer and was finished on time. It became a stepping stone for Rajendra Nath, which was to lead him from one successful task to another. Gradually, he rose to prominence in the field of engineering. Henry Kimber, the then Chief Engineer of the Calcutta Corporation, invited him to remain at the waterworks and supervise the maintenance of the filter and settling tanks. Rajendra Nath readily agreed to the offer and during his tenure as maintenance contractor at Palta he took on small construction jobs under the PWD in Calcutta and Chinsura.[33]

Maintenance work was almost entirely of a routine nature and once the routine was established, nominal supervision was all that was required. Rajendra Nath perfected the machinery at the Palta Waterworks to such an extent that he felt quite secure of his contract work and found ample time on his hands that could be utilized profitably elsewhere. Then, he set out in search of large construction projects. Rajendra Nath's commercial career started to become large scale with the setting up of T. C. Mookerjee & Co., with Bhutnath Mookerjee as partner.[34]

He ultimately succeeded in obtaining a large contract in Hooghly for the construction of law courts, and several small repair jobs. Rajendra Nath was associated with the Calcutta waterworks from the very beginning. At about this time, the Corporation of Calcutta sanctioned a scheme for the laying of a 40-inch (100-centimetre) diameter main pipe line from Palta to Calcutta, at an estimated cost of over 5 million rupees. On behalf of his firm, Rajendra Nath secured the contract for laying the main water pipe after competing against six European competitors.[35] As a result of his experience, along with his skill, foresight, and innovations, Rajendra Nath's firm was able to complete the contract within 18 months and to the full satisfaction of all concerned.[36] In a short time, he came to be known as the foremost authority on waterworks in Bengal.

The Government of the United Provinces of Agra and Oudh contemplated a series of waterworks installations in the chief towns, and, with 10 years of experience in the field of waterworks, Rajendra Nath submitted a tender for the proposed waterworks at Agra. In Calcutta he was well received, but in upcountry areas, however, British officials were more entrenched in their prejudices. Although he provided the lowest tender and was strongly recommended by the Agra Municipality, it was not accepted by the government and the contract was given to a European firm. The rejection could only be explained on the grounds that the tender had been submitted by an Indian.[37] And yet such was Rajendra Nath's reputation that when tenders were being submitted for the much bigger waterworks scheme at Allahabad his help was sought by a number of English businessmen in Calcutta, each of whom wanted to secure his services as a paid employee. He summarily rejected all offers.[38]

A British engineer, Acquin Martin, suggested a partnership and Rajendra Nath readily agreed to the proposal. They secured the contract for what was the biggest project of its kind in north India at that time. Rajendra Nath supervised the work while Martin imported the equipment from Britain. The construction of the waterworks was completed on time and being the first waterworks installation in the United Provinces to be completed, the occasion of its formal opening was considered worthy of a ceremonious visit from the then Viceroy, Lord Lansdowne (1888–94). Just before the formal opening ceremony, an unfortunate incident occurred which again demanded a high level of engineering skill and self-confidence. Rajendra Nath once again proved his worth. His biographer narrated the incident as follows:

> On the evening prior to the ceremony, Rajendra Nath suddenly received an urgent summons from the superintendent of the engine-house saying that the Keralabagh pump was refusing to function and therefore not a drop of water could be pumped into the settling tanks. The programme was to fill up the settling tanks by noon the next day and from there lead the water into the filters. An ornamental fountain was especially installed with a pipe connection to the filters, and it was intended that the fountain should begin to play as the opening ceremony was being performed.... On receiving the message, Rajendra Nath hurried to the engine-house and remained there the entire night, helping the engine-room staff, but the pumps were obdurate and refused to work. At about four o'clock in the morning, exhausted and fagged out but with his brain still actively searching for a possible source of error, Rajendra Nath suddenly alighted on the reason: that perhaps the pumps were not working owing to the accumulation of air in the pipes. A hole was ordered to be drilled at the top of the bend and soon a hissing sound was heard, followed by a jet of water through the drilled hole. The defect remedied, the pumps began to function properly and water was rushed to the settling tanks with extra speed and thence on to the filters.[39]

Lord Lansdowne opened the waterworks and congratulated Rajendra Nath personally on the successful completion of the work. Martin and Mookerjee worked together on other schemes, and in 1892 started a new concern based on equal shares. This was the beginning of the great Indo-British organization known as Martin & Co.[40] The subsequent story of the firm was one of continued achievements. After initially specializing in waterworks, within a few years Rajendra Nath took the initiative in developing light railway lines to improve internal communications in Bengal, and Martin & Co. spurred the establishment of more than half a dozen companies for this purpose, one after the other.

Rajendra Nath understood that one of the greatest needs of the province was communication and there were hardly any connecting links between Calcutta and the outlying districts, except for the main Eastern Bengal Railway line. Rajendra Nath, on behalf of his firm, offered services to the administration as a contractor for the construction of light railway lines on the understanding that

> during the construction period, or immediately after, his firm would establish a joint stock limited liability company with the guarantee of a minimum dividend rate to the shareholders, this guarantee being issued under the imprimatur of the local municipality or district board, or jointly under the authority of the Government of India and the local administration.[41]

Figure 2.1 Howrah–Sheakhalla Light Railway, a dream project of Rajendra Nath Mookerjee

Source: *Martin Burn Limited* (Calcutta: Martin Burn, not dated).

The first light railway line constructed under this scheme was the Howrah–Amta Light Railway (1897–8). The great impetus behind the development of this feeder line was to bring the surrounding district of Howrah within easy reach of the trading centre and this very soon created a popular demand for similar feeder lines all over the country (see Figure 2.1).[42] The completion of the Howrah–Amta Tramways (the popular name) was followed by the construction of the Ranaghat–Krishnagar line and the Barasat–Basirhat line. The latter was of special interest to Rajendra Nath, as it brought his village of Bhabla within easy reach of Calcutta. Not long afterwards, he received requests from the Behar area (present-day Bihar) for the construction of similar feeder lines in that province. Thus, the Bukhtiarpur–Behar and Arrah–Sasaram lines were developed by Martin & Co.[43] Girish Chandra Das, who in 1891 obtained a B.E. from the Bengal Engineering College, Sibpur, became the chief engineer of these light railways.[44] The success of Rajendra Nath attracted widespread attention and jealousy. The European business community of Calcutta was apprehensive, and this reaction found expression in the pressure being brought upon the Railway Board to discourage the development of feeder lines under the guarantee of government or local authorities. Finally, the feeder line policy under the guarantee system was officially discontinued.[45]

Another new initiative embarked on by Rajendra Nath was the designing and building of houses and palaces, and this reached its acme with the contract for the Victoria Memorial in Calcutta, the foundation stone of which was laid by King George himself in 1911.[46] Anukul Chandra Mitra, another alumnus of the Sibpur engineering college, was the engineer-in-charge of the construction of the Victoria Memorial Hall.[47] After the waterworks came the light railway constructions and the emergence of Martin & Co. as designers and builders. Almost all the striking and noble buildings which were built in the city during the first two decades of the twentieth century were planned by Rajendra Nath. The Mysore Memorial, the Esplanade Mansions, and the Chartered Bank Buildings, to name only a few, are amongst the most notable contributions he made as a civil engineer.[48] Rajendra Nath thus began his career as a builder and his most deep-rooted inclination had always been to construct something durable. Under his competent guidance, the company's fame as a pioneer among architects and builders quickly spread across the land and even overseas.

Rajendra Nath's reputation as a keen businessman with a strong common sense and sensible views on public affairs was steadily growing and he was made a C.I.E. in 1909 as a 'Captain of Industry in Bengal'. Under the Morley Reforms he was first offered a place on the Lieutenant Governor's Executive Council, which, however, owing to certain legal difficulties he was unable to accept. Mookerjee was nominated as the Sheriff of Calcutta in 1911 and honoured with a knighthood the same year at the Coronation Durbar at Delhi. In 1922, Sir Rajendra Nath was conferred a K.C.V.O. for the successful execution of the Victoria Memorial Hall.[49]

In 1910, Sir Rajendra presided over the All-India Economic Conference at Allahabad and his presidential address furnished the starting point for a demand to conduct an exhaustive economic and industrial survey of India's potential wealth,[50] an enquiry that was ultimately conducted six years later by the Indian Industrial Commission (1916–18), of which Sir Rajendra was a member.[51] The idea of setting up a central organization of Indian engineers was mooted during this period and Sir Rajendra, the then acting chairman, warmly supported the proposal. On 13 September 1920, the Institution of Engineers (India) (IEI) came into being and Sir Rajendra Nath Mookerjee became its first president (1920–1).[52]

The distinguishing characteristic of the IEI in the interwar period was its emphasis on Indianization and industrialization. This was referred to by Sir Rajendra is his inaugural address. Rajendra Nath saw the formation of the IEI as heralding an era of equality, lauding 'the spirit of comradeship and co-operation in which British engineers have extended the hand of fellowship to their Indian colleagues'. He also saw the institution as a means of promoting 'the efficiency and training of Indian engineers', the better for them to harness India's plentiful natural resources in the cause of industrialization.[53] In fact, Rajendra Nath's election as president in the first full year of the institution's functioning was itself, as Aparajith Ramnath identifies, symbolic of the twin priorities of industrialization and Indianization.[54] Unlike most of those who had represented Indian engineering in the past, he was not a colonial government officer. Instead, at a time when 'native' engineers had limited opportunities, he had developed a successful career as an engineer-businessman.

Sir Rajendra Nath also presided over a committee of engineering experts which presented a unanimous report on such a technical and controversial subject as the Hooghly Bridge. For decades the problem of bridging the Hooghly River had been at the forefront of the city politics of Calcutta. When the government invited several expert engineers to sit together and collaborate in designing a new bridge over the river, one might have expected that there would be as many designs as there were members in the committee. However, Rajendra Nath acted as a unifying force and their famous report presented not only a practical solution to the problem but also a model for similar reports in future.[55]

Both as an engineer and as a businessman, Rajendra Nath had developed a deep and abiding interest in education. At the request of the Government of Bengal, he conducted an enquiry into the need for technical education in Bengal. His association with numerous committees[56] brought him into close contact with the realities of the problem. Rajendra Nath realized that the existing facilities for technical education in Bengal were meagre. As early as 1910, he had pleaded for the establishment of a central technical college in India, rather than sending Indian students abroad for technical training.[57] Sir Rajendra had boldly asserted that 'there is nothing inherent in our blood which permanently disqualifies us from becoming sound and practical engineers'. To the students of the Bengal Engineering College, Sibpur, he had often provided practical advice, and his admirable summary in 'Fourteen Points' for engineering students[58] still remains significant. He was also instrumental in the opening of the East Indian Railway's Kanchrapara Workshop for Indian apprentices.[59]

Sir Rajendra Nath Mookerjee believed in the concept of an industrial future for India and had intense faith in the potential capabilities of his countrymen to absorb the commercial traditions and practices that had proved successful elsewhere, thus gradually helping India to become a first-class industrial nation.[60] The Indian Science Congress elected him as president for the 1921 session, a notable tribute to his eminence in the engineering profession. In his address, Sir Rajendra confined his remarks to the relationship between science and industry – science he referred to as organized knowledge and industry its practical application. He appealed for 'bridging the gap between the laboratory and the shop'.[61]

In an address delivered in Bangalore before the South Indian Science Association in 1928, Sir Rajendra defined the relationship of science to economic progress.[62] In his scheme for industrialization, he perceived the essential necessity for developing friendly cooperation between capital and labour and a harmonious blending of indigenous and foreign capital, as well as an alliance with Western practice in technical matters. He had no time for the 'vain prejudices of a narrow-minded *Swadeshi*, which mistakenly advocates the exclusion of foreign experts'. It was not impossible for an Indian to achieve great prominence in a modern technical profession, argues Daniel Headrick, but it was extraordinarily rare, and could only happen outside the normal career path; for Mookerjee, this was by associating with a British engineer. Thus, the lives of the eminent technicians were determined by politics. Sir Rajendra's success was not due only to his merits as an engineer and contractor, Headrick observes, but also to his partnership with Martin, which gave him opportunities perhaps denied to other Indian entrepreneurs.[63]

Sir Rajendra Nath's firm, Martin & Co., also emerged as a leader in the production of pig iron and steel, at least before the establishment of the Tata Iron and Steel Company (TISCO). The Bengal Iron and Steel Company, managed by Sir Rajendra's firm, had been producing pig iron from 1889 onwards, despite the long government refusal to extend any help. Along with Sir Martin, Sir Rajendra Nath Mookerjee contributed to the success of Bengal Iron at Kulti. Since then, the firm had been producing pig iron for the domestic market and had already established that the production of pig iron was a highly profitable business in India; however, the manufacture of steel was altogether a much more difficult proposition.[64] When the First World War put the profitability of the iron and steel industry in India beyond doubt, Sir Rajendra joined G. H. Fairhurst in founding the Indian Iron and Steel Company (IISCO) at Burnpur in 1919. Due to the collapse of the steel boom in the early twenties, IISCO was forced to confine its production to pig iron.[65] But it was also clear that the future lay in steel and not in iron products, for there was a progressive substitution of steel for iron.[66] Thus, IISCO could not take up such a pioneering role as undertaken by TISCO due to its inability to produce good quality steel.

It was also during the stewardship of Martin & Co., especially by Sir Rajendra Nath Mookerjee, that electricity-generating and waterworks installations were erected, bringing power to new industries and water for many parched areas. A pioneer again in the generation and distribution of domestic and industrial power in India, the Electricity Department of the firm was inaugurated in 1915. In the first half of the twentieth century, the department operated as many as nine electric supply companies and undertakings in different parts of the country.[67] A few well-established Indian business groups, such as the one led by Rajendra Nath, successfully achieved integration with European business ethics and cultural values. Rajat K. Ray denies that he belonged to the comprador groups in the strict sense of the term.[68] Rajendra Nath began his career as a 'maintainer engineer', and later his contribution in heavy engineering and construction work was decisive for the growth of a domestic industrial production system which was no longer entirely subordinated to the colonial import–export sector. It had so far been dominated by European management agencies. Sir R. N., as he was popularly known, summed up his views in these words:

> Our political friends are busy translating their aspirations into terms of constitutions and are thinking about majorities, electorates and votes. I ... picture an India of busy workshops, smoky factories, sanitary dwellings for the work-people and eager money-getters.[69]

Prafulla Chandra Ray and His Bengal Chemical and Pharmaceutical Works

This section probes the corpus of work and activity associated with Prafulla Chandra Ray (1861–1944), considered by many to be the founder of the tradition of modern chemistry in India. In 1888, the University of Edinburgh awarded him a doctorate for his thesis on 'Conjugated Sulphates of the Copper-Magnesium Group: A Study of Isomorphous Mixtures and Molecular Combinations'.[70] It is interesting to note how Ray, on his return to India, decided on his first research challenges. These had to do with the application of chemical knowledge to the extraction of chemicals that were hitherto being imported from England. His entrepreneurial activities began early, in the 1890s. While teaching in the Chemistry Department of the Presidency College in Calcutta, he wondered how the natural products of Bengal might be used to feed its poor. The industrial production of necessities was his solution. The history of European industrialization showed him that 'industry and scientific pursuits have gone hand in hand, both advanced *pari passu*, the one helping the other.... The history of the gigantic progress of industry achieved in Europe and America is a history of the triumphs of research in the laboratory'.[71] In 1893, the Bengal Chemical and Pharmaceutical Works (BCPW) was conceived as an industry with an in-house research laboratory that would have the capacity to develop efficient processes for manufacturing chemicals.

Prafulla Chandra's first attempt at producing citric acid from lemon juice had to be dropped, as it was not economically viable.[72] He soon realized that pharmaceutical preparations had a readier market. Prafulla Chandra examined Calcutta's drugstores to understand the volume of drugs imported from Britain. The premises for his 'work' were located at 91 Upper Circular Road, his rented apartment, and the laboratory was the outhouse of the residence, which was intended to be the kitchen. He used to work during the evenings after returning from college and looked after all aspects of the operation – performing the manifold functions of chemist, purchaser, salesman, and compounder. Most of the preliminary experiments on the preparation and testing of products to ensure their conformity with British Pharmacopoeia (BP) standards were done in his spare time in the Presidency College laboratory.[73]

But here, Prafulla Chandra was on unfamiliar technical ground. During his earlier visit to England, he had found that pharmaceutical preparations were closely guarded secrets. He started from the basics, reading books on British pharmaceutical preparations and texts such as the *Pharmaceutical Journal*, *Chemist and Druggist*, and Cooley's *Cyclopaedia of Recipes*. Working with much perseverance, he solved the problem of procuring and locally producing some of the basic ingredients, such as sulphuric acid and phosphates of soda. He soon found that most European drugs could be produced locally.[74] These he bottled in second-hand jars procured from local *bikriwallas* (scrap merchants) and vendors. But manufacturing BP products proved to be easier than selling them. Some drug firms expressed admiration for such a novel venture, others heaped ridicule on his efforts, but all agreed on one point – *deshi* (indigenous) drugs would not be bought by customers; it was only *bilati* (foreign) drugs of reputed firms that were in demand. However, Bengal Chemical eventually got its first break with an order from Butto Kristo Paul & Co. a leading Indian chemist and druggist firm.[75] Customers gradually began to accept his products, and the first modern Indian pharmaceutical establishment made its presence felt.

Amulya Charan Bose, one of his assistants, began a vigorous propaganda campaign among doctors. Soon, physicians such as Nilratan Sarkar and Radha Gobinda Kar were prescribing Ray's medicines. Their appeal to chemist and druggist stores began to show results.[76] Amulya Charan added another dimension to Prafulla Chandra's work by drawing his attention to the preparation of *kaviraji* (Ayurvedic) medicines. Amulya had consulted several *kavirajs* (practitioners of Ayurveda) and collected from them the formulae and recipes for Ayurvedic preparations, such as of *kalmegh* (*Andrographis paniculata*) and *vasak* (*Adhatoda vasica*). If selling *deshi*-manufactured BP preparations had been difficult, selling indigenous drugs was nearly impossible. Prafulla Chandra himself hawked the streets of Calcutta carrying sample 'phials' of Bengal Chemical preparations in his portfolio – Syrup of Vasaka, Ajowan Water, and so on.[77] It was then that Dr Kartik Chandra Bose came to his assistance.

Dr Bose, a gold medallist from the University of Calcutta and a successful medical practitioner, had a chamber within the shop complex of B. K. Paul & Co. It was Kartik Bose who induced Bhutnath Paul to allow Bengal Chemical's indigenous preparations a fair trial in his shop. Bhutnath was reluctant, even though the medicines had been prepared by a professor of chemistry, a D.Lit. from Edinburgh, but they had neither the refinement of the bottles, labels, or packaging of imported drugs nor the standardized stamp of a foreign pharmacopoeia. The efficacy and acceptability of such drugs could not be assured. However, Dr Bose argued that Syrup of Vasaka and Ajowan Water were common Ayurvedic medicaments used in every household in Bengal – one was a common remedy for coughs and colds, the other for indigestion. If such medicines were scientifically prepared by a reputable chemist in his laboratory, there could be no reason to doubt their efficacy. Dr Kartik Bose's support even extended to the point of promising Bhutnath Paul that if he accepted the six phials brought by Prafulla Chandra, Dr Bose would personally prescribe them to his patients. Thus, the ice was broken. Within two days the medicines were sold out and there were fresh demands for supplies.[78] This proved a great success, for they were easy to prepare in small workshops and could serve a large market. Aqua Ptychotis was manufactured using crudely constructed apparatus, while *vasak* was merely boiled in containers suspended over ordinary *chullas* (ovens) in order to extract *vasak* syrup. Such rudimentary equipment could hardly suffice in the longer term. Supply began to lag behind the increasing demand as sales picked up. Medical men, mostly peers of Prafulla Chandra, began to prescribe indigenous preparations and large numbers of shops began to stock Bengal Chemical products.[79]

Eventually, in 1900, the firm was converted into a limited liability company.[80] Manufacturing continued at 91 Upper Circular Road. The company now recruited some very able men who helped in its expansion and growth. Chandra Bhusan Bhaduri, a demonstrator of chemistry at the Presidency College, provided invaluable service. He quickly introduced innovations, and crude equipment was gradually replaced. Steam pans, disintegrators, vacuum stills, filter-presses, and other modern adjuncts of a modern pharmaceutical factory were introduced.[81] A plot of land was procured at Manicktala, in the suburbs of Calcutta, to expand operations. One contemporary journal reported an interesting incident:

> During this time, horse-driven trams were gradually giving way to electric trams. The stables for the horses were falling into disuse. Near Cornwallis Street was a large stable for horses. The stable shed was no longer in use and was bought by a Marwari, who was a patient of Upen Sen [a leading *kaviraj* who was later to become one of the directors of BCPW]. On the latter's advice, Dr. Kartik Bose bought the shed at a nominal price from the Marwari. This was shifted to Maniktala and was used in the construction of a factory building.[82]

In 1905, the manufacturing concern was shifted to the new factory site, but the offices remained in the city. The same year, construction began on the installation of a 4-ton sulphuric acid plant (chamber process: 72–74 per cent). Since its inception, the basic strength of Bengal Chemical was its spirit of innovation, along with its ability to adapt and modify. The entire sulphuric acid plant was designed and engineered by Chandra Bhusan Bhaduri. The lead chambers were entirely constructed by Bengal Chemical scientists.[83] By 1907 work was completed and production began. It was not only in the installation of plants or the adaptation of machinery but in all other respects that Bengal Chemical strove to be self-sufficient. In the years to come Bengal Chemical would have its own printing department, with modern machines supplying their printed materials, a saw mill for producing packaging boxes, its own waterworks, fed by a 5-inch tube-well sunk and maintained by its staff, its own power plant, an engineering department, and its own private fire-brigade – the members of which were regularly drilled and paraded in order to maintain efficiency.[84]

The partition of Bengal in 1905, along with the Swadeshi Movement and the boycott that followed in its wake, created a market for goods produced by *swadeshi* enterprises. Sections of the Bengali scientific community subscribed to the programme of *swadeshi*, or constructive modernization, the focus of discussions being on scientific and technical education appropriate to the needs of Indian society and, in tune with the programme of industrialization, the need for plans to be drawn up by the growing Indian industrial interests.[85] Prafulla Chandra was closely associated with these developments. A chemical industry developed along modern lines, with BCPW utilizing indigenous raw materials, local labour, and building its own machines and plants as far as possible. If profit was a motivating factor, even more so was a deep sense of service to the nation.[86]

At the Indian Medical Congress held in Calcutta in 1908, Bengal Chemical had a stall at which the preparation of Indian drugs was exhibited. This stall attracted a good deal of attention. Strong representation was made by the Council of the Congress, which called for the official recognition of some of these drugs. The BP authorities were eventually prevailed upon to include a list in the addendum to their existing list of pharmaceutical products.[87] The official seal was thus extended to some of these drugs. By 1910, BCPW had begun full-scale production of chemicals, pharmaceuticals, and toilet preparations. Some proprietary medicines were introduced to the market; the production of surgical tools and scientific instruments was also taken up. Between 1902 and 1910, Bengal Chemical would increase its sales from 34,423 to 262,654 rupees.[88]

The Indian chemical and pharmaceutical industry received its greatest boost during the two world wars. Bengal Chemical's enterprises equally benefitted from this progress. Since its inception, independent research had been important to BCPW. Due to the exigencies of the war, research and adaptation were given a further impetus. With normal lines of supply dislocated, the government increasingly had to depend on BCPW to supply the eastern war front with essential chemicals and drugs. Additional chambers had to be constructed in the sulphuric acid plant to meet increasing demands.[89] Lead-coated iron sheets were required for the expansion of the sulphuric acid chambers. Their lack of availability was tackled with ingenuity by the Bengal Chemical scientists.[90] Sodium thiosulphate, which was in great demand in government stores, was manufactured on a large scale by a process developed by BCPW chemists. Caffeine was extracted from tea dust by means of a quickly improvised process and most of the caffeine was exported. In their workshop, along with other apparatus, fire extinguishers were also constructed.

The story of the fire extinguisher is interesting. At the insistence of the insurance company, BCPW decided to buy several fire extinguishers, and asked for a discount from the foreign suppliers on account of the size of the order. The sales agent refused, claiming that the production was a 'major enterprise'. Satishchandra Dasgupta, who was then the factory superintendent, took up the challenge. He bought only one item and examined its technical properties; he then produced a replica. A patent was obtained and by 1913 BCPW was able to sell their fire extinguishers at half the price of imported ones. There was great demand for these fire extinguishers during the war years and Bengal Chemical supplied an average of 500 items each week to government military stores.[91]

In 1916, in order to meet the increased civilian and military demand for surgical dressings, the company began the manufacture of sterilized surgical dressings. Here too the creative genius of Bengal Chemical scientists proved successful. The manufacture of bandages and sterilized dressings was comparatively easy, but to compress and pack them required recourse to a sophisticated machine. The import of machinery was impossible due to war conditions. However, the problem was solved with ease; no less than four machines were constructed to do the work. The contemporary journal *Bharatbarsha* reported:

> An ordinary hacksaw was converted into an automatic knife, to cut the rolls of bandages into required lengths, ordinary oil drums were subjugated to the purpose of a disinfecting chamber, and the compressing machine was made from bits of steel bars and screws. Two and half yards of gauze, 36 inches wide, was compressed into a package 2.62 inches×1.62 inches×1.38 inches and packed specifically for delivery to government stores.[92]

These innovations were developed even though the Bengal Chemical scientists had no idea of how to construct a packing machine. Dr P. C. Ray was very satisfied with the activities of BCPW and remarked,

> Today the standard of civilization is measured by the output of machinery in the country and the standard of efficiency of a factory is measured by the quantity and quality of the output. By this standard alone the staff and the work force of BCPW is most efficient; but that would be nothing remarkable did we not know that these young chemists, raw

> and inexperienced – and inefficient – the product of a non-practical University, have trained themselves to a pitch of excellence that they are not only able to compete but have become dominant in their special fields. It is worth ruminating on.[93]

The volume of sales of the company's spirituous preparations increased to such an extent that a bonded laboratory had to be established in 1916. In addition, BCPW supplied these goods at much lower rates than those associated with imported ones. It was the spirit of *swadeshi* that helped the company to expand its market. However, it was not the case that patriotic consumers were subjected to higher prices or inferior quality.[94] Bengal Chemical was unique in this respect. The phenomenal growth of the company should not be attributed merely to *swadeshi* sentiments, or to the boost provided by an international war.[95]

To accommodate the increasing demands, the company considered other means of increasing expansion. During the First World War, the market for sulphuric acid was buoyant. A new sophisticated plant was, therefore, thought to represent a profitable investment. Sulphuric acid was the mother of all industries; it was essential for the manufacture of certain chemicals, necessary in the workshop for treating surgical instruments, for bleaching surgical cotton, and was also marketed as basic sulphuric acid.[96] A new factory site was purchased at Panihati in 24 Parganas, on the Barrackpore Trunk Road. An order was placed for a new sulphuric acid plant in 1920 with J. F. Carmichael & Co. Ltd, Engineers and Contractors, New York.[97] The materials needed for the new plant were sent by Carmichael, along with detailed construction plans, with the actual installation being undertaken by BCPW itself. The company preferred to depend on foreign construction firms only for those sophisticated parts that were not available in the country. Where items were available within the country, or could be produced indigenously, foreign orders were not placed. For example, it was calculated that lead plugs could be manufactured more cheaply by Bengal Chemical than could be supplied by Carmichael. Lead plugs were therefore made in the BCPW workshop according to required specifications. A generating plant was installed and a 40-foot water-storage tank was built to supply water to the chambers.[98] The distillation of coal-tar was commenced in 1922 and the large-scale manufacture of alum started in 1924.

However, this boom was followed by a sudden decline in the post-war period, when the industry was faced with an uncooperative colonial regime. This was also the time when foreign companies were keen to regain the markets they had lost during the war. The war had led to the growth of a massive capacity in the chemical industries of the West.[99] Since most industrialized countries were now suffering from overproduction, those such as the USA, France, Germany, and England sought to protect their markets through the introduction of high import tariffs. This simply served to leave colonial markets such as India open to foreign exploitation. In order to meet the unfair competition, Bengal Chemical was forced to sell its products (especially sulphates) at a price that virtually wiped out profits. The manufacture of certain products had to be curtailed. Magnesium sulphate was a case in point. Salt was produced regularly by BCPW, but the declining price of refined salt meant that production was no longer profitable. Only when there was a temporary shortage in the market was BCPW in a position to undertake the infrequent production of salt.[100]

Government policy, foreign competition, unfair tariffs, along with the difficulty and cost of buying plant and machinery from abroad, all resulted in a fearsome burden for BCPW. Far from increasing production, the company was not able to operate its works at full capacity.[101] However, a determined Bengal Chemical, under the guidance of Sir P. C. Ray, gradually transcended the barriers imposed by the state and its apparatus. By 1929, BCPW as well as manufacturing heavy chemicals had begun to develop pharmaceutical preparations, surgical dressings, toilet preparations, scientific instruments, along with 300–400 varieties of fine chemicals a year. The company's heavy chemicals were mainly used in such industries as galvanizing – in demand from the government for galvanizing telegraph poles, tanning, the production of aerated water, and so on.[102] Therapeutic sera, vaccines, and injectable drugs were very much in short supply during the war years. To move the country towards greater self-sufficiency in relation to these products, the management of Bengal Chemical opened a modern Biological Department in 1929, with a well-equipped laboratory and attached stables. It was the noted policy of the company to send its staff to foreign countries, not so much to buy technology products as to develop their 'know-how'. The services of H. Ghosh were secured for the department and he was sent to Europe for practical training in the field of improved and scientific methods of manufacture. After his return in 1931, the manufacture of gland products commenced, and the production of vitamin preparations was taken up in the following year.[103]

With the passing of time, the Panihati factory expanded rapidly. A bigger and more improved type of sulphuric acid plant was installed there in 1931. Acharya Ray's account of the event is as follows:

> The sulphuric acid plant, with Glover's and Gay Lussac's Towers installed, is perhaps the biggest of its kind in India. The firm at present employs 2,000 hands and its net assets amount to half a crore of rupees.[104]

In 1932, a Bio-Chemical Department was opened for the study of vitamins and the manufacture of vitamin products, under the guidance of Dr Bires Chandra Guha. One of the important experiments that were undertaken was the photo-chemical synthesis of vitamin B.[105] In 1934, the company began manufacturing soap at Panihati and printing ink at Manicktala. The soap-making process at Panihati was as sophisticated as that of the multinational Lever Brothers Company, which was already operating in India. The machinery, most of which was imported, was the same as that used by foreign firms, albeit on a smaller scale (see Figure 2.2).[106] The Printing Ink Department produced a host of letter press and lithographic inks (black and coloured), inks for offset and rotary printing, as well as colours for artists and draftsmen.[107] In 1937, in order to achieve a more organized and larger scale research facility, Sir Prafulla Chandra Research Laboratory was established at Manicktala.[108]

In the post–First World War period, as mentioned earlier, the situation became difficult. There was competition within the country. More acute was the aggressive competition of Western firms, which were continually underselling their products in the Global South countries in order to recapture the ground lost during the war, and thus forcing the indigenous firms out of business. Taking advantage of the conspicuous absence of quality control measures within the country, some of the Western firms were virtually inundating the Indian market with cheap, substandard preparations. Agents of the foreign firms were swarming around the practitioners with 'high sounding but worthless literature' linked to equally worthless drugs.[109]

Bengal Chemical was prepared to fight in order to address the adverse situation. The first step it took was to improve its sales promotion capability. Advertising outlay was increased. The company refocused its efforts on the local market, particularly on the production of indigenous drugs. In 1934, it published a booklet in Bengali entitled *Deshiyo Oushad* (Indigenous Medicine). It stressed the scientific verification and quality control processes that were applied to drugs produced in BCPW factories, particularly in relation to the use of modern machines: 'None of the medicines are mixed by hand. Everything is prepared by machine; everything is bottled by machine.'[110] The company was aware of the vital necessity to secure the cooperation of doctors in the development of the drugs trade. Bengal Chemical now recruited several medical representatives in order to influence the decisions made by medical practitioners. Among others, Dr B. C. Roy eulogized the progress made by BCPW in the manufacturing of various chemicals from indigenous raw materials (for example, caffeine from tea sweepings) at the 5th All-India Medical Conference held at Meerut in 1938.[111] Bengal Chemical started publishing a booklet, *Swastha Prasanga* (Health in Context), in Bengali, which was freely distributed by representatives of the company in *mofussil* districts. This provided a comprehensive list of common ailments and their specific remedial medicine, as produced by BCPW.

For an Indian firm such as BCPW, faced with the constant battle to survive in the face of international pressure in the pharmaceutical trade, and with the need to make production cost-effective, fundamental research took a backseat, an activity that Ray had always stressed as representing the crucial element in modern science-based industrialization. A conflict between science and industry, a term Pratik Chakrabarti uses,[112] was also becoming visible within BCPW. M. C. Bakshi, a student of the Science College, developed a process for manufacturing zinc chloride using raw zinc waste materials from the galvanizing works. P. C. Ray engaged him at the Manicktala factory to develop the process further. However, the general manager and the superintendent of works did not regard this development favourably. Initially, Bakshi was provided with no formal appointment, even though he continued to work. It was only in 1937 that he was recruited as a chemist in the Research and Development (R&D) Department, but the directors did not consider it justifiable to allow him any royalty or commission for his work.[113] Zinc chloride was an essential preservative for starch, which was used for the sizing of thread used in cotton mills. Efforts were made by Bakshi to secure orders for zinc chloride from some of the local mills but most favoured foreign brands. With the outbreak of the Second World War, however, once the supply lines with Europe were interrupted, BCPW's zinc chloride found an immediate market. To meet the huge demand, further expansion of the zinc chloride unit at Panihati was undertaken.[114]

The process of caffeine manufacture from tea waste was further perfected by Shrish Saha, another graduate of the Science College. But the directors imposed severe restrictions on the amount that could be spent on such experiments. It was again on Prafulla Chandra's initiative that Sailendra Mohan Chakravarty was appointed to take on the task of manufacturing caustic soda and bleaching powder. Such an increase in expenditure as incurred by Prafulla Chandra was looked on with displeasure and there was growing tension between him and the management of BCPW. In fact, despite the caustic chloride being prepared by Chakravarty, the Panihati factory began to lodge complaints that the goods were of substandard quality. The installation of a new type of cell for the manufacture of caustic chloride was not sanctioned by the directors. Its production was finally discontinued on the grounds that the cost of production at BCPW was higher than the available market price.[115] Within a few months, Imperial Chemicals, a multinational company, began the manufacture of caustic chloride at Rishra, near Calcutta.[116]

Figure 2.2 Manufacture of soap at Panihati, BCPW
Source: Fifty Years of Bengal Chemical, 1901–1951 (Calcutta: BCPW Ltd, not dated).

Throughout the 1930s, despite declining sales, profits continued to be high and BCPW directors and shareholders were satisfied with this achievement. A separate Research Fund, as requested by Prafulla Chandra, was regarded as a bad investment by the directors. Even after the Prafulla Chandra Research Laboratory was created (1937), it was found 'unnecessary to maintain a permanent Reserve Fund'.[117] Prafulla Chandra had consistently insisted that a research fund should be established as a means of ploughing back profits.[118]

A compromise was no longer possible. In fact, there seems to have been a concerted move to prevent Acharya Ray, as he was known, from being re-elected to the Board of Directors.[119] In July 1939, Prafulla Chandra signed the annual report of the company after adding a note of dissent:

> I sign this report subject to my note of dissent. For the last two years and more I have been impressing on the directors – my colleagues, the supreme necessity of reducing the amount of dividends but evidently to no effect. Bengal Chemical was first established in 1892 and has now been well high half a century in existence. We were the pioneers in this field, but during this long period we have wasted much precious time

> with the result that several chemical industries started by Europeans and other enterprises have sprung up all around us and have encircled us. We cannot afford to lower the standard and physiologically standardized products at competitive market prices.
>
> I regret to say that one obsession with our directors has been to offer large fixed dividends to shareholders and thus to increase their ravenous appetites. The net result has been that there is no reserve fund properly so called in gilt-edged securities. We should have, by this time, a crore of rupees as a reserve fund and we could have then ventured to start three or four industries on a large scale, but we are precluded from taking any such steps.[120]

Prafulla Chandra died on 16 June 1944, only four years after his resignation from the Board of Directors of BCPW. His Bengal Chemical and Pharmaceutical Works was one of the first attempts to replicate the success of European science-based industries on Indian soil. While building up the works, he always attributed his pioneering efforts to those instances of personal zeal and innovation that marked European enterprises.[121] Prafulla Chandra's BCPW was a demonstration to his countrymen that miracles could also be achieved in their country.

Inspired by his own practical and commercial acumen for industrialization, Prafulla Chandra was extremely critical of the obsession with technical institutes and education. In his evidence to the Indian Industrial Commission of 1916–18, he remarked, '… in a backward country like India what is required is the direct encouragement of industrial habits and enterprise amongst the people by the establishment of pioneer and demonstration factories rather than the establishment of highly developed technological research institutions.'[122] Prafulla Chandra had hit on a vital point, that science did not produce industries; it only assisted their development and it was often the industrial base that encouraged scientific investigations. His recommendation to the delegation was simple: '… the students who have passed through the technical and industrial schools should be taken on as apprentices in factories and workshops and the Government should make it a rule that workshops and factories which are patronized by the Government should take on a certain number of apprentices.'[123] Prafulla Chandra believed that practical knowledge acquired in workshops was sometimes more helpful to industries than the knowledge acquired by students in technological institutes. His experience with Bengal Chemical, which was as much an entrepreneurial venture as a scientific one, confirmed his ideas. Prafulla Chandra observed (1932),

> Some fifteen years ago, we took on a young man who had only qualified on a junior course from the Engineering Department of the National Council of Education. Being in close touch with chemical engineering, he has grown in knowledge and experience with the gradual expansion and growth of our firm. He has acquired skills in his specialist field. We had no hesitation in entrusting him with the task of setting up the sulphuric acid plant.... Now, in a technological institute, a miniature plant (as is undertaken in junior course class experiments) is shown as an illustration of the manufacture of sulphuric acid. Miniature models of the *Taj Mahal* are often shown in exhibitions. One can no more erect a Taj from the toy model than one can construct an acid plant from the miniature models.[124]

Conclusion

The industrialization that began in the colonial period acted as a catalyst in the creation of industrial zones, which consistently played a role in successive waves of capitalist enterprise in postcolonial India. In the presidency towns of Calcutta, Bombay, and Madras, there was an institutional consolidation of Indian entrepreneurs. In turn, they established schools, colleges, universities, technical-training institutions, hospitals, and public utilities such as electric-power generation. Surprisingly, the Bengalis, who had remained, with only rare exceptions, almost indifferent to business after the disappointing experience of the 1840s,[125] slowly succeeded in overcoming their reservations, and during the early twentieth century several Bengali-owned and Bengali-managed firms were established in more advanced fields of manufacture. This is evidenced by the careers of both Sir Rajendra Nath Mookerjee and Dr Prafulla Chandra Ray.

An alumnus of the Bengal Engineering College, Rajendra Nath first formed a Bengali contracting firm specializing in light engineering jobs and completed a large pipe-laying contract for the Calcutta Corporation in record time. He later met Acquin Martin, who like Rajendra Nath was interested in engineering schemes. Martin, therefore, joined hands with him to form Martin & Co. It soon grew into a reputable engineering firm specializing in waterworks, light railways, design and building, iron works, and electricity. So valuable was Rajendra Nath's contribution to the development of Martin Burn & Co. that after Martin's death he became the senior partner and undisputed leader of the firm.

The combination of engineering and entrepreneurship was almost uncharted territory for the Bengalis in the latter half of the nineteenth century. Although the discipline represented only an entry ticket to the lower strata of the PWD, Rajendra Nath swam against the tide and proved there was nothing inherent in the Bengali character that prevented them from becoming successful engineers as well as entrepreneurs. Another Bengali whose industrial initiative seems to have been inspired by his professional training was Prafulla Chandra Ray. His BCPW was one of the most successful attempts to develop a modern science-based industry in the last quarter of the nineteenth century. But about the linkage between technical knowledge and industry, Prafulla Chandra's perspective was different from Rajendra Nath's. The latter advocated for the establishment of a central technical college as early as 1910. But any inclination on the part of Bengali intellectuals to establish technical institutes annoyed Prafulla Chandra. He advised scientists and engineers to develop their awareness of the intricacies of the market and become entrepreneurs. However, Rajendra Nath, later in his career, appealed for a bridging of the gap between the laboratory and the shop.

All these episodes represent examples of only sporadic entrepreneurial ventures, launched by professionally trained persons, which required immense insights into the manufacturing processes of their firms. Nevertheless, they are indicative of how Indians with the requisite capabilities and knowledge of industrial transition in the West were able to identify new opportunities, even in unconventional lines. Undaunted by the government's indifference to India's industrial development and despite explicit discrimination on occasion against its industrial interests, the new breed of entrepreneurs, capable of perceiving and exploiting new opportunities, continued to grow. The technological approaches of the promoters of these industrial ventures provided ample evidence that they were gradually developing a sense of technological autonomy. The record of companies such as BCPW, for example, which were engaged in the production of goods requiring intricate technologies and entrepreneurs with appropriate attitudes and the personal command of technical expertise, supports this theory. Now the mature Bengali entrepreneurs tackled the techno-scientific developments with confidence. For example, by the first half of twentieth century, residents of Calcutta, the second city of the empire, had access to or familiarity with electricity, the prime mover of the twentieth century. The Government of Bengal appointed an Enquiry Committee to investigate the charges levied for electrical energy supplied to consumers by the Calcutta Electric Supply Corporation Ltd. (CESC) in 1935. The Bengal National Chamber of Commerce, established in 1887 to promote the commercial interests of the community, wrote a letter to the committee expressing their opinion:

> While urging for a reduction of rates, the Committee did not overlook the fact that the benefit of a low rate had already been given by the Company to the large industrial consumers requiring supply at or above 6000 volts. The cost of distribution of electricity to big industries at such a high voltage was exceedingly small, electricity in such cases coming straight from the generating station to the consumer without the intervention of sub-stations with rotating or static machinery and consequent over-head capital charges. While however, the Committee were glad that the Supply Corporation had considered the special claims of the industries in this respect, they objected strongly to the Company's policy of charging unduly high rates for domestic consumption....[126]

Thus, they had a clear road map for industrial development backed by modern technology.

Notes

1 *The Statesman*, 30 August 1916.

2 Quoted in Anirban Ganguly and Avadhesh Kumar Singh (eds), *Syama Prasad Mookerjee: His Vision of Education* (New Delhi: Wisdom Tree, 2017), 79–81.

3 Henry Etzkowitz (ed.), *The Triple Helix: University-Industry-Government Innovation in Action* (New York and London: Routledge, 2008).

4 Andrew Russell and Lee Vinsel, 'Hail the Maintainers', *Aeon*, 7 April 2016, available at https://aeon.co/essays/innovation-is-overvalued-maintenance-often-matters-more (accessed on 12 July 2018).

5 Tirthankar Roy, *Traditional Industry in the Economy of Colonial India* (Cambridge: Cambridge University Press, 1999).

6 Daniel Headrick, *The Tools of Empire* (New York: Oxford University Press, 1981), 205.

7 Michael Mann, *South Asia's Modern History* (London and New York: Routledge, 2015), 272–3.

8 Parimal Ghosh, *Colonialism, Class and a History of the Calcutta Jute Millhands, 1880–1930* (Hyderabad: Orient Longman, 2000).

9 Dietmar Rothermund, *An Economic History of India* (New York and London: Routledge, 2002, 2nd edn).

10 B. R. Tomlinson, *The Economy of Modern India, 1860–1970* (Cambridge: Cambridge University Press, 1993), 92–6.

11 Tirthankar Roy, *The Economic History of India 1857–1947* (New Delhi: Oxford University Press, 2011, 3rd edn), 183–212.

12 Morris D. Morris, 'The Growth of Large-Scale Industry to 1947', in *The Cambridge Economic History of India II*, ed. Dharma Kumar (Cambridge: Cambridge University Press, 1982), 556–72.

13 Ibid., 600.

14 Ibid., 573.

15 K. Otsuka, G. Rains, and G. Saxonhouse, *Comparative Technology Choice in Development* (New York: Basil Blackwell, 1988), 71.

16 Dwijendra Tripathy, 'Colonialism and Technology Choices in India', *The Developing Economics* 34, no. 1 (1996): 87. See also Dwijendra Tripathy, *Historical Roots of Industrial Entrepreneurship in India and Japan* (New Delhi: Manohar, 1997).

17 Rajnarayan Chandavarkar, 'Industrialization in India before 1947: Conventional Approaches and Alternative Perspectives', *Modern Asian Studies* 19, no. 3 (1984): 623–8.

18 Frank Harris, *Jamsetji Nusserwanji Tata* (Bombay: Blackie and Son, 1958, 2nd edn), 219–41. See also N. Benjamin, 'Jamsetji Nusserwanji Tata: A Centenary Tribute', *Economic and Political Weekly* 39, no. 35 (2004): 3873–5; Prasannan Parthasarathi, 'Trade and Industry in the Indian Subcontinent', in *Reconceptualizing the Industrial Revolution*, ed. Jeff Horn, Leonard N Rosenband, and Merritt Roe Smith (Cambridge: The MIT Press, 2011), 271–90.

19 Ian Inkster, 'Prometheus Bound: Technology and Industrialization in Japan, China and India Prior to 1914 – A Political Economy Approach', *Annals of Science* 45, no. 4 (1988): 399–426.

20 Amiya Kumar Bagchi, *Private Investment in India 1900–1939* (Cambridge: Cambridge University Press, 1972), 6.

21 T. Roy, *The Economic History of India*, 116.

22 Ibid., 149.

23 Amit Bhattacharyya, *Business, Politics and Technology* (Kolkata: Readers Service, 2005), 101.

24 *Hindusthan Standard*, 14 December 1946. According to a government report, this company was one of the four companies that produced machines of grade I category. *Report of the Indian Tariff Board on the Machine Tools Industry* (Delhi: Government Press, 1947), Appendix VI.

25 The Seshasayee brothers, who trained as electrical engineers in the United States, played a pioneering role in the rural electrification of south India in the 1930s and later set up the prestigious Fertilizers and Chemicals Travancore Ltd (FACT) just before independence. They depended entirely on American technology. See Dwijendra Tripathi and Makranth Mehta, *Business Houses in Western India* (New Delhi: Manohar, 1989).

26 Amit Bhattacharyya, *Swadeshi Enterprise in Bengal: The First Phase 1880–1920* (Kolkata: Readers Service, Second Edition, 2008).

27 Surendra Mohan Basu in an interview with Sudhakanta Dey. *Arthik Unnoti* 2, no. 7, Kartik 1334 B.S. (1927): 439.

28 S. P. Sen (ed.), *Directory of National Biography*, Vol. III (Calcutta: Institute of Historical Studies, 1974): 166–7.

29 In the *Bengal Engineering College Centenary Souvenir Volume*, it is seen that Rajendra Nath Mookerjee was one of the ex-students of the Bengal Engineering College in the year 1883 and obtained a B.C.E. qualification. See 'Glossary of Records', *Bengal Engineering College Centenary Souvenir* (Calcutta, 1956), 128.

30 Deb Kumar Ghosh, *Sir Rajendra Nath Mookerjee: A Pen Portrayal* (Calcutta: The Institutions of Engineers, 1984), 8.

31 Under the chief supervision of Leslie, several construction projects at the Waterworks, such as the extension of filters, settling tanks, and so on, were in progress. From the observations and remarks of Rajendra Nath, the Englishman felt sure that he would be capable of undertaking assignments as a contractor. A satisfied Leslie offered him some contracts if the latter would agree to do the work at scheduled rates. Rajendra Nath accepted the offer but on the condition that the entire job would be given to him. P. C. Mahalanobis, 'Sir Rajendra Nath Mookerjee: First President of the Indian Statistical Institute 1931–1936', *Sankhya: The Indian Journal of Statistics* 2, no. 3 (1936): 238.

32 K. C. Mahindra, *Sir Rajendra Nath Mookerjee: A Personal Study* (Calcutta: Martin & Burn Ltd, 1933), 67.

33 *Calcutta Municipal Gazette* XVIII, no. 5 (24 June 1933): 201.

34 *Calcutta Municipal Gazette* XVIII, no. 6 (1 July 1933): 267.

35 Mahindra, *Sir Rajendra Nath Mookerjee*, 95–8.

36 *The Statesman*, 16 May 1936, 9.

37 Rajendra Nath's inquisitiveness in the field of engineering sciences was so high that he examined the drawings of the Agra waterworks scheme minutely and discovered several errors therein. A. J. Hughes, special waterworks chief engineer of Agra Municipality, realized the engineering skills of Rajendra Nath and instructed that necessary alterations should be made to the drawings. Although Rajendra Nath failed to secure the bid, they became good friends and in course of time this friendship proved beneficial for Rajendra Nath. Mahindra, *Sir Rajendra Nath Mookerjee*, 104–15.

38 Mahalanobis, 'Sir Rajendra Nath Mookerjee', 238.

39 Mahindra, *Sir Rajendra Nath Mookerjee*, 116.

40 *The Statesman*, 16 May 1936, 10.

41 Mahindra, *Sir Rajendra Nath Mookerjee*, 137.

42 *Banik* 8, no. 5, Bhadra 1340 B.S. (1933): 135.

43 *Martin Burn Limited* (Calcutta: Company Publication, not dated), 5A.

44 Girish Chandra was also the Engineer-in-Charge of the construction of the High Court at Calcutta. *Bengal Engineering College Centenary Souvenir*, 35.

45 Martin & Co. sponsored two light railway companies after the decision of the Railway Board, but they did not undertake the construction work. *Banik*, 136.

46 Mahindra, *Sir Rajendra Nath Mookerjee*, 143–45.

47 Anukul Chandra, who later became Rai Bahadur, was from the '1900 batch' of Sibpur Engineering College. *Bengal Engineering College Centenary Souvenir*, 35 and 88.

48 *Martin Burn Limited*, 1–19.

49 Sudhanshubikash Roy Choudhury, 'Sir Rajendra Nath Mookerjee', *Banik* 8, no. 6, Aswin 1340 B.S. (1933): 161–6.

50 *The Statesman* declared the presidential address of Sir Mookerjee as 'an intellectual treat'. *The Statesman*, 16 May 1936.

51 *Report of the Indian Industrial Commission, 1916–18* (Calcutta: Superintendent Government Printing, 1918), 3.

Sir Rajendra also acted as the chairman of the commission for some time during the absence of Sir Thomas Holland, the permanent incumbent.

52 H. Nandy (ed.), *IEI Marches On* (Kolkata: Institution of Engineers, 2002), 64.

53 'Presidential Address: The Institution of Engineers (India)', Calcutta, 23 February 1921, quoted in N. Mukherjee (compiled), *A Collection of Addresses and Speeches by Sir Rajendra Nath Mookerjee* (Calcutta: The Art Press, not dated), 44–51.

54 Aparajith Ramnath, 'Engineers in India: Industrialisation, Indianisation and the State, 1900–47', PhD thesis, Centre for the History of Science, Technology and Medicine, Imperial College, London, 2012, 90.

55 *New Bridge between Calcutta and Howrah, Appendix to the Report on the Committee of Engineers, February 1922*, Vol. II (Calcutta: Bengal Secretariat Book Depot, 1922), 1.

56 Apart from the Indian Industrial Commission, Sir Rajendra Nath was associated with the Transport Committee and Railway Committee (1921), the Bengal Retrenchment Committee (1923), the All-India Retrenchment Committee (1924), the Indian Coal Committee (1924–5), and the Royal Commission of Indian Currency and Finance (1925–6), among others.

57 'In the present condition of our country we should recognize that to develop any industry successfully, we must have, first and foremost, expert knowledge as well as men of undoubted practical experience in the particular industry which we desire to establish.' 'Presidential Address Industrial Conference, Allahabad 1910', quoted in Mukherjee, *A Collection of Addresses and Speeches*, 2–3.

58 *Speeches at Prize Distribution Ceremonies and on Educational and Technical Subjects*, quoted in Mukherjee, *A Collection of Addresses and Speeches*, 105–10.

59 'Memorandum submitted by the Government of Bengal to the Indian Statutory Commission', *Report of the Indian Statutory Commission*, Vol. III (Calcutta: Majesty's Stationary Office, 1930), 49.

60 *Address Delivered at the Annual Convocation of the University of Patna, November 29, 1919*, quoted in Mukherjee, *A Collection of Addresses and Speeches*, 25–6.

61 Sir Rajendra Nath Mookerjee, 'Presidential Address, Eighth Indian Science Congress, Calcutta, January 1921' (unpublished monograph, Indian Science Congress Association, Calcutta), 2.

62 Quoted in Mahindra, *Sir Rajendra Nath Mookerjee*, 163.

63 Daniel Headrick, *The Tentacles of Progress* (New York and Oxford: Oxford University Press, 1988), 360–74.

64 *Indian Industrial Commission: Inspection Notes 1916–18 (Confidential)* (Calcutta: Superintendent Government Printing, 1918), 25.

65 N. R. Srinivasan, *History of the Indian Iron and Steel Company* (Burnpur: IISCO, 1983), 27.

66 Amiya K. Bagchi argues that a company producing only pig iron would have to depend on a highly fluctuating export market, whereas a company producing steel could depend on a large internal market if foreign competition could be overcome. Bagchi, *Private Investment*, 294.

67 Agra Electric Supply Co. Ltd, Benaras Electric Light & Power Co. Ltd, Jubbulpore Electric Supply Co. Ltd, United Provinces Electric Supply Co. Ltd, Bareilly Electricity Supply Co. Ltd, Saugor Electricity Supply Co. Ltd, Upper Jumna Valley Electricity Supply Co. Ltd (Managing Agents); the Fyzabad Electric Licence and the Jaunpur Electric Licence (Managers & Agents). *Martin Burn Limited*, 14–15.

68 Rajat K. Ray, *Industrialization in India* (Delhi: Oxford University Press, 1979), 294.

69 Quoted in R. C. Ray, 'Sir Rajendra Nath Mookerjee: The Story of His Life', *Calcutta Municipal Gazette* XVIII, no. 7 (8 July 1933): 10.

70 Dhruv Raina, *Images and Contexts* (New Delhi: Oxford University Press, 2011, 2nd imp.), 71.

71 P. C. Ray, *Life and Experiences of a Bengali Chemist*, Vol. I (Calcutta: Chuckerverty, Chatterjee & Co. Ltd, 1932), 92.

72 'Acharya Prafulla Chandra Ray Mahashoy-er Gabeshona', *Prabasi* 8, no. 6, 1317 B.S. (1910): 333.

73 *Acharya Prafulla Chandra Ray Birth Centenary Volume* (Calcutta: Calcutta University, 1962), 72.

74 Ray, *Life and Experiences*, 103.

75 For the manufacture of BP preparations, Bengal Chemical had to purchase large quantities of raw materials such as iodine, balsam of tolu, and so on, from Butto Kristo Paul & Co. Bhutnath Paul, the proprietor, was surprised to discover a large quantity of iodine (7 pounds) on the invoice of a single customer. An ordinary dispensary would hardly require 1 pound of iodine in one month or even one year. When the purpose

of the iodine and tolu was explained to him by Bhutnath's agent, he was pleasantly surprised. He had previously been approached by Bengal Chemical for a trial of their BP preparations, but the attempt had been in vain. On being made aware of the situation, B. K. Paul & Co. at once placed an order for 1 hundredweight of Ferri Iodine and 1 hundredweight of Ferri Sulpha. Thus, BCPW set out on its journey. Ray, *Life and Experiences*, 106.

76 Atiken's Tonic, Syrup of Hyphosphite of Lime, Tonic Glycerophosphate, Parrish's Chemical Food, and so on, were resolutely prescribed by patriotic medical practitioners. Anuradha Roy, 'Growth and Development of the Chemical Industry in Bengal 1900–47', unpublished PhD thesis, Jadavpur University, Kolkata, 1994, 239.

77 *Masik Basumati*, *Bhadra* 1375 B.S. (1968): 788.

78 Viswakarma, *Laxmir Kripalabh Bangalir Sadhana* (Kolkata: Ananda, 1969), 364–5.

79 *Masik Basumati*, Aswin 1375 (1968): 909–12.

80 On 12 April 1901, Acharya Prafulla Chandra Ray, along with Sri Chandra Bhusan Bhadury, Sri Bhutnath Paul, Dr Kartik Chandra Bose, Sri Charu Chandra Bose, and the widows of Amulya Charan and Satish Chandra, formed a limited liability company, which was named The Bengal Chemical & Pharmaceutical Works Limited. Dr P. C. Ray imposed only one condition – the shares should be issued only to Bengalis. *Fifty Years of Bengal Chemical, 1901–1951* (Calcutta: BCPW Ltd, not dated) 11.

81 Ibid., 13.

82 *Masik Basumati*, Aswin 1375 B.S. (1968): 1103.

83 P. C. Ray, *Essays and Discourses* (Madras: G. A. Natesan, 1918), 315–16.

84 Ray, *Life and Experiences*, 110.

85 Dhruv Raina and S. Irfan Habib, *Domesticating Modern Science* (New Delhi: Tulika, 2004), 83–181.

86 In Bengal the one thing needful was not so much the establishment of Technological Institutes as the initiative, the dash, the pluck, the resourcefulness in our youths that go into the making of a businessman or an entrepreneur or a captain of industry. The college-bred youth has been found to be a hopeless failure; there is no driving power in him; at best he can only shine as a tool or an automaton. How to bring bread to the mouths of the ill-fed, famished young men of the middle classes?

In this way, Prafulla Chandra explained the motives behind his setting up of BCPW. Ray, *Life and Experiences*, 92.

87 Ray, *Life and Experiences*, 105.

88 'Ekti Swadeshi Karkhana', *Prabasi* 12, no. 1, Baisakh 1319 B.S. (1912): 83.

89 *Chronology of Important Events* (Calcutta: BCPW, not dated).

90 Ray, *Essays and Discourses*, 316.

91 A. Roy, 'Growth and Development of the Chemical Industry', 246.

92 Sri Jaladhar Sen, 'Bengal Chemical & Pharmaceutical Works', *Bharatbarsha* 7, no. 1, Aswar 1326 B.S. (1919): 111.

93 P. C. Ray, *Essays and Discourses*, 317.

94 Sumit Sarkar observes that 'indigenous goods should be selected by consumers even if they were more expensive than and inferior in quality to their imported substitutes, and that it was the patriotic duty of men with capital to pioneer such industries even though profits might be minimal or nonexistent'. Sumit Sarkar, *Swadeshi Movement in Bengal 1903–1908* (Ranikhet: Permanent Black, New Edition, 2010), 92.

95 Hemendra Prasad Ghosh, a contemporary journalist, recalls,

> The ambition of the Acharya was to make India self-sufficient in her need for medicines and toilet requisites. I remember how one day, on his way to the maidan he came to the *Basumati* office and, placing two small containers on my table, said – 'This is the latest.' It was Carbolic Tooth Powder, prepared as a replacement for the Calvert's product, which was then extensively used by our young men. On learning the fixed price, I said that it could be raised by two pice. He said: 'No, the remotest chance of competition must be removed.'

Acharya Prafulla Chandra Ray Birth Centenary Souvenir Volume, 173.

96 J. P. de Sousa, *History of the Chemical Industry in India* (Bombay: Technical Press Club, 1961), 22.

97 A. Roy, 'Growth and Development of the Chemical Industry', 249.

98 *Fifty Years of Bengal Chemical*, 17.

99 This trend has in fact been referred to as the 'Chemists' war. See Edmund Russell, *War and Nature* (New York: Cambridge University Press, 2001).

100 *Indian Tariff Board: Evidence Recorded during an Enquiry on Heavy Chemical Industry*, Vol. I (Calcutta: Government of India Central Publication Branch, 1930), 240–6.

101 Pratik Chakrabarti, 'Science and Swadeshi: The Establishment and Growth of the Bengal Chemical and Pharmaceutical Works, 1938–1947', in *Science and Modern India: An Institutional History*, ed. Uma Das Gupta (New Delhi: Pearson Longman, 2011), 130–2.

102 *Indian Tariff Board: Evidence*, 245.

103 *Fifty Years of Bengal Chemical*, 17.

104 Ray, *Life and Experiences*, 334.

105 Dr R. N. Chopra, Professor of Pharmacology at the School of Tropical Medicine, Calcutta, was pleased to see the new Bio-Chemical Laboratory. He once remarked: 'The standard of products manufactured, I can say from personal experience is up to those produced by renowned firms in Great Britain and America.' *Advance Therapy* 8, no. 2 (April 1936): 37. It was a quarterly journal published by the BCPW.

106 A. Roy, 'Growth and Development of the Chemical Industry', 262.

107 *BCPW Price List of Printing Ink* (Calcutta: BCPW, 1946).

108 *Chronology of Important Events.*

109 *Advance Therapy* 9, no. 1 (January 1937): 54. These agents toured the country distributing free samples of their doubtful wares.

110 *Deshiyo Oushad* (Calcutta: BCPW, 1934), 1.

111 *Advance Therapy* 11, no. 1 (January 1939): 21.

112 Pratik Chakrabarti, 'Science and Swadeshi', 134.

113 This was a severe deviation from the earlier stance of the company, when BCPW had followed a policy of paying royalties to a chemist. In 1918, Satish Chandra Dasgupta had earned as much as 50,000 rupees in commission from selling the fire extinguishers he designed. *Acharya Prafulla Chandra Ray Birth Centenary Souvenir Volume*, 76.

114 *Minutes of the Meeting of Directors*, BCPW, 4 January 1940.

115 *Minutes of Meeting of Directors*, BCPW, 18 May 1939.

116 Advertisement of Imperial Chemical Co., *The Statesman*, 15 January 1940.

117 *Minutes of Meeting of Directors*, BCPW, 6 February 1940.

118 On one occasion, Ray remarked,

> Take again the several Electric Firms in America and England and on the Continent. The articles and appliances they annually manufacture, if valued in pounds sterling, will amount to hundreds of millions. Here too the enormous development has been made possible by the harmonious cooperation between existing industries and laboratory researchers.

Ray, *Life and Experiences*, 330–1.

119 *Minutes of Meeting of Directors*, BCPW, 18 May 1939.

120 'Note of dissent by Sir P. C. Ray', *BCPW Annual Report, 1939* (Calcutta: BCPW, 1939), 67.

121 Ray, *Life and Experiences*, 96.

122 *Indian Industrial Commission, Minutes of Evidence 1916–17*, Vol. II (Calcutta: Superintendent Government Printing, 1918), 35.

123 Ibid., 38.

124 Ray, *Life and Experiences*, 332–3.

125 Suvobrata Sarkar, *The Quest for Technical Knowledge* (New Delhi: Manohar, 2012), 165–73.

126 *Bengal National Chamber of Commerce: Report of the Committee for the Year 1935* (Calcutta: BNCC, 1936), 135–6.

3

Electrification

The Shaping of a Technology

> The demand of electrical energy in this great city [Calcutta] has recently increased very rapidly, and energetic steps have had to be taken by the Electric Supply Corporation, under the Chairmanship of Lord Meston, to keep pace with the requirements of their area with its population of one and a half millions. In 1925 100 million units were sold. Last year this output reached 148 millions while the estimate for the current year is 168 millions. Truly remarkable progress.
>
> The leading developments to be noted with regard to the general supply in the city are the recent completion of the transfer of the Tramway Company's load to the Electric Supply Corporation and the substantial progress made in the electrification of the Jute Mills and other industries.
>
> —A. T. Cooper, a professional engineer with wide experience of electrical problems in India (1929)[1]

The historians of technology, dealing with colonial South Asia, mostly discuss the new infrastructural and transportation technologies, and the modernization narrative from the mid-nineteenth century onwards. Surprisingly enough, this scholarship is not very vocal about perhaps twentieth century's most dynamic technology – electricity. The saga of electrification and its interface with colonial society is mostly unwritten. Sunila Kale explains this gap – electric power emerged as a new technology only near the end of the nineteenth century and thus left a tiny record in the colonial archive, unlike the long histories of canal irrigation and railroads, to document the recent past.[2] Although this technology arrived in India just after it was first introduced in London and New York in the 1880s, the electricity networks expanded here only in the early twentieth century.[3] Akhil Gupta remarks, as there is no 'sensual way' to experience electricity, thus from the beginning it is a social and cultural thing, 'not something that belongs to the natural world, however that might be constructed'.[4] Historically a young form of power, electricity became conducive for lighting purposes, and thus gradually outshined other forms of energy.

A technology is not merely a combination of machines with certain purposes, but part of our society. Electrification is not a helpless force moving through history, but a social process that differs from one time frame to another and from one culture to the other. In the highly industrialized Western societies, electrification was not a 'thing' that came from outside and had an 'impact'; rather, it was an internal development shaped by its social context.[5] But for India it came as a colonial baggage. Here the electrification process had two aspects. First, as a technology that was introduced by the colonial government, it had served the needs of the British Empire. Second, as a technology that inherited the nature of transforming society and economy, it had brought visible changes in the socio-economic milieu too.[6] Although electrification was a social construction, not all groups in a society had the same influence in laying its foundations. In the years between the 1880s and the 1940s, a dialogue on electricity took place within Indian society in which some voices were more persuasive than others. Electrification was a political issue, an element of spectacle, a means of transportation, a motive force, and a source of profit. The purpose of the chapter is to know the process of the development of electricity in a colonial setting, Calcutta, the capital of British India until 1911, and the role of the innovators, bureaucrats, and the foreign electric company in the background of colonialism.

Historicizing Electricity

In his pioneering work on the development of electrical systems in three highly industrialized cities, Thomas P. Hughes first introduces the model of system formation and growth, a four-stage process involving invention and development, technology transfer, system growth, and system momentum.[7] His extensive study illuminates the relationship between electricity and local circumstances – social, political, economic, and geographical. He argues that the electricity system was influenced by combinations of circumstances which vary from nation to nation. In doing this, Hughes has also posed a major historiographical question: Are systems the basic units of study for the discipline? Since electricity, as a modern technology, was not born and developed in India, simple application of a social constructivist approach may be problematic. Drawing from the social constructivist theory, a recent study examines the role of legal, economic, political, and environmental factors in determining the course of development of electricity in the Madras Presidency under British colonial rule. According to the author, the combination of circumstances that influenced the development of electricity in a colonized territory was quite unusual in many ways and considerably shaped its ultimate character.[8]

William J. Hausman, Peter Hertner, and Mira Wilkins present the historical narrative of multinational companies acting as 'drivers of globalization' by enhancing electrification all over the world, including India. The foreign direct investment, they argue, played a major role in the process of global electrification, supplying modernizing infrastructure more widely and more efficiently than would otherwise have been the case. The enterprises that pioneered foreign direct investment in this sector were the electrical manufacturers and banks, but eventually complex holding companies and clusters of firms specializing in the financing, construction, and operation of electric utilities emerged and came to dominate international investment in electric utilities. Over time, they played a major role in stimulating electrification. They provided management, technology, knowledge, and experience, along with capital. They built generating plants, and constructed transmission and distribution lines. They created networks of power. They led in, according to the authors, technical rationalizations. Finally, direct investors contributed in an important way to electrification within the world economy.[9]

David Arnold and Erich Dewald argue that technology's social fashioning is a difficult concept to employ in an Asian colonial context than in relation to autonomous European and North American industrial societies. These were neither designed nor manufactured locally, but in the West. The social construction of these technologies in a colonial or semi-colonial setting perhaps takes in a different form. How various technologies were locally accepted or rejected depended on significant local emendation and reinvention to conform to local cultural norms and social usages.[10]

Universal access to electricity continues to remain elusive even after seven decades of Indian independence. This is despite electricity being central to the conceptualization of Indian modernity by early nationalists and planners. Most recently, Sunila Kale has presented a political history of the Indian electricity sector from 1947 until 2003, when the Electricity Act was enacted. She offers three in-depth case studies of the states of Maharashtra, Odisha, and Andhra Pradesh, telling the story of the history of electrification and electricity supply in each. She argues that in those parts of the countryside that were successfully electrified in the decades after independence, the gains were due to neither nationalist idealism nor merely technocratic plans. Instead, rural electrification occurred either when rural constituencies became politically influential in state governments or when farmers started demanding a larger share of development resources.[11]

Was there something unique about Calcutta and its plan that led to the electrification of a colonial-metropolis almost simultaneously with other Western industrial nations? Colonial Calcutta had its own combination of circumstances which influenced the local development of electricity. In the long journey from small oil engine generation facilities to the gigantic Mulajore Generating Station (1940), electricity projects faced various upheavals and emerged as one of the biggest thermal networks. In the initial years of the twentieth century, the colonial government did not fully realize the potential of electricity and decided to leave it to local governments and private agencies. The Calcutta Electric Supply Corporation Ltd (CESC), with its head office in London, played the most vital role – it debated and resolved various technical questions, such as load factor, fuel sources, operation of generating stations, and electricity supply to industry, traction, and population centres (see Figure 3.1).. However, based on the shifting agenda of the empire, electricity was assigned new functions from time to time. Could the electrification of Calcutta create new conditions? What impact did it have on the socio-economic condition of the city? What was the role of bureaucrats and specialists in the electrification of Calcutta? Was there any impact of this modern wizard on the mode of transportation in Calcutta? As technology is socially constructed and 'grows symbiotically with society', both shaping and being shaped by it,[12] the interface between electricity and the social life and material culture of Calcutta must be fascinating.

Figure 3.1 Laying the underground cables of the CESC (1920s)

Source: Pradeep Gooptu, Head, Corporate Communications, CESC.

Early Diffident Steps

Although in the 1830s, Dr William Brooke O'Shaughnessy, Professor of Chemistry at the Calcutta Medical College, lit charcoal lights by battery,[13] it was only with the advent of the steam-run dynamo that electric lighting became practicable. Carl Louis Schwendler, Superintendent Electrician of the Government Telegraphs and a founder of the Calcutta Zoo, was the first to successfully implement it.[14] In 1877, Schwendler was asked by the government to make a detailed investigation of the possibilities of lighting Indian railway stations by electricity. His remarkable report, based on trial runs, appeared in 1881. With a second-hand 25 horsepower (HP) slow-speed steam engine, Schwendler ran four 'dynamo electric machines' at Howrah Station, each of which lit a carbon arc lamp for two good sheds, with zinc reflectors lined with silvered glass.[15] In 1881, Schwendler achieved another remarkable feat by setting up an electric railway for joyrides in the zoo. On Christmas Day, the inaugural run of the electric railway took place in the presence of the then Lieutenant Governor of Bengal and his suite and over a thousand spectators.[16] The machine came from Vienna Zoo where it was used at an exhibition during the summer of 1873. The motive power electricity was produced by a 10 HP stationary engine situated outside the zoo and an electro-magnetic machine was fixed in the driving carriage and connected to the axle of one pair of wheels.[17]

Thus, the 1880s onwards, Calcutta and its residents became gradually familiar with the marvel of electricity. A few private companies, both foreign and Indian, demonstrated their skills on several occasions in this new technology. Prominent among them were P. W. Fleury & Co (builders and electrical engineers), Dey, Sil & Co., and so on. The contemporary press was in a jubilant mood.[18] On 13 July 1882, Mr P. W. Fleury, proprietor of the P. W. Fleury & Co, illuminated his house at Dhurmtollah Street by means of incandescent electric light.[19] In 1883, the whole premises of the Great Eastern Hotel was illuminated by electric lights. The Indian Electric Light Company oversaw the incident. The hotel authorities expected more customers would turn up to see the novelty.[20] One should remember that in the last decade of the nineteenth century, electricity was used by very few people in Calcutta and it was generated either by steam or oil engines by the users within their own premises. They were not licensed producers and therefore could not sell the energy they produced in the market for public consumption. The first street of Calcutta to be lit by electricity was the newly built Harrison Road in 1891. Messrs Kilburn & Co. undertook to light it from dynamos set up at the Halliday Street Pumping Station and the municipal consultant was the renowned scientist Jagadish Chandra Bose.[21] In 1905, the authorities reverted to gas, and the Halliday

Street plant was sold off. But the absence of a suitable license for generation and distribution was a major obstacle for the electricity manufacturing industry.

Colonel REB Crompton: Inventor-Entrepreneur

Rookes Evelyn Bell Crompton (1845–1940) was one of the pioneers who founded the British electrical industry. Inventor, electrical, mechanical, and automobile engineer, soldier, and businessman – he was all these and more. The people of India remember him as the one who mechanized army transportation,[22] helped not only the Government of India in drafting the first Electricity Act, but also experimented with the generation of the first unit of hydroelectricity in Darjeeling, and initiated thermal power generation in Calcutta.

The momentous discovery of electromagnetic induction by Michael Faraday in 1831 practically remained confined to the laboratory until a few brilliant engineers like Edison, Crompton, and others emerged to put this principle to use through strenuous trial and error. In 1878, Crompton founded the firm of REB Crompton & Co., Chelmsford. Since motor transport had not yet become a commercially viable proposition, Crompton focused on electricity, which at that time virtually meant lighting. In those days in Britain, public power supply was non-existent and every lighting installation had to be independently sustained.[23] He developed improved versions of the dynamo to provide power for the lighting of individual installations. Not satisfied with catering only to existing needs, Crompton developed new products for newer applications. Gradually, he began supplying his own arc lamps, switch board, and dynamos. The combination of imaginative product development and sound commercial sense served him well and his business flourished. At the International Exposition of Electric Lighting held in Paris in 1881, Crompton sent a comprehensive selection of self-focusing arc lamps, generating sets, and switchboards manufactured at his Chelmsford workshop and won the first gold medal ever given for lighting equipment.[24]

In 1896, Colonel Crompton was invited by the Government of India to assist in the preparation of an Electric Lighting Act.[25] Electricity in Calcutta, as elsewhere in the world, was first used more for lighting purposes. Its use by the manufacturing and other industrial organizations was a later phenomenon. While it is not clear as to when and to what extent electricity was initially used by the British in India, the fact that the colonial government had passed an all-India Electricity Act as early as 1887 is indicative of its growing importance in the eyes of the state. The Electricity Act of 1887 was only a 'General Act', because all it did was 'to take power for the Governor General in Council to make rules for the protection of persons and property and for the prevention of injury to telegraph lines, from the appliances or apparatus used in the generation or supply of electricity'.[26] In 1891, the Bengal government reported that a number of proposals had been made by private entrepreneurs for the establishment of works for the supply of electric light to the city of Calcutta.[27] But since the Act of 1887 had no provision for the issue of licences, it became necessary to consider whether further legislation should, by a general Imperial Act, be made applicable to the whole of India or by a Local or Special Act for only Calcutta. The latter alternative was recommended to accelerate processing of proposals. However, the discussions with the Government of India went on for four more years before the Bengal Legislative Council passed the Calcutta Electric Lighting Act, 1895. By this Act, the 'Local Government may from time to time license any company or person to supply electricity for any public or private purposes within any specified area of Calcutta'.[28] With the passing of the Act, the Bengal government invited tenders to illuminate the Belvedere, Alipore, with electricity by both 'direct supply' and 'accumulated' systems.[29] The Act applied to only Calcutta in the first place, though there was power to extend it to other municipalities, and this was done in the case of Howrah, Dacca, and Darjeeling. The Howrah Bridge, which connects that town of Howrah with Calcutta, was unfortunately found to be situated in no municipality, and the Howrah Bridge Electrical Lighting Act, 1902, had to be passed to meet this defect.

The Modern Wizard's Formative Stage

Colonel Crompton's long acquaintance with India, especially at the government circle, enabled him to overcome many difficulties, including local prejudices and superstitions against the use of that strange and potent force, electricity. He undertook several hazardous journeys to survey the far-flung areas of the city with a view to working out feasibility reports for electrification and industrial development. To escape the humid heat of summer in Calcutta, the Britons used to migrate to the 'salubrious climate' of the hill station of Darjeeling at an altitude of nearly 2,000 metres. Although the former princely state of Bikaner holds the record of ushering in the era of electricity in the subcontinent, Crompton helped Darjeeling to earn the distinction of possessing India's first water-turbine driven hydroelectric generating station.[30] The power station was situated at Sidrapong (1897) and at the heart of this were two turbo-dynamos of 100 HP each (Crompton-Brunton Copper Alternator) situated between the hospital and Kotwalla *jhora* (spring), about 3 miles from the town and 3,500 feet lower.[31]

The plant was intended primarily for street lighting and private houses.[32] Not satisfied with having successfully installed a major hydroelectric project, Crompton set his goal for yet another challenge – thermal power. The scene of action now shifted to Calcutta.

The Calcutta Electric Lighting Act, 1895, threw open the doors to competition. Initially several firms applied for licences to supply electricity. In March 1896, Messrs Kilburn & Co., agents to Indian Electric Co. Ltd, submitted their scheme 'for the supply of electric light and power to Calcutta, including the working of the Calcutta Tramways by electricity' to the Bengal government. Another tough contender was Messrs A. J. Bolton & Co., agents to the Elektricitaets Gesellschaft of Berlin. On 29 December 1896, J. W. H. Glass, Secretary to the Government of Bengal (PWD), announced:

> In exercise of the powers conferred by Section 3, Chapter II of the Calcutta Electric Lighting Act No. IX of 1895, the Lieutenant-Governor of Bengal is pleased to grant to Messrs Kilburn & Company, of No. 4, Fairlie Place, Calcutta, acting on behalf of the Indian Electric Company, a license to supply electricity within the area of Calcutta....[33]

Thus on 7 January 1897, Messrs Kilburn & Co. secured the coveted Calcutta Lighting License for a period of 21 years. In February 1897, special meetings of the Indian Electric Co. Ltd were held in London where it was resolved to change the name of the enterprise to the Calcutta Electric Supply Co. Ltd,[34] popularly known as the CESC. Crompton himself was involved in the formation of the CESC and had personally chosen the site for the station.[35]

The CESC contemplated using aerial lines in the streets of Calcutta supported on iron posts. The electric company assured the Bengal government that 'by this system of distribution, which consists throughout of bare copper conductors insulated and supported by porcelain insulators, we get over the difficulties and uncertainties which undoubtedly exist in this climate in using conductors buried in the ground'. According to them, the underground cables were not feasible in the humid condition of Calcutta as 'conductors buried in the ground must be insulated with materials such as India-rubber or Lead covered, both of these materials having been found to be attacked when buried in the earth in India'.[36] Such a scheme was unique so far as India was concerned at the turn of nineteenth century. But the system had been carried out extensively in America, Canada, and Europe. The power company proposed to generate and distribute 2 million units of electrical energy per annum. But at that point in time, such a huge amount of energy was beyond the consumption capacity of the city. So, the CESC considered arranging with the Calcutta Tramway Company (CTC) to supply them the excess energy, which they could convert to electricity as motive power for their haulage. The electric supply company had a unique recommendation for the working of the tramways: 'the trolly wire system of conductors placed overhead, the trolly-wire being supported by central posts of a handsome design which carry the trolly wires by means of double brackets'. But this did not materialize at that juncture;[37] the electrification of the Calcutta tramways had to wait until 1902.

In their proposed scheme submitted to the Bengal government for supplying electric light and power to Calcutta, the electric company gave a detailed description about the technicalities:

> Generating Station– this will be situated near the Sealdah Station on the side of the present Tramway company's yard; here we propose to erect a substantial building and chimney shaft, later to be 160 feet high; this building will contain four sets of boilers and steam dynamos each complete in themselves, and each about 450 HP.
>
> Storage Plant– In each of the three stations we supply electric storage in the shape of accumulators to furnish electricity for the greater part of the lighting.
>
> Trunk Mains– The electrical energy will be conveyed from the generating station to the storage stations and to several principal points on the tramway lines by main line conductors consisting of bare copper strips strained and supported in brickwork culverts substantially built in brickwork and cement and made watertight: by this method of construction the whole of the principal lines and mains are readily accessible; we provide powerful pumping plant to free these culverts of water at times of flood, so that we can make sure that in no time will there be an interpretation of supply due to this clause.[38]

They proposed to supply all electricity 'on the low pressure continuous current system'. The actual price the company intended to charge for lighting purposes was eight annas per unit, which was lower than the rate charged for electricity in the city of London then. Such a price for electricity, the company hoped, could favourably compete with the cost of lighting with gas. Colonel Crompton was closely associated with the whole process. He wrote,

> The first few days were given to inspecting and testing the works at Calcutta. It was decided that the works should be started, and public supply given on April 6, and as my chief engineer, Scott Moncrieff, had been married only a few days before, I took over most of the work. We also worked out the tariff prices both for lighting and for power for driving *punkah* fans, work which had always been performed at higher cost and less efficiently by coolies.[39]

But everything was not a cakewalk for Messrs Kilburn & Co. The company had to fight tooth and nail the Corporation of Calcutta in matters of granting licence. One William Graham, Municipal Commissioner, shared his experience: 'After the London Schemes, there was a great deal of litigation by everyone in all parts of London who lived near the Central Station. They complained of the noise and vibration, which was so great as to bring down their houses.' If the power company were to install very heavy machinery in Calcutta, he requested putting in a clause in the 'provisional order', in the line of the London Electric Lighting Provisional Order (1890), to prevent any nuisance on the part of the company.[40] But a more formidable opponent was C. H. Reynolds, Director General of Telegraphs in India. His objection was against the overhead wires proposed to be erected by the electric company. In his note to the government, Reynolds categorically said,

> The streets in Calcutta are very generally planted with trees, and these trees to my mind cannot but be a constant source of danger to overhead wires. When our lines carrying weak, harmless currents are broken by trees, we repair them, with the result of a little delay to messages, but the case is different with overhead wires carrying powerful currents on which public are dependent for locomotion and for light in their houses, to say nothing of the danger of coming into contact with such wires....[41]

He understood that the CESC wanted to use 'bare wires on the ground of economy', but cautioned about the security and convenience of the general public. The power company was not in the mood to backtrack. Ultimately Crompton had to intervene. He discussed the matter with Major P. Cardew, Electrical Adviser to the Government of India. This melted the ice and the electric company was permitted to use 'either insulated metallic returns or un-insulated metallic returns of low resistance' for the supply of electricity.[42]

In the meanwhile, Colonel Crompton also assisted the Bengal government to strengthen the laws related to generation and supply of electricity. Several licences were successively granted in 1896 and the following years to the same company for various areas of supply in Calcutta.[43] These licences were based on the antiquated model of the British Provincial Order of 1889, and J. W. Meares observed, 'As they were only licenses, not confirmed by legislation, a large portion of each document was of doubtful validity, as affecting third parties.'[44] The CESC wanted to extend the area of supply, saying that they were receiving applications for supply to premises just beyond the limits of the districts covered by their existing licence. There was an intense debate within the government circle about the feasibility of the plan. Several officers objected, while others were in a go-ahead mood.[45] Finally, Messrs Kilburn & Co., on behalf of the CESC, was permitted to supply 'electricity for any public or private purpose, throughout the specified area of supply, by means of the low tensions, continuous current system, distributing by means of distributing mains' by enacting the Calcutta Electric Lighting Act, 1899.[46] Calcutta was situated on the banks of the River Hooghly. There was a special clause in the Act to save the river: 'Nothing in this license shall authorize the undertakers to lay, or place, any electric line, or works, in the River Hooghly, or affect in any manner the powers or privileges of the Commissioners of the Port of Calcutta.'[47] Construction began in right earnest, but by the beginning of 1899 the work of electrification of Calcutta was nowhere near finished. Serious doubts were raised in London as to the feasibility of meeting the deadline to start electric supply to Calcutta by the end of April 1899. Once again, Crompton intervened to personally supervise and accelerate the pace of work. He made critical pragmatic changes and injected new impetus into the venture in order to bring it back to schedule.[48]

Links to a New World

The first generating station of the CESC commenced operation at Emambagh Lane, near Princep Street, from 17 April 1899. This station was equipped with 'Crompton' dynamos, 'Willans' reciprocating steam engines, and 'Babcock and Wilcox' boilers. Following the most up-to-date practice then functioning in England, it was decided to adopt the three-wire system of distribution (Edison system of distribution), supplying direct current (DC) to consumers at 450 and 225 volts.[49] The plant in Emambagh Lane 'consists of three boilers of 500 horse-powers which can be extended to 800 horse-powers, if desired, with eight dynamos and a storage battery'.[50] Colonel Crompton had not only designed the plans and made the blueprints for operation, but also programmed the optimum efficiency of the plant.

A month after the commissioning of the Emambagh Lane powerhouse, a decision was taken to have electric connection at the Government House in May

1899, with the stipulation that the job must be completed before Lord Curzon, the then Viceroy, returned to Calcutta from his official tour of north India. The Government of India accordingly sanctioned 48,075 rupees with the request of speedy completion of the project.[51] The Director General of Telegraphs wanted to introduce electrical power into the workshops at Calcutta in the place of steam power and asked for necessary permission, stating that

> the advantages of electrical power over steam power are now so thoroughly recognized that it does not appear necessary to go into details to prove that in a place like Calcutta, where electrical power will be available close to our Workshop in a few months, it is the best form of energy to adopt.[52]

With this intention, the Telegraph Department proposed to purchase a plant 'locally' from Messrs Kilburn & Co., who was also interested in assisting the installation of the same. The government sanctioned the local purchase of the necessary plant for the introduction of electrical power into the Telegraph Workshops at Calcutta in 1901.[53]

The experience in Calcutta gave rise to several specific technical questions that had not been anticipated by the Bengal government under the Calcutta Electric Lighting Act, 1895. It was found that the period of 21 years was not long enough to attract capital for electrical undertakings. The government was willing to extend the period of the licences to 42 years, but this was not possible under the existing Act.[54] Thus, the Government of India was forced to reconsider the whole question of supply of electrical energy and adopt a procedure that could be applied to the whole of British India. The various local governments as well as the promoters of electrical enterprise were generally in favour of legislation by an Imperial Act.[55] After detailed consideration of the many issues involved, a more elaborate All India Electricity Act was passed in the year 1903, which shaped the future of the electricity manufacturing industry. The Act of 1903 was aimed at mainly regulating the generation and supply of electricity for both industrial and domestic purposes. It addressed issues such as (*a*) who may be allowed to produce and supply electricity, (*b*) what norms should the suppliers follow with regard to protecting consumers safety, (*c*) what should be the rates charged to the consumers, and (*d*) how much of control should the government have over the suppliers.[56] These four issues constituted the core of the colonial government's policy towards this emerging industry, whose development shaped the very nature and structure of various economic activities, particularly in the industrial sector, in the later years.

After Calcutta, it was the turn of Madras, another stronghold of the British in India. Though Colonel Crompton never visited the city, he was instrumental in setting up the Madras Electric Supply Company just like what he had done for the CESC. He also advised the local authority for the Madras Tramway and even supplied the tramway motors. The experience gained in Calcutta served as the basis for Crompton & Co. to establish their business in Madras City.[57]

Electricity reached Calcutta almost simultaneously with its acceptance in Europe. Thermal generation was first started in the city on a commercial scale by the CESC and with the passing of the Calcutta Electric Lighting License 1901, additional areas were placed under the purview of the company.[58] When electricity first came to Calcutta no one could have imagined that the days of the hand-pulled *punkah* (fan) were numbered. The popularity of the electric fan ensured immediate success for the electric supply company and provided the 'day load', essential to the economic working of an electric supply station.[59] For example, in 1902 the Governor-General in Council sanctioned an additional grant to install electric ceiling fans at the Imperial Library in Metcalfe Hall, Hare Street.[60] Government buildings, both offices and private residences, were fitted with electrical appliances very soon.[61] The nine Government Houses, including that in Calcutta, were supplied with electricity by 1904 and provision was made to recover charges for electric lights and fans in the residences of governors, lieutenant governors, and heads of local administrations.[62]

But the lower level of the administration was not as lucky to have the comfort of electric fans in summer! As in the case of Imperial Secretariat Buildings, where the noise of the *punkha*-pulling machine distracted the day-to-day work, a proposal was made 'for substituting electric ceiling fans in place of the existing *punkhas* pulled by electric motors in the clerks' rooms'. But the proposal was rejected on the ground that '... as *punkhas* are required for a very brief period each year, the Government of India have decided not to incur the proposed expenditure'.[63]

In 1904, the Head Engineer of the Calcutta Mint applied to the Bengal government to receive electric current from the CESC for 'one 25 HP and one 20 HP motors at a pressure exceeding 450 volts' for driving machinery at the mint. He also assured that his intention was 'to enclose the apparatus in a separate casing, to cut it off entirely from everyone, except the man in charge of it'.[64] Subsequently, permission was granted. The Superintending Architect of the Victoria Memorial requested the CESC for electric connection at his office on the site of the memorial buildings in June 1904. The supply company accordingly applied to the Bengal government for a temporary licence to erect an overhead mains to the site of the Victoria Memorial, situated at the Calcutta Maidan, outside their licensed area. The permission was granted.[65]

Granting temporary licence to erect electric mains was usual in those days. As on another occasion, the CESC permitted the erection of an overhead mains to a skating rink at the Calcutta Maidan with the help of a 'temporary license'.[66] As the electricity business expanded, the Bengal government had to sanction new licences or revise the existing ones to further the cause. The electric supply company applied for a licence for the supply of electricity to the Eastern Bengal State Railway's loco sheds at Narcoldanga. But this was outside the area of supply of the company. Granting a special licence for such a small area was not feasible, so extending the Calcutta Electric Lighting License (1901) the plot was incorporated and thus the CESC was able to supply electricity there.[67] On the occasion of the Indian Industrial Exhibition (1906), the electric company was authorized to erect a special pole at the Lower Circular Road for the supply of electricity to the venue with the clause that they would remove the same after the end of the exhibition.[68]

Calcutta witnessed the biggest public display of electricity, perhaps for the first time, on the occasion of the visit of Their Royal Highnesses the Prince and Princess of Wales on the night of 3 January 1906. One contemporary newspaper reported:

> The whole of that portion of the Maidan which is bounded by the Outram Avenue on the North, by Chowringhee and the Cathedral Road on the East, by the Casuarina Avenue on the West, and by the Grass side on the South will be hung with thousands of lamps, and it is believed that the Bengal Club, the Army and Navy Stores, and other buildings on that portion of Chowringhee will also be illuminated on that evening.[69]

For lighting purposes, the Government of India sanctioned a sum of 86,063 rupees and the CESC was in charge of the event. The charge was met by a 'corresponding reduction in the allotment of Rs. 60,000 for the development of the Veterinary Institution in the Scientific and other Minor Department's budget for the year 1905–06'.[70] The growing demand for electric current for lights as well as fans necessitated the enlargement of the Emambagh Lane station from time to time, and the extension of the distribution mains. Additional DC generating stations were opened in different parts of the city: Alipore in March 1902 (750 kilowatts [kW]), Howrah in May 1906 (165 kW), and Ultadanga in September 1906 (1,200 kW).[71]

Witnessing History on Wheels: Electric Tramways

On 11 April 1898, the following item appeared in the *Amrita Bazar Patrika* under the headline 'Proposed Electric Tramway in Harrison Road':

> At a meeting of the General Committee of the Calcutta Corporation, the Chairman submitted for consideration a letter from Messrs Kilburn & Company on the subject of laying an electric tramway in Harrison Road. The correspondence, he said, tended to show that the Committee were not prepared to negotiate in August last. A further letter had since been received, and he proposed to discuss the situation with Messrs Kilburn and Company, and lay the result before the Committee. Mr. Baker thought there were serious objections to entering into negotiations on the subject, because a tramway along Harrison Road would be an intolerable nuisance. As long as the poles of electric lighting remained in the centre of that road, it would be impossible to have a tramway on either side. Baboo Nolin Bihari Sircar reminded the Committee that there was a similar application from the Tramways Company, which had been refused. Mr. Baker added that the same proposal made to the Port Commissioners, who refused to consent as far as their jurisdiction was concerned. The application was rejected.[72]

Calcutta Tramways was sought to be developed as the first organized mass transport. In 1896, Messrs Kilburn & Co. sought the permission of the Calcutta Corporation for the introduction of electric propulsion in the tramcars. They came to terms with the CTC in addition to the supply of electricity to the general public. The Calcutta Corporation was critical of the proposal and asked for clarification on several points from the tramways company before entering into any agreement with them.[73] The tramcars were at first drawn by horses; owing to the severe strain to which the horses were subjected in the Indian hot weather, casualties were heavy, and the substitution of mechanical traction was desirable, both from economic and humane considerations. In 1882, the company was allowed, as an experimental measure, to run steam-engines in Chowringhee for a year.[74] The next logical step was electricity. J. R. Maples, the then Managing Agent, CTC, tried hard to convince the corporation and argued in favour of this new technology: 'We have no statistics at command where electric traction and electric lighting have been worked from a single installation, although the combination is being introduced in several cities in Europe. If lighting and traction are each separately remunerative, it is obvious that their combination must give economy in production.' He continued,

> It has been urged that gas traction should be given a trial.... The closed double-deck cars with outside uncovered seats used with the gas engines are quite unsuitable for the climate of Calcutta.... Electrical traction will enable cars to be run in any weather as long as there are passengers to be carried, and the delays now inseparable from frequent horse-changing will be avoided.[75]

Finally in 1899, the CTC entered into an agreement with the corporation to introduce electric traction. On 27 March 1902, the first electric tramcar ran from Esplanade to Kidderpore, and on 14 June that year to Kalighat.[76] By the end of the year, the conversion to electric traction, with overhead or aerial wires, was completed, no doubt to the relief of the wretched horses, which died in great numbers each year during the hot weather.

A. K. Roy, the Census Commissioner (1901), was optimistic with the developments:

> Electric Tramways, and Electric Lighting of the main thoroughfares of the Town, for which the requisite contracts have already been completed, and the requisite plant has already been imported and partly erected by the contractors, will, if carried out in conjunction with the large schemes of improvement that are in contemplation, and towards which preliminary action has already been taken, completely change the aspect of the town in the course of a few years....[77]

But everybody was not in a jubilant mood. A contemporary journal, the *Indian Mirror*, reported:

> The subject of the Tramways overhead electric traction in Calcutta must engage the serious attention not only of the residents of Calcutta, but also of all who have business or any other relations with the metropolitan city. The system is fraught with danger, and this has been emphasized by the recent loss of life, but still the journal learns that the matter is going to be hushed up, powerful European commercial interest being at stake.[78]

The completion of the electrification process accounted for the phenomenal growth of the Calcutta tramways. By 1905, their system covered 46 miles of single track. The company possessed a large power station fully equipped with all modern machinery for the supply of electrical energy at Nonapookur. The power generated from this station could be used for the purpose of supplying energy for electric traction only. They also had four depots in different parts of Calcutta. The service added 'most materially to the comfort and convenience of the Calcutta public'.[79] The Calcutta Tramways (Howrah) Act, 1905, paved the way for the introduction of electric tramways within the municipality of Howrah. To connect their said generating station in Calcutta to the sub-station of Howrah with cables, the CTC had to cross the River Hooghly and the necessary permission was granted.[80] Subsequently, tracks were laid in Tollyganj, Belgachia, and Harrison Road in 1903, Bagbazar in 1904, and Lower Circular Road, Alipur, Behala, and Howrah in 1908. Later extensions were to Rajabazar (1910), Park Circus (1923), Rashbihari Avenue (1928), Upper Circular Road and Galiff Street (1941), and Gariahat (1943). Tracks were also laid along the new Howrah Bridge in 1943.[81] Tramcars were for long virtually the only form of mass transport in Calcutta.

The inspection of the overhead wires of the tramways was an issue which engaged the Calcutta Corporation, the CTC, and the Bengal government in prolonged administrative and legal ordeals. Concerned with the electrical apparatus attached with the cars and of the overhead wires, the Calcutta Corporation requested the Bengal government for a thorough examination. As their right to inspect the overhead wires was not clear, the corporation also requested the government to issue the necessary instructions to the government Electric Inspector to inspect and report on the same.[82] At the request of the Bengal government, R. J. Browne, Electric Inspector, made a special inspection of the entire 61 miles of the overhead equipment and submitted his report in November 1911. He was totally satisfied with the tramway company's overhead construction and remarked that the Calcutta Corporation had no powers with respect to the overhead electrical equipment, which rested in the hands of the Bengal government alone.[83] At this, the Bengal government authorized Browne to make an annual inspection of the electrical equipment connected with the tramways and report to it in future.

Really indeed, electric tramway was the symbol of modernity of the twentieth century. As in 1938, H. D. Bhattacharya, Professor of Dhaka University, rightly observed,

> Thirty-eight years ago, when I first came to Calcutta from a village, there was no electric tramcars and taxis and buses, nor even restaurants and 'bioscopes'... no urban attraction.... As if by a stroke of magic, the old city has shed most of its ugly features. If the dead of those times were to come to life today, what a strange contrast would meet their eyes![84]

Strengthening the Network and Capacity Expansion

A letter written by the Secretary to the Government of Bengal (PWD) to his counterpart at the Government of India in July 1906 reveals the following:

> ... an application has been received from Messrs Nixon & Co and John Fleming & Co, Bombay for the grant of a license for the supply of electric energy in bulk. The area of supply comprises a tract of country on both sides of the river Hooghly from Uluberia and Budge-Budge on the south to the East Indian Railway Bridge across the Hooghly, excluding the portion within the Municipalities of Calcutta and Howrah.[85]

Such a 'bulk supply' scheme was the first of its kind in the province and the Lieutenant Governor was interested. Messrs Nixon & Co. wished to supply electricity on a large scale, while the CESC supplied electricity on a comparatively small scale. But a licence could not be granted under the Indian Electricity Act, 1903, for the supply of electricity in bulk, the Government of India appointed a committee to investigate the matter. The most important question in front of the committee was 'whether in the disputed area electrical power chiefly required for mills, factories, etc. i.e., for power purposes proper, or chiefly for lighting and fans, and to a limited extent only for workshops, etc.'[86] The Electric Company of Bombay informed the government that their proposed customers were mainly big jute mills, flour mills, cotton mills, and so on, and so the supply of electricity in bulk was necessary.[87]

At this the Managing Agent, CESC, wrote to express their objection to the Bengal government. But since hitherto the power company had made no attempt to supply energy in bulk to mills and factories, in the opinion of the Lieutenant Governor, the objection of the CESC did not carry much weight.[88] The Imperial Government also preferred the industrial supply of energy to factories, which was more important than the supply of energy for traction, lighting, and fans. Finally, the Hooghly River Electric License (1907) was granted to Messrs Nixon & Co. and Messrs John Fleming & Co. for the supply of electric energy to the Hooghly district of Bengal.[89] There was something for the CESC too. The Calcutta Electric License (1907) was granted to them for the supply of electrical energy in Calcutta and additional areas in its environs. By this licence, the other licences granted to them between the years 1896 and 1904 had been revoked. With this, the electric company was authorized to place any electric supply line above ground across any street in Calcutta and they had to pay an annual rent of 1 rupee for every pole to the Corporation of Calcutta.[90]

Two years later, the Indian Electricity Bill, 1909, was introduced which extended to the whole of British India, including British Baluchistan and Santhal Parganas. The dual system of control under the previous Act was corrected and the local government was vested with full powers to control and grant licences. But there were still a few points that needed to be rectified. As Babu Sita Nath Ray, Secretary, Bengal National Chamber of Commerce, pointed out,

> in the former Act of 1903, energy was defined as electrical energy expended at a greater than 25 watts, which excluded electric energy in electric bells, telephone, etc.; but in the present Bill the definition includes every use of electric power, and would have the effect of interfering with the use of the energy in domestic and scientific apparatus. If the former definition is not restored it will be necessary to take out license even for an exhibition of the Rontgen rays.[91]

The electric company expressed their concern about the increasing power theft. According to them, 'the usual method employed for stealing energy being that of tapping the licensee's wires at a point where they enter a consumer's premises, joining a wire at this point and connecting the other end of this wire to the consumer's wire above the meter'.[92]

The practical working and administration of the electrical industry disclosed numerous defects. One such point was the supply of electricity in bulk. It was appreciated that the 1903 Act was unable to cope with the current state of scientific progress and the rapid expansion of the industry, and, thus, a thorough revision was needed.[93] Thus, the Indian Electricity Act, 1910, came into existence and remained unaltered in most of its important provisions for half a century before it was copiously amended by the Indian Electricity (Amendment) Act, 1959. The Indian Electricity Act, 1910, laid down the law relating to 'the supply and use of electrical energy' in India and regulated the procedure for the grant of licences to electrical undertakings, prescribing obligations in respect of the execution of works and delivering supplies, and regulated the relations between the licensees and the consumers.[94]

With the rapid increase in demand for power for jute presses and mills, the CESC decided to install an alternating current (AC) plant at the Ultadanga station to deal with the pressing needs of consumers of the northern areas of Calcutta. Supply from this station was available from September 1910.[95] Now, the electric company applied for the sanction of the local government to supply electrical energy for power and other purposes at a standard pressure of 6,000 to 6,600 volts to meet the demands of large consumers, such as the jute presses. The supply was made by means of a 'three-phase alternating current at a periodicity of 50 cycles'. The Bengal government granted the necessary permission with the condition: 'The word Danger, both in English and in the vernacular, shall be affixed in a conspicuous position near every motor, switchboard or regulator apparatus in connection with the supply.'[96] To attract large consumers, the CESC proposed certain special rates of electricity.[97] The approval was made on the condition that the supply should be taken on one and the same premises. The rate was also fixed by the government in consultation with the company.

By now the advantages of having a large central station generating AC at high voltage and supplying sub-stations in different parts of Calcutta where AC could be converted to DC were felt.[98] The River Hooghly, the lifeline of Calcutta, on both banks of which industrial units had sprung up, could provide the water necessary to run a large power plant. A site had been selected at the riverside at Cossipore and the company entered into an agreement with the owners of the land. But lawsuits between various stakeholders of the land in the Calcutta High Court made the whole arrangement complicated. At this, the power company solicited the assistance of the Bengal government to acquire the 27 *bighas* of land for the proposed generating station.[99] The government set up a one-member enquiry committee to investigate the matter. The committee in its report assured the government about the feasibility of the project. The proposed station was required to generate electricity to meet the increased demands of the public for energy. The demand was so high that the CESC was at that time refusing new applications for motive power. The government acted swiftly, and work started at the site. Cossipore – the first central thermal generating station – was commissioned in 1910, with an initial installed capacity of 15 megawatt (MW), generating AC at 6,000 volts from July 1912.[100] In order to supply electrical energy throughout Calcutta from this new generating station, it was necessary to place high tension cables under the Eastern Bengal State Railway Line at Chitpur. Accordingly, the CESC applied to the railway company, but the latter denied permission and suggested the erection of overhead cables. At this, the electric company requested the Bengal government for necessary permission. The then Electrical Inspector of the Bengal government was also in favour of placing high tension cables under the track for proper functioning of the power system. The government accepted the proposal of the CESC as the public supply of electricity had to be ensured.[101] Cossipore indeed marks the beginning of a new era in the history of the CESC. The next step was the new sub-stations where the 6,000 volts AC from Cossipore could be transformed into DC. These were built at Jackson Lane in the business quarter; at Wellesley Street in the 'European' section; and at Prinsep Street, opposite the company's first station at Emambagh Lane. The machinery used at these sub-stations was 'Bruce Peebles' motor converters.[102] Subsequently, the old DC generating stations at Howrah, Ultadanga, and Alipore were converted into sub-stations. A new sub-station was built entirely on piles on the River Hooghly and was called the Bank Sub-Station.[103]

Thus, urban demand was the main driving force behind the emergence of a centralized thermal power station. The CESC had become the main provider of electricity to industrial works, government establishments, and private consumers. There were a few exceptions where the protagonists were permitted to generate electricity for their own purposes. For example, the East Indian Railway Company had electricity generation plants at Jamalpur, Howrah, Bamangachi, Lillooah, Asansol, and Giridhi within the province of Bengal. These installations were used primarily for the working of the railway workshops. In addition, the railway company supplied energy for fans and lighting to the residents of railway towns at a nominal rate. R. J. Brown, the Electrical Advisor to the Government of India, informed the Bengal government about private generation and distribution of electricity by the East Indian Railway Company. After enquiry, the Bengal government exempted the railway company from obtaining a license for the same in 1911.[104]

In the meanwhile, the Calcutta Improvement Trust (CIT) was established (1911) by the Bengal Legislative Assembly to improve 'city health and housing on a great scale, the laying out of new suburbs with their sewerages, water and lighting systems, and the provision of bridges, parks, cemeteries and all adjuncts'.[105] Naturally, they had to negotiate with different foreign business companies involved in providing urban amenities to the city, including the CESC. The CIT was to construct new roads and improve existing ones.[106] After the completion of the work and inspection by an engineer appointed by the Calcutta Municipal Corporation, these were to be handed over to the corporation. In fact, the officials of the CIT and the corporation tried to manipulate the terms and conditions regarding street lighting as both the Oriental Gas Company and the CESC used to compete for the public lighting of the city during the early years of the twentieth century. The following resolution taken at the Second Meeting of the Joint Conference (6 March 1920) between the CIT and the corporation states: '... in view of the comparison of cost, electric lighting be adopted in Scheme V. As regards future schemes, the method of lighting to be adopted will depend upon the relative cost in each case.'[107] So, there were tripartite agreements between the CIT (construct roads, and so on), the Calcutta Municipal Corporation (owner of roads), and the CESC (service provider).

But uneasy situations continued to arise. A dispute arose between the CIT and the CESC regarding the underground cables in Russa Road. Due to the sinking of the level of the road, the cables had become exposed to the surface level. The Chief Engineer of the CIT was of opinion that 'the main could be safely lowered in its present position'. But the CESC opposed the idea saying 'it was necessary to lay a new main under the footpath of the new road'.[108] Again, in 1923, S. R. Das, the Advocate-General of Bengal, objected to the idea of compensation by any government body (including the CIT) to the different private utility companies in case of removal and replacement of their lines, cables, posts, and so on, in the larger public interest.[109] Such questions continued to haunt the relationship of these two organizations for several years. But despite that the usual business went on. The annual report of the CIT for the year 1936–7 declared:

> Southern Avenue: Electric lighting has been installed in the roads north of Southern Avenue and everything is in readiness for lighting the remaining roads to the south as soon as necessary connections are given by the Calcutta Electric Supply Corporation.[110]

Voice of Consumers

The last three decades of the nineteenth century saw some major developments: underground water pipes and drains in some areas from the 1870s; a pontoon bridge across the Hooghly River in 1874; horse-drawn trams from 1880; gas lights on the streets; the first telephones in 1882; and a few motor cars from 1896. In this context a statement of Jotindra Mohan Tagore, British Indian Association President, is worth a mention (1865): 'The Town cannot afford for that elaborateness which the Engineer has designed. All that the inhabitants want is wholesome water for drink, and it was the duty of the Municipality to consider whether it could not be supplied at a moderate expense.'[111] The groundwork for urban development and the consensus for change had already been laid by some earlier renovations of the city, the major among those being, perhaps, the modern system of sanitation and water supply. This probably enabled electricity to be accepted more easily.

Although usually highly appreciative, consumers from the very beginning also criticized the company's service. One James Cleghorn, resident of 57, Ballygunge Circular Road, complained to the government against the CESC. He had been using bare lamps as regulators for his fans. The electric company began charging him lamp rates, which was higher, for the fans. The Electric Inspector visited the place and charged Mr Cleghorn with 'improper use' of electrical energy under the law.[112] On another occasion, the contenders were Messrs Andrew Yule & Co. and the CESC. The dispute had arisen over certain differences caused by the slow reading of meters. These meters were installed to register the three-phase current supplied to Messrs Yule & Co. at the following places: the City Flour Mill, the Central Jute Press, the Monarch Flour Mill, and the Chitpore Press.[113] The power company on various occasion charged extra money from them on the alleged grounds that 'either the meters were inaccurate or the connections thereto incorrect'. The government this time supported the consumer. It is a fact that electricity, as a source of light and motive power, boosted productivity. But in the beginning electricity was, in fact, widely regarded as a fearsome djinn that came to life at the flick of a switch. Communication to inform and educate the public on the immense benefits of this modern wonder was begun by the CESC. It took the forms of advertisements in the press, handouts like blotting papers with messages inscribed on them, and door-to-door canvassing.[114] The canvassers went from house to house trying to sell electricity to consumers as late as the 1930s. These were the symbols of a new technological culture ushered into Calcutta with electricity.

The supply of current for lights, fans, and power increased from 412,950 units in 1900 to 21,081,928 units in 1915. During the period 1911–15, that is, after the introduction of the new plant at Cossipore, the annual profits of the CESC rose from 95,597 pounds to 162,922 pounds.[115] By this time several individuals, local authorities, and organizations had started criticizing the power company over their rates. Prominent among them were the Calcutta Corporation, the Anglo-Indian Association, and so forth. Pointing to the rates charged by other electric companies in Britain and India, they accused the Calcutta company of overcharging.[116] In 1916, the Bengal government appointed a committee to enquire into the question of charges levied by the CESC.[117] With no Indian member on board, the committee questioned the basis of comparison between different stakeholders. All praise for the power company, it suggested 'a further reduction in the cash price per unit for lighting'. But the committee was against any coercive method by the state as it would be detrimental to the steady growth of the electrical industry.[118] Unhappy with the developments, the then Chairman of the CESC, P. V. Luke, wrote to the Bengal government, 'As our present charges are already far below the maximum, such a reduction could not benefit the consumers, which it would amount to a disparagement of the policy of the Company which my Board claims we done nothing to deserve.'[119] Finally, it was decided to reduce the flat-rate charge to the public from 3¾ annas to 3½ annas per unit for consumption up to 60,000 units.

Technological Momentum

The First World War (1914–18) had an enormous impact on the development of technological systems, particularly in the colonial context. As far as the growth of electricity was concerned, the war situation worked in two ways, as recently shown by two scholars: first, as a negative force, the war context delayed the long-term development of the electricity system and, second, as a positive force, it accelerated industrial development, especially war-based industries, which in turn generated more power demand.[120] As one government report reads,

> War conditions, such as restricted lighting, restricted coal output and shortage of labour, have caused very many British companies to raise their rates by 10 or 15 percent in the last year. These factors have not affected the CESC appreciably; but the difficulty of obtaining new plant and the prohibition of the manufacture of copper wire must necessarily limit the possible expansion of the business.[121]

The Electric Supply and Traction Federation of India was formed to promote the interests of electrical undertakings in 1918. While the larger undertakings such as the CESC and the various Tata hydroelectric companies were not affiliated to it, the federation represented the smaller undertakings effectively.[122] It objected to the special low rates enjoyed by the government in its electricity bill.[123] Since it was the guarantee of supply given by the government which in many cases assured the initial prospects of the electrical undertakings, in the opinion of the government, it was justified to enjoy special rebate. Not simply that; big consumers like the government, Calcutta Corporation, Baranagar Jute Mill, and so on, helped the CESC to reduce their cost of generation, and thus benefitted the general public to enjoy a moderate rate. If refused, the government threatened to install their own generating station and that would impact the supply company as its main expenses would remain unaltered and the general public would have to pay higher rates.

The Bally-Utterpara Electric License was granted to the CESC in 1920. With this, several adjacent areas of Calcutta were supplied with electricity.[124] Calcutta witnessed one of the largest electrical installations in the city during the Calcutta Exhibition (December 1923) held at the Eden Gardens. The entire power installation was carried out by the Russa Engineering Works, a well-known electrical firm of the city, and the consulting engineers were the Messrs G. Bartholomew & Co. The supply and distribution of electricity had been carried out by the CESC and they also loaned the necessary materials required for that to the exhibition authorities. In order to meet the requisite demand, special arrangements were made – the exhibition site was directly connected to the Cossipore Power Station. A sub-station of considerable magnitude was built in the exhibition area near the Auckland Road entrance and the necessary switchgear and transformers were also installed there. From the technical information mentioned in an official publication of the exhibition, one can assume the magnitude of the entire project:

> The supply is transmitted to the Sub-Station at a pressure of 6000 volts 3-phase Alternating Current and transformed down to 400 volts 3-phase and 225 volts single-phase by means of two 450 K.V.A. oil cooled transformers; five heavy overhead feeders have been erected from the sub-station to the various parts of the Exhibition. In addition to the Alternating Current supply Direct Current has been provided for the Engineering section. In addition to convey an idea of the extent of the supply arrangements it may be mentioned that over 10 tons of bare copper wires have been utilized for the purpose of providing the supply.[125]

In 1920 the CESC proposed the erection of two special cables across the Hooghly River to serve the sub-station at Howrah, situated on the west side of the river, from their Cossipore generating station at the east side and asked for the necessary permission. An agreement was signed between the Secretary of State for India and the CESC to carry aerial conductors supported by masts on each side of the river.[126] If the River Hooghly was Calcutta's lifeline, the Calcutta Dock was the city's very heart. The port commissioners had their own generators for lighting up the docks but later found it more convenient to rely on the CESC for the rapidly developing load.[127] In 1926, when the electric company decided on further expansion, the site of the Southern Generating Station at Garden Reach with an initial capacity of 22.5 MW was once again selected on the riverbank. The capacity of the station was subsequently augmented to 110 MW and eight turbo-generator and fifteen boilers were installed in the station.[128]

But technologically, the most important link between the River Hooghly and the CESC was formalized in 1929 when a decision was taken to build a tunnel under the river to carry cables from one bank to the other. Miss Eileen Homan, daughter of Mr F. T. Homan, Chief Executive of the CESC, inaugurated the project and work commenced on the underground tunnel between the Southern Generating Station and the Botanical Garden, Howrah.[129] This unique engineering feat, one of the most interesting carried out in the city, was completed in 1931. The contemporary press congratulated the CESC with enthusiasm. *Commercial Gazette* reported:

> In order that the increasing demand for power purposes on the Howrah bank of the river Hooghly may be met from the Southern Generating Station, the Board decided to construct a tunnel under the Hooghly for the purpose of carrying the mains from the Southern Station. On the 16th December 1929, the first sod in connection with the construction was cut by Miss Eileen Homan. The tunnel was completed in September 1931 and it is anticipated that the work of laying the cables through the tunnel will shortly commence. The tunnel is approximately 690 yards long, the Station end being located to the west side of the circulating water pump house, the other end being located at the Botanical Garden, Sibpur. The tunnel is some 90 feet below ground level and is 6 feet in diameter, made up of cast-iron sections reinforced by concrete. In the construction of the tunnel, British supervision was provided throughout, but Indian labour alone was employed. The supervision staff suffered much from the heat and humidity in the tunnel, particularly during the rainy season, when the temperature at times rose to 99° F with 100 percent humidity. The Southern Station will shortly be in the position to deal with all power demands emanating from the Howrah bank of the Hooghly.[130]

In the meanwhile, the CIT also carried out its usual job – road construction and making necessary infrastructure for street lighting. In the case of electricity, as we know, the service provider was the CESC. For example, in the case of Central Avenue, Beadon Street, and Grey Street, the CIT stated in 1933: 'The poles for the electric lighting of the main road have been erected but the reflectors and lamps have not been fixed. It is hoped that the installation will be completed and put into lighting at an early date.'[131] On another occasion (1938):

> Improvement Scheme No XXXIII (Southern Avenue): Arrangements are being made to install mercury vapour lighting in place of ordinary tungsten filament lamps in Southern Avenue between Russa Road and Lansdowne Road so that the Corporation and the Trust may arrive at a definite decision as to whether this type of lighting is suitable for main roads in Calcutta where alternating current is available.[132]

In the year 1908, the CESC opened their first office in Calcutta, at first at the Dalhousie Square and later at the Old Post Office Street until 1931. But after several years of operation, a larger accommodation became necessary as a result of the rapid expansion of their business. This coincided with the demolishing work of the CIT around the Old Post Office Street. The foreign power company purchased a 'large area of surplus land near the Chowringhee end'[133] and erected Victoria House,[134] an excellent architectural manifestation that still exists.

Looking at the busy industrial complex on both sides of the River Hooghly today, it is difficult to imagine how this modern wizard called electricity acted as an agent of development and progress. Between the two world wars, the electric supply company completed the construction of the Mulajore Generating Station to meet the demand of the growing industrial production and commenced work on the New Cossipore Generating Station to augment the capacity of the old station at Cossipore. Although the New Cossipore Generating Station commenced operations in 1950, only after the independence,[135] the Mulajore Generating Station was perhaps the last engineering feat dedicated to the service of Calcutta before 1947. Due to the disturbances caused by the Second World War, no directors of the CESC from London could be present at the venue for the inauguration, but war condition could not prevent the growth of the electrical industry. F. T. Homan, the Chief Executive of the CESC, introduced the project to the large gathering assembled for the inauguration.[136] Sir John Herbert, Governor of Bengal, performed the opening ceremony and declared:

> This is not only because as Governor of the Province I am glad to see our resources of electrical energy so materially augmented but because the opening of a great plant such as this is an act of faith – faith that the great industries which have come into being an and about Calcutta will continue to thrive and expand in the future as they have done in the past. The fact that the men who have been responsible for building up the Company from its comparatively small beginning 42 years ago to its present gigantic dimensions have had the confidence and courage to bring into being this vast plant which I am to open to-day is, I think a good omen for the future industrial development of this area and for the part which electricity may be expected to play in this development.[137]

Everywhere there was more access to electricity in the 1930s because of the foreign manufacturing company's role, but the rise was small in relation to the huge population. Thus, the CESC in 1934 purchased the property and goodwill of the Bhatpara Power Co. and obtained the permission of the Bengal government to take over its licence. The energy it sold increased from 230 million kilowatt hour (kWh) in 1934 to 395 million kWh five years later. The area the company served had 1.5 million people, but at the beginning of 1940 merely 57,415 houses had electrical wiring, a bare fraction of the houses in the area.[138] In short, there was a modest spread of electrification despite the international connection of the power generation company with their networks of various knowledge workers.

Conclusion

The electric utility industry has been and remains extraordinarily capital intensive, particularly in the transmission and distribution functions. Multinational enterprises and international finance were deeply involved in the electric light and power industry at its birth and in the subsequent years. The power generation companies that participated in the spread of electricity were influenced by considerable economic, political, and social change as they served as important catalysts in the transformation of electricity from a luxury to a necessity.

In elucidating the context in which electricity developed in colonial Calcutta, this chapter has emphasized various aspects. Multinational enterprises go where there are opportunities. In a colonial setting, the CESC was able to assemble capital and direct it to productive purposes without much challenge. Of greater importance is that they introduced technology, management, and experience and raised productivity. Their role is indeed very important, as argued by William J. Hausman and others, but here a few points deserve notice. Of course, London served as the model for electrification to the CESC, but the local situation of Calcutta influenced the growth of the power system to a considerable extent – the aerial and underground cable story can be a good reference point.

Calcutta, the capital of the British India until 1911, became the model for the rest of the country in terms of electrification. Among the foreign power companies, the CESC was directly involved in the Madras Presidency and several American and European companies in the Bombay Presidency and other parts of India. Here, the colonial state decided the ways of utilization and implementation of the electricity system; foreign enterprises decided what was to be manufactured and marketed; and the bureaucrats and intellectuals debated what technology was appropriate for society – together they shaped the course of the development of electricity with different ideas. R. H. G. Johnston, a Deputy Collector who served in several districts of Bengal, wrote on the 'insatiable appetite' of the electric power-stations of Calcutta for coal. His concern was the large amount of coal being transmitted to Calcutta from the Asansol and Raniganj sub-divisions for thermal power generation and the huge 'rail freights' thus wasted. This was probably not really an economic proposition. He proposed, '... why not build the power-station at pit-head and transmit the power to Calcutta by high tension line?'[139]

Most of the technologies related to electricity came from England and the foreign power company never tried to produce these locally. As a business strategy, they could have created conditions conducive to the production of these technologies in the colony itself. They brought the necessary technologies along with the human capital to supervise the local unskilled workforce. Their intention was profit-making, not the integration of 'modern' technology into the 'native' knowledge system. This no doubt inhibited the indigenization of electrical technology in the colonies. But Indians were not mere spectators; there were ripples in their minds from the beginning itself, and by the 1920s, Indians were able to domesticate this modern technology to a considerable extent. Surendranath Ghosh, Chief Electrical Engineer of the Tata Iron & Steel Co. Ltd, once remarked (1924),[140]

> The management of the Tata Iron and Steel Co. has been quick to realize the advantages of electric drive. Some of the advantages are ease of control, increased safety, increased production and economy; therefore, electric drive is now applied to most machinery used in the production of steel. The steel industry represents one of the largest fields for the endeavours of electrical engineers.

He continued,

> When steel plants first started to electrify, the generating units which they used were of small capacity and were usually engine-driven. The increasing use of electrical apparatus in the mills has made it necessary to enlarge greatly the generating stations. The power plant has now become a very important part of the entire plant and demands a great deal of attention of the engineering forces of the Plant.

Notes

1 A. T. Cooper, 'Recent Electrical Progress in India', *Journal of the Royal Society of Arts* 77, no. 3994 (June 1929): 743.

2 Sunila S. Kale, 'Structures of Power: Electrification in Colonial India', *Comparative Studies of South Asia, Africa and the Middle East* 34, no. 3 (2014): 454–5.

3 J. W. Meares, one of the pioneers of Indian electrical industry, shared his experience in 1929: When he went to India in 1896, the only public lighting installation was in the Eden Gardens, Calcutta, and it consisted of Jablockhoff candles. That system came into use in the 1870s, and disappeared in the next decade, but was still in operation in Calcutta even in 1896. When he argued with the Bengal government that modern

lighting should replace those candles, the official reply was, 'What is the matter with them? They have been working for thirty years, and will go on working for a long time. Why replace them?' It was found afterwards that those candles cost three times higher annually than the modern electric lamps! Quoted in Cooper, 'Recent Electrical Progress in India', 759.

4 Akhil Gupta, 'An Anthropology of Electricity from the Global South', *Cultural Anthropology* 30, no. 4 (November 2015): 556.

5 David E. Nye, *Electrifying America* (Cambridge: The MIT Press, 1990), 138.

6 Y. Srinivasa Rao, 'Electrification of Madras Presidency', unpublished PhD thesis, IIT Madras, 2007, iv.

7 Thomas P. Hughes, *Networks of Power* (Baltimore and London: John Hopkins University Press, 1983).

8 Rao, 'Electrification of Madras Presidency'.

9 William J. Hausman, Peter Hertner, and Mira Wilkins, *Global Electrification* (Cambridge: Cambridge University Press, 2011).

10 David Arnold and Erich Dewald, 'Everyday Technology in South and Southeast Asia: An Introduction', *Modern Asian Studies* 46, no. 1 (2012): 1–17.

11 Sunila Kale, *Electrifying India* (Stanford and California: Stanford University Press, 2014).

12 Wiebe E. Bijker, Thomas P. Hughes, and Trevor J. Pinch, 'Introduction', in *The Social Construction of Technological Systems*, ed. Wiebe E Bijker, Thomas P. Hughes, and Trevor Pinch (Massachusetts: MIT Press, 1987), 1–6.

13 O'Shaughnessy observed, '... when a powerful battery current is directed through pieces of well burned charcoal these ignite and shed a light of such brilliancy that it transcends every other mode of illumination.' W. B. O'Shaughnessy, *Notes on Natural Philosophy, First Series on Galvanic Electricity* (Calcutta: The Baptist Mission Press, 1841), 99.

14 Louis Schwendler, 'Precis of Report on Electric Light Experiments', *Proceedings of the Journal of the Asiatic Society of Bengal* (March 1879): 81.

15 Louis Schwendler, *Report on the Electric Light at the East India Rly Coys Station*, Howrah (Calcutta), 1881, in Sidhartha Ghosh, *Kaler Sahar Kolkata* (Kolkata: Ananda, 1991), 116.

16 *The Statesman*, 3 January 1882.

17 Biren Roy, *Marshes to Metropolis* (Calcutta: NCE, 1982), 265. This was just two years after Werner Siemen's first demonstration of an electric railway at the Berlin Exhibition of 1879!

18 *The Statesman*, 29 June 1881, reported:

> Electric Light: We hear that Messrs Mackinnon Mackenzie and Co.'s Garden Reach Cotton Mills are to be lighted with electric lights. The inauguration is to take place within a day or two, when the representatives of most of the

commercial firms of Calcutta are invited to be present. Thirty-six lights will be lend their brilliancy to the ground illumination, under the superintendence of the Electric Light Company.

19 *The Statesman*, 15 July 1882.

20 *The Statesman*, 14 May 1883.

21 P. Thankappan Nair, 'Civic and Public Services in Old Calcutta' in *The Living City*, Vol I: *The Past*, ed. Sukanta Chaudhury (Calcutta: Oxford University Press, 1990), 231.

22 Colonel Crompton introduced the first self-propelled road vehicles in India, the 'Road Steamers'. His first steamer-driven vehicle, the *Blue Bell*, is now in the London Science Museum. Another, the *Primer*, later used to haul a train of road wagons, arrived in Calcutta in 1870 and was taken to Delhi for trial. Arunabha Dasgupta, *Colonel Crompton's India* (Bombay: Tata Press, 1990), 14–20.

23 Leslie Hannah, *Electricity before Nationalisation* (Baltimore: The John Hopkins University Press, 1979), 17.

24 Paris Exhibition, 1899: Gold Medal awarded to Crompton & Co Ltd for their Exhibit of Electrical Machinery, which comprised the Lighting of the entire British, American, and a great portion of the French Sections. The Jury appointed to judge the Electrical Exhibits found that our Machines gave a commercial efficiency of 94 percent; a result which we believe has not been attained in any Dynamo hitherto constructed for Arc Lighting. The output of these Machines was 1,300 volts and 27 amperes. (The IET Archives.)

25 Available at http://www.theiet.org/about/libarc/archives/featured/crompton-india.cfm (accessed 2 June 2011).

26 Public Works Department (hereafter PWD), Civil Works: Telegraph, September 1897, Nos 5–14, NAI.

27 V. R. Muraleedharan, 'The Electrification of Madras City 1905 to 1914', Paper presented at the Third World Economic History and Development Conference, University of Manchester, 13–15 September 1991, 2.

28 PWD, MPI, File No. 5E/1/1895, Proceed No. A A/1–5, August 1895, WBSA.

29 Ibid.

30 John Willoughby Meares, one of Crompton's subordinate and later Electrical Engineer to the Bengal government, remarked in his autobiography,

> The problem before me was to build a reservoir of 40,000 cubic feet capacity, for one-fifth of the sum which a PWD engineer said it would cost; then to bring water to it from two streams through several miles of galvanised iron channel laid either in dense jungle or on almost vertical cliffs; to connect the reservoir with a smaller one as a forebay; to lay two steel pipes down a steep hillside to a small power house; to erect and test the turbo-generators and their switchgear after building this power house; to put up a 3 mile overhead transmission line, 3 or 4 sub-stations in the town, and lights in all the streets.

J. W. Meares, *At the Heels of the Mighty: Being the Autobiography of Your Obedient Humble Servant*, 1934, 69, The IET Archives.

31 PWD, MPI, File No. 5E/1/1904, Proceed No. A A1to37 and KW, WBSA.

32 PWD, Civil Works Miscellaneous, July 1899, Nos 6–9, NAI. There were four different types of aerial line, namely the bare high-tension line, the insulated high-tension line, the heavy-house lighting distribution, and the street and minor-house lighting distribution.

33 PWD, MPI, File No. 5E/1 of 1897, Proceed No. A 1–79, January 1897, WBSA. See also *Amrita Bazar Patrika*, 5 April 1898.

34 The capital of the company was 100,000 dollars divided into 20,000 shares of 5 dollars each. The object of the company was 'to carry on, in the Empire of India and elsewhere the business of an electric light and power company in all its branches'. PWD, MPI, File No. 5E/3 of 1899, Proceed No. A 1–11 and KW, May 1899, WBSA.

35 Messrs Kilburn & Co. informed the Bengal government that their scheme for lighting had been prepared after consultation with Mr Crompton who came out from England especially for the purpose. PWD, MPI, File No. 5E/1 of 1897, Procced No. A 1–79, January 1897, WBSA.

36 Ibid.

37 J. W. Meares claimed in his autobiography, 'The original intention was to combine the new project, for supplying Calcutta, with the electrification of the old horse – and steam-tramways, though eventually this did not materialise.' Meares, *At the Heels of the Mighty*, 89.

38 PWD, Civil Works Miscellaneous, November 1896, Nos 7–46, NAI.

39 R. E. Crompton, *Reminiscences* (London: Constable & Co. Ltd, 1928), 158–9.

40 PWD, MPI, File No. 5E/1 of 1897, Proceed No. A 1–79, January 1897, WBSA.

41 PWD, Civil Works: Miscellaneous, November 1896, Nos 7–46, NAI.

42 PWD, MPI, File No. 5E/1 of 1897, Proceed No. A 1–79, January 1897, WBSA.

43 For example, the Calcutta Electric Lighting License 1896, and so on. PWD, MPI, File No. 5E/ 1 of 1897, Proceed No. A 1–32, February 1898, WBSA.

44 J. W. Meares, *The Law Relating to Electrical Energy in India and Burma* (Calcutta: Thacker, Spink & Co., Sixth Edition, 1941), 12.

45 Electrical Engineer to the Bengal government, J. W. Meares observed, 'I think it will be greatly in the public interest if powers are granted to the Corporation to supply electricity.... In Ballygunge and Alipore it is to be expected that many persons requiring power....' While A. H. MacCarthy, Under-Secretary to the Bengal government (PWD), noted, 'I do not think that the area coloured red in the map can be thirsting for electric light at present.' PWD, MPI, File No. 5E/3 of 1899, Proceed No. A 1–11 and KW, May 1899, WBSA.

46 Ibid.

47 Ibid.

48 Crompton, *Reminiscences*, 165.

49 Sumantra Banerjee, 'Hundred Years of Electricity in Calcutta', *Indian Journal of Power and River Valley Development* 52, no. 7 and 8 (2002): 119–25.

50 PWD, MPI, File No. 5E/4/1900, Proceed No. A 1–6 and KW, October 1900, WBSA.

51 PWD, Civil Works Miscellaneous, May 1899, Nos 27–33, NAI.

52 PWD, Civil Works Miscellaneous, A Proceedings, August 1901, Nos 5–11, NAI.

53 The Despatch No. 16PW, dated 11 May 1899, placed electric light installations entirely in the hands of local firms. This equally applied in the case of electric motor installations. Ibid.

54 PWD, MPI, File No. 5E/4/1900, Proceed No. A 1 and 2 and KW, December 1900, WBSA.

55 PWD, MPI, File No. 5E/4/1900, Proceed No. A 1–22 and KW, August 1900, WBSA.

56 Meares, *The Law Relating to Electrical Energy*, 13.

57 Muraleedharan, 'The Electrification of Madras City 1905 to 1914', 2–3.

58 PWD, MPI, File No. 5E/7/1901, Proceed No. A 12–30 and KW, June 1901, WBSA.

59 PWD, Civil Works Miscellaneous, A. Proceedings, April 1904, Nos 1–14, NAI.

60 Home, Public, A. Proceedings, August 1902, Nos 55–59, NAI.

61 For the private residences of government officials, special scrutiny was conducted after 'the example of Indore, where an electric installation was put up at the instances of one Government officer, and his successor has promptly objected to pay....' PWD, Civil Works Miscellaneous, A. Proceedings, June 1902, Nos 10–12, NAI.

62 PWD, Civil Works Miscellaneous, A. Proceedings, April 1904, Nos 14–28, NAI.

63 'The Octavius Steel's system consists of electric motors pulling the ordinary pole *punkhas* be means of levers and usual ropes.' PWD, Civil Works Miscellaneous, A. Proceedings, December 1905, Nos 14–22, NAI.

64 PWD, MPI, File No. 5E/17/1905, Proceed No. B 31–33, February 1905, WBSA.

65 PWD, MPI, File No. 5E/24/1904, Proceed No. B 11–16, July 1904, WBSA.

66 PWD, MPI, File No. 5E/97/1905, Proceed No. B B/49–51, November 1905, WBSA.

67 PWD, MPI, File No. 5E/9/1904, Proceed No. A 1–11, April 1904, WBSA.

68 PWD, MPI, File No. 1E/82/1906, Proceed No. B B57–59, December 1906, WBSA.

69 *The Englishman*, 29 November 1905.

70 PWD, MPI, File No. 11/12/1906, Proceed No. A A43–85, January 1906, WBSA.

71 *1899–1999: A Century of Power to Calcutta, the Living City*, a CESC release.

72 *Amrita Bazar Patrika*, 11 April 1898.

73 Cost of electricity to run 1,878,529 car-miles; depreciation of electric plant; maintenance and renewal of line; repairs of machinery and plant, and so on. PWD, MPI, File No. 5E/1/1897, Proceed No. A 1–79, January 1897, WBSA.

74 '"Hauled by Steam" – On Saturday morning, we had the satisfaction of seeing a trial trip with another of the engines totally imported by the Tramway Company, and the result was most encouraging.' *The Statesman*, 6 February 1882.

75 PWD, MPI, File No. 5E/1/1897, Proceed No. A 1–79, January 1897, WBSA.

76 *The Statesman*, 25 June 1902.

77 A. K. Roy, *A Short History of Calcutta, Census of India, 1901*, Vol. VII, Part I (Calcutta: Bengal Secretariat Press, 1902), 86.

78 *Indian Mirror*, 20 June 1902, *Report on Native News Papers in Bengal*, January–June 1902, 256.

79 PWD, MPI, File No. 1E/7/1906, Proceed No. A 22–53 and KW, April 1907, WBSA.

80 Ibid.

81 Nair, 'Civic and Public Services in Old Calcutta', 235.

82 PWD, MPI, File No. 1E/14/1911, Proceed No. A 1 and 3, July 1911, WBSA.

83 PWD, MPI, File No. 1E/14/1911, Proceed No. A 53–57, December 1911, WBSA.

84 H. D. Bhattacharya, 'Calcutta – Then and Now', *Calcutta Municipal Gazette* XXIX, no. 1 (1938): 35.

85 PWD, Civil Works – Electricity, A. Proceedings, May 1907, Nos 1–19, NAI.

86 PWD, Civil Works – Electricity, A. Proceedings, January 1907, Nos 1–5, NAI.

87 PWD, MPI, File No. 1E/5/1907, Proceed No. B B40–41, May 1907, WBSA.

88 PWD, Civil Works – Electricity, A. Proceedings, May 1907, Nos 1–19, NAI.

89 The systems which may be adopted for the supply of electrical energy are – (a) a two or three wire direct current supply at a distribution pressure not exceeding 600 volts between outer-wires; and (b) a single phrase or poly-phase alternating current supply at a pressure not exceeding 10,000 volts between phrases. (PWD, MPI, File No. 1E/5/1907, Proceed No. A A1–67 and KW, May 1907, WBSA.)

90 PWD, Civil Works – Electricity, A. Proceedings, October 1907, Nos 1–4, NAI.

91 PWD, MPI, File No. 1E/44/1909, Proceed No. A A1–32, November 1909, WBSA.

92 Ibid.

93 Naushir Bharucha, *The Indian Electricity Act, 1910* (Bombay: Bombay Presidency Association, 1967), 2.

94 *The Indian Electricity Act, 1910* (Calcutta: Superintendent Government Printing, 1922), 1–65.

95 PWD, MPI, File No. 1E/12/1910, Proceed No. A 1–4, April 1910, WBSA.

96 Ibid.

97 The special power rate was applicable for those who had not less than 10 kilowatts installed either in one motor or as an aggregate of motors of not less than 1 kilowatt each. PWD, MPI, File No. 1E/9/1909, Proceed No. A A1–2, August 1909, WBSA.

98 The electricity used in homes comes from large electricity generating stations. These utilities transmit electricity to regional sub-stations, which then distribute it to consumers. Because transmission lines resist current flow, the current loses energy as heat. The amount of power lost depends on current flow. Direct current (DC) flows in one direction; alternating current (AC) regularly reverse its course. Lata Seth and Anuj Chawla, *Know about Science: Electricity* (New Delhi: Dreamland, 2014), 8.

99 PWD, MPI, File No. 1L/1/1910, Proceed No. A 1–17 and KW, March 1910, WBSA.

100 Oerlikon steam turbine sets, Babcock & Wilcox and Stirling boilers, and British Thomson Houston switchboards were installed initially. Subsequently, larger turbo-alternator sets manufactured by Metropolitan Vickers and English Electric Company were installed at this station. Banerjee, 'Hundred Years of electricity in Calcutta', 120.

101 PWD, MPI, File No. 1E/17/1911, Proceed No. A 1–20 and KW, October 1911, WBSA.

102 *History of Calcutta Electric Supply Corporation Limited (1897–1912)* (London EC: no pub., November 1913), 17.

103 PWD, MPI, File No. 1M/3/1915, Proceed No. A 1–6, May 1915, WBSA.

104 PWD, MPI, File No. 1E/3/1911, Proceed No. A 1–5, September 1911, WBSA.

105 E. P. Richards, *Calcutta Improvement Trust: Report by Request of the Trust on the Condition, Improvement and Town Planning of the city of Calcutta and Contiguous Areas* (Hertfordshire: Jennings and Bewley, 1914), 19. Partho Datta opines that the CIT was perhaps for the first time a consciously planned intervention for an Indian city that would include 'much more than sanitation and conservancy'. Datta, *Planning the City* (New Delhi: Tulika, 2012), 201.

106 It was entrusted with the engineering works related to road construction along with street lighting. In their annual financial statement, one can find expenditure on works related to electricity under the head 'Engineering Works'. These were: (*a*) electric supply contingencies, (*b*) shifting overhead tramway poles, (*c*) alteration to electric supply cables, (*d*) taking up and relaying electric supply cables, (*e*) shifting electric cables and poles, and so on. *Annual Report on the Operations of the Calcutta Improvement Trust for the Year 1912–1913* (Calcutta: CIT, 1913), 40.

107 *Annual Report on the Operations of the Calcutta Improvement Trust for the Year 1919–20* (Calcutta: CIT, 1920), 64–9.

108 *Annual Report on the Operations of the Calcutta Improvement Trust for the Year 1916–17* (Calcutta: CIT, 1917), 21–2.

109 The CIT asked the opinion of the Advocate-General regarding the rebuilding of the Kidderpore Bridge and the removal of electric cables of the CESC thereon. The power

company asked for compensation from the CIT. *Annual Report on the Operations of the Calcutta Improvement Trust for the Year 1922–23* (Calcutta: CIT, 1923), 50.

110 *Annual Report on the Operations of the Calcutta Improvement Trust for the Year 1936–37* (Calcutta: CIT, 1937), 27.

111 Judicial (Judicial), March 1865, Proceedings No. 114, WBSA.

112 PWD, MPI, File No. 1E/6/1911, Proceed No. A 1–30 and KW, May 1911, WBSA.

113 PWD, MPI, File No. 1E/12/1915, Proceed No. A 1–4, July 1915, WBSA.

114 *Jugantar Patrika*, 8 January 1939. 'Aro beshi alo' (More Light): An advertisement by the CESC.

115 PWD, MPI, File No. 1E/4/1916, Proceed No. A 1–2, March 1917, WBSA.

116 The present maximum rates are eight annas per unit for lighting and four annas for fans, while the actual rates charged by the Company are seven and four annas for lighting and fans respectively. With rebates for prompt payment the actual cash rates are much lower and are five annas and annas, respectively.

PWD, MPI, File No. 6C/1/1912, Proceed No. A 7–8 and KW, April 1917, WBSA.

117 The members were J. Donald (President), J. W. Meares, A. K. Taylor, and W. Stather Hale. Ibid.

118 Unless those adventurers come forward, obtain concession and float a concern there seems little likelihood of an increase in India in those electrical facilities which prevail so largely in all other countries, to the greater comfort and well-being of the population. These adventurers, will, we fear, not forthcoming if there is any likelihood of unreasonable interference in their operations. (Ibid.)

119 PWD, MPI, File No. 1E-11, Proceed No. A 1918, July 1918, WBSA.

120 Srinivasa Rao and John Lourdusamy, 'Colonialism and the Development of Electricity: The Case of Madras Presidency, 1900–47', *Science, Technology and Society* 15, no. 1 (2010): 49.

121 Committee appointed to enquire into the question of the charges levied by the CESC, Ltd, for electric current supplied in Calcutta. PWD, MPI, File No. 1E/4/1916, Proceed No. A 1–2, March 1917, WBSA.

122 Meares, *The Law Relating to Electrical Energy*, 9.

123 PWD, MPI, File No. 1-E-7, Proceed No. 6–7B, March 1920, WBSA.

124 The area of supply under the Act: North– by Bhudra Kali, South– by Mali Panchghara lane, Jaliapara Road, East– by the Hooghly River, West– by the East Indian Railway. *The Bally-Utterpara Electric License, 1920* (Calcutta: The Bengal Secretariat Book Depot, 1920), 2–3.

125 *Calcutta Exhibition: Official Hand-book & Guide* (Calcutta, 1923), 262.

126 PWD, MPI, File No. 1-E-5, Proceed No. A 9–12, May 1920, WBSA. The cables were very heavy, weighing 12 tons each. They were laid under the pontoon bridge, which

gave them protection from injury caused by ships dragging their anchors when going up and down the tide.

127 *The Calcutta Port Trust* (Calcutta: Thacker, Shink & Co., 1920), 17–29.

128 A. T. Cooper remarked in 1929:

> The first section of a new Southern Power Station laid out for an ultimate capacity of 150,000 kilowatts came into operation at the end of 1926. This is equipped with stoker-fired water-tube boilers and turbo-alternators generating at 3-phase 6000 volts, circulating water being taken from the river Hooghly. The Southern Station is linked up with the older Northern Station at Cossipore by means of two 6000 volt trunk feeders laid along separate routes.

Cooper, 'Recent Electrical Progress in India', 743. See also Banerjee, 'Hundred Years of Electricity in Calcutta', 121.

129 *Story of Electricity in the City of Calcutta*, CESC Release, 1979.

130 *Commercial Gazette*, 5 September 1932, 17.

131 *Annual Report on the Operations of the Calcutta Improvement Trust for the Year 1933–34* (Calcutta: CIT, 1934), 21.

132 *Annual Report on the Operations of the Calcutta Improvement Trust for the Year 1938–39* (Calcutta: CIT, 1939), 24.

133 *Annual Report on the Operations of the Calcutta Improvement Trust for the Year 1929–30* (Calcutta: CIT, 1930), 11.

134 'Behind is Victoria House, the handsome and imposing building of the Calcutta Electric Supply Corporation, surmounted by a dome on which is a globe that becomes an illuminated beacon during the early hours of the night.' John Barry, *Calcutta 1940* (Calcutta: The Central Press, 1940), 25.

135 *Jugantar Patrika*, 4 January, 1950. Dr K. N. Katju, the Governor of West Bengal, inaugurated the power station.

136 *Story of Electricity in the City of Calcutta*. There were 5 turbo-generators and 18 boilers with a pressure of 350 psi and temperature of 700°F. This is presently the oldest CESC power plant.

137 Quoted in *The Statesman*, 16 January 1940.

138 Hausman, Hertner, and Wilkins, *Global Electrification*, 216.

139 Johnston continued,

> This would certainly deprive the railways of a lucrative load but might be a better proposition for the country as a whole. There would be fairly high cost of a heavy transmission line but there would be the great saving on rail freights. Thermal generating stations need large quantities of cooling water for their condensers and I thought this could be done by damming the Barakar river and making a lake. Several advantages could follow, fishing, water-supply, water conservation, some measure of Damodar flood control and amenity as well as condenser cooling.

I did mention these ides to the Government of Bengal in reporting on the Damodar floods but the suggestions seemed to rouse little interest.

Johnston Papers, *Reminiscences of India, 1915–46*, Box 1, p. 75, CSAS, University of Cambridge.

140 Educated at the Queen's College, Benares, Surendranath received his technical training at the Manchester School of Technology, Manchester, UK. He acted as a lecturer and demonstrator at the Civil Engineering College, Sibpur, before joining Tata's firm as the Chief Electrical Engineer in 1914. Surendranath Ghosh, 'The Electrification of the Tata Iron Works at Jamshedpur', *The Calcutta Review*, June 1924, 496–518. http://www.southasiaarchive.com/Content/sarf.120137/211256/010 (accessed on 22 January 2018)

4

Domesticating Electricity

> When electricity first came to Calcutta, it was a fearful object to most of the rich and affluent of the city. They assumed that for new electric connection they had to make a hole in the wall and that could be risky. Thus, tried hard to avoid such things! My father was the first who discarded such phobia by applying for electricity and subsequently got the connection in our locality. The incident acted as a catalyst and after that many applied for electric connection. As that was like big advertisement for them, a pleased electric supply company relieved my father from remitting the connection changes.
>
> —Purnima Debi on her father, Gaganendranath Thakur (1900?)[1]

> Realizing the need of a journal on electricity in vernacular, we started *Bijoli* few months back. We earnestly hope that our initiative would be recognized by the Bengali entrepreneurs who involve in the business of electricity and things electrical in and outside Bengal. We also hope that the journal would be helpful to them. We want to see our fellow Bengalis to excel in electricity industry and our journal would be the mouthpiece of such emerging entrepreneurial activities.
>
> —*Bijoli*, in an editorial published in 1933[2]

The introduction of electricity transformed life fundamentally. At first, a luxury good, electric light and power generation, both symbols of modernity, soon became a basic need everywhere in the world. The subject of electrification has fascinated business and economic historians along with scholars with an interest in technology: analysing strategies of manufacturing companies from different perspectives, the interaction between social and cultural factors and the process of electrification, the history of electrical technology, and many more aspects. But the literature mostly caters to the Global North.[3] Alongside capital, land, and labour, energy – especially electricity – is the key input for contemporary capital accumulation. Poor quality power supply damages the industrial and commercial interests of the state and thus casts doubt on the extent of the state's 'pro-business tilt'. Elizabeth Chatterjee rightly opines that the power sector provides a crucial lens on Indian political economy.[4]

The harnessing of electricity has been considered one of the driving technologies behind modern capitalism and industrialization. What makes the question of electricity more interesting is the wide variety of uses it offers society – illumination, agricultural, communication, medical, and industrial. Besides, electricity generation and supply is itself an industry. The history of electricity in Calcutta begins effectively in 1899. Before that, electricity had been generated on a small scale for display or private luxury, but commercial generation commenced on 17 April 1899 under the Calcutta Electric Supply Corporation (CESC). The company, originally called the Indian Electric Company Ltd, had been set up in London in 1897. The first generating station was erected at Emambagh Lane, near Prinsep Street, heralding the beginning of thermal power generation in India. In the early years, electricity was treated with suspicion, and had to be popularized through advertisements and even door-to-door canvassing. Who could imagine that within two decades, Calcuttans would be crying for more electricity? Its first big power station was set up at Cossipore in 1912, followed by the Southern Station at Garden Reach (1926) and the Mulajore Station in the northern suburbs in 1940.[5] The study of technology is arguably best seen as a study of social life and material culture. How did the traditional Bengali society respond to the latest technological change in the early twentieth century? How did electricity influence the industrial culture of the city? Can one trace any correlation between the emergence of electrical engineering as a new discipline, industrialization, and the electrification of Calcutta? Thus, this chapter outlines the impetus provided by the Bengali public for the adoption of modern technology, including electricity, its impact on the industry, and the emerging trends.

Historiography of the Electric Power Industry

Technological projects, such as electricity, born and expanded in a peculiar context may or may not suit other contexts. It is evident from the archives of the history of technology that the context was an important deciding factor for the development, design, and transfer of technology.[6] The reception of technology was not just related to its physical suitability to an alien environment. Factors such as technological utility, organization, technical knowhow, economic viability, and legal, cultural, and political factors played a determining role. Apart from these, in the colonized context, colonialism too had a major role in the selection of technology. The model for the development of electricity in Calcutta was basically designed keeping in mind the interests of the colonial government. Nonetheless, the trajectory was continuously shaped and reshaped in the course of time based on the changing circumstances. At the outset, colonial political and economic ideology appears to have been the major determining force for the development of electricity.

Nevertheless, the local context played an equally significant role in determining its development.

In her pioneering work, Judith Tendler argues that research on the technological configuration of an electric power project is a valuable source of information in the study of opportunities for economic development.[7] Thus, she narrates the intervention of the state in the electric power sector of Brazil – due to political pressures, the basic electricity rate was fixed during a period of substantial inflation and the situation led to underinvestment in power generation by the private foreign utility.[8] Yet there was impressive growth in power capacity, according to Tendler, mostly due to government investment. Richard B. Du Boff characterizes electrification as the most complex and sweeping technological change in manufacturing during the first half of the twentieth century. He further argues that electricity was responsible for bringing about the reorganization of production processes and management with a resulting increase in productivity.[9]

Another milestone in this archive is Thomas P. Hughes's magnum opus, *Networks of Power*. He discusses the two waves of industrialization that swept across the Western world during the late eighteenth and early twentieth centuries. According to Hughes, the second era of rapid industrialization (Germany and the United States) is not as well defined in the literature as the first (England and Scotland). But when future historians will probe its phenomena, electric power (especially high-voltage transmission) and the universal system of electric light and power shall figure prominently in their interpretations.[10] He continues that during the formative years of the electrical industry, the existence of a substantial number of engineering institutions influenced the growth of the industry, and the rise of the industry shaped electrical engineering institutions. The training and education of the electrical technicians, engineers, and scientists who filled the increasing number of positions offered by electrical utilities and manufacturers occurred on multiple levels during these periods.

Later studies, however, underline several defects in Hughes's approach. Prominent among them is David E. Nye. He complains that Hughes's account illuminates only one aspect of the subject: the story of power generation and transmission. He never focuses on electricity's meanings and uses for ordinary people. Nye argues that technological history is often written from the point of view of the insider. Yet most people are not inventors, engineers, or utility employees, and for them a device is only real once they begin to incorporate it into everyday experience. Nye further argues that the electrification of America, his area of study, is thus far more than the story of inventions; it involves 'a popular absorption in the potentialities for personal and social transformation'.[11]

In the Indian context, the tone is set by Y. Srinivasa Rao in his study on the electrification of the Madras Presidency. The colonial economic and political priorities came into conflict with the functions which the Indians wanted the electricity system to perform. This disjunction influenced the development of the electric power system. According to him, the combination of circumstances that influenced the development of electricity in a colonized territory was quite unusual in many ways and considerably shaped its ultimate character. Introduction of electricity transformed the structure of industry in India. All the pre-electricity sources of motive power gradually disappeared under the sway of electricity. This was due to, as Rao argues, the scale of production, cheapness, and cleanliness of electricity.[12]

Electricity and Urbanization

'In those days there were neither gas lamps nor electricity; even the kerosene lamp, when it came dazzled us with its brilliance.... Night Calcutta in our childhood days was not so lively. Now after sunset, another day starts, i.e., day with electric lights.' Rabindranath Tagore thus explains the marvels of electricity while looking back at the days of oil lamps.[13] Electricity was considered a panacea for basic urban problems and one of the important means in the management of urban space. Around the start of the twentieth century, British residents of Calcutta were writing more about the city than ever before. As one contemporary noted,

> Life in Calcutta is no longer what it was in the 'good old days'.... There is everything to remind her citizens ... that she is the capital of the British Raj ... a new Calcutta is rising in our midst.... On every hand the electric car and the electric fan tell of the advent of a new era....[14]

When the electric supply company first started their business, they were apprehensive about the acceptance of electricity by Indians. But all their fears proved groundless and electricity was gradually very successful. Although there were apprehensions about this new technology among the general public, a good number of them welcomed it enthusiastically.

Jotindra Mohan Tagore, for example, wished to install electric current in his garden house, Emerald Bower, at the Barrackpore Trunk Road as early as 1904. The electric supply company at that time had been erecting poles on that road, and Jotindra Mohan approached them. But as his house was situated outside the supply area, the company expressed their inability. An enkindled Jotindra Mohan this time requested the government: 'It will be a very great convenience to me if

I can have current for lights and fans, which I wish to install in my house.'[15] The Bengal government finally agreed to the supply of electric current outside the supply area of the CESC to Tagore's garden house by the company. But due to some unknown reason the process was delayed, and electricity reached Emerald Bower only in 1908 when the project of erection of posts for carrying overhead mains was conducted on the Grand Trunk Road by the CESC.[16]

Even before the private generators of electricity had started illuminating the streets of Calcutta, they had made a mark in the lives of the elite of the city as an exciting new amusement. This is evident from the following newspaper report:

> A brilliant night at Belvedere– The handsome reception rooms ... were never seen to better advantage than on the occasion of the ball given by Sir Alexander and Lady Mackenzie on Thursday night. In the ball room alone there were ... 5 handsome cut-glass electriliers, each of 12 lamps, suspended in the centre of the room, besides 18 wall brackets, each comprising 3 lamps. The adjoining boudoir was fitted with bracket lamps, while the staircase and vestibule were lighted with cut-glass pendants. In the same way, the supper room was fitted with bracket lamps besides coloured lamp shades which together lit up the apartment very effectively.[17]

Another journal announced:

> Electric Installation at Belvedere: The Lieutenant-Governor of Bengal has granted an allowance of Rs. 100 per month, for six months, to Messrs F and C Osler, for their supervision of the installation of electric lighting apparatus at Belvedere, in view of the excellent way in which the work has been done and the superior quality of the appliances fitted up.[18]

Electricity in Calcutta, as elsewhere in the world, was first used mainly for lighting purposes. Its use by the manufacturing and other industrial organizations was a later phenomenon. Street lighting began as a measure of safety and such it has largely remained. Until July 1857, the streets of Calcutta were lighted exclusively with oil lamps. Since then, when the Oriental Gas Company first secured its foothold in Calcutta, gas lights had been, if not the only, at least the best form of illumination.[19] Street lighting is regarded as one of the most indispensable functions of municipal bodies all over the world. Thus, this was one of the statutory duties of the Calcutta Municipal Corporation.

The first electrically illuminated street in Calcutta was Harrison Road. After the completion of the road in 1891, the municipal authorities arranged with the contractors, Messer Kilburn & Co., for its lighting by electricity for an annual payment of 9,750 rupees.[20] The dynamos were set up at the Halliday Street Pumping Station at a cost of 92,000 rupees. Low-tension overhead cables supported on posts were used for transmitting the energy. In September 1895, the Lieutenant Governor of Bengal enquired about the danger of overhead light wires in Harrison Road. Experts commented that an overhead system was not suited to a crowded thoroughfare like Harrison Road, and an underground concentric two-conductor cable was preferable. It recommended concentric cables cased in lead.[21] Finally, it switched to underground cables. In 1895–6, the substitution of overhead by underground cables caused a temporary suspension in the electric lighting of this road. Kilburn & Co. continued to light Harrison Road with electricity until 1905–6 when the CESC took it over. The offer of the company to light the street with 70 Lucas lights, at an annual charge of 8,228 rupees, was accepted, and the plant at Halliday Street was sold.[22]

Civic life in Calcutta is now unthinkable without street lighting. In the first decade of the twentieth century, electric lights were installed on numerous streets of the city: Harish Chander Mukherjee Road in 1904; Old Ballygunge Road, Hazra Road, Mott's Lane, Clive Street, Amherst Street, Roy Bagan Street, Wellington Square, and Medical College Street in 1905; Durmahatta Street next year; Wellesley Square in 1907; New China Bazar Street in 1908, and gradually the whole of Calcutta.[23] The electric supply company used to apply to the Electrical Inspector of the province with a blueprint for permission to lay an electric supply line at a street. The Electrical Inspector then forwarded the application to the Bengal government, which consulted the Director General of Telegraphs about the feasibility of the plan.[24]

In the beginning, the power company intended to use aerial lines in the streets supported on posts. By this system of distribution, according to them, the difficulties in maintaining underground cables in the humid climate of India could be solved. The use of overhead wires was completely alien to India at that time and thus faced severe criticism in the government and public circles. The then Director General of Telegraphs, C. H. Reynolds, warned the government about 'the danger to the public of having naked overhead wires carrying powerful currents' and suggested the use of 'lead-covered underground cables'.[25] Referring to the overhead electric traction in Calcutta, the *Rangalaya*, a contemporary Bengali journal, wrote: 'We are against such traction. The copper conducting wire overhead may break down or hang down in tempests and kill passers-by.'[26] Thus, in the early years of electricity in Calcutta the conductors for distributing current from the generating stations to consumers were partly underground and partly overhead. Underground cables were laid in the main streets and more densely populated areas, while overhead wires were erected in the outskirts.

At the end of 1912, there were 250 miles of underground and 124 miles of overhead mains, a total of 354 miles. The general idea was to replace the overhead lines with the costlier underground cables as demand grew.[27] For a pioneer enterprise like the CESC, with practically no experience of underground cables in a tropical climate and in a spongy soil like that of Calcutta, the selection of the underground cabling system in some crowded areas presented many difficulties. Most of the cabling was done according to what was then known as the V. B. System, consisting of rubber insulated cables laid in bitumen-filled cast-iron troughs.[28]

Even though electricity had come to the city commercially in 1899, gas seems to have had an edge over it as a medium of street lighting. In 1907, tenders were invited for lighting the city by gas, electricity, or another illuminant. Two tenders for electric lighting were received, but the Calcutta Corporation finally decided to accept the tender of the Oriental Gas Company.[29] A new contract with the gas company was made to improve the lighting of the Calcutta Maidan by high-power lanterns.[30] In 1909–11, the advisability of improving the lighting of the more important places was considered by the corporation. A noteworthy improvement in electric lighting was effected from 1914 when the new fringe areas (Manicktala, Ultadanga, and so on) were lighted with 34 100-watt electric lamps.[31] High-power Keith lamps of 1,000 candle-power and the latest type of high-power electric lamps were fixed that year on Corporation Street and Chowringhee Road respectively to compare the efficiency and economy in the expenditure between gas and electricity. The CESC, which conducted this experiment at its own cost, demonstrated the advances of electricity over gas. But electricity had to compete tooth and nail with gas. On the recommendation of the Public Utilities and Market Standing Committee, the corporation concluded a new agreement with the Oriental Gas Company for a period of five years as late as 1939.[32]

But in the conflict between gas and electricity, the victory of the latter was inevitable. Being a superior technology, electricity as an illuminating device stood ahead of gas. The introduction of metal filament glow lamps after 1915 by the CESC added to the charm.[33] This was recognized in the official arena. The Special Committee of the Calcutta Corporation appointed to consider the arrangements of the city lighting observed: '… as regards illumination and cost, electric lighting is better and cheaper than gas.'[34] The electric company received exceptionally favourable treatment from the government too, which had conceived and encouraged electricity generation very much as an industry in itself and had therefore evolved a fairly elaborate policy to govern and shape the various electrical undertakings. The Bengal government appreciated the role of the CESC several times as 'a great portion of the population of an Indian town is of a class which would never be able to pay for installing and hiring electric lights and fans' without the generosity of the supply company in the matter of pricing.[35]

The Calcutta Improvement Trust (1912) preferred electricity to gas in illuminating most of the parks and streets it constructed.[36] The advent of electricity had an impact on the designing of buildings. Architects henceforth had to draw their designs to accommodate an electricity supply plan.[37] The CESC began to play an increased role in the lighting of the streets of the city. It had become the main provider of electricity to government establishments, industrial works, and the centralized street lighting system. Street lighting as a public facility, on the one hand, and electric light at individual houses and shops, on the other, gave a new look to the streets of the city. There was an increasing demand from both government and domestic sections of the city. Within the urban limits itself, thermal electricity gained popularity and there was rapid expansion of the consumer base of the power company.

Symbol of a New Culture

On 13 January 1901, *The Statesman* reported on the various utilities of electricity, perhaps the most fascinating among which was the newly installed electric-driven passenger lift at the Government House, Calcutta.[38] Indeed, it was a novelty that was introduced at the turn of the century at the Viceroy's House. After that there was no looking back; the electric lift quickly mingled with the culture of Calcutta. Provision was made for this new technology in both public and private premises of the city. Permission was granted to the CESC in October 1905 to supply 'electric current for one 7 HP motor at a pressure 450 volts' for a passenger lift at the premises of the South British Insurance Co., Clive Street.[39] An agreement was signed between the government and the power supply company in 1908 for the supply of electric current at a pressure of 450 volts at the new Chartered Bank Buildings situated on the same street to run lifts.[40] Again in August 1908, similar authorization was granted to the supply company for driving a passenger lift at the Presidency General Hospital, Bhowanipur.[41] Provision was made for an electric lift in the new Civil Secretariat Buildings on Council House Street.[42] When the Indian Electricity Act, 1910, was under discussion, the question of making provision for the periodical inspection of electric lifts was raised.[43] Finally, it was incorporated in the new Electricity Act.[44] Thus, gradually people became accustomed to the use of this public utility propelled by electricity.

Calcutta, being the second city of the British Empire next to London, offered the most fertile field for the growth of electricity, as is amply evident from the history of its early years. A newspaper reported on 6 December 1898 that electricity on trial basis was being supplied to the Bank of Bengal, the Bengal Club on Chowringhee, and several private residences.[45] The Calcutta High Court decided on 19 August 1899 to opt for electric fans instead of *punkhas* with the hope that the job would be completed by the next year. The government sanctioned 15,000 rupees to replace *punkhas* at Fort Williams on 28 May 1902. A month earlier, the government-owned Army Clothing Factory at Alipore decided to bring electricity at a cost of 19,000 rupees.[46] Like the posed studio photograph, the *punkah-wallah* (fan puller), along with his friend the lamplighter, was part of a vanishing lifestyle of the city.

As early as 1883, the entire premises of the Great Eastern Hotel were illuminated by electric lights. The Indian Electric Light Company was in charge of the event.[47] Twenty-five years later, the successor of the same company, the CESC, supplied electric current for a 5 HP motor 'at a pressure exceeding 250 volts viz. 450 volts at the terminals of the machine' for driving a refrigerator at the same hotel.[48] New electric poles for the Automatic Starting Chronograph were introduced at the Calcutta Race Course on the Maidan by the Calcutta Turf Club in 1908.[49] The same year, the government sanctioned 9,400 rupees for lighting the Bronze and Silver Mint; this was in addition to what had already been included in the original estimate for working and lighting the Calcutta Mint by electricity.[50] The growing theatre movement was part of the Bengali culture of the twentieth century. With the advent of electricity, this major form of entertainment also underwent severe transformation.[51] In 1908, the authorities of the Empire Theatre applied to the government along with the CESC to receive electric current at 450 volts to the main switchboard of the theatre. The switchboard was placed on a platform about 10 feet off the stage floor, accessible through a ladder. R. J. Browne, the then Electrical Inspector, visited the spot and accordingly sanction was given.[52] The sway of electricity could not leave the Indian Museum untouched. A proposal was raised to wire the galleries of the museum for better functioning with electric light in 1913. Administrative sanction came the next year for the installation of electric lights at the Indian Museum, Calcutta (established in 1866), at an estimated cost of 7,600 rupees.[53]

It is interesting to note how electricity intersected with modern medicine, which was another form of scientific modernity that had come with colonialism. Developments of modern medicine had a very direct and crucial relationship with electricity. In a modern hospital, apart from providing power for lights and fans, electricity was indispensable for general maintenance as well as surgical operations. Perhaps the biggest discovery at the end of the nineteenth century was X-ray, which revolutionized modern medicine and was also among the blessings of electricity. Of all the photographs ever taken, probably none generated a greater sense of admiration and disbelief than a widely publicized 1895 depiction of a hand. A phenomenon generated by Wilhelm Rontgen in a tube in a laboratory created rays that could penetrate the skin and reveal the structures beneath it – rays whose nature was unknown, and hence they were described as X.[54] The picture announced a new technology that propelled medicine into a visual age.

The first X-ray photograph in India was probably taken by H. T. D. Jacob in Calcutta in January 1897, by means of 'a Crookes three inch tube and induction coil'; the exposure time was approximately 20 minutes (see Figure 4.1).[55] The next year, the Government of India sanctioned five sets of apparatus for producing Rontgen X-rays, to be obtained from England at an estimated cost of 100 pounds for supply to the five Medical Store Depots.[56] The experts who were consulted by the Director General of Stores, India Office, cautioned about the low-priced apparatus: 'Although it will admit of bones in the hands and feet being photographed, is useless for the more important work required of it in hospitals.' As one set of Rontgen X-ray apparatus would not meet the requirements of the 32 stations and 62 regimental hospitals of Bengal, the Lieutenant General commanding Bengal, Indian Medical Service, requested the sanctioning of an additional set of portable apparatus for the Medical Store Depot, Calcutta. The additional apparatus arrived after four years.[57] Although Calcutta was the first city of the empire that witnessed this technological marvel, Madras first started using X-ray at the hospital level. Somewhere around 1900, the Madras General Hospital secured its first X-ray apparatus.[58]

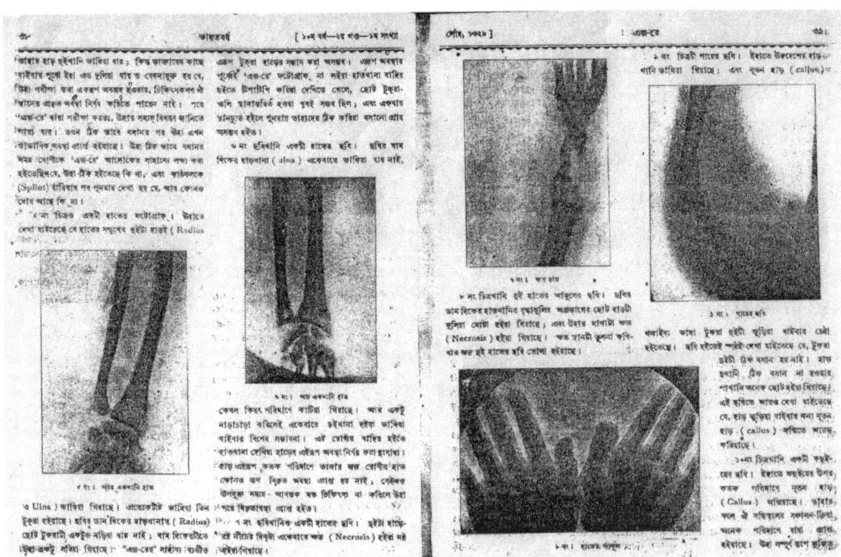

Figure 4.1 An article on X-ray by Dhirendra Nath Bandopadhyay

Source: *Bharatbarsha* 10, no. 2, Poush 1329 B.S. (1922): 33–41.

An X-ray apparatus was installed at the Calcutta General Hospital in 1903 and worked most satisfactorily. The Calcutta Medical College also had a second-hand portable X-ray machine. A proposal was made to exchange it for a new apparatus belonging to the Military Department received from England on the condition that 'the apparatus will not be worked by anyone not acquainted with the working of X-ray apparatus and that it will be kept primarily for instructional purposes'. Thus, the Calcutta Medical College received the new X-ray machine in 1904.

At first everyone was sceptical about this new technology. One government correspondent observed:

> The use of the Rontgen X-ray apparatus as a surgical appliance is very recent, and perhaps the Principal Medical Officer and the Director-General, Indian Medical Service, were unwilling to recommend any large expenditure on this apparatus until they know more about it. This is a feeling the Government of India need not object to. It is economically better to be a little behind the day than too much in front of it.[60]

Gradually, the medical professionals viewed X-ray examinations as superior to all other forms of medical analysis. The Government of India decided to supply up-to-date X-ray apparatus to the hospitals.[61] The X-ray challenged the supremacy of the stethoscope by introducing a new form of realism – the photograph. The reaction of the public was equally enthusiastic:

> The X-ray is one of the most valuable aids which has come into the hands of the medical man in recent years to aid him in the different field of diagnosis. It was remarkable coincidence that the rapid development of this new diagnosis method came just about the time of the Great War; and its universal application in those days for determining the exact position of bullets in the wounded must have saved many thousands of endangered lives.... In view of the wonderful ways in which a patient's condition may be accurately diagnosed by X-rays, it is surely very foolish to begrudge the fee for an X-ray examination when the doctor considers it advisable.[62]

Calcutta's tramcars were at first drawn by horses. Horse power, with all its elegance and adventure, had its share of uncertainties too.[63] Close to the arrival of the electric age in the city, a special committee was set up in 1897 to look into the possibility of electrification of the tramways and their recommendations were accepted.[64] The old tram tracks were fully repaired to make them suitable for electric traction, and in December 1902 the horses bowed their heads to the progress of the 'modern wizard'.[65] The Calcutta Tramway Company (CTC) had its own generating stations at various points in the city. Unlike Bombay and Madras, where tramway systems were an integral part of the electric supply undertakings and their public for the first time experienced electricity from them, the CTC was only authorized to generate and supply electricity for the tramcars in Calcutta.[66] The Bengali intelligentsia welcomed the move jubilantly.[67] As Khitindranath Thakur, cousin of Rabindranath Tagore, the Nobel laureate, once remarked,

> Electric tram ushered a new era in our country. In the beginning very, few could have understood the scientific laws behind such marvel! With the arrival of the electric tramways, the once popular hackney-carriage disappeared completely. Due to separate sitting arrangements, first class for the elites and second class for the masses, the *bhadralok* of Calcutta comfortably avail tram service. One can see the judges, barristers and lawyers of the Calcutta High Court return from there sitting in the first-class compartment. What an arrangement to maintain the deference![68]

The next logical step was railway electrification. The subject was discussed at length in official circles from the 1914 onwards in Calcutta. The government even considered the electrification of the Sealdah to Kanchrapara section. But the proposal was shelved due to the outbreak of the First World War. This was again revived after the war and the Secretary, Railway Board, requested the agents of Bengal Nagpur, East Indian, and Eastern Bengal Railways to discuss and submit their views regarding the desirability of electrifying certain sections of the railway lines near Calcutta (1919). The Railway Board also issued orders to all state-worked railways to equip all passenger stock with electric light and to discontinue the use of gas for train-lighting.[69] The public was aware of the developments and thus optimistic. One Hemendra Prasad Ghosh wrote,

> The suburban train networks of Calcutta should be electrified. It will be of great help for the office-goers and other daily passengers. Electrification will save time by increasing the speed and frequency of the local-trains. Recently a proposal was raised in Calcutta … but we are uncertain whether it shall see the light of the day or not![70]

Hemendra Prasad was right. In the Indian Railways, electric traction was first introduced between Bombay Victoria Terminus (VT) to Kurla Harbour (16 route kilometres) in 1925.[71] The electrification of the Howrah–Burdwan section of the Eastern Railways was taken up during the First Five-Year Plan period and completed in 1958, only after independence.

A Transformer: Electricity and Industrial Development

Rabindranath Tagore once remarked: '... steam and electricity shall be our nerve and muscle.'[72] The introduction of steam significantly affected the industrial scenario of British India, but it was electricity that accelerated the production process and the development of large-scale industries. But economic historians of India have not given adequate attention to this technology so far.[73] Electricity was instrumental in stimulating the development of many older industries along new lines. In many cases, it also gave impetus to the emergence of whole series of new industries.

The public of Calcutta experienced this new technology at least from the last decade of the nineteenth century onwards and the credit definitely goes to Shibdas Sil, the proprietor of the Dey, Sil & Co. – Electricians, Electrometallurgists and Brass Founders. *The Statesman* reported in 1885:

> In our Friday's issue we mentioned a novelty in marriage processions, which was the innovation of the electric light. The procession having taken place at night, the light, a *Serrin* 1,500 candle-power, was most effective and successful. The electrician who arranged the apparatus is a rising young member of scientific Bengal, Mr. Sil, of the firm of Dey, Sil & Co., in Wellington Street....[74]

He was the pioneer Bengali entrepreneur in the electrical industry. From an advertisement of the company published in 1895 (Figure 4.2), one can get the following information:

> Electric Light Stationary – Electric Light Portable, of 1,500 candle-power, sufficient to illuminate brilliantly a quarter mile straight space, are supplied in Town and Moffusil for Illuminating Marriage Processions, court-yards, Halls, Gardens &c. These lights have been carried along with more than 200 Marriage Processions with unequalled success, since 1883, and have been honoured with numerous testimonials of Gentries, Nobilities, Rajahs, and Princes. Estimate for Permanent Electric Lighting Installations Arc and Incandescent System for Illuminating Palaces, Buildings, Halls, Parks etc. are furnished on application, Dey, Sil & Company.[75]

Apart from arranging for lights at meetings, parties, wedding processions, and so on, they manufactured a wide range of apparatus: carriage lamps lit by batteries of their own device, sewing machines and table fans worked by electric motors.[76] These were displayed at important gatherings – including the Second National Congress of 1886,[77] and the 1888 annual conversazione of the Mahomedan Literary Society, and won high praise from eminent scientists as well as the Viceroy himself.[78] This pioneer Bengali electrical firm was in operation until 1912, although on a reduced scale.

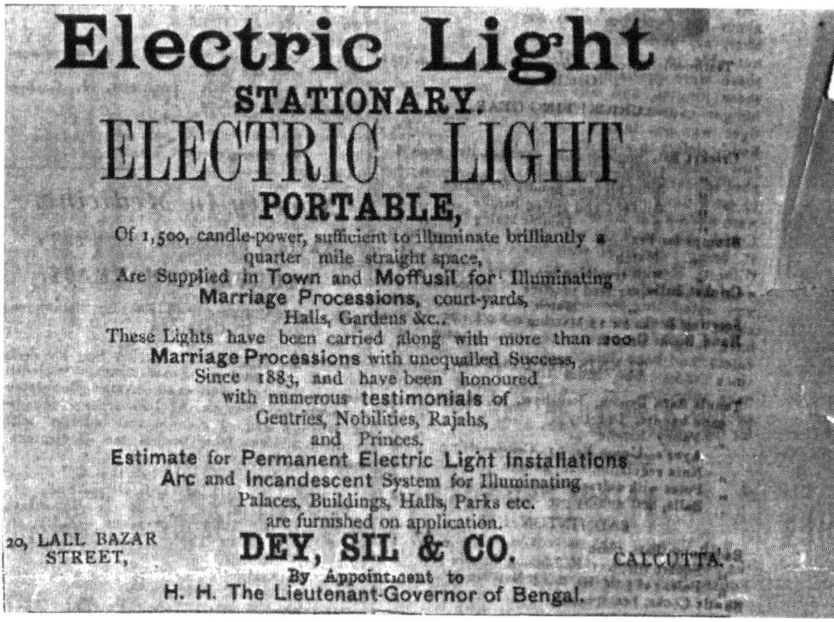

Figure 4.2 Dey, Sil & Co. – the pioneering Bengali entrepreneurs in the electrical industry

Source: *The Statesman*, 5 November 1895.

For the business class, especially Indians, the economic viability of electricity was the main reason for choosing electricity over gas, oil, and animate forms of energy. As soon as they realized the power of electricity, they chose this new technology rejecting the earlier versions. In those days, to get a new electric connection a joint application of the consumer and the undertaker was necessary.[79] Very soon the department of the Bengal government concerned with electricity was flooded with such joint applications. In the colonial scheme, electricity was used in prisons for two important reasons: first, to control the inmates and, second, to establish some industrial units there. In one such case, the authorities of the Alipore Central Jail intended to use electricity to run a 22 BHP motor for better efficiency of the jail workshop.[80] One Surendra Narain Singha Chowdhury, proprietor of the Bengal Soap Factory, applied for electric current for one 7½ HP motor for manufacturing soap. The government was perhaps a little late in sanctioning the request; at this he again requested for the approval of his scheme at an early date 'as the work of the factory is suffering a heavy loss for the stoppage of the work for about a month'.[81]

The manager of the Bengal Silk Mills Co. Ltd asked the permission of the government to connect with the network of the CESC, which was within a couple of hundred yards of their premises but outside the supply area of the power company. The manager wrote: 'We have had no trouble about getting the Gas Supply.... Now we think it a distinct hardship that we cannot have the same privileges as the Calcutta people because we are a short distance outside the boundary....'[82] The government granted the necessary permission to erect an electric supply line from the west side of the canal at Ultadanga Bridge to the Bengal Silk Mills situated at the Manicktollah Municipality.[83] We have plenty of such examples where the small and medium business ventures gradually switched to electricity. The Eagle Engineering Co. put an application to the government to get electric current for one 4½ HP motor which was used for driving drilling machines. They also assured the government that for the safety of the general public, they would enclose the apparatus in a separate casing.[84] Permissions were granted in all such cases after proper inspection by the Electrical Inspector.

The mechanization process that had already been initiated with the introduction of steam power prepared the ground for the speedy modernization brought about by the electrification of existing industries. The important industries served by the electric grid were the jute mills, cotton mills, paper mills, hydraulic presses, and so on, situated on both sides of the River Hooghly.[85] For industrial purposes, the Bengal government permitted the supply of electric energy in bulk and placed the industrial supply ahead of the supply of energy for traction, lighting, and fans in the priority list by the first decade of twentieth century.[86] This made the power market of Calcutta more lucrative to the private supply companies. Perhaps for the first time the CESC felt the heat of severe competition and although they emerged victorious in the end, they had to provide certain special rates for the big consumers of electricity like the various industries.[87] But this in turn helped to strengthen the power supply industry. The big factories provided the 'day load' to the CESC and thus benefitted the public by helping to lower the cost of generation.[88]

However, R. P. Adams, Chief Inspector of Factories, complained about the CESC:

> It is, moreover, a notorious fact that, in Calcutta where fuel is cheaper than in almost any other city in the world, the rates charged by the Electric Supply Corporation for small power users, are so high that the factories have invariably considered it cheaper to install their own small steam plant. These small installations are, however, far from economical, and are expensive to maintain.[89]

According to him, the oil mills and rice mills, which had sprung up recently in Tollygunge, suffered badly. Here one should notice an interesting point – many times these mills were closed because of power failure or power shortage. None of them maintained any kind of alternative power resources at their premises. Before the electrification of the large-scale industries, two agencies were responsible for the shutdown of industry: one was management (lock out) and the other was labour strike. But with the advent of electricity, a third agency, namely technology, joined the list.

It is important to note that for the initial two decades of the twentieth century, the colonial government employed electricity more for administrative and military purposes than for improving manufacture and commodity production. It did not utilize electricity as an economic instrument until the Indian Industrial Commission (1916–18) recommended the acceleration of industrialization in India. The committee identified limited availability of power as one of the constraints in India's restricted industrial growth.[90] It was underlined that industrial and agricultural development would largely depend on the availability of electricity.

Once the value of electricity was proven, thanks to the Industrial Commission's report, the colonial government recognized its potential in extracting resources from the colonies and intensified investigations into the large-scale hydro and thermal power sites throughout India. However, due to the lack of experts in hydrology to identify hydroelectric power sites, unfamiliarity with electricity among the natives, and economic difficulties, the provincial governments did not show adequate interest in investigating power sites.[91] When the British government asked the provinces to conduct investigations, they did not respond enthusiastically. Nevertheless, the process started, and a few reports were submitted. But experts called these reports unscientific and inaccurate.[92] The Industrial Commission's recommendations envisioned the British government as the ultimate authority of power resources in India. The constitution of the Hydro-Electric Survey of India (HESI) points to the colonial government's priority in exploring hydroelectric sites. But most of the industrial sites of the country, including Calcutta, were situated at great distances from those parts of the country where the natural features exhibited possibilities for the generation of water power.[93] Apart from that, most of the coal deposits were in Bengal and Assam. This also acted as a stimulus for the growth of thermal power in Calcutta.

In this context, the much-acclaimed Hindi film *Swades* (2004) is worth a mention. It tells the story of Mohan (Bollywood star Shah Rukh Khan), a US-based NASA employee who returns to India and settles down in his childhood village to improve the deplorable condition of the village. With his money, technical acumen, and a few local recruits, he builds a small hydroelectric plant on a hillside just outside the village. We had such enterprising gentlemen in early twentieth-century Calcutta too. Consider, for instance, the Shillong Hydro-electric Ltd; although situated in Assam, the protagonists of this hydroelectric scheme were mostly Bengalis. When the proposal first arose in the government circles in 1905, it was part of the Bengal Presidency. J. W. Meares, the then Electrical Adviser to the Bengal government, even identified the Beadon Falls and its adjacent areas as a proposed hydroelectric site in 1908. But the proposal did not see the light of day. Many years later, Ramanath Roy, a local entrepreneur, revived the plan and formed a joint-stock company, the Shillong Hydro-electric Ltd. Subsequently, Dr Bidhan Chandra Roy, a famous doctor of Calcutta and later the Chief Minister of West Bengal in independent India, associated himself with the project and provided the necessary funds. His younger brothers, Subodh Chandra Roy and Sadhan Chandra Roy (electrical engineer), were also closely involved. But the role of one Khitichandra Sanyal, an electrical engineer, was perhaps the most crucial.[94] Work started in right earnest at the Beadon Falls in 1921 and two years later Shillong witnessed the first glimpse of electric light in October 1923. In those days the work was an example of the high standards of hydraulic and electrical engineering managed entirely by Bengali entrepreneurs and technologists.

Whereas lanterns were meant mainly for villages and partly for towns, electric lamps catered to the needs of the latter. While electric lamps were introduced in Calcutta by foreign businessmen in the early twentieth century, Bengali manufacturers invested in this product in large numbers in the 1930s. The most notable name in this sector was the Bengal Electric Lamp Works (BELW), popularly known as Bengal Lamp. It was formed in 1932 as a private company at Kasba, in the southern fringe of the city, and the proprietors were Suren Roy, Kiran Roy, and Hemen Roy – three brothers. Both Suren and Kiran were educated in Germany and later while Suren Roy joined the College of Engineering and Technology, Jadavpur, as Professor of Electrical Engineering, the younger brother Kiran became the Secretary of the Managing Committee of the same college.[95] At first, they started on a small scale and initially turned out 200 lamps a day. The formative stage was naturally hard, and they had to struggle a great deal to get a foothold in the market. In the latter half of 1932, the private company was converted into a public limited concern with an issued capital of 300,000 rupees.[96] The company declared its objective as the manufacturing of electric incandescent lamps of all descriptions – neon lamps, neon light tubes, and other electrical appliances:

> Electric Lamp is the very symbolic manifestation of the use of electricity. The ultimate and the only chief end of electricity lies in its conversion to light energy. Electric lamp is the only medium by which this useful purpose can be brought into effect. It is now an open fact that we are fast approaching into the heart of an electrical era. The consumption of Electric Lamps is consequently growing very rapidly side by side with the increasing number of new Electric Supply undertakings cropping up all over India.[97]

Most of the directors and shareholders of this company were highly trained engineers and scientists. Several of them were associated with educational institutions and industrial ventures in the city.[98] Gradually, the company installed new machines and started turning out 1,000 lamps every day. The production of vacuum lamps was followed and accompanied by that of gas-filled lamps by March 1934, which were initially of 60 watts to 100 watts, but later increased to 200 watts.[99] The steady progress of Bengal Lamp is attested by the fact that within two years of its inception, the company could extend its market network from Bengal to such distant areas as Madras, Bombay, the United Provinces, and Punjab. Its lamps were of high quality. These had to pass many outside tests such as those of the Government of India, the Lighting Department of the Calcutta Corporation, the CESC, and many mills. It was the intrinsic quality of its lamps that earned many medals and first-class certificates for BELW and enabled it to grow despite keen competition from foreign and indigenous manufacturers (see Figure 4.3).[100]

Figure 4.3 Bengal Electric Lamp Works, popularly known as Bengal Lamp

Source: *Calcutta Municipal Gazette*, Ninth Anniversary Number, 25 November 1933.

One of its main customers was the government. The number of lamps supplied to the government increased from 28,000 in 1935–6 to 80,000 in 1936–7, and the demand had been rising without a break. Dividend was first given to all the shareholders for the financial year 1937–8. The prospectus of the company for the year 1941 read:

> For example I.S.D. sales alone went up from about 20000 pieces in 1935–36 to nearly 300000 pieces in 1939–40. Today the Company's products are not only accepted as the Country's National Lamp, but are also popular in countries like Ceylon, Africa, Malaya Peninsula and other neighbouring countries. During the current year, this Company's products are the only National Lamps approved by I.S.D. for the use

> of Railways, Army, Public Works Departments and other Public and Semi-public bodies.[101]

Prafulla Chandra Ray, a great chemist and himself an entrepreneur, thus praised Bengal Rosney, the *swadeshi* electric lamp manufactured by Bengal Lamp:

> I have been to the recent exhibition at the Sradhyananda Park and was delighted to find it illuminated throughout with 'Bengal' electric lamps manufactured at Calcutta. The bulbs have stood the test of continued use for over a couple of months and are still going on all right. This is one of the few rare instances of a successful indigenous industry.... Both in quality and in price the articles turned out compare favourably with imported goods. The organisers and workers are some of my past pupils and also of the Bengal Technical Institute who have got high scientific training to their credit.[102]

Bengal Lamp survived after independence (1947) as well.

Evolution of Electrical Engineering

The advent of a new technology necessitated the introduction of new institutional facilities. Referring to large-scale technologies such as the electric supply systems in Europe and America, Thomas Hughes argues that when the new system gains momentum, a supportive context, or culture, forms rapidly. Human capital and institutions developed to keep pace with the advancement of technology.[103] As per this hypothesis, such supportive systems are supposed to emerge in colonized countries also and they did. In the case of Calcutta, supportive systems like a community of experts, electrical engineers, and institutional facilities evolved in tandem with the electricity system.

During the early days of the electricity system, when it was beginning to gain popularity, a lack of expertise in organizing the system was felt. As the network widened and as the power generation stations increased, it became inevitable for the colonial government to create an electrical engineering community within India as importing all engineers from London was a costly option. Hence the government started the electrical engineering course at the Bengal Engineering College, Sibpur, although at a very elementary level in the beginning. An official correspondence of 1896 reveals the following:

> The Lieutenant-Governor is endeavouring to establish at Sibpur a training class for electricians competent to find employment under the various firms who are now engaged in developing this class of business in Calcutta and elsewhere. It is largely with a view to the instruction of this class that the scheme was originally started by the College authorities.[104]

Thus, a full practical course in electrical engineering was already introduced at the Civil Engineering College, Sibpur, in the previous year.[105] While delivering a lecture on 'Electric Traction', J. W. Meares inspired the students of Sibpur about electrical engineering:

> I am very pleased to be able to congratulate the students who have taken up the special electrical classes on the success of those who have preceded them in obtaining appointments. This has been invariably the case, I believe, and the demand has actually been in excess of the supply up to the present time. And yet it may be safely be said that the electrical era in India has scarcely commenced; for so far as I know there are, excluding private plants, only three public electric-supply stations and one tramway system actually working, and about half-a-dozen more schemes in contemplation on under construction. This province is well to the fore in the matter, and Calcutta as is only right holds the first place with its extensive installations....[106]

A proposal for a complete electric lighting installation at the college was initiated in 1895. Dr P. Bruhl, Professor of Physics, prepared an estimate for the installation, which was to serve as a means of practical instruction to the students of electrical engineering. The modernization of the workshops through the introduction of an electric power plant in place of the old steam-power drives again served a similar purpose.[107]

A combined Electrical and Mechanical Engineering Department was started at the college in 1902. This department used to conduct both theoretical and practical classes in electrical engineering for the professional group of the Bachelor of Engineering degree course in civil engineering.[108] The University of Calcutta granted affiliation to the B.E. degree in all branches of engineering, namely civil, mechanical, electrical, and mining, of the college in 1911. In the session of 1912–13, the Electrical Engineering Department was separated from the Mechanical Engineering Department. The degree course in electrical engineering was introduced in the year 1935–6, and the first batch of electrical engineering graduates under the University of Calcutta received their degrees in 1936. The same year, the department also undertook the training of Bengal Nagpur Railway apprentices. In 1943–4, evening coaching classes in electrical engineering were arranged here for several Royal Air Force units stationed in and near Calcutta for two years.[109]

The Indian Industrial Commission visited the college in 1916–17. B. Heaton, the then principal, in his testimony before the commission, remarked:

> The mechanical and electrical engineering course of its present lines is quite a recent departure.... It is thought that if picked lads to be taken into the college after having completed four years of an apprentice course satisfactorily they will be of more immediate value to employees on passing out of Sibpur than those who have only been through a college course.[110]

Electrical engineering as a subject was introduced but it took a long time to initiate research in electrical engineering; a small community of Indian electrical engineers came up but colonial engineers retained the upper hand. Finally, electrical technology was transferred and marketed but technology manufacturing was not encouraged.[111] Given the disadvantageous position, very few Indian entrepreneurs tried to establish electrical industries on their own financial capacity or applied for state aid. The Indian Industrial Commission in its report perhaps captured the lacuna best:

> In the past, the education of engineers has been too much influenced by the immediate requirements of the PWD, without regard to the future or to those other interests in India which can be handled only by engineers. The greater part of the work done in the college is the training of upper subordinates, lower subordinates, surveyors and draftsmen.... In the four principal colleges, increasing attention has, in recent years, been paid to the provision of instruction in mechanical and electrical engineering; but the measures adopted are inadequate and are conceived on altogether too narrow lines to meet the needs, present and prospective, of a rapidly expanding industrial system.[112]

It was not only the colonial government which stressed the need for better institutional facilities for effective maintenance of technological projects. The local intellectuals and politicians, who were also aware of the significance of investing in human capital formation, recognized the necessity of achieving self-sufficiency in the industrial sector, stimulated by higher technical education. When their consistent demand failed to expand the scope of technological training, the Bengali intellectuals came up with their own model. The alternative crystallized as Jadavpur college (National Council of Education, or the NCE) in the first half of the twentieth century. There was a demand for trained professionals from India's emerging industrial class too.

The Jadavpur college offered a four-year degree course in electrical engineering from 1910 onwards. A graduate in this discipline knew the design, construction, operation, and maintenance of electrical machinery and could take charge of electric supply schemes, illumination, electric railways, communication, and so on.[113] The faculty members, many of whom had obtained foreign training, of the Electrical Engineering Department were associated with the leading business firms of the city in various capacities. At the same time, the industrial entrepreneurs dealing with electricity were involved with the college. Power and water for the workshops, laboratories, college buildings, hostels and staff-quarters, and so forth, were supplied from a power plant 'consisting of one 106 B.H.P. 4 cylinder Crude Oil Engine directly coupled to a D.C. Generator and one 75 B.H.P. Bellis Morcom Compound Steam Engine and generating set fed with steam from a Bebcock Wilcox Water-tube Boiler and other accessories'.[114] These two engines alternatively supplied power to the college campus and were also used for instructional purposes. The power plant was designed by the professors of the Electrical Engineering Department with the active help of the students.

The first few decades of twentieth century saw a massive electrification programme, both thermal and hydro, in India. The construction of these power production sites was itself considered an industry. These were also centres of employment generation in two ways: direct and indirect. Directly it provided employment at the site itself and indirectly by providing electricity, as a motive power, to industries. Several electrical engineers from Jadavpur were involved in these projects in various capacities. They were associated with industrial concerns such as Bengal Lamp, General Electric Co., Indian Iron & Steel Co., National Iron & Steel Co., Siemens (India), and so on. Some of them distinguished themselves in their professional fields.[115] Benoy Kumar Sarkar, a renowned economist, rightly observed:

> The socio-economic structure of Bengal as of all India had been used to the profession of the lawyer, the medical man, the office clerk, and the school or college teacher of literary and philosophical subjects. The scholars that were turned out of the Government's Engineering College

> at Shibpur were chiefly civil engineers skilled in building of roads and houses for municipalities and elsewhere. It is the N.C.E engineers who commenced enriching the society with new professions nurtured by the tonic of machinery. The country began to get acculturated to technocracy, mechanics, chemical operations, electrical energies and so forth.[116]

Response and Resistance

At the request of the government, Louis Schewendler, Superintendent Electrician of the Government Telegraph, carried out an experiment of illuminating Indian railway stations with electricity amid protest by the Oriental Gas Company in the 1877. Ultimately, three years later, two platforms of the Howrah Station were lighted with four carbon arc lamps powered by 25 HP dynamos. A point which Schwendler emphasized in his report on station lighting was the efficiency and ingenuity of the 'native *mistri*' in mastering a new technology. He especially mentions the engine-driver who set right the irregular speed of a dynamo with the help of a mercury speedometer. 'The whole trial', concludes Schwendler, 'has proved that there is no difficulty whatever in the working of the electric light in this country by trained natives.'[117]

Thus, there was no dearth of inquisitiveness in the traditional Bengali society at the end of the nineteenth century. Although the electrification project was not yet launched officially in Calcutta, by that time it was a matter of serious discussion in the intellectual circles of the city.[118] Here one incident is worth a mention. An attempt was made to light the Old Howrah Bridge with a private source of electricity. One Jawaharlal Dhar, a self-made electrician, actively participated in the project. He was personally known to Mr Fischer, Managing Agent of the Indian Electric Light Co. Aware of his technological curiosity, Mr Fischer recruited Dhar at a salary of 100 rupees. When the electrification of the Eden Gardens was carried out by the company, he also worked there. But due to a minor dispute with one of the German engineers of the project, Dhar left the place. Later, he joined the Emerald Theatre and produced electricity to light the premises with the help of a steam-driven machine. The major invention of this self-styled engineer was the safety-door lock for which he received patent right from the government. Dey, Sil & Co., the leading electrical firm, became the distributor and Jawaharlal Dhar used to get the royalty from the invention.[119]

The Bengal Legislative Council enacted the Calcutta Electric Lighting Act, 1895, which contained a note of dissent by Surendranath Banerjee:

> I would add a proviso to section 14 of the Bill to the effect that, when a local authority considers it necessary to alter the position of any street or the under-ground pipes and drains, and other works, such local authority may require the undertakers to shift the electric lines at the expense of the undertakers. The Gas Company shift their pipes on the requisition of the Corporation free of cost. I do not approve of some of the provisions relating to punishments for injuring electric works. Whoever maliciously causes electricity to be diverted or wasted is deemed guilty of theft under sub-section (3) of section 26. Under the Penal Code, malicious or wanton waste of property amounts to mischief. There is no reason why waste of electricity should be treated as theft, simply because it is larceny under the English Law. I think it ought to be dealt with as mischief in consonance with the provisions of the Penal Code.[120]

This may be rightly observed as the beginning of a prolonged tussle between imperial interests and nationalist aspirations within the larger technological milieu.

In Calcutta, the entire urbanization process was initiated by the British out of imperialistic motivations. Hence, the lighting scheme can also be viewed as a part of that infrastructure which was imported into India to facilitate further expansion. Electricity was a source of income to the government in two ways. First, electricity installation and distribution itself was an important revenue generation mechanism for them. Second, import of electrical technology and its associated business by the British companies was another source of income. This can be seen from the simple fact that the Oriental Gas Company, CESC, and CTC were all British-owned private companies based in London. But the course of development of the technology was also influenced by the people who were at the receiving end. The Calcutta Corporation, which played a constructive role in building a nationalistic vision, had contributed to this process to a significant degree.[121]

The triumph of the Swaraj Party in the municipal elections of 1924 opened the doors of the Calcutta Corporation to the nationalist Indians led by C. R. Das (1870–1925). But the corporation possessed neither the financial resources nor the administrative jurisdiction for implementing their full programme. It had no power to do anything in the field of electric and gas supply, which was contracted to British companies.[122] Despite all these limitations, the corporation tried to stimulate indigenous industries. The corporation workshop took up in earnest the manufacture of electric fans, gas mantles, iron pipes, boilers, and so on, all of which it had hitherto imported from Britain.[123] In this venture into *swadeshi* enterprise, the corporation attained no striking success, but

Indian firms were exhibiting an interest in the new manufactures. Inevitably, European big business in Calcutta was angered by the role of the corporation. Particularly serious, from the point of view of European big business, was the sharp conflict between the Congress-controlled Calcutta Corporation and the British-incorporated CESC.

From the beginning of the Civil Disobedience Movement (1930), the Swarajist corporation had continuously pressurized the CESC, which had a monopoly of electric supply in Calcutta, to reduce the rates of electricity.[124] In 1930, the corporation managed to persuade the British company, by a fierce public agitation, to reduce the rate from 3 annas per unit to 2 ½ annas per unit. This did not satisfy the corporation, which argued that the rate be further reduced, to 2 annas per unit. Further agitation induced the government to reduce the rate to 2 annas per unit.[125]

Towards the end of the 1930s, another kind of opposition began to emerge among the political, business, and educated elite communities. This was against the domination of the British electrical company. Not content with the reduction in the rates of electricity, the corporation went on to propose an end to the monopoly of electric supply by the CESC.[126] At the beginning of the Civil Disobedience Movement, a Bengali engineer, Dr B. N. Dey, was appointed as Chief Engineer by the corporation (see Figure 4.4). He immediately drew up a scheme for the generation of electricity by the corporation which calculated that 'if the gas lamps of the city were converted into electric lamps and each burner was replaced by 75-watt electric lamps, Calcutta will get 51 percent better lighting and the net annual saving to the Corporation will be about Rs. 3,65,000.'[127] On the basis of Dr Dey's plan, the Calcutta Corporation submitted to the government for its sanction an electricity scheme under which the corporation would produce its own electricity, at rates lower than those charged by the British company.[128] While the government maintained a stony silence on the scheme, the corporation continued to make energetic preparations for its implementation. The mouthpiece of the corporation reported:

> A beginning has already been made by the installation of two powerful electric generations in two of the principal pumping stations of the city. When the connecting cables have all been laid the electricity thus rendered available for distribution will be used for different purposes – driving pumps, lighting streets, lighting the Stuart Hogg Market, the Central Municipal Office and other places.[129]

Figure 4.4 Dr B. N. Dey, who prepared an economical electricity generation and supply scheme

Source: Calcutta Municipal Gazette XV, no. 21 (30 April 1932): 958.

The government had been sitting tight over Dr Dey's scheme, as it affected the vested interests of British capital. Not just that; when in 1938 the Calcutta Corporation erected a sub-station at the Stuart Hogg Market to supply electricity to a portion of the Central Municipal Office, an angry CESC sent a legal notice to the corporation, termed the incident 'a breach of the contract', and wanted to even discontinue their service to the entire building.[130] The CESC was perhaps furious over the fact that the Calcutta Corporation was sympathetic towards the agitation of the supply company's workers that had surfaced around 1937 and had extended its wholehearted support to it.[131] The first session of the All-India Electric Supply Workers' Conference at the Mohammed Ali Park was presided over by A. K. M. Zakarian, the then mayor of the Calcutta Corporation.[132] The corporation even exerted continuous pressure on the Government of Bengal for the option to purchase the CTC and the CESC on the expiry of their license in 1938. But that did not materialize at that point in time. Rajat Ray demonstrates the change in the balance of forces in the arena of municipal politics in terms of the the vastly improved position of the CESC vis-à-vis the Calcutta Corporation after the new Muslim ministry came to power in 1937 on the basis of the Government of India Act of 1935.[133] The Fazlul Huq ministry, supported by the European bloc in the

Legislative Assembly, proved the most effective guarantee of those vested foreign interests that had so long been under pressure from the Swarajist corporation.

Science and Culture, a leading journal, once remarked:

> Almost every civilized country in the world has come to regard the supply of electricity as a public utility concern and has taken steps for full development of its power resources, for adequate control of the production of electrical energy and for ensuring the public of a cheap supply and protecting them from profiteering and exploitation.[134]

But Calcutta was perhaps an exception and the result was obvious: 'The rate at Calcutta was about eight times greater than that at London….' The private supply companies in India enjoyed several special privileges over their counterparts in England. The CESC even had monopoly in this sector. Despite that, the rate of electricity was so high in Calcutta. According to the journal, cheap and abundant power supply was of utmost importance considering that the industrial efficiency of a nation entirely depended upon it. The power resources should be regarded as national assets and it further recognized that the development of cheap and abundant power was a prime duty of the state.[135] The logical culmination of such demands was nationalizing the power sector.

The demand for nationalization was further accelerated by the National Planning Committee (NPC), appointed under the chairmanship of Jawaharlal Nehru in 1938. The Power and Fuel sub-committee recognized that a well-organized national system of generation and distribution of electrical power could be achieved only if the entire enterprise of production as well as supply of this energy was made a public utility concern. The interim report of the sub-committee was presented by Dr Meghnad Saha, the great Indian astrophysicist and chairman of the sub-committee, on 12 May 1940. An extract from the resolutions presented is as follows:

> We agree with the view that the rates for energy in India are unduly high, and power has been very adequately developed, and this has stood in the way of promotion of industries, particularly electro-chemical and electro-thermal ones … the State should develop a definite National Power and Fuel Policy. As the generation and distribution of electricity is a public utility of great importance, the State should ultimately own it and the control and management of it should be exercised by the Electricity Boards. In order to implement the National Policy on Power,

> it is necessary to create Provincial Electricity Boards, and one Central Electricity Board. The Hydro-electric Survey of India should be an all-India body.[136]

The desire for Indianization was not fulfilled immediately even after independence. Two decades later, when the directors of the CESC decided that the industrial supply of power to Calcutta would have to be managed and controlled by an Indian company, only then was the control of the company transferred from London to Calcutta in 1970. Surprisingly, this was entirely different from the rest of the country. While planning for the post-war organization of the power supply industry in Burma (1945), the Government of Burma acknowledged that 'public ownership of the generation and distribution of electricity in Burma should be the ultimate aim of Government'.[137] The generation, bulk transmission, and distribution of electricity in the Central Provinces were placed in the hands of the government, 'as a prelude to the nationalization of all electricity undertakings in the province', in 1950. The Government of Madras also passed an Act 'enabling the Government to take over all electricity undertakings in the province'.[138] But a confident CESC proposed new issue of sterling capital to rejuvenate their business even in 1949–50![139]

Conclusion

Since electricity's invention in the late nineteenth century, the spread of electric utilities has come to signify the advance of modernity. The representation of electricity in colonial Calcutta was no different. What makes the question of electricity so interesting is the wide variety of uses it offered society. An agent of social change and industrial development, electricity thus provides a deeper understanding of modern technology in a traditional society. This chapter is therefore a synthesis of two different aspects of technology and society. First, it is concerned with the material practice of technology – how people responded to new technologies and how the technologies themselves were made to fit into the local physical environment. Second, it investigates the more abstract role of ideas, cultural beliefs, and the contributions of technology towards a growing sense of nationalism and identity. But the literature often describes technological modernity as a single standard story of movement – from the cultural and economic domain of the West, the birthplace of modern technology, towards the non-Western world through the agencies of colonial regimes or the distributive networks of international business organizations.

However, this does not seem to be the only model of technological modernity. Scholars generally use the social construction theory to describe complex technological systems such as electricity. While adopting this theory, it is also necessary to identify issues that arise from the distinctive kind of non-Western context. Here probably Arnold rightly argues that the primary stage of social construction of various modern technologies occurred in the industrialized West and then they underwent a second stage of socialization in the colonial context.[140] The basic form might remain the same, but as various electric innovations were transferred from the West to 'native' elites and indigenous masses, the cultural significance of these electrical utilities might change. After appropriating this new knowledge, many enterprising Indians came up with their own models, competed successfully with their Western counterparts, and demanded better avenues to further the cause of industrialization. For a quick example, Bengal Lamp, specializing in the production of electric bulbs, was the brainchild of three Bengali brothers. As the electric blubs were slowly becoming indispensable to the growing middle class, taking advantage of the situation they were instrumental in ushering in a new era in the electric bulb manufacturing industry of the country. At the same time, they were closely associated with the Jadavpur engineering college, which is one of the preferred destinations of post-secondary Indian students even today. Bengal Lamp, an indigenous industrial venture based on a highly sophisticated technology of its time, proudly declared:

> Dr. H. L. Roy, Dr. Ing (Charlottenburg) A.B. (Harvard) and now Senior Professor in charge of the Chemical Engineering Department of the famous College of Engineering and Technology, Bengal (at Jadabpur) as Hony. Consulting Chemist has been rendering us great help in the matter of chemical problems of our factory. A very competent Board of Directors consisting of Experienced Engineers, Merchants and Banks ensures the thorough management of the company. Some of our Directors are also directors of Electric Supply Companies elsewhere and some are actually commanding over a network of organised sale of electric lamps and thus ensuring a sure market for our manufactured products. The most significant of all being the Managing Directorship of Prof. S. K. Roy, M.E.E. (Harvard) M.A.I.E.E., who has shown distinct ability as Director of several other companies.[141]

However, such association between academia and industry is rarely visible in our times.

Notes

1 Purnima Debi, *Sri Gaganendranath Thakur* (Kolkata: Sahitya Bharati, 2012), 12. Gaganendranath, an eminent cartoonist, was the nephew of Rabindranath Tagore.

2 *Bijoli* 1, no. 2 (October 1933): 45. This was the first illustrated Bengali monthly dealing with electricity and things electrical. The editor was Basudeb Bandopadhyay.

3 Julie A. Cohn, *The Grid: Biography of an American Technology* (Cambridge, MA: The MIT Press, 2017).

4 Elizabeth Chatterjee, 'The Limits of Liberalization: The Power Sector', in *Political Economy of Contemporary India*, ed. R. Nagraj and Sripad Motiram (New Delhi: Cambridge University Press, 2017), 52–53.

5 Sumanta Banerjee, 'Hundred Years of Electricity in Calcutta', *Indian Journal of Power and River Valley Development* 52, nos 7 and 8 (July–August 2002): 119–25.

6 Bernhard Rieger, *Technology and the Culture of Modernity* (Cambridge: Cambridge University Press, 2005), 1–7.

7 Judith Tendler, *Electric Power in Brazil* (Cambridge: Harvard University Press, 1968), 27.

8 By utilities we understand the electricity supply systems operated primarily as suppliers of power for public use, as distinguished from industrial and transportation agencies generating primarily for their own use. N. B. Guyol, *The World Electric Power Industry* (Berkeley and Los Angeles: University of California Press, 1969), xv.

9 Richard B. Du Boff, *Electric Power in American Manufacturing* (New York: Arno Press, 1979), 37.

10 Thomas P. Hughes, *Networks of Power* (Baltimore and London: John Hopkins University Press, 1983), 175.

11 David E. Nye, *Electrifying America* (Cambridge and London: The MIT Press, 1990), 382.

12 Y. Srinivasa Rao, 'Electrification of Madras Presidency, 1900-1947', unpublished PhD thesis, IIT Madras, 2007, 194–95.

13 Rabindranath Thakur, 'Jiban Smriti', *Rabindra Rachanabali*, Vol. 11 (Kolkata: Government of West Bengal, 1989), 101.

14 H. E. A. Cotton, *Calcutta Old and New* (Calcutta: W. Newman & Co., 1907), iv.

15 PWD, MPI, File No. 5E/17/1904, Proc. No. B 16–18, May 1904, WBSA.

16 PWD, MPI, File No. 1E/16/1908, Proceed No. B B19–25, September 1908, WBSA.

17 *The Statesman*, 17 January 1897.

18 *Amrita Bazar Patrika*, 6 July 1897.

19 Sarmila Sarkar (née Mitter), '*The Urbanization of Calcutta in the Nineteenth Century*' (MPhil dissertation, Jadavpur University, Kolkata, 1991), 104.

20 S. W. Goode, *Municipal Calcutta* (New Delhi: Macmillan, Reprint Edition, 2005), 319. The lamps were to be of 1,200 candle-power (c.p.), and the contractors were to superintend the lighting for three months.

21 PWD, Civil Works: Miscellaneous, November 1896, Nos 7–46, NAI.

22 Goode, *Municipal Calcutta*, 320.

23 Index of the MPI (1888–1924), PWD Series, WBSA.

24 PWD, MPI, File No. 5E/59/1905, Proceed No. B B1–4, July 1905, WBSA.

25 PWD, MPI, File No. 5E/1/1897, Proceed No. A 1–79, January 1897, WBSA.

26 *Rangalaya*, 5 April 1902, *Report on Native News Papers in Bengal*, January–June 1902, 212.

27 Subhas Samaddar, *Kolkata Kalaha-katha* (Kolkata: Sahitya Prakash, 1990), 45.

28 This was the vulcanized bitumen or V. B. System. *Story of Electricity in the City of Calcutta*, CESC, 1979. This booklet has been released on the inauguration of the Titagarh Generating Station.

29 Goode, *Municipal Calcutta*, 318.

30 PWD, MPI, File No. 1M/8/1912, Proceed No. A 1–10 and KW, June 1912, WBSA.

31 Sarmila Sarkar (née Mitter), '*The Urbanization of Calcutta in the Nineteenth Century*', 114.

32 That in view of the desirability of maintaining two alternative systems of street lighting, at least, for the main thoroughfares, and also in consideration of the fact that there is no prospect in the near future of dispensing altogether with the use of gas as an illuminant, the Committee recommends that a new Agreement be concluded between the Oriental Gas Co Ltd....

Calcutta Municipal Gazette XXIX, no. 15 (11 March 1939): 608.

33 PWD, MPI, File No. 1E/4/1916, Proceed No. A 1–2, March 1917, WBSA.

34 *Calcutta Municipal Gazette* XV, no. 4 (19 December 1931): 172a. However, the committee identified one obstacle: 'It is bound to take several years to convert gas lamps throughout Calcutta into electric lamps.'

35 PWD, MPI, File No. 6C/1/1912, Proceed No. A 7–8 and KW, April 1917, WBSA.

36 Partho Datta, *Planning the City* (New Delhi: Tulika, 2012), 202–8.

37 S. Preston, Secretary to the Government of India, PWD, once wrote to his counterpart in the Bengal government for modification of the system of distribution and measurement of the electrical energy supplied to the treasury and imperial buildings in Calcutta. Under the existing arrangement, there were a large number of meters scattered all around and thus led to a good deal of unnecessary wiring and considerable confusion. PWD, Civil Works – Miscellaneous, A. Proceedings, April 1904, Nos 11–12, NAI.

38 *The Statesmen*, 13 January 1901.

39 PWD, MPI, File No. 5E/95/1905, Proceed No. B B19–20, October 1905, WBSA.

40 PWD, MPI, File No. 1E/47/1908, Proceed No. B B/58–60 and KW, July 1908, WBSA.

41 PWD, MPI, File No. 1E/51/1908, Proceed No. B B/38–40, August 1908, WBSA.

42 PWD, C.W. – B, August 1909, File, NAI.

43 PWD, Electricity, March 1909, A. Proceedings, NAI.

44 J. W. Meares, *The Law Relating to Electrical Energy in India and Burma* (Calcutta: Thacker, Spink & Co., Sixth Edition, 1941), 19.

45 *The Statesman*, 6 December 1898. An advertisement released by F&C Osler & Co. announced that the firm was ready to take on 'the installing of electric light in Calcutta' for houses and commercial establishments.

46 Banerjee, 'Hundred Years of Electricity in Calcutta', 121.

47 *The Statesman*, 14 May 1883.

48 PWD, MPI, File No. 1E/52/1908, Proceed No. B B/53–55, August 1908, WBSA.

49 PWD, C.W. – E, March 1908, Part B, NAI.

50 PWD, C.W. – B, February 1908, Part B, NAI.

51 This is very much evident in the pages of the Bengali literature. Sunil Gangopadhyay, *Pratham Alo*, Vol. II (Kolkata: Ananda, 1997), 551. Gangopadhyay wrote: 'There were other changes in the theatre since Bharat had seen it last. Electrical lighting had already taken place of gas jets. Now the electric fans add the comfort of the audience very much. One would astonish by seeing the marvel of electricity.'

52 PWD, MPI, File No. 1E/65/1908, Proceed No. B B58–59, December 1908, WBSA.

53 PWD, C.W. – B, December 1914, Part B, NAI.

54 Stanley Reiser, *Technological Medicine* (New York: Cambridge University Press, 2009), 22.

55 Available at http://archives.theiet.org/detail.aspx?parentpriref=110000274 (Accessed on 21 June 2012).

56 Home, Medical, A. Proceedings, November 1898, Nos 201–204, NAI. Bengal, Punjab, Madras, Bombay, and Rangoon.

57 Home, Medical, December 1902, Part B, NAI.

58 T. W. Bernard Paper, MSS. EUR C26111, India Office Records, Asia, Pacific and Africa Collection, BL.

59 Home, Medical, A. Proceedings, July 1904, Nos 40–41, NAI.

60 Home, Medical, A. Proceedings, November 1898, Nos 201–204, NAI.

61 Home, Medical, A. Proceedings, October 1913, Nos 98–100, NAI.

62 'How X-rays Help the Doctor', *Calcutta Municipal Gazette* XXIX, no. 9 (28 January 1939): 378.

63 Goode, *Municipal Calcutta*, 328.

64 PWD, MPI, File No. 5E/1/1897, Proceed No. A1–79, January 1897, WBSA.

65 *Mahajan Bondhu*, Baishak 1309 B. S. (1902): 68–70. One contemporary observed,

> When the tram authority introduced the first electric tram cars, they arranged a free-ride for the general public of Calcutta. The elders went to enjoy the fun-ride, but we are not permitted to accompany them. From the balcony of our house, we saw the wonder run of electrically driven tram cars.

Debi, *Sri Gaganendranath Thakur*, 51.

66 PWD, MPI, File No. 1E/7/1906, Proceed No. A 22–53 and KW, April 1907, WBSA.

67 *Bijoli*, in 1934, summed up succinctly the functioning of electric tramways. *Bijoli* I, no. 6 (February 1934): 260.

68 Khitindranath Thakur, *Kolikatar Chala-phera* (Calcutta: Adi Brahma Samaj, 1337 B.S. [1930]), 90.

69 *Indian Railways Administration Report, 1913–14* (New Delhi: Government pub., 1914), 21.

70 *Sahitya* 30, no. 4, Srabon 1327 B.S. (1920): 235.

71 During the pre-independence period, it remained confined to 388 route kilometres around certain sections of the Great Indian Peninsula, and the Bombay, Baroda, and Central Indian Railways; and it is only in the post-independence period that further electrification was taken up. *India in 1929–30* (Calcutta: Government of India Central Publication Branch, 1931), 184.

72 Rabindranath Tagore, 'Sadhana', in *English Writings of Rabindranath Tagore*, Vol. 2, ed. S. K. Das (New Delhi: Publication Division, 1996), 304.

73 Morris D. Morris, 'The Growth of Large Scale Industry to 1947', in *The Cambridge Economic History of India*, Vol. II, ed. Dharma Kumar (New Delhi: Orient Longman, Reprint Volume, 2008), 599–600.

74 'A Novelty', *The Statesman*, 1 February 1885.

75 *Amrita Bazar Patrika*, 1 December 1895.

76 Jitendranath Ray, *Banglar Kalkarkhana O Karigari Bidyar Ihihas* (Kolkata: Dey's, 2005), 155.

77 *The Statesman*, 1 January 1887.

78 *The Statesman*, 29 January 1888.

79 PWD, MPI, File No. 5E/1/1897, Proceed No. A 1–79, January 1897, WBSA.

80 PWD, MPI, File No. 5E/14/1904, Proceed No. 9–12, April 1904, WBSA.

81 PWD, MPI, File No. 5E/56/1904, Proceed No. B 4–6, January 1905, WBSA.

82 PWD, MPI, File No. 5E/2/1905, Proceed No. B B1–5 and KW, March 1905, WBSA.

83 PWD, MPI, File No. 5E/25/1905, Proceed No. B B13–16, May 1905, WBSA.

84 PWD, MPI, File No. 1E/1/1910, Proceed No. B 82–84, January 1910, WBSA.

85 PWD, MPI, File No. 1E/5/1907, Proceed No. A A36 and KW, May 1907, WBSA.

86 PWD, Civil Works – Electricity, A. Proceedings, May 1907, Nos 1–19, NAI.

87 PWD, MPI, File No. 1E/9/1909, Proceed No. A A1–2, August 1909, WBSA.

88 PWD, MPI, File No. 1-E-7, Proceed No. 6–7B, March 1920, WBSA.

89 *Indian Industrial Commission, Minutes of Evidence 1916–17*, Vol. II (Calcutta: Government Printing, 1918), 326. The CESC, however, in their letter to the President, Industrial Commission, refuted the charge (Letter No. 17698, 2 December 1916).

90 *Report of the Indian Industrial Commission 1916–18* (Calcutta: Superintendent Government Printing, 1918), 64–70.

91 Srinivasa Rao and John Lourdusamy, 'Colonialism and the Development of Electricity', *Science, Technology and Society* 15, no. 1 (2010): 34.

92 J. W. Meares, Chief Electrical Engineer, CESC, complained about the indifferent attitude and scientific inaccuracy of the investigation reports. Meares, *Water Power* (Calcutta: Thacker, Spink & Co., 1935), 7–8.

93 *Report of the Indian Industrial Commission*, 68.

94 Ananda Kishore Das, 'Shillong Hydro-electric Limited', *Arthik Unnoti* 2, no. 2, Jaistha 1334 B.S. (1927): 145–48.

95 Ray, *Banglar Kalkarkhana*, 159.

96 Amit Bhattacharya, *Swadeshi Enterprise in Bengal 1921–47* (Kolkata: Setu, 1995), 130.

97 *Prospectus of the Bengal Electric Lamp Works*, 15 October 1932, 2, Office of the Registrar of Companies, Kolkata.

98 Some of the early directors and shareholders: S. K. Roy, Professor of Electrical Engineering, College of Engineering and Technology, Jadavpur (also the Managing Director of Bengal Lamp); J. N. Lahiri, Director, The Bengal Belting Works Ltd; A. K. Ganguli, Manager, The Scientific Instrument Co. Ltd; U. Ghose, Proprietor, Bangia Diasalai Karjalay; H. C. Guha, Professor, College of Engineering and Technology, Jadavpur; H. L. Roy, Professor, College of Engineering and Technology, Jadavpur (later he became the Managing Director of Bengal Lamp). 'Memorandum of Association of the Bengal Electric Lamp Works, Ltd', *Declaration on Registration of Company*, 24 March 1932; Office of the Registrar of Companies, Kolkata.

99 *All India Industrial and Commercial Directory, 1938–39* (Bombay, 1939), 76.

100 Bhattacharya, *Swadeshi Enterprise*, 131.

101 *Prospectus of the Bengal Electric Lamp Works Ltd*, 31 March 1941, 6, Office of the Registrar of Companies, Kolkata.

102 *Calcutta Municipal Gazette*, Ninth Anniversary Number, 25 November 1933.

103 Thomas P. Hughes, *Networks of Power*, 140.

104 PWD, Civil Works – Miscellaneous, April 1896, Nos 1–7, NAI.

105 *First Quinquennial Review of Education in Bengal, 1892–96* (Calcutta: Government Printing, 1902), 106. To meet the expenses of electric installation, students were levied one rupee each for 10 months of the year.

106 J. W. Meares, *Electric Traction* (Calcutta: Bengal Secretariat Press, 1902), 1.

107 S. N. Sen, *Scientific and Technical Education in India* (New Delhi: INSA, 1991), 394. Similarly, an electrical plant was installed at the Behar School of Engineering in 1905. Home, Education, A. Proceedings, Nos 2–3, December 1905, NAI.

108 Home, Education, A. Proceedings, Nos 80–84, October 1901, NAI.

109 *Bengal Engineering College Centenary Souvenir* (Calcutta, 1956), 56–7.

110 *Indian Industrial Commission, Minutes of Evidence 1916–17*, 250.

111 The Centenary Souvenir of the B.E. College confessed, 'Available records do not show any systematic or connected history of research work in this College during the period 1856 to 1900. No specific record is again available for the period 1915 to 1947.' *Bengal Engineering College Centenary Souvenir*, 80.

112 *Report of the Indian Industrial Commission*, 106.

113 The electrical engineering course was comprehensive enough to comprise steam engine, boiler, turbine, strength of materials, hydraulics, thermodynamics, and so on, as well as electrical measuring instruments, AC and DC machines, power-plant engineering, telegraphy, and telephony. Poulami Sarkar, 'Towards Swadeshi Technology', MPhil dissertation, Jadavpur University, Kolkata, 2000, 104.

114 *College of Engineering and Technology, Bengal, Prospectus Session 1944–45* (Jadavpur: Secretary, NCE, Bengal, not dated), 3.

115 See the *NCE Annual Reports*, 1920s and 1930s.

116 Benoy Kumar Sarkar, *Education for Industrialization* (Calcutta: Chuckervertty, Chatterjee & Co., 1946), 125.

117 Siddhartha Ghosh, *Kaler Sahar Kolkata* (Kolkata: Ananda, 1991), 116.

118 The *Amrita Bazar Patrika* reported on 11 April 1878: 'A lecture on "Electrical discharge and their effects" will be delivered by Dr. Mohendra Lal Sarker at 4 P.M. at the Science Association.'

119 Jawaharlal Dhar, *Sachitra Kolikata-Rahasya* (Kolkata: Paraspathar, Reprint Volume, 2012), 85–9.

120 PWD, MPI, File No. 5E/1/1895, Proceed No. A A/1–5, August 1895, WBSA.

121 Thomas Hughes argued that in England, for example, Joseph Chamberlain's municipal socialism which guarded the public from exploitation by private agency was cited as the main reason for the backwardness of the electricity system. Thomas Hughes, *Networks of Power*, 227–61.

122 Despite such adversities, the Calcutta Corporation was vocal against the CESC from the beginning, especially regarding the tariff and overhead electric traction. PWD, MPI, File No. 6C/1/1912, Proceed No. A 7–8 and KW, April 1917, WBSA.

123 *Calcutta Municipal Gazette* XV, no. 2 (5 December 1931): 80.

124 *Calcutta Municipal Gazette* XV, no. 4 (19 December 1931): 172a.

125 *Bijoli* I, no. 7 (March 1934): 360.

126 Rajat Ray, *Urban Roots of Indian Nationalism* (New Delhi: Vikas, 1979), 146.

127 *Calcutta Municipal Gazette* XXIX, no. 4 (17 December 1938): 170.

128 *Calcutta Municipal Gazette* XV, no. 21 (30 April 1932): 958.

129 Amal Home (ed.), *The Imperial Silver Jubilee Commemoration Volume, Souvenir Number of CMG* (Calcutta: Calcutta Municipal Corporation, 1935), 106.

130 *Calcutta Municipal Gazette* XXIX, no. 13 (25 February 1939): 534–7.

131 *Jugantar*, 5 Aswin, 1344 B.S. (1937): 10.

132 Zakarian reportedly said, 'The high prices which is undoubtedly charges from the consumers and the scant courtesy it apparently shows to the grievances of the workers are ominous features in the administration of this otherwise efficient business organization (CESC).' *Calcutta Municipal Gazette* XXIX no. 14 (4 March 1939): 571.

133 Ray, *Urban Roots of Indian Nationalism*, 194.

134 *Science and Culture* I, no. 7 (December 1935): 367. The journal was published on behalf of the Science News Association, Calcutta. It was the brainchild of Meghnad Saha, scientist par excellence and nationalist.

135 *Science and Culture* III, no. 11 (May 1938): 595.

136 K. T. Shah (ed.), *Power and Fuel* (Bombay: Vora and Co., 1947), 128–31.

137 *Minutes of the Governor's London Committee and Other Papers on the Distribution of Essential Civil Services in Burma Including Electricity*, MSS Eur F145/22: March–June 1945, India Office Records, Asia, Pacific and Africa Collection, BL.

138 *Nationalization of Electricity Undertakings in the Central Provinces*, November 1949 (L/E/8/7699), India Office Records, Asia, Pacific and Africa Collection, BL.

139 *Calcutta Electric Supply Corporation Ltd: Proposed New Issue of Sterling Capital*, July 1948–April 1950 (L/E/8/7067), India Office Records, Asia, Pacific and Africa Collection, BL.

140 David Arnold, *Everyday Technology* (Chicago and London: The University of Chicago Press, 2013), 6–8.

141 *Prospectus of the Bengal Electric Lamp Works*, 11 May 1934, 3, Office of the Registrar of Companies, Kolkata.

5

Assimilation of Technological Ideas

> If the Government really desire to remove the wants of the Indian people, it should send Indian youths to England in order to have them taught in the working of machinery. India is suffering heavy loss for the want of knowledge. The manufacture of jute cloths is very profitable. But educated Indians do not engage in that profitable business. Manchester drains away the wealth of this country by making cloth out of its jute. The writer complains that every European country levies duties upon goods imported from India. Even, London, the home of free trade, levies duties upon Indian gold and silver plates. This oppression will not cease until India begins to manufacture articles with the aid of machinery.
>
> —*Charu Varta*, Bengali periodical, 24 March 1884[1]

> Among the various exhibits of the Calcutta Exhibition, the mechanical appliances of Ghatak Iron Works deserve mention. These include the rice-husking machine, flour-husking machine, pump, etc. Late Jagadishwar Ghatak, the father of the present proprietor Babu Umapati Ghatak, first introduced rice-mill in Bengal almost thirty-five years ago. Today rice-mill is a flourishing industry throughout Bengal. The Ghatak Iron Works also first established match factory in Bengal and invested huge amount of money to strengthen the industry. Many aspirant young men learnt the art from them and started match industry successfully. Their match-making machine was the centre of attraction in the Calcutta Exhibition of 1923–24 and won gold-medal and felicitation. Their inventive capacity is commendable.
>
> —*Arthik Unnati*, a monthly journal in Bengali, reported in 1928[2]

The history of technology is not merely a history of the machines. It is much more than that: an inquiry into the application of the human imagination. The history of technology can also be written in terms of the ways people associate with and yet at the same time seek to keep themselves aloof from technological objects. Modern technologies, starting from the electric telegraph to the modern-day computer, originated in the West. However, this does not mean that their histories were uniform across the globe – only replicas of the Western models. Since the late nineteenth century, our society witnessed the incorporation of numerous technologies and transformations therein. The purpose and connotation assigned to modern technology are not same everywhere: identical technologies can take on entirely different meanings once they are transferred to different societies and cultural areas, regardless of their source of origin.[3] A recent study demonstrates the ways in which railways enmeshed with the everyday experience of thousands of Indians from the mid-nineteenth century onwards, and how ordinary Indians (including elites) responded by adapting and challenging this new technological tool. Significantly, it illustrates how such technological presence in everyday Indian lives 'materially shaped India's history'.[4] 'Everyday' for the author is a broad concept that includes individuals and their negotiation with 'new' technologies, and the social consequences thereof. As the recent historiographical shift constitutes a demand to move away from 'grand technologies', including railways, this study takes a middle ground in the growing debate about different technologies and their varied impact on colonial Indian society. It concurrently examines the 'individual, private and domestic' as well as the 'broad use of the idea of transgression, including within it those acts through which people actively inhabit the large-scale technological abstraction that they routinely face'.[5] Big and small technologies were not separate in their origin, action, and politics. Although the widespread use of various technologies – big as well as small – by the Indian population was a calculated move, promoted by the state and the industry, once it became a domestic item it was no longer a colonial instrument alone. The common people exercised a good amount of agency over several of these technologies and shaped them partially, altering the actual meanings attributed to them by the state.

Thus, technological advancement more precisely resembles a structure to which every society brings its own imagination: its own sense of 'social ownership and cultural belonging'. The transmission of techno-scientific knowledge between the West and the East has been the subject of several recent historical studies. While scholarly attention focused on the diverse means by which knowledge diffused outside Europe and to the process of its introduction, attempts to understand the adoption of the transmitted knowledge and its adaptation to its new habitat were also undertaken.[6] Was the newly received technical knowledge used in its original form or implemented within the framework of traditional technology or practice, or did it undergo some transformations? How did they affect not just economic life and productive processes but also the ways in which people worked? To what extent did they become part of the new ways of thinking? How far did modern technology become the harbinger of all-round development?

Debate over Technology

The late nineteenth century saw the rise of Indian nationalism and the entry of Indians in techno-scientific education, research, and debate. By the turn of the twentieth century, India's technological imaginary encompassed a great diversity of different ideas and perspectives. Many Indian interlocutors, belonging to different disciplines and walks of life, contributed to the new quest for techno-scientific knowledge. One of the first to realize the necessity of rearticulating science in national terms was Mahendra Lal Sircar (1833–1904). The first effort towards institutionalizing Indian interest in Western science was his Indian Association for the Cultivation of Science (IACS), which after a great deal of effort and controversy was inaugurated in 1876.[7] Even as Sircar was treading a delicate path in dealing with the colonial government, a challenge came from within, in the form of a parallel movement launched by the Indian League, founded by Motilal and Sisir Ghosh. Its aim was to establish an institute for technical training which would prepare Indian youth for immediate employment in industries.

The then Lieutenant Governor, Richard Temple, himself was inclined more towards technical education than original scientific research. It is not surprising that the *zamindars* of the Indian League endorsed his preference for technical over scientific education. They proposed to inaugurate its technical institute as a memorial to commemorate the visit of the Prince of Wales to India.[8] At the request of the League and the Director of Public Instruction, Dinanath Sen, the then headmaster of the Dacca Normal School, prepared a proposal for the school of industry or practical science.[9] Dinanath described in detail the necessity for such an institution, its objective, and its mode of instruction in his proposal. According to him, the reasons behind the backwardness of India in the industrial sector were 'the high pay necessary for employing European Engineers or Superintendents, the cost and risk of importing Europe-made machinery, and the difficulty of having Machines, when out of order, cheaply and expeditiously repaired on the spot'.[10] His prescription to solve the problem was to create a class of well-trained mechanical engineers and skilled workmen among the youth who would devote their energies to the discovery of cheap and suitable indigenous raw materials and chemical agents for manufacturing operations. The existence of such a class of men would give a great impetus to the introduction of scientific methods in the manufacturing industry. Dinanath's scheme of teaching is worth a mention here:

> Departments of Instruction – In order to combine sound theoretical instruction with thorough practical training, the school should have three departments: (1) for theoretical instruction in the class under professors; (2) for practical training in Mechanical Engineering, under professional workmen, in a workshop furnished with a Smithy, Foundry and all necessary Hand and machine tools; and (3) for practical training

> in Manufacturing, Chemical and Metallurgical processes, in a Museum of apparatus, illustrative of those branches of Industry, under instructors, who should be trained for the purpose, at the expense of the school.[11]

He was interested mainly in mechanical engineering, since for civil engineering there already existed the Bengal Engineering College, Sibpur.

A few days after the publication of Dinanath's proposal, one Pratap Chandra Ghosh condemned the plan and voiced his objection in an open letter that appeared in the *Hindu Patriot*. Pratap Chandra believed that educating the native artisan class was the crying need of the country, rather than creating a class of Western-educated engineers.[12] Dinanath chose the same journal to answer Pratap Chandra and his other critiques. According to him, the skill of the native artisan class was acquired through a long course of training as apprentice under the elders of their families. So their artisanal skill was the result of a hereditary aptitude generated by the same occupations being followed by the same families from generation to generation. No school could teach them such skills. He rightly said,

> … unless we could avail ourselves the two great advantages of European manufactures, first the extensive application of science to practical industry and second the adoption of the large system of production, and completely remodel our arts and manufactures on the European plan, there was no hope for the productive industry of this country.[13]

Dinanath lamented that the Indian workmen were familiar with only portions of any branch of study, and being devoid of any knowledge of theoretical principles, they did not know how to proceed further. India's great want therefore, he continued, was one of educated engineers, who would be able to take charge of mills, factories, and workshops and run them with the aid of country workmen and artisans. Hence, the Indian League, according to Dinanath, wanted to establish the 'European system of mechanical engineering and manufactures'.

This was the maiden plan authored by an Indian individual to promote engineering education. Although very promising and practical in the contemporary context, the scheme remained unheeded. What is more unfortunate is that in the scholarly discussion on Indian attainment in modern techno-science, Dinanath and his scheme never got their due share!

An entrepreneur, Behary Lall Ghose, proposed a scheme for a polytechnic institution near Calcutta in 1897 and, like Dinanath Sen, he never received the intellectual limelight. But his memorandum, which combines scientific instruction with practical training, submitted to the government was in all sense a complete blueprint for such an institute. In the then gloomy economic condition, Ghose argued, the foremost necessity was 'the introduction and extension of technical education and workshops with the double aim of reviving some of the useful indigenous arts, and planting on our soil, and cultivating, foreign industrial arts, manufactures and trades for the products of which there is a considerable demand in our country'.[14] The government engineering colleges, in spite of their long existence, were unable to fulfil the objective and therefore he appealed for the establishment of the polytechnic with a detailed lesson plan.[15] The mode of instruction of the proposed institution was Bengali and 'instruments, machines and implements will be gradually supplied and along with their use, construction will be explained and knowledge of principles and of the nature of laws of motive power, so far as it relates to practical application, will be inculcated'.[16] Behary Lall was aware of the link between machinery and the material civilization and therefore he gave the utmost importance to the construction of machinery in the institute. Not just that, he even considered science as taught at the University of Calcutta, Calcutta Medical College, and especially at the IACS 'of little avail in the concerns of life'. The proposed polytechnic would train the youth in the application of the sciences to the arts and expand their inventive power to set up industries.

Behary Lall knew that to sustain the intellectual rigour created by the proposed institution, he simultaneously had to enhance the Bengali readership in technology. For this purpose, he already started a journal, *Viswakarma*, and a series of books under the title of *Karigar Darpana* – both in Bengali. The book series, meant for teaching purposes, dealt with practical science, art, and industries of a useful nature, construction of principal machines, new discoveries and inventions, and manufacturing articles. The journal was meant for the general public and tried to stimulate 'a taste for, and spread a knowledge of the arts'.[17] Who was this Behary Lall Ghose? In his memorandum, he gave a self-introduction too. He previously worked at the Calcutta Mint as an Assistant Foreman and later at the Oriental Gas Co. He had developed a great taste for the mechanical and industrial arts from his childhood. At the time of submitting his plea for the polytechnic, Ghose launched his own business firm, B. L. Ghose & Co., which dealt in electric light supplying, electroplating, gilding, gas-fitting, plumbing, and so on. He was a self-made man who devoted 22 years of his life to the practical study of several industries and spent a huge amount on experiments and instruments.

In February 1876, Bholanath Das, an alumnus of the Bengal Engineering College, submitted a note accounting for the decline of his college.[18] At the time of its establishment (1856), the Government of India offered around 40 guaranteed appointments for the students of the college. This incentive compelled many bright students of the Presidency College 'to throw away his metaphysics and law for the exact sciences'. But the subsequent amalgamation of the Civil Engineering College with the Presidency College in 1864, a 'reduction from a position of rivalry to one of subordination', was a sad mistake. Bholanath was also unhappy with the change of the duration of study from three to five years at the college. He did not understand why if in England a term of three years was found to be enough to train an engineer and at Roorkee even two years' training was enough, did the authorities of the Calcutta college make the process so lengthy? He had faith in the capabilities of the Bengali students: 'It cannot be that the Bengalis are so slow in acquiring a scientific education that they would take five years, while the alumni of the sister college in the North-West Provinces would take only two.'[19]

Bholanath emphasized that unlike in England where engineering as a profession was established on a solid footing, in India engineering was still in its infancy. Thus, the private enterprises to which it gave birth were scarcely recognized here. So, government concessions to the would-be Indian engineers, according to him, were a must. In the absence of private enterprises, government employment was the only ray of hope to them. But on several occasions, the authorities preferred men with practical experience over the fresh graduates. Bholanath had the remedy:

> ... if the engineering students are fortunate enough to combine a sufficient practical with their theoretical knowledge, they can prove to a certainty that they are still better fitted for the service and for the profession generally. It is therefore absolutely necessary that the course of studies should be both of a theoretical and practical nature.[20]

An optimistic Bholanath requested the detaching of the Civil Engineering section from the Presidency College and providing 'it a habitat of its own'. He dreamed of a proper recognition for his alma mater. In the year 1880, the Calcutta Civil Engineering College moved to Sibpur and was renamed the Bengal Engineering College. Many new branches of engineering – mechanical, electrical, mining, and so on – were gradually introduced there. Bholanath must have been very happy with such developments!

The Indian men of science also took up the question of technical education because they thought it was the precondition for economic development. Pramatha Nath Bose (1855–1934) was probably the first to talk about science-based industries and the need to remodel the university curriculum accordingly.

He specialized in geology at the University of London and later joined the Geological Survey of India (GSI).[21] In 1886 he published a pamphlet on techno-scientific education in Bengal which attracted wide notice and is said to have inaugurated the movement for technical education in Bengal. Pramatha Nath found the teaching at the Bengal Engineering College, Sibpur, very elementary in nature and only serving the requirements of a civil engineer. For the successful industrial application of scientific principles, however, the instruction must be far more advanced. He recommended setting up a Central Technical Institute at Calcutta.[22]

Pramatha Nath was worried about the exploitation of Indian resources exclusively by Western capital and enterprises. So, he called for some sort of higher technical education to enable Indians also to come up with industrial ideas. What kind of technical education? He elaborated: '… not the education given in the so-called technical schools in which carpentry, and similar petty trades are taught, but the education based upon natural science which is imparted in the technical institutes of Europe.' He continued that the Western civilization was based upon natural science, while their Eastern counterpart was upon mental and moral science. If he had a choice, he would opt for the latter. The practical applications of natural sciences were responsible for incalculable misery to the extra-European world.[23] But in the prevalent conditions, the Asiatic had no alternative. They must ape the West or perish. So, he ardently invoked the paramount importance of natural science in modern civilization which was essentially industrial.

Fierce nationalism had transformed a geologist like Pramatha Nath into a historian. From physical mapping he shifted to cultural contours. His search for the distinct Indian tradition of techno-science resulted in his monumental work, *A History of Hindu Civilization during British Rule*, in three volumes. While tracing the history of technology in India, he referred to the long tradition of her technological expertise:

> Remains of temples, roads, bridges and reservoirs testify to the engineering skill of the Hindus in pre-British times. But, though some Sanskrit books on engineering subjects have come down to us, they had long before the establishment of British rule ceased to be taught in schools.[24]

He had made a critical estimate of the impact of the West on Indian culture: the colonial rule brought in a degenerating influence on Indian society and culture that had a glorious past. Of course, restrictions in the Hindu society regarding the caste system, Pramatha Nath argued, made it stagnant.[25]

Thus, he held the Brahminical system responsible for neglecting physical science 'to a most serious extent' and thought that 'the Hindu civilization carried the germs of its decay within it'. But he would never agree with the contemporary colonial mindset that Indians are 'utterly incapable to any original work in natural science'.[26] He could see no reason why 'with an improved system of scientific education, and with just and sympathetic treatment of the young men trained in India, they will not be able to take place in the modern scientific world'.[27] Pramatha Nath quoted the successful example of Japan pursuing science with an eye to industry, but only forgot to mention that Japan was not a colony! But he did realize (at his own cost[28]) that a just and sympathetic treatment was not always possible in a colony.

During the last two decades of the nineteenth century, technical education superseded almost every other educational issue. Technical education was the only remedy and thus every fund-raising opportunity was utilized to enhance the technical skills of the Indian youth with an eye to industry. An Indian Industrial Association was formed in Calcutta in 1891. Its principal members were Pramatha Nath Bose and Trailokya Nath Mukherjee. They arranged a series of popular lectures and experimented with indigenous raw materials but without much success.[29] The Association for the Advancement of Scientific and Industrial Education of Indians, founded by Jogendra Chandra Ghose in 1904, further sought to improve Indians' technical skills by financing their training abroad.[30] He received donations from many leading men in Bengal, including Europeans. Jogendra Nath was perhaps the only influential person who opposed the boycott of foreign goods and naturally could manage some official patronage for the association.[31] In 1905, 16 students were sent; the next year the number rose to 40, and by 1907, the figure was almost double. An analysis of the subjects that these students took up abroad shows the industries which the educated Bengalis then thought were suitable for local development.[32] No doubt this was an ambitious scheme and one may be interested in examining the careers of the foreign-trained Bengalis after their return to the country. A few examples are:

> K. C. Nandi returned after distinguishing himself in Glasgow in Mechanical and Electrical Engineering. He was elected a Research Student of the Glasgow University and a member of the Society of Mechanical Engineers, London, which in itself was a great honour. He has been engaged as the Chief Engineer of the Cooch-Behar State. G.

> C. Sen returned after a distinguished University career in England and after learning the manufacture of dyes and the allied industries of Calico-printing, Colour-making and Paint-making in Leeds and Germany. He stood first in the competitive examination of the City and Guilds, London. He has been engaged as Professor of Dyeing and Colour Chemistry in the Bengal Technical Institute and as a Dyeing expert in the Banga-Laksmi Cotton Mills. He has also started a Dyeing and Bleaching factory on his own account which is yielding him profit. J. K. Das Gupta joined the University of Glasgow where he stood first in the B.Sc. Examination, distinguished himself in Mechanical and Electrical Engineering and secured several splendid certificates from his professors and the engineering firms where he worked. He has been, on his return, engaged as Professor of Mechanical and Electrical Engineering in the Bengal Technical Institute. P. C. Roy returned from Japan after fully qualifying himself in the manufacture of matches. He has been employed in the Bande Mataram match Factory started by Rashbehari Ghose. R. Dutt returned after fully qualifying himself in the manufacture of soap and essential oil after both theoretical and practical training in France, and Germany. He has been employed by the Indian Perfume Co., Calcutta.[33]

They were among the first-generation Bengali students who visited various foreign countries with the help of scholarships. Technological self-sufficiency for building an independent industrial base was of the utmost importance. The search for alternative techno-scientific models, bypassing Britain, by the Bengali intellectuals was established on an institutional footing with the formation of this organization.

From Appropriation to Assimilation

Certain sections of the Bengali elite were convinced that industrialization had a connection with the growth of techno-scientific knowledge. The Dawn Society was founded by Satish Chandra Mukherjee in 1902. The *Dawn Magazine*, the mouthpiece of the society, attempted to combine the roles of the traditional and modern technicians to make them the primary agents of social transformation. Indian artisans were central to the industrial transformation of India.[34] But it was felt that they required better tools and implements, financial support, and knowledge of market trends and fashions. This would necessitate training in modern techno-science, with the state providing the infrastructure through technical schools.[35] It was felt that an effective strategy of industrialization could only be premised upon a system of technical education that was sensitive to the demands of the local context. The *Dawn Magazine* consistently warned against the uncritical transplantation of Western industrialism and searched for an 'Indian path'.[36] The strategy for Indian industrialization could emerge only when her traditionally skilled artisans were drilled in modern technical knowledge.

The early twentieth century had witnessed a significant development in Indian nationalist politics: *swadeshi* – the urge to develop an indigenous industrial base opposed to the import of foreign industrial goods. Nationalism articulated a vision of a new political, social, and economic future. Here modern techno-science occupied a crucial position: The attempts to locate Western science and technology within the cultural traditions of India, and the hunt for a better future were the two aspects that dominated Bengali thought during these periods. Somewhere the search for legitimacy of techno-science in the Indian tradition and the search for a future engineered by that modern knowledge, Pratik Chakrabarti argues, are linked.[37] Visions of the future were often articulated in terms of the past tradition. However, an ideology of disjunction with the past or tradition was also inherent in that vision. For example, a prominent section of the intelligentsia believed that a new industrial India could emerge through the ushering in of a completely distinct culture based on modern knowledge.

The need for revamping and reformulating the technical education programme was uniformly acknowledged by the Bengali interlocutors. The history of the Dawn Society and the subsequent National Council for Education (NCE) reveals many of the complexities of the relationship between technical knowledge and industrialization.[38] The NCE initiated a new techno-scientific culture through further dialogue between tradition and modernity. The nationalist scientific and technical education was to be supplemented by literary studies. The knowledge of science was to be complemented by knowledge about the country – its literature, history, and philosophy – and incorporating the best oriental ideas with the modern ideals of the West.[39] It was through the dual course – a critique of European industrialism and an alternative techno-scientific educational culture – that the NCE sought to initiate its discourse on Indian industrialism. This scheme was soon contested by some scientists and engineers who questioned the need for this literary supplement to techno-scientific training. In their view, science and technological training must drop the cultural and moral components.[40] Although within the NCE, industrialization was still very much a 'moral' agenda, as pointed out by Raina and Habib,[41] these attempts to drop the cultural and literary components were significant. This was an early instance of the *bhadralok*'s attempt to secularize techno-scientific education.[42]

However, the question of an Indian future based on modern technical knowledge was yet to be resolved. Strong doubts about an industrial future persisted. Many prominent Indian scientists had expressed such apprehensions. Prafulla Chandra Ray (1861–1944) was closely associated with the NCE, a pedagogic programme committed to economic self-reliance. He was extremely critical of the existing educational system that was out of touch with practical needs and was driving students in disproportionately high numbers towards clerical and legal jobs. Moreover, these favoured destinations too were becoming overcrowded, with declining capacity for further absorption. Not just that; the young generation of business families preferred to abandon the family business in favour of service. Not confining himself to only accusing the government for its education policy, Prafulla Chandra was equally self-critical. The controls of the business sector, the agricultural sector, and even the railway construction works throughout Bengal were in the hands of non-Bengalis. Two essential elements to ensure success in trade and commerce, according to Prafulla Chandra, were sadly lacking in the Bengali character: 'a spirit of enterprise and a business instinct'. They were impatient and always after quick results; as Prafulla Chandra ridiculed, 'he is for reaping without sowing'.[43]

Why were entrepreneurship and business acumen missing in the Bengali character? Was our history responsible for the remorseful state of techno-scientific growth in India? Such questions bothered Prafulla Chandra. Living in an era when scientific progress had become the great denominator of nationhood, he was convinced that a nation needed its own rational tradition, particularly in science. For a nationalist scientist like him, the absence of a scientific base for industrial growth in India was a major issue. Thus, Prafulla Chandra's turning towards the history of science was more than pedagogic, argues Dhruv Raina, as it directly influenced the existing industrial culture: it was a way of analysing the country's strengths and weaknesses and acted as a road map for future industrial development.[44] The fruit of his research was the two-volume work, *A History of Hindu Chemistry*.

The history of techniques, Prafulla Chandra argued, offered ample evidence of the existence of strong empirical traditions of metallurgy and other technical crafts in India. The Iron Pillar of Delhi was a testimony to this tradition of metallurgy. But why did this empirical-technical tradition fall into decline? Prafulla Chandra linked the decline of India's scientific spirit to increasing caste rigidities in the society – the separation of intellectual exercise and manual application of that knowledge. Thus, the how and why of phenomena were lost sight of, leading to a general decline in the spirit of scientific enquiry.[45]

Prafulla Chandra identified the serious obstacle in the progress of techno-science in India: 'reluctance to take part in industrial concerns'. The scientific principles underlying manufacturing processes could be learnt at any technical institute, but the actual manufacturing knowledge (production as well as marketing) could only be acquired in the industrial ventures. Prafulla Chandra quoted the example of B. M. Das, a tannery expert in the National Tannery and Government Tanning Research Institute, to show that schools and colleges did not develop an industrial culture; this had to be acquired in the real life of business.[46] For him, the learning-while-doing approach was far better than a mere training from some technological institute. This explains Prafulla Chandra's criticism of the popular obsession with technical institutes and education.

The great paradox in Prafulla Chandra's perception of modern technology was perhaps, on the one hand, his scientific skills and advocacy of heavy industry and, on the other, a harmonization with the Gandhian *charka* – a symbol of cottage industry in India. Prafulla Chandra was deeply influenced by Gandhi and argued that industrialism was intrinsically related to imperialism.[47] To survive in India, he argued, the chemical industry had to operate on a large scale. On the other hand, he promoted the *charka* and argued about the evils of European industrialism.[48] He was in favour of the modern scientific industries in place of the old cottage type industries – as the latter involved inefficient techniques and wastage.[49] He appreciated and tapped the advantages of science-based industrialization. Yet Prafulla Chandra could also sympathize with the *charka*, appreciating immediate and local needs. An interesting feature of Prafulla Chandra Ray's life was that despite his admiration for modern techno-science, he never looked upon it as a universal remedy for all problems.

Like Prafulla Chandra, our next protagonist to help us understand the Bengali psyche vis-à-vis modern technology is Pramatha Nath Bose. A champion for the cause of techno-scientific education, he in his later life drifted from his earlier standpoint. Pramatha Nath initiated a gigantic step towards Indian industrialization by persuading Jamshedji Tata to establish the largest heavy industry in colonial India – the Tata Iron & Steel Co., or TISCO.[50] After retiring from the GSI (1903), he took charge as the Principal Geologist of Mayurbhanj State at the request of Mohini Mohan Dhar, the Dewan of the native state. The state had never been surveyed before and he was the first geologist to examine it. He brought to the notice of the world the mineral resources of Mayurbhanj for the first time in his famous paper, 'Notes on the Geology and Mineral Resources of Mayurbhanj'. From the survey it appeared to him that 'the chief mineral wealth of the State consists in its iron-ores, which are possibly among the richest and most extensive in India'.[51]

It is said that Pramatha Nath first disclosed his discovery to some of his Bengali industrialist friends hoping that a son of the soil would come forward. But that was not to be. However, he was instrumental in facilitating the terms between the firm Tata Sons & Co. and Maharaja Ramchandra Bhanja Deo, on behalf of Mayurbhanj State. Pramatha Nath stressed the advantages of Mayurbhanj, rich in iron-ores and near the Bengal coal fields, as a promising site.[52] After several extensive explorations by the experts of the firm along with Pramatha Nath, Sakchi was chosen for the proposed factory located in the eastern part of Mayurbhanj.

Thus, Pramatha Nath played a vital role in the foundation of TISCO, an institution of national importance. The company fired the first coke ovens in 1911. It may be said that the establishment of TISCO was the product of a perfect blend of the knowledge-capital of Pramatha Nath with the organizational commitment and finance-capital of Jamshedji Tata. Pramatha Nath also had the satisfaction of witnessing a trend that he had been earnestly looking for since the eighties of the nineteenth century, that is, academia and industry exchange – the foundation of TISCO immensely furthering the cause of techno-scientific education in India. The students of the Bengal Technical Institute, for the foundation of which Pramatha Nath was largely responsible and of which he was the honorary Rector, were provided employment there on a substantial scale.[53] Thus, TISCO since its foundation absorbed a large section of the trained manpower that had received technological education in India or abroad.

However, one may find a sudden change in the mental and intellectual world of Pramatha Nath in the early years of the twentieth century. In the recent years, he observed, there was a positive attitude towards technical education among the public. It was a great illusion that '... with the progress of technical education and with persistent endeavour, India will gradually become studded with factories after the manner of the flourishing countries of Europe owned and managed by Indians'.[54] Once an ardent propagator of technical education, he now considered institutional training in technology as insufficient. But in the present context one could not avoid such advanced training.[55] Modern industries were largely supplemented by labour-saving machinery and appliances. Technical education on Western lines was indispensable for this method. Bose termed it as the 'Positive Method' of regenerating India's decaying industries. Even such education was insignificant unless modern industries sprang up to absorb the men with advanced training in technology. But from the beginning, Pramatha Nath argued that a formidable hardship in the way of indigenous enterprise was the scarcity of capital.

Pramatha Nath was becoming more and more apprehensive about the nature of modern industrialism. Once a votary of modern science and technology, he came to believe that the world's misery was largely due to the unbridled and thoughtless application of technology to modern industrialism. He highlighted the evil alliance between education, industry, war, and wealth.[56] Until the ancient Hindu culture was not established, Pramatha Nath thought, it would be unwise to demolish the existing institutions for techno-scientific education. Although he believed the present system of education was an economic blunder and nurtured 'parasites', yet without setting up the alternative model, that is, the Hindu model, on a solid footing, he wanted to carry on with the existing technological training institutes.[57]

Like the contemporary intellectuals, Pramatha Nath was also deeply influenced by Mahatma Gandhi. His *swarajya* proposed to reverse the conditions of modern progress and dared to challenge the ideals of the Western civilization. Pramatha Nath opined:

> I am quite at one with him in regarding it as a curse. No one would be more heartily glad than me to see the end of the Frankenstein created by Western industrialism. But, I am afraid, Mahatma Gandhi has grievously under-estimated the vitality of the monster, and is too sanguine of success within an incredibly short time.[58]

He was right. The djinn was already out of the bottle – the djinn of industrialization! For all his critique of the moral standards of modern industrialism, he never abandoned that model and worked for the establishment of the first heavy manufacturing industry in India, that too under Indian control. Pramatha Nath's identity in the colonial setting as a nationalist-geologist in a rapidly industrializing world had apparently confined his choices for the future.

Subaltern Technologists

Examining the world of popular healing in South Asia, two scholars recently looked at the way it is marginalized by the state and medical establishments while at the same time being very important in the everyday lives of the poor. They analyse a world of 'subaltern therapeutics' that both interacts with and resists state-sanctioned and elite forms of medical practice.[59] In this context, it is perhaps fitting that we begin here with a discussion of non-Western traditions of technology and the choices before them during our period of discussion. In many of these societies, science traditionally enjoyed a higher status than most forms of technology. The intellectual sections in these societies often looked down upon technology as an inferior form of activity. Traditional Indian society was not an exception – the scholar-gentry and artisans lived in exclusive social and cognitive worlds and problems of application were shared not between, but only within such groups.[60]

In the traditional society, science as a part of philosophy was the exclusive preserve of the erudite elites – the Brahmins. The Indian social structure, caste for example, as identified by Indian luminaries, was responsible for the cleavage between mental and manual work and the resultant stagnation.[61] Technology, despite its place in the cosmology, was confined to the manipulators of things – the artisans. Theologically also, even today, the Hindu goddess of learning, Saraswati, enjoys a higher status than the god of technology, Viswakarma.[62] Did colonial intervention merely mark the earlier fault line between the hand and the mind?

The first volume of *Subaltern Studies*, edited by Ranajit Guha, was published with a provocative opening statement: 'The historiography of Indian nationalism has for a long time been dominated by elitism – colonial elitism and bourgeois-nationalist elitism.'[63] The social history of science and technology in India has always been top-heavy. It is the celebration of the career of renowned scientists and technocrats.[64] They are, no doubt, important. However, there also existed substantial indigenous efforts, outside the focus of any intellectual limelight, in the field of technology. The achievements of these men devoid of formal technological training, whom we may loosely term 'subaltern technologists', deserve mention.

This 'House of Unknown Fame' features a long list and its luminaries can be found in the early nineteenth century itself. Amitabha Ghosh has identified Goluk Chunder, a Bengali blacksmith of Titagar, as the 'first Indian engineer'.[65] Goluk built a steam engine in 1828. In Serampore, the first self-contained industrial complex of Bengal, paper manufacture received a real breakthrough in 1820 with the introduction of steam power.[66] Many contemporary Europeans tried hard to make a prototype of the imported engine. But it was Goluk who ultimately succeeded in copying it. The steam engine made by him was put on display during the Annual Exhibition of the Agri-Horticultural Society at the Town Hall of Calcutta in January 1828. The *Calcutta Gazette* reported on 17 January:

> A Curious model of a Steam Engine, made by Goluk Chunder, Blacksmith of Tittaghur, near Barrackpur, without any assistance from European artists, was likewise exhibited; and although not coming within the immediate sphere of the society's exertions was considered so striking an instance of native ingenuity and imitative skill as to deserve encouragement. A donation of fifty rupees was, therefore, presented to the ingenious Blacksmith.[67]

Was there any practical utility of the steam engine made by him? George Smith, the biographer of William Carey, made a mention of it: '... the steam engine was useful for irrigation of lands made upon the model of a large steam engine belonging to the missionaries at Serampore.'[68] But unfortunately, nothing more about the first Indian engineer is known.

Thus, the steam engine, in those days an imported technological innovation from Britain, produced ripples in the minds of the local people. And in the early nineteenth century itself, one Goluk Chunder, without any knowledge of modern mechanics, was able to make a prototype of the steam engine successfully. Electricity too, another technological innovation, did not remain virgin for very long! In the age of industrial revolution, to cope with the ever-increasing need to speed up communication in step with the steamships and railways, the new science of electricity found its first practical and large-scale application in the telegraph. It was with the introduction of the electric telegraph system that the profession of electrical engineering came into existence.[69] The first Indian electrical engineer, Shiv Chunder Nundy, came from the field of the electric telegraph.

Shiv Chunder, at a very early age, joined the Refinery Department of the Calcutta Mint in 1846. His rise in the professional career shows that he was entirely a self-made man. His technical aptitude came to the notice of W. B. O'Shaughnessy, the chemical examiner of the mint, and Nundy was selected as his 'personal assistant'. Together they carried out several experiments in O'Shaughnessy's laboratory.[70] When, in 1851, the Company Bahadur authorized the construction of the first telegraph line in India and selected O'Shaughnessy to lead the task, he immediately placed Nundy as the 'in-charge' of the assignment. Thus, the mint-man became a telegraph-man, a transformation that would last for the rest of his life. The very next year, work on the 21-mile-long first section was completed and Nundy was closely associated with the project. It was Nundy who sent the inaugural message from Diamond Harbour, received in Calcutta by Lord Dalhousie and O'Shaughnessy.[71] Immediately afterwards, Nundy was appointed as 'Inspector' in charge of the line. He also had to instruct and train other signallers. He was afterwards given the additional charge of the post office at Diamond Harbour. Subsequently, he constructed about 900 miles of lines, from East Barrackpur to Allahabad, from Benares to Mirzapur, from Mirzapur to Seonee, and from Calcutta to Dacca.[72] Such responsibilities are enough to secure Nundy the distinction of an engineer proper.

During the turmoil of 1857, Nundy was in charge of the headquarters in Calcutta and in order to secure the communication between Calcutta and Bombay, he laid down a portion of the alternative line from Mirzapur to Seonee via Jubbulpur.[73] Nundy became an Assistant Superintendent of the Indian Telegraph Department

(1866) and retired on a special pension in 1884, in which year he was made an Honorary Magistrate. He had been awarded the title of 'Rai Bahadur' the preceding year. [74]

Many Indians made significant attempts to diffuse and disseminate knowledge about technology in the public sphere in Indian languages. Electric telegraph and railways perhaps first captured the imagination of the Bengali intellectuals in the nineteenth century. One Kalidas Moitra of Serampore wrote two separate treatises on these technological innovations in Bengali as early as 1855.[75] Apart from original works on the telegraph and the railways, he also published on the principles of anatomy and physiology.[76] Moitra, in his book on telegraphy, claimed that though several authors had written on electricity and chemistry in the *Tattobodhini Patrika*, the *Bibidhartha Sangraha*, and the *Satyapradip Patrika*,[77] his monograph was the first attempt in Bengali to cover the entire subject of electricity. He provided guidelines for experiments like principles of magnetism and chemical reaction using household items. He named telegraph stations as *adda*s, or 'chatting spaces', and described O'Shaughnessy's single needle signalling instrument at length, probably in hopes of Indian replication.[78] Moitra provided a preliminary outline of systems of signalling in Bengali along with the original English. He also offered here an elaborate discussion on the Puranic or classical Indian time and Western time. Arguing for the superiority of the Western division of the day into 24 hours, he provided a guide to both Western and Indian time calculation as well as homogenizing time calculation.[79]

Although an ardent follower of Western technology, one can discern a heavy strain of revivalist tenor in some of Moitra's writings. For example, he attempted to prove that ancient Indians used steam power in his *Baspiya Kal O Bhartiya Railway*.[80] Thus, he constructed his argument based on the views of many early nineteenth-century Indian nationalists, that ancient Indian culture was the amalgamation of both spiritual knowledge and scientific truths. At the same time, Moitra was aware of the exploitative nature of colonialism and contended that the British state's strategic need to transport troops rapidly was behind the growth of the railways in India.[81] He admitted honestly that he borrowed various technicalities of the steam engine from several English works. For Moitra, the machine was equal to modernity, and the telegraph and the railways were the best examples of that. He urged his countrymen to learn a European concept – that time was money. Deep Kanta Lahiri Choudhury perhaps rightly remarks that Kalidas Moitra was a curious combination of 'early nationalist egotism and conservative radicalism'.[82]

Sitanath Ghosh of Jessore manufactured an air pump and power loom that were exhibited at the Hindu Mela in the 1870s. The young Sitanath entered the Calcutta Medical College for his aptitude in scientific pursuits but was unable to complete his study due to ill health. He privately studied electricity and later joined as the editor of the *Hindu Patrika* published from Calcutta in which he printed many scientific papers.[83] The fifth session of the Mela (1871) was significant from the point of view of technological innovation. Here, Sitanath for the first time demonstrated his cotton spindle which produced yarn and twisted mechanically in three places without manual effort at each turn, though the thread lacked uniform thickness. He also showed his loom, but it was not not yet a finished product.[84] Sitanath also delivered a lecture on various issues of science and technology even before he demonstrated his inventions. In fact, he made his first appearance on the platform of the National Society, which was created at the fourth session of the Mela in 1870, in conjunction with the Mela.[85] The first lecture was given by Sitanath on machinery, about his new air pump and power loom. The latter could produce the work of four persons through the simple operations of one operator. On the same platform, he gave his speech on electricity.[86] Impressed with his lectures on 'Electricity and Magnetism' at the National Society, Debendranath Thakur offered Sitanath the editorship of the prestigious journal *Tattobodhini Patrika* in 1872. In the subsequent years, he regularly contributed on electricity in that journal.[87]

At the tenth session of the Hindu Mela (1876), Sitanath demonstrated his cotton weaving machine and a loom that could be run by draught animals, steam, or manual labour. The first was an improvement on the *charka* and produced treble the amount of yarn done by the latter. The loom could produce in a single effort over 20 yards of cloth.[88] The cloth was not yet of fine quality but could compete with Manchester in future if given due encouragement.[89] The weaving machine made him famous. Many wealthy persons, including the Rani of Betia, offered huge sums of money to buy his weaving machine. But Sitanath was determined not to sell it. He also invented a wheat-pounding machine, a mechanical plough that could be drawn with the help of one bullock, and a mechanized boat. His other inventions were writing and press ink. He gave the formula to his friend Amrita Lal Roy who later became well known using the formula as A. L. Roy's Ink. Another invention, a scientific amulet, was given to one Brajamohan Kar for marketing and he also made a good business out of it.[90] Inspired by the concept of the Hindu Mela, Sitanath organized an annual agricultural and educational fair in his native village, Roygram, in Jessore district. There too he demonstrated his technological skills, this time in the form of telegraph lines set up from the river front to the fair site to welcome the dignitaries.[91]

Sitanath's greatest scientific achievement, in his opinion, was the magnetic healer, which he described in his book on medical magnetism. Here, he even depicted himself as the founder of Electropathy, or the magnetic system of treatment in India. He derived the principle from the daily prayer (*anhik mantra*) of the Hindus and from the *Vishnu Purana*. The trident over temples was based on the theory of magnetism to prevent their collapse from lightning strikes. 'It has been found that', wrote Sitanath, '... the human body is a magnetizable object though far inferior to iron and steel.' In 1880, he opened his chamber at the Mechhua Bazar Street, Calcutta, and started treating patients using electricity and magnetism. He claimed that '... every description of indisposition known is partially or entirely removed as it is serious or light'.[92] As we know that technology was a technique informed by scientific knowledge, Sitanath was a technologist in its true sense – for he did not rest satisfied with the theoretical principles of electricity alone; he applied that knowledge to invent his greatest apparatus, the magnetic healer.

Jogesh Chandra Ray, lecturer of science at the Ravenshaw College, Cuttack, applied his scientific acumen to build technological devices (see Figure 5.1). He always insisted on the practical demonstration of theoretical knowledge while teaching, and tried to keep the college laboratory up to date for the benefit of the students. For better instruction in physical sciences, he even manufactured various instruments.[93] Jogesh Chandra was a prolific writer and contributed to the leading journals of Calcutta – both English and Bengali. He also realized that there was a serious lacuna in science teaching in the Indian colleges and schools, which was the absence of good quality books in Bengali. So, he concentrated on writing Bengali books on science subjects for students.[94]

Jogesh Chandra was a multi-talented character. From scientific subjects to literature, his canvas was vast. He was an elected fellow of the Royal Microscopical Society (1901) and the Royal Astronomical Society (1902).[95] One can devote an entire treatise on him! Here we shall discuss Jogesh Chandra's accomplishments in the field of technology. He always tried to apply his scientific aptitude for the betterment of society. His inquisitiveness dragged him towards different branches of knowledge – the first perhaps was fabric-printing. From a casual reading of the *Journal of Indian Arts*, Jogesh Chandra developed an interest in the subject and devoted almost two years experimenting with colours.[96]

Figure 5.1 Jogesh Chandra Ray, Lecturer of Science, Ravenshaw College

Source: Jogesh Chandra Ray, *Atmajebani* (An Autobiography) (Bankura: Anandakumar Roy, 2002).

Jogesh Chandra's major invention was the wind-mill which made him famous. He published the result of his research in the *Sahitya Parishad Patrika* and it demonstrated his engineering skills.[97] In the year 1923, he applied for patent on two of his appliances – one was 'an improved hand mill' and another was 'an improved lift pump for liquids'. The government sanction came the very next year. His hand-mill consisted of a stationary upper stone and a revolving lower stone, with an arrangement for maintaining a gap between the stones, which could be regulated at will. In the ordinary grinding mill used in Indian households, the lower stone remained fixed while the upper stone rotated. Splitting pulses without pulverizing them was difficult to perform by the old grinding machine, which tended to crush the pulses rather than split. This difficulty, Jogesh Chandra claimed, had been overcome in his improved hand mill entirely.[98]

Jogesh Chandra's another feat, his improved lift-pump for liquids, was perhaps more interesting. The following description, quoted from the testimony of the inventor to the Patent Office, ascertains the nature of his invention:

> This invention relates to a lift pump which is capable of raising water from any depth and which can be worked by means of levers operated by foot, or by hand, or jointly by foot and hand, or with the addition of a suitable gear of bullock power. Ordinary suction pumps cannot raise water from depths below twenty-five feet. This defect has been overcome in my invention by using a long pump barrel, of which one end is submerged in water and the other end extends right up to the delivery point. A long-stroke piston is used and the portion of the barrel below the piston functions as an ordinary suction pump, while the portion above acts in the manner of a force pump. Another defect in common hand pumps is the rapid wear of the pump bucket or hide cup. This has been overcome in my invention by dispensing with the hide cup or any other packing for the piston and by using a loose piston which is long enough to prevent any considerable side-slip or leakage past it of water. Leather or hide is not necessary for any of the working parts, which is an advantage....[99]

A man with such technological inclination must have some standing on technical education too. On several occasions, Jogesh Chandra made the demand for better facilities to train the 'Architects and Engineers'.[100] According to him, such education was needed as could enhance the resources of the country. He realized the inherent gulf between mainstream education and technical training – the former was for Brahmins whereas the latter was meant for the Shudras. Jogesh Chandra ridiculed the popular demand for technical education.[101] Mere training in pottery, carpentry, and so on, was not enough. Industrial application of technical knowledge was necessary. There was little effort to increase the inventive capacity of Indian students in the engineering colleges. Behind the achievements of Germany and America in the modern world were only their inventive skills. Jogesh Chandra knew that a Newton or Darwin rarely appeared, but at least we could manufacture an Edison or a Rontgen in our country.[102]

The lack of adequate industry to absorb the science students was an acute problem of the country. The only successful industrial application of scientific knowledge, Jogesh Chandra pointed out, was a pharmaceutical works, the BCPW. He was upset about the trend of acquiring foreign technical training, which he thought was incapable of altering the industrial scenario. Jogesh Chandra reminded us of two points: technical education alone was not the gateway to industry, and without knowing the country no one could succeed in running an industry with his foreign degrees in technology.[103]

It is evident from his autobiography that Jogesh Chandra Ray was a well-known figure of early twentieth-century Calcutta. He had personal contact with the contemporary intellectuals – Rabindranath Tagore, Jagadish Chandra Bose, Gooroo Das Banerjee, C. V. Raman, and Prafulla Chandra Ray, to name a few. He was also a regular contributor to various prestigious journals of the time. The University of Calcutta conferred on him an honorary DLit degree in 1956. In that sense, Jogesh Chandra was the most privileged person in the list of our subaltern technologists. But as the word 'subaltern' suggests, he remains absent from the academic discussion on Bengali attainments in modern techno-science even today.

The last luminary of our 'House of Unknown Fame' is Bepin Behari Das, a self-taught mechanic who can safely be termed as the first builder of an Indian motor car. When motor cars first appeared in early twentieth-century Calcutta, the famous coach-builders of the time like Steuart & Co. or Dykes & Co. found little difficulty in reorienting their expertise to build elegant car bodies.[104] But these initiatives were entirely dependent on foreign technologies and expertise. Indian engineers were not yet ready to think in terms of car manufacturing. But a miracle happened, and the protagonist was a self-taught mechanic deprived of any advanced training in technology. Bepin Behari Das, working in a small shed near Ballygunge-Bondel Road crossing, Calcutta, built all the components of a car, including its body and chassis, except for the tyres, spark plugs, carburettor, and magneto. 'Swadeshi', as named by its builder, was a '15 hp. L-head 4-cylinder 5-seater and 4 door touring model car'.[105] Bepin Behari sold his first car to Benaras Hindu University in 1931. One D. P. Khaitan, Councillor of Calcutta Corporation, noted in 1933 that the car was still running and was used by Pandit Motilal Nehru and Pandit Madan Mohan Malaviya.[106] Thus, the first car manufactured by an Indian was used by the leading Indian nationalists of the time!

The Calcutta Corporation entrusted Bepin Behari with the task of building a second car for them at a cost of 3,000 rupees. Arrangements were made to pay him 300 rupees per month as advance for six months on the condition that

> any defect being disclosed in any part or parts of the car during the period of two years, he will examine the same and should any fault be due to defective material or workmanship, he will repair the defective part or supply a new part in place thereof free of charge.[107]

However, he would not be held responsible for tyres, tubes, speedometer, or any electrical equipment not manufactured by him. The car would be 12½ feet in length for which 'an imported car would cost Rs. 5 or 6 thousands'.[108] It is interesting to note that when the delivery of the car was a little delayed, almost all the councillors expressed serious doubts about Bepin Behari's capability and were convinced of the misuse of public money. Luckily, he was supported by the then mayor of the corporation, Santosh Kumar Basu, and a few others and the project continued.[109]

At the end of the day, Bepin Behari again proved his technological skills. After the first trial run of the 'Swadeshi Motor Car' on the roads of Calcutta, the editor of *Advance* happily noted in 1933,

> ... last week an event, which will perhaps stand out as epoch-making in Indian industrial history, took place, comparatively quietly when the first motor car manufactured in Bengal by a Bengali, was passed by the police for registration and awarded the number 35977. The car did up to 35 mph. and the ease in steering and its good acceleration were praised by the correspondent.[110]

But Bepin Behari's endeavour found little appreciation and patronage. He built another car for Gwalior State which ran satisfactorily for many years.[111] He was engaged with another car-making project at the time of his death in 1938. Bepin Behari Das was only 55 then.[112] His example reveals that not only the British government but also the Indian elites thought little of the people below in the technological hierarchy created by the modern state.

It would be wrong to assume that the persons dealt with here were the only examples of creative aptitude in the field of technology in Bengal. One can cite many instances of humble technologists toiling their hands far removed from the glare of intellectual limelight. Modern 'Viswakarmas' were scattered all over the country. But one must know the local languages to read the contemporary texts to recognize their attainments.

Emerging Technologies and the Bengali Imagination

This history of technology relies heavily on vernacular texts[113] because neither the technologists routinely participated in the written culture nor the technological texts represented professions that did not enjoy high prestige. But by the end of the nineteenth century, a large section of the Bengali intelligentsia identified technology as a necessary means to improvement, both moral and material.[114] The examination of the contemporary Bengali journals dealing with matters of technology reveal that a variety of these technologies had originally emerged in the West. These were re-suited in the course of colonial rule. The re-situation of the technological practices led to their reformulation as well.[115] For any kind of technology, perfect transplantation in a different culture is impossible. Indigenous traditions of local knowledge and concepts of technology infiltrated Western techno-scientific practice in some form or the other. One of the primary means of reformulation and dissemination of such technological knowledge in Bengali were the contemporary journals – both technical and popular. Over the course of the period under discussion, several popular techno-scientific journals were published that provide various visions with regard to modern technology and indigenous society (see Figure 5.2).

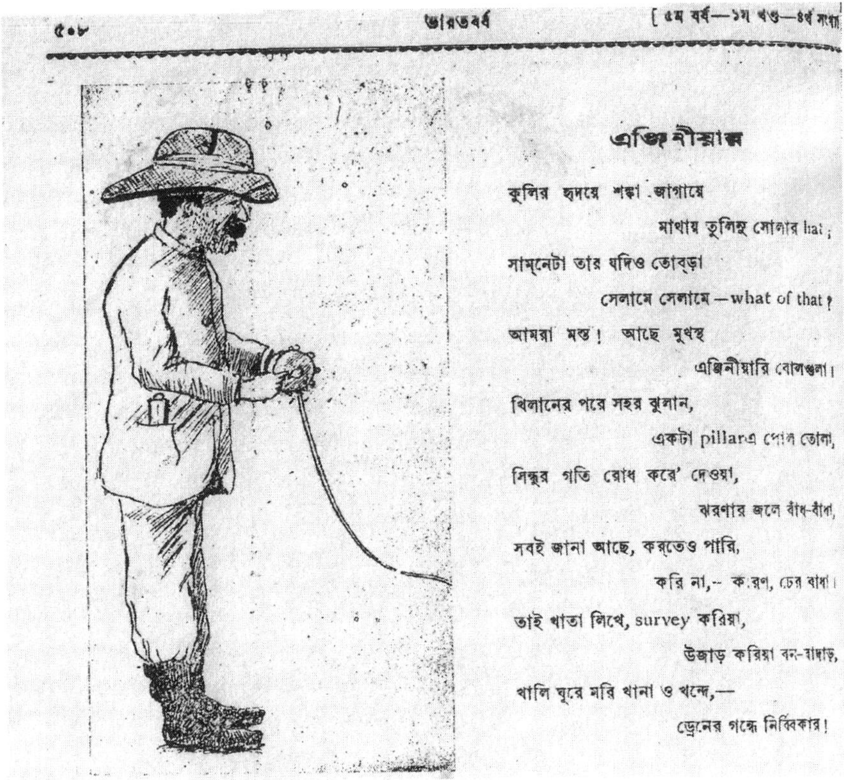

Figure 5.2 A limerick on the 'Engineer' published in the *Bharatbarsha* (1917)

'Striking fear in the coolie's heart/I put on my hard hat; The front is dented though/ groveling and scraping – but what of that? We are the invincible! We have crammed/ all the set phrases of engineering; The city rests on frames/bridges poised on pillars; The gushing river to be tamed/the running stream to be fettered; All is known, all possible/ but by several hurdles stopped; So copy in hand I survey all/haunting the forests and the dungeons I stumble into pits and falls/unperturbed by the foul drains.' (Translation by Arpita Chattaraj Mukhopadhyay.)

Also significant is the speed and seriousness with which the latest advances in European knowledge were followed in the recipient society. Not just that; they articulated such knowledge and made their presence felt in the early decades of the twentieth century itself. One Jawaharlal Dhar invented a machine to generate solar electricity and claimed, 'Our machine is not a true-copy of any foreign-made machine.'[116] That electrical power was to be the key to a modern industrial economy excited the erudite Bengalis. In an article read at the annual conference of the Chaitanya Library, the author emphasized, 'Machines help to boost the productivity of any industry. We shall advise our countrymen to learn the art of electricity, because future is here. The current industrial trend indicates the acceptance of electricity as main motive power over the others.'[117]

It was the era of *swadeshi* and one journal in a self-critical tenor questioned the attitude of the Indian workers. Of course, technical backwardness was a lacuna, but their work ethic was also not above suspicion. Round-the-clock supervision was needed where Indian workers were involved and that in turn enhanced the manufacturing cost of a product.[118] On another occasion, the journal identified the step-motherly attitude of the government towards indigenous industry and, inspired by the successful examples of Germany and Japan, asked for protection at least in the formative stage. Technical knowledge in any branch of industry was essential, but such knowledge, the journal lamented, was difficult to acquire through our educational system. However, a preliminary training was crucial before sending students abroad for a technical course. Otherwise, they were unable to relate their foreign training with the Indian reality.[119]

The bone of contention was the colonial education system. Unhappy with the government pedagogy, one Umeshchandra Mitra wrote,

> The education imparted so far under the British Raj was responsible for all-around deficiency. The goal of this education was to produce only clerks and pleaders. We need vocational education (*arthakari siksha*) to rectify the odds. But the character of vocational education has been changed. Previously it successfully produced medical and legal professionals, but presently these favourite destinations are also overcrowded. So, we need something different. We need to spread modern agricultural and techno-scientific education among our countrymen.[120]

The dearth of Indian participation in technological affairs haunted the intellectuals. On one occasion Jogesh Chandra Ray commented,

> The harmony between the creativeness of an engineer and laboriousness of a worker is essential for the invention of a machine. Unfortunately, the non-existence of country-made machine does not bother us much. The lack of demand for our own machine resulted in the spread of foreign-made machines in our households – sewing machine, bicycle, gramophone, and many more. In an agricultural country like India nobody turns up with his invented husking machine! We need a determined technologist who will feel the lacuna and engage in research.[121]

The narratives of the twentieth-century Bengali journals were different from their nineteenth-century counterparts due to a conceptual modification of the Bengali psyche over technology. Earlier, their demand was mainly confined to a better training facility in Western techno-science. But in the early twentieth century, after appropriating the new knowledge, they wanted to be self-sufficient in the realm of technology. Self-reliance was the new mantra.[122] *Bharatbarsha*, a contemporary journal, lauded the generous grant of Sir Tarak Nath Palit and Dr Rashbehari Ghosh to the University of Calcutta. For industrial development, they argued, such benevolence on the part of the Indians was urgently needed.[123]

In the second decade of the twentieth century, the country's preference for 'natural history' sciences was replaced by public sponsorship of industrial technology (see Figure 5.3). The Great War convinced them of the need to foster tertiary industrialization that would provide war-related necessities. The Bengali press was in constant vigil:

> In most of the European countries like Germany and France research in pure science is the top-most priority of their universities. England has so far neglected both science education and research. They had suffered its obvious consequences in the last war. So, they are now serious about it. Scientific research directed towards industrial development is their slogan now.[124]

Taking stock of the existing situation, they urged for immediate investment in scientific research if India wanted to survive in that tumultuous world economy. To them that was not wastage of public money, but investment for the future.[125] The euphoria generated by the Indian Industrial Commission (1916–18) was short-lived, and its recommendations were shelved by the British government.[126] One Pashupati Bandopadhyay emphasized that the mythological references to iron-made weapons established the point that India had a long tradition of iron industry. In the recent past too, iron was exported to Europe from Asia. But now the direction of trade had changed. The remarkable expansion of the iron industry in the Western hemisphere was possible due to the deindustrialization of India, especially in the iron industry. Bandopadhyay continued,

> India is a huge repository of iron-ore. Due to the lack of enterprise and self-confidence our iron-industry is suffering. Tata company, although pioneer iron-industry in India, depended on foreign technical assistance. Our universities are unable to fulfill the requirements for the expansion of iron-industry. Re-modeling them according to the foreign universities and establishment of more such industries by the enterprising Indians are the two conditions urgently needed for the prosperity of iron-industry.[127]

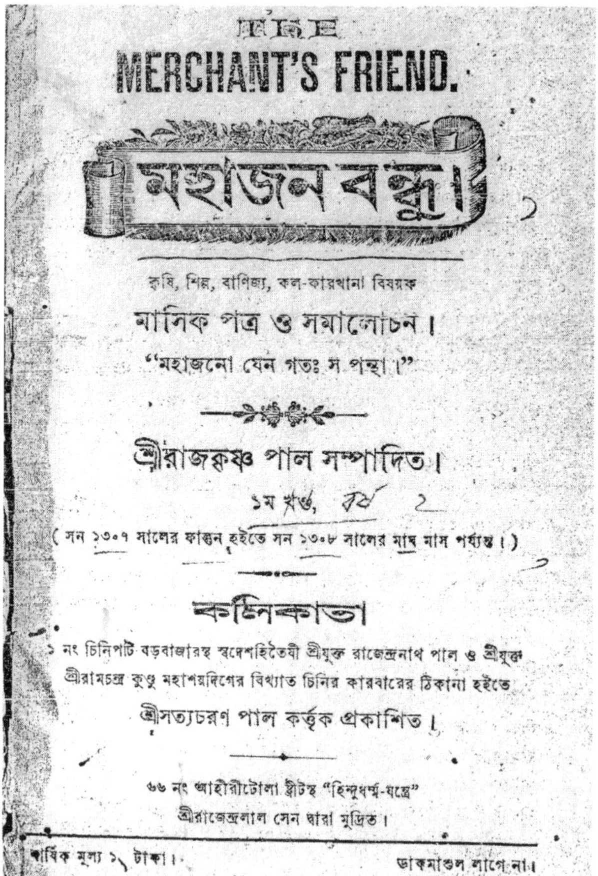

THE

MERCHANT'S FRIEND.

মহাজন বন্ধু।

কৃষি, শিল্প, বাণিজ্য, কল-কারখানা বিষয়ক

মাসিক পত্র ও সমালোচন।

"মহাজনো যেন গতঃ স পন্থা।"

শ্রীরাজকৃষ্ণ পাল সম্পাদিত।

১ম খণ্ড,

(সন ১৩০৭ সালের ফাল্গুন হইতে সন ১৩০৮ সালের মাঘ মাস পর্য্যন্ত।)

কলিকাতা।

১ নং চিনিপটি বড়বাজারস্থ স্বদেশহিতৈষী শ্রীযুক্ত রাজেন্দ্রনাথ পাল ও শ্রীযুক্ত শ্রীরামচন্দ্র কুণ্ডু মহাশয়দিগের বিখ্যাত চিনির কারবারের ঠিকানা হইতে

শ্রীসত্যচরণ পাল কর্ত্তৃক প্রকাশিত।

৬৬ নং আহীরীটোলা ষ্ট্রীটস্থ "হিন্দুধর্ম্ম-যন্ত্রে"

শ্রীরাজেন্দ্রলাল সেন দ্বারা মুদ্রিত।

বার্ষিক মূল্য ১৲ টাকা। ডাকমাশুল লাগে না।

Figure 5.3 *Mahajanbandhu*, a monthly Bengali periodical of the early twentieth century

Courtesy: Centre for Studies in Social Sciences, Calcutta.

The British model was inadequate. The new icons were Japan and Germany, and the new watchword was science-based industry. Inspired by the Japanese education model, one Jogesh Chandra Dutta asked: 'Can't we follow the Japanese educational system?'[128] He elaborated that behind the recent industrial development of Japan, their education system played the most crucial role. They followed the American system but modified it according to their societal needs. Earlier, the medium of instruction in Japan was English as it was in Indian schools. Although they gained fluency in English, the intellectual depth of the Japanese students in various technical subjects was below average. The assimilation of techno-scientific knowledge through the foreign language was difficult – realizing this they turned to their mother tongue.[129] Of course, the process of translation and appropriation was a rigorous exercise, and unlike Japan, we were reluctant to do so. Later, Jogesh Chandra discussed the technical education system of Japan at length.[130]

In the first quarter of the twentieth century, there was some optimism in the air. Fascinated by the marvel of electricity, one interlocutor wrote,

> In the meanwhile, Germany identifies another technological innovation for their industry. They attempt to reduce the industrial use of coal as much as possible. Electricity now has been replacing coal. They started using electricity to run the railway engine also. Not even that it is now the major motive-power in the German industry. The world is now transforming from the coal-age to electricity. The best advantage of industrial application of electricity is that the powerhouse (the place where electricity is generated) can be located in the far of places from the site of the factory, easily up to two hundred miles.[131]

An interesting characteristic of the period was the firm approach towards industrialization – the celebration of modern technology as the creator of a new industrialized world. It is in this context that we might locate Benoy Kumar Sarkar (1887–1949), the most prominent social scientist of the period before independence. A champion of *swadeshi* industrialization and technology, Sarkar and his *Arthik Unnoti* (Economic Progress) became the mouthpiece of an emerging 'technocratic' India. While discussing 'Shilpa, Banijya, Shilpalaya' (Industry, Commerce, and Technical Institutes), Benoy Sarkar emphasized,

> This is not my intention to criticize the degrees like, B.Sc., PhD, B.L, etc. These are all, of course, beneficial. But in the present circumstances, these are not enough. Along with these, we need other kinds of degrees,

> diplomas and training for our youths. For that we need different types of institution – ordinary intermediate, B.A., or B.Sc. is unable to fulfill the present requirements.[132]

Whatever the terminology used to define such institutes, these should be established with an eye to the local requirements. The curriculum should be framed in such a way as to stimulate the wealth-generating capacity of that locality. Sarkar urged that instruction be imparted in drawing, the inner mechanism of machines, ingredients, and market-study at the proposed institutes (see Figure 5.4).

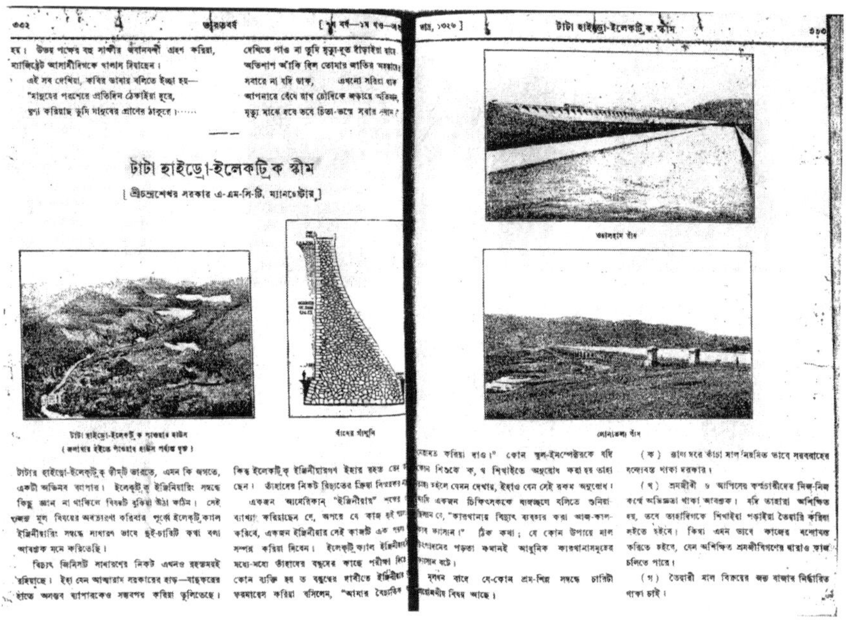

Figure 5.4 An article on the Tata hydro-electric scheme by Chandrasekhar Sarkar, *Bharatbarsha* (1919)

Courtesy: Centre for Studies in Social Sciences, Calcutta.

In another editorial, Sarkar identified the Swadeshi Movement and the First World War as the two events that created huge opportunities for Indian engineers, chemists, technologists, and entrepreneurs. In the prevalent situation, the government would promote skilled Indians for their own benefit. Sarkar encouraged the Indian youth to exploit their skills in turn and strengthen the economy. He had enormous admiration for technology:

> … while talking on business and entrepreneurship; by and large I portray the story of the machines, tools and technology. Beyond machines and technology, I don't have any interest. This country can be economically strengthening only with the application of machinery in industry and wide spread of technological skills among our countrymen.[133]

While delivering the presidential address at the Economics Section of the Dhaka Youth Conference, Sarkar commented that a successful industrial venture demands something extra. For any science industry, the services of engineers and chemists are indispensable. But they may not have knowledge about the market. An experienced manager can fill the gap. Thus, a modern industrial enterprise means a correct union between engineers, chemists, and managers with market-knowledge.[134] To make the Bengali youth technologically proficient, Sarkar wanted to reshuffle the university curricula. His mantra was education for wealth generation of the country.[135]

It is impossible to ignore Rabindranath Tagore while discussing Bengali literature in any format. He was not only a poet and a lyricist but also a thinker who impacted the trends in the social and political thought of his times. Rabindranath wanted India to smell the West, taste it, and understand the differences within it. He realized that imperialism was only one aspect of the West, that there were other West(s) that one could talk to and assimilate – including science and technology.[136] Rabindranath was convinced that the present deplorable state of the economy and the backwardness in the realm of technology were linked. Earlier, Bengal had prosperity – at least the sugar factories and looms could provide testimony to their technological attainment. Bengal received the first fruit of English education in our country. But that was literary in character; a techno-scientific outlook was absent. The result was obvious; our technicians forgot to handle tools and machines. Rabindranath emphasized that the knowledge of technology and encouragement to the Bengali youth were essential for industrialization.[137]

Electrification is a science-based high technological innovation that demands not only educated technicians, scientists, enormous amount of capital, and industrial capability, but also an enlightened public as consumers. It was true for Calcutta as well. Although apprehensive in the beginning, Bengalis not only welcomed electricity but also launched a monthly journal, *Bijoli*, on the subject by the third decade of the twentieth century (see Figure 5.5). In an article, the journal succinctly captured the victory of electricity over other forms of power:

> The invention of steam certainly inaugurated a new age for human-being. However, we have now a source of power which is much stronger than steam. This is nothing but electricity. The process of our thinking and work-pattern, in terms of technology, started changing with the invention of electricity.[138]

Women were regular contributors to *Bijoli*. They thought electricity revolutionized the *andarmahal* (the inner, private section of the house) of the Bengali household.[139] Apart from the general topics on electricity, the latest electrical innovations of the day were also featured in the journal. One Bhupen Ganguly, an expert in the science of electricity and managing director of Ms Ganguly & Chatterjee Ltd, wrote on 'Air Conditioning',

Figure 5.5 *Bijoli*, an illustrated Bengali monthly dealing with electricity and things electrical

Courtesy: Bangiya Sahitya Parishad Library, Kolkata.

> In the summer season to get rid from the heat we use hand-fan or electric fan. In both the cases we can regulate (increase and decrease) the flow of wind. But we cannot control the temperature of the atmosphere. Many believe that scientific cooling is not good for health. However, Indian men of medicine have given clean chit to scientific cooling. The newly established *All India Institute of Hygiene & Public Health* of Calcutta and several textile factories already adopted cooling through electricity. This sufficiently proves the safety of such method. Air-conditioning is a separate branch of engineering. Here the level of heat, humidity, pressure and flow of wind in our atmosphere can be controlled scientifically. The main composites of an air-conditioning machine are a water pump, a fan and a spray chamber.[140]

Others discussed the 'X-ray', 'Telephone', 'Street-lighting', 'Electricity in agriculture', 'High unit rate of electricity in India', and so on.[141] In *Bijoli*, one can get a perfect blend of popular and technical writings on electricity.

While discussing the triple engagement between modern technology, industrialization, and Bengali attainment, the entrepreneurs emerged as major protagonists. Aditya Mukherjee recently argues that one of the most striking features of post–First World War India was the extent to which Indian capitalists constituted themselves as a class.[142] In the year 1887, the entrepreneurs of Bengal were organized under the banner of the Bengal National Chamber of Commerce & Industry (BNCCI), which would be distinct from the relatively better organized European-dominated Bengal Chamber of Commerce. Naturally the latter served the interests of the Europeans. In the first annual meeting of the BNCCI (1888), Rai Budree Das Bahadur, President of the Chamber, declared,

> Indigenous native labour, enterprise, and capital properly directed can accomplish much, and if the Bengal National Chamber can give their attention in that direction, and induce and help the educated natives to follow commercial pursuits, their efforts will be crowned with the most successful results, and it will not be long before the country will grow in national resources, wealth and prosperity.[143]

The annual reports of the BNCCI are important source material through which one can get a glimpse of the world view of the Bengali entrepreneurial class in terms of technology. But this is not a descriptive catalogue of the BNCCI that can be found elsewhere.[144] It will only introduce the readers to the issues that captured the attention of the Bengali entrepreneurs in the late years of the Raj.

The BNCCI played an important role in developing public opinion in favour of technical education. Two annual prizes of 50 rupees each were sanctioned for the successful candidates of the Government Commercial Institute and the Calcutta Technical School.[145] The BNCCI had a strong commitment to society as well. In 1932, it sent a representation to the Bengal government urging them on the necessity of taking immediate steps to ensure the supply of electric current at concession rates to the non-government hospitals of Calcutta. As these hospitals were large consumers of electric energy, there was nothing unusual in claiming redemption in charges from the electric supply company on their part.[146]

The BNCCI was anxious that although TISCO had benefitted from the scheme of protection, it was unable to fulfil the expectation regarding increase in output. It had remained the only company of its kind in the country manufacturing steel, though there was enough room for one or two more. The protection granted to the fabricated steel industry, they thought, had not been able to attract Indian enterprise and capital to the industry. The steel industry being by its very nature a key industry, its development was linked to the emergence of other subsidiary industries in the country. Thus, the scheme of protection granted to the steel industry was unable to fulfil one of its principal objectives. The BNCCI asked for simultaneous protection to the basic industry (steel) and other subsidiary industries (engineering).[147] On another occasion, the BNCCI strongly opposed the government move to withdraw protection granted to the enamel industry as that would lead to its ruin. Although Indian goods were of superior quality, 'uneconomically' cheap Japanese enamel ware threatened its existence altogether. The cancellation of protective duty would worsen the already alarming situation.[148] The most outstanding handicap of the small- and middle-sized industries in Bengal, the BNCCI identified, was undercapitalization. There was also no marketing organization to help those concerns. The most effective means of stabilizing the position of small- and middle-sized industries, according to them, was an improvement in technology, and the better organization of marketing methods. It was, however, more important to work out ways and means for the establishment of industries in new directions.[149]

The Government of Bengal appointed a committee to enquire into the charges levied for electricity supplied to consumers by the CESC in 1935. In response to the general invitation for public opinion on the subject, the BNCCI responded that the rates levied by the CESC for the supply of electric energy were excessively high and called for substantial reduction. They believed that in view of the cheapness of coal and labour in Calcutta the cost of generating electricity for a monopolistic concern like the CESC should be very low.[150] They also requested the reduction of the electricity charges levied on small industrial concerns. The existing rate was indeed too high for them, particularly in facing the challenge of cheap imported goods. The BNCCI predicted that a reduction in rate would probably induce the non-users of electricity more and more to use electric energy in their manufacturing operations.[151] On another occasion, they welcomed the move of the government to establish a bio-chemical laboratory in Calcutta. The pharmaceutical industry of India, they argued, was still in its infancy, and effective steps should be taken to stop the manufacture and sale of adulterated and inferior drugs. The BNCCI also urged the government to protect both the indigenous drug industry and the consumers from imported 'dangerous' drugs.[152]

In 1937, the Government of Bengal introduced 'A Five-Year Plan for Industrial Development of Bengal' based on two fundamental considerations – (*a*) utilizing the existing natural resources of the province and (*b*) employing the huge available manpower running into lamentable waste – and harnessing both for productive work. The government paid greater attention to the smaller and cottage industries through a scheme of research, demonstration, and propaganda to be organized through specialized technical institutes. The BNCCI, however, considered that bypassing the prospect of large-scale and medium-sized industries, it was next to impossible to formulate a plan for the industrial development of Bengal.[153] On several occasions, the BNCCI emphasized the need for starting the basic industries. But what industrialization meant during all these years was the production of secondary or consumer goods excluding entirely the primary goods. They identified the major hurdles – the absence of machineries and raw materials, and low level of technological aptitude.[154]

The BNCCI expressed its concern over the shortage of electric supply in various parts of the province which led to the forced reduction in the output of many industrial concerns with large war orders. At the time of the Second World War, the quota for diesel oil was restricted for every province by the government. It created immense confusion, as the BNCCI pointed out in 1942: 'A large number of industrial concerns in the mofussil who had been obtaining power for their manufacturing processes either from their own diesel engine plants or from supply of electrical energy by the local supply companies were experiencing considerable difficulties on account of the limited supply of diesel oil.'[155] The BNCCI requested the government to intervene to save the Indian industries, especially the smaller ones. The government, although admitting concern over the situation, expressed its incapacity in the prevailing turmoil. The BNCCI had a genuine concern about the electric supply industry.[156]

When the Council of Industrial & Scientific Research appointed an Industrial Research Planning Committee in early 1944, the BNCCI readily acknowledged the importance of scientific and industrial research in any scheme of post-war reconstruction planning. They identified the existing deficiencies in the scope and organization of industrial research in India: the inadequate supply of trained technologists, shortage of money, absence of machineries and raw materials, and so on. Most of the industries in India, being organized into small and medium sizes, did not have resources to conduct any research work. The big industrial concerns were involved only in 'short-sighted research'. The BNCCI also identified the need for liaison between universities and private industries for furthering the cause of industrial research.[157]

The Government of India announced its post-war industrial policy in the year 1945. The government proposed to bring under central control several industries which were, under the existing constitution, within the jurisdiction of the provinces. It also indicated the lines along which they proposed to nationalize several industries. Welcoming the move, however, the BNCCI emphasized:

> ... two important pre-requisites for the successful implementation of any policy of industrial development. The first was the establishment at the centre of a truly constituted National Government enjoying the confidence of all sections of the community and also divested of all foreign control. The second was the abolition of the principle of 'commercial safeguards' by which a large number of non-nationals had acquired control over Indian industries.[158]

Such a declaration only ascertains the nationalist character of the BNCCI. They further suggested that the government should consider the possibilities of extending the supply of electricity to the industrial concerns in the *mofussil* areas that were expected to start production as part of the post-war development programme.[159] Thus, throughout the thirties and forties of the twentieth century, the Bengali entrepreneurs propagated one idea: modern technology needed to be appropriated so that a national programme of industrialization could be launched. This coincided with the larger intellectual temper of the society.

Towards Technological *Swaraj*

By the 1930s, the colonial government was faced with two important but difficult tasks of immense urgency: first, to restrain the rising tide of nationalism and maintain political control over the country and, second, to manipulate India's resources to meet the economic and strategic requirements of the empire.[160] The new middle class that had emerged out of the colonial experience also appropriated the right to speak on what the Indians had received at the end of a century and a half of British rule and responded accordingly. Technology was recognized as a necessary means to the desired end of industrialization through which Indian economic development would be achieved.[161]

Meghnad Saha, a pioneer astrophysicist and a celebrated student of Prafulla Chandra Ray, campaigned for the large-scale application of science and technology to national reconstruction. The *Science and Culture* group, especially Saha, believed that the Soviet model was ideal for India and set about transplanting it on Indian soil.[162] The younger generation of the Congress – both Jawaharlal Nehru and Subhas Chandra Bose – shared similar ideologies. An opportunity arrived for Saha when Bose was elected President of the Indian National Congress (January 1938–May 1939). He was a few years junior to Saha in the Presidency College, Calcutta. They developed a proximity in the following years.[163] In an address to the Indian Science News Association, a brainchild of Saha, Bose remarked in 1938,

> The movement for Indian emancipation has reached a stage when Swaraj is no longer a dream – no longer an ideal to be attained in the distant future.... Limited though the powers of those governments are, they have yet to handle the problems of reconstruction within their respective domains. How are we to solve these problems? We want, first and foremost, the aid of science in this task. The problem we have to face is not industrial recovery, however, but industrialisation. Whether we like it or not, we have to reconcile ourselves to the fact that the present epoch is the industrial epoch in modern history. There is no escape from the industrial revolution. We can at best determine whether this revolution, that is industrialisation, will be a comparatively gradual one, as in Great Britain, or a forced march as in Soviet Russia. I am afraid that it has to be a forced march in this country.[164]

The exigencies of the First World War revealed electricity as a vital agent of industrial production all over the world. This concern for developing the sources of energy, especially electricity, was felt with equal seriousness in India. The *Science and Culture* group took up the issue with a missionary zeal under the leadership of Meghnad Saha. What he then tried to do was find an institutional system that would guarantee not only an efficient production of energy but also an equitable distribution of it. As in the case of coal and mineral oil, the journal was prompt in realizing the value of electricity for the material progress of the country, but here the colonial policy was one of torpor and laissez faire.[165] Despite her abundant potential for power generation, India's record was very poor.[166] During a symposium on India's power supply, Meghnad Saha attacked the private electricity generation and distribution companies that had been granted licences for the purpose. Despite the improvements in technology, which enabled a ton of coal to produce four times as much energy as it did two decades earlier, there was no corresponding reduction in the rates charged. The CESC produced electricity at a cost of 0.35 annas per unit for domestic purposes. The charges were nearly six times higher than the cost of production. An analysis of British supply companies confirmed that nowhere was the ratio more than two or three times the cost of production.[167] Thus, the journal bitterly criticized the colonial policy allowing uncontrolled exploitation of coal and its failure to protect and develop the sources of fuel and power scientifically.[168]

Education attracted attention in *Science and Culture*, which was convinced that teaching had to be now approached with a new purpose and logic.[169] Saha had taken up the cause of the revival of university education. He identified universities, rather than technical institutes, as the hubs of such a mission. He envisioned a close collaboration between universities and industries, and between 'pure' and 'applied' science.[170] The *Science and Culture* group advocated a forced march to industrialization, the nationalization of power and fuel, the multipurpose development of rivers, the establishment of scientific surveys and research laboratories, the training of personnel in techno-scientific knowledge, and the development of education with an eye to industry.[171]

The National Planning Committee (NPC), masterminded by Meghnad Saha, was the first attempt by Indian nationalists to embark on a path of systematic and planned industrialization. In 1937, he persuaded the then Congress president, Subhas Chandra Bose, to constitute a national-level planning committee. This materialized at the end of 1938 under the chairmanship of Jawaharlal Nehru. As many as 29 sub-committees were formed, with economist K. T. Shah as secretary, to address different areas of national reconstruction, including agriculture, industries, power and fuel, population, labour, irrigation, communication, health, and education.[172]

Meanwhile, under the chairmanship of Meghnad Saha, one of the earliest to understand the importance of energy to India's progress, another sub-committee presented a blueprint for a 'definite National Power and Fuel Policy'. The ambition for large-scale industrialization in India had been handicapped, they argued, by the lack of the power necessary for driving and working complicated machinery. Therefore, if she wanted to realize her growing industrial ambitions, India must find adequate energy. Electricity was very costly in the country and development of industries, which required cheap and plentiful supply of power, was retarded because of that. A well-organized and well-distributed national system of generation and distribution of electrical power, they argued, could be met only if the entire enterprise of production and supply of this energy was made a 'Public Utility Concern'.[173]

While several sub-committees offered suggestions on technical training and development in their respective fields, a separate sub-committee, again under Saha, was set up to deal with technical education and research. The provision of the highest degree of technical education, and the organization of scientific research, must necessarily be an integral part of the educational sector in the national plan.[174] Here the sub-committee recommended a polytechnic, rather than a mono-technic, system to provide a deep grounding in the general sciences and mathematics, and emphasized upon industrial and technological applications. Such institutions were to be joint concerns of the central and provincial governments. The location and number of courses would depend on the industries to be set up in different parts of the country.[175] The Saha sub-committee criticized the complete absence of research in the Indian engineering colleges:

> Every educational institution of the university standard should be equipped with men, machines, and instruments for carrying on advanced research work. At present no engineering educational institution in India has research work as a part of its programme. Civil Engineering is the oldest engineering subject taught in this country, but even in this line all plans and designs of bridges, big buildings, and new cities are done by foreign firms in foreign countries. Professors in engineering colleges in co-operation with Government Engineering Departments should be entrusted with works of this nature.[176]

Although the NPC lost impetus once the Congress ministers resigned following the outbreak of the Second World War and ceased to function with Nehru's imprisonment in 1940, the committee marked the beginning of the party's active commitment to state planning and the use of science and technology to serve nation-building goals. Since the purpose of the NPC was to formulate plans and not to implement them, in the opinion of Jagdish Sinha, it is unfair to look for a direct outcome. But its work must be viewed as part of the freedom movement and seen as an indigenous endeavour to achieve a degree of self-reliance which ultimately could not be achieved in the absence of political freedom.[177]

To these new nationalist demands the British government awoke rather late. It witnessed silently the debate that surfaced in the *Science and Culture*, the rumblings of the Indian intellectuals and entrepreneurs, and the formation of the NPC.[178] But the scenario changed fundamentally with the onset of the Second World War. A government report read:

> If we are to improve our standards of living after the war and to maintain our position in the world, research in many categories will have to be undertaken on a scale not hitherto contemplated in peace-time. The resources upon which we depend for our schemes of reconstruction and social betterment will have to be used and developed with the maximum vision, intelligence, and enterprise. This can only be ensured by the application of active and well-directed technological research firmly based on the foundation of scientific discovery.[179]

This was also what nationalists like Saha were demanding, yet their motives were different. From the British point of view, it was a reassertion of constructive imperialism. But the likes of Saha would not accept an 'empire-driven development'.[180] They would not settle for anything less than *purna swaraj* (total self-rule) and complete control over the policy of techno-science and their implementation.

In the context of academia–industry interface, Nalini Ranjan Sarkar (1882–1953), our last protagonist, deserves mention. He had served as the Finance Minister of both undivided Bengal and post-independence West Bengal, and was one of the few personalities from the province who had made a mark in mainstream national politics as well as in the contemporary commercial organizations and had also represented a number of government committees.[181] A true nationalist, Nalini Ranjan was always vocal about the defects of the educational system of Bengal. On the East Bengal Education Week (1940), he commented,

> The numbers undergoing a technical or commercial education have gone by leaps and bounds, but opportunities for employment in technical and commercial lines have not at all kept pace with this increase. The result is wide gap between the numbers who have qualified for such occupations and the actual volume of employment available for them. At the same

> time, it cannot unfortunately be denied that our educational system makes no perceptible attempt to foster a bent for independent career or provide opportunities for imparting a commercial bias to students.[182]

The industrial skills of a worker could be improved effectively by technical training. In the present circumstances, Nalini Ranjan thought, foreign technical training was one option and another was the simultaneous attempt to build a high-grade school of technology in India.[183]

On another occasion, while discussing the post-war reconstruction programme, he underlined how complicated the case of India was in the absence of a national government. His remedy was 'a conscious and planned development of our economic resources'. Due to the shortage of capital, Nalini Ranjan wanted to give preference to the consumer goods industry over the capital goods one. At the same time, he did not forget to highlight the significance of the capital goods or basic industries. There were certain basic industries, such as power, whose development was a precondition for the growth of the consumer goods industry. According to him, at that time, the early initiative should be directed towards the development of power – he preferred hydroelectricity.[184] Inspired by the successful example of Japan, Nalini Ranjan assigned a prominent role to cottage industries in his reconstruction planning.[185]

The Indian Institutes of Technology (IITs) are the premier academic institutes of technology in India. Originally envisioned as 'Higher Technical Institutes' for the post-war reconstruction of the country, these institutes are only the latest demonstration of the development process initiated during the colonial period and successfully pursued after independence. In 1945, a 22-member committee was constituted to consider the development of higher technical institutions for the purpose of the post-war industrial development of India. The chairman of this high-level committee was none other than Nalini Ranjan Sarkar and the committee subsequently became famous as the Sarkar Committee.[186] He was an obvious choice because of his long association with the issues of technical education and industry in Bengal and the belief that he could influence the government's policies on education.

The Sarkar Committee recommended 'not less than four Higher Technical Institutions, one in the North, one in the East, one in the South and one in the West will be necessary to satisfy the post-war requirements' and 'the one in the East should be set up in or near Calcutta at an early date', among others. Accordingly, the Eastern Higher Technical Institute, later IIT Kharagpur, was the first to be set up in 1950 at the Hijli Detention Camp in modern-day West Bengal.

Undergraduate instruction (four years) was the main branch of study. In view of the inadequate facilities for post-graduate study and research in technology, the committee recommended the inclusion of facilities for both in these proposed institutes. To be modelled on the Massachusetts Institute of Technology (MIT), the idea of the IITs was a clear break from the existing structure of technical education in the country and was intended to provide high-grade technologists necessary for industrial development.[187]

However, not everybody was happy with the proposed Indian version of MIT. Benoy Kumar Sarkar expressed serious doubts about its feasibility in the Indian context: 'It is nothing short of hallucination to imagine, or senseless verbosity to broadcast from Imperial heights, that a CIT [California Institute of Technology] or MIT is a question of practical politics within Indian boundaries.' But, on the other hand, he argued, the highest level of engineering institutes in the country like the Jadavpur college had each been functioning as an MIT or CIT in a fundamental pedagogic sense. Although the room for improvement at Jadavpur was immense, he appealed to the alumnus of the college to make generous grants:

> Modest buildings and low salaries have not prevented the Jadavpur Campus from turning out Engineering and Technology graduates of the MIT stamp.... Jadavpur College – the existing Indian MIT of today – can become a more efficient MIT in case a few million Rupees can be spent within five years. Let the MIT-wallahs, both official and non-official, ponder over this reality. The modest demand for Rs. 5,000,000 has been before them for some long time in the interest of Greater Jadavpur.[188]

Conclusion

This chapter is an outline of the contours of the debate that took place in early twentieth-century Bengal in the context of emerging technologies and the growing demand for industrialization. This concern for industrialization and its deficiencies became one of the primary sites for the critique of colonial exploitation. In the process, technical education was perceived as an important instrument in the realization of the goal of industrial development, as it directly fulfilled the needs of technical manpower required by a potential nation. Of course, there were people without formal training in technology who excelled in the field. But in the course of time, we tend to forget them. The contemporary erudite section also seldom recognized the self-taught Viswakarmas. There was a 'de-link' between the 'intellectual technocrats' and the 'subaltern technologists'. Even the intellectuals differed on the question of technology and industry. They debated over the role and place of technical education in the process of industrialization. But one thing is apparent – the culture of technology, at least in the context of Bengal, was not confined to the upper strata of society alone. Through the vernacular publication, this culture was disseminated deep into the society.

In the heyday of national reconstruction, these debates intensified. Now the question of a future independent India was at the forefront. The new watchwords were planning, industrialization, institutionalization, and scientized technology. Planning was no doubt a complex exercise and that too under foreign domination. Every Indian scientist and technologist sought solutions for the country's reconstruction, but their methods differed. The model of *charka* or heavy industry, pure or applied research, USSR or USA, thermal or hydroelectricity, and many more occupied their minds. But there was one consensus: a sound technological base was necessary for rapid industrialization and the subsequent economic development of the country. In 1947, British India was partitioned, and in bloodshed and turmoil the new states of India and Pakistan were born. In this context, Nalini Ranjan Sarkar, also the chairman of the newly formed All India Council for Technical Education (AICTE), made a very relevant statement:

> I may be permitted to refer to another point in this context which concerns not only the present but also the future of technical education. The air is thick with rumours of divisions and partitions, of separate sovereign states and a host of other fissiparous tendencies. This has, again, introduced further confusion and other uncertainties. But here too, whether there are divisions and partitions or separate sovereign states or a loose union of the type provided in the Cabinet Mission Scheme, the task of creating the machinery for the provision of technical education may well be conducted on a basis of co-ordination between provinces and states. For this is a task too vast for a single province or state to undertake in a satisfactory or comprehensive manner. The necessity is also too abiding and permanent to be influenced by every passing wind of politics. This whole question of technical education deserves to be lifted to a higher plane where considerations of politics or any other considerations will not hamper work in a sphere which is of equal urgency to all provinces and states alike.[189]

Notes

1 *Report of the Native Papers Bengal*, January–June 1884, 375.

2 *Arthik Unnoti* 3, no. 10, Magh 1335 B.S. (1928): 725.

3 David Arnold, *Everyday Technology* (Chicago and London: The University of Chicago Press, 2013), 5–6.

4 Ritika Prasad, *Tracks of Change: Railways and Everyday Life in Colonial India* (New Delhi: Cambridge University Press, 2015).

5 Ibid., 11.

6 S. Irfan Habib and Dhruv Raina (eds), 'Introduction', in *Social History of Science in Colonial India* (New Delhi: Oxford University Press, 2007), xxxi.

7 Pratik Chakrabarti, *Western Science in Modern India* (Ranikhet: Permanent Black, Paperback Edition, 2011), 150.

8 Minute by Richard Temple, 18 April 1876, General, Education, No. 3, April 1876, WBSA.

9 *Amrita Bazar Patrika*, 10 February 1876.

10 Dinanath Sen, *A Scheme for the School of Industry or Practical Science Proposed to be Established in Calcutta* (Calcutta: Minerva Press, 1876), 1.

11 Ibid., 3.

12 Quoted in Sidhartha Ghosh, *Kaler Sahar Kolkata* (Kolkata: Ananda, 1991), 211.

13 *Hindu Patriot*, 6 March 1876.

14 Home, Education, File No. 14–88, October 1897, NAI.

15 Section I: Class 1- Drawing: Sub-Class a) Architecture, b) Mechanical, c) Engineering; Class 2- Engraving: Sub-Class a) Wood, b) Metal, c) Ivory, d) Stone; Class 3- Modelling & Plastic Arts; Class 4- Lithography; Class 5- Photography; Section II: Class 6- Electricity: Sub-Class a) Telegraph, b) Telephone, c) Electric Light, d) Electro-Plating, Gilding and Typing; Section III: Class 7- Machinery-in general: Sub-Class a) Steam Engine, b) Manufacturing Machines and Tools; Class 8- Agricultural Machinery; Class 9- Railways and Tramways; Section IV: Class 10- Metallurgic Arts: Sub-Class a) Iron, b) Steel, c) Brass, d) Copper, e) Tin, f) Zinc, g) German Silver; Class 11- Country Basins; Class 12- Steel Cutlery and Edge Tools; Section V: Class 13- Printing: Sub-Class a) Type-Casting, b) Stereo-Typing, c) Book-Binding; Class 14- Paper and Parchment, Millboard & Stationary; Section VI: Class 15- Illumination: Sub-Class a) Safety-Matches, b) Candle, c) Oil, d) Gas, e) Magnesium Light; Section VII: Class 16- Pottery: Sub-Class a) China, b) Stone ware, c) Earthen ware, d) Tera cotta, e) Mosaic, f) Pavement Tiles; Section VIII: Class 17- Glass Manufactures: Sub-Class [Flint, Crystal, Plate, Window, Bottle, Enameling, Staining]; Section IX: Class 18- Horological Instrument: Sub-Class [Watch, Clock, Turret clock, Astronomical clock, Chronometer]; Class 19- Jewellery: Sub-Class [Goldsmith,

Silversmith, Imitation Gems]; Class 20- Musical Instrument: Preparing English instruments & Constructing native instruments; Section X: Class 21- Building Materials- Sub-Class [Marble and stone working, Cement, Lime, Ornamental Mouldings cast in plastic and cement]; Section XI: Class 22- Perfumery: Scented waters oil and filters; Class 23- Distilling and Brewing; Class 24- Sugar refining; Class 25- Bread and Biscuit; Section XII: Class 26- Manufactures: Sub-Class [Gums, Ink, Soap]; Class 27- Dyeing and Calico Printing; Class 28- Bronzing and Lacquering; Section XIII: Class 29- Naval Architecture: Sub-Class [Dock Works, Boat making]; Class 30- Furniture and Wood Works: Sub-Class [Bamboo cane and Reed works]; Class 31- Coach Building; Section XIV: Class 32- Manufacture: Sub-Class [Leather, Hides, Saddlery, Boot and Shoes]; Class 33- India Rubber and Guttapercha; Section XVI: Class 34- Manufactures: Sub-Class [Cotton, Silk, Wool, Flax, Hemp, Hosiery, Gloves, Hats and Caps]; Class 35- Carpets, Velvets, Lace & Linen; Class 36- Needle works; Section XVII: Class 37- Manufactures: Sub-Class [Locks, Pins, Buttons, Needles, Pens, Pencils, Toys, Tinsel works, Horns, Ivory, Bones].

Ibid.

16 Ibid.

17 Ibid.

18 Quoted in Francis J. Spring, *Technical Education in Bengal* (Calcutta: W. Newman & Co., 1886), 27.

19 Ibid., 28.

20 Ibid., 29.

21 Subhayu Chattopadhyay, 'Pramatha Nath Bose (1855–1934) and Indian Geology', PhD thesis, Jadavpur University, Kolkata, 2008, 69–88.

22 P. N. Bose, *Essays and Lectures on the Industrial Development of India* (Calcutta: Newman & Co., 1906), 75.

23 It is the steam and electricity, and the numerous infernal compounds invented by Chemistry, which enable the greater powers of the West to deprive the weaker peoples of the world of their independence and to exploit and enslave them. The weak have been more or less exploited by the strong in all ages and all over the globe, but never so scientifically, and, therefore, so systematically, so universally and so relentlessly.

Ibid., 140.

24 P. N. Bose, *A History of Hindu Civilization during British Rule*, Vol. III (Calcutta: W. Newman & Co., 1896), 112.

25 P. N. Bose, *A History of Hindu Civilization during British Rule*, Vol. I (Calcutta: W. Newman & Co., 1894), lxxx.

26 Note by H. B. Medlicott, Director, GSI; Revenue-Agriculture, Surveys, Proceeding No. 25, September 1880, NAI.

27 P. N. Bose, *A History of Hindu Civilization*, Vol. III, 98.

28 In 1903, Pramatha Nath was superseded as Superintendent of the GSI by Thomas Holland, three years junior to him. Bose resented the injustice done to him and resigned from the GSI. See S. Chattopadhyay, '*Pramatha Nath Bose*', 91.

29 Deepak Kumar, *Science and the Raj* (New Delhi: Oxford University Press, 2nd edn, 2006), 210.

30 *Industrial India* II, no. 2 (February 1905): 28.

31 *Industrial India* II, no. 3 (March 1905): 65–7.

32 Electrical engineering 6, applied chemistry 5, mechanical engineering 12, pharmacy 2, dyeing 4, leather tanning 7, agriculture 12, cotton weaving 4, sericulture 5, pencil making 6, soap manufacture 2, button manufacture 2, rubber manufacture 2, and so on. J. G. Cumming, *Technical and Industrial Instruction in Bengal, 1888–1908* (Calcutta: Office of the Superintendent Govt. Printing, 1908), 28.

33 *Industrial India* V, no. 2 (February 1908): 126–7.

34 'India's "Industrial Revolution": What It Means and Involves—II', *The Dawn and Dawn Society's Magazine*, New Series VII, no. 10 (October 1911): 342–6.

35 'The Indian System of Training Workmen for the Manual Industries', *The Dawn and Dawn Society's Magazine*, New Series I, no. 2 (November 1904): 75.

36 'Advanced Economic Thought in the West: How to Solve the Labour–Capital Problem', Editorial, *The Dawn* III, no. 6 (January 1900): 147–52.

37 Pratik Chakrabarti, 'Science in India in the Twentieth Century', in *Science, Technology, Imperialism and War*, ed. Jyoti Bhusan Das Gupta (New Delhi: Pearson Longman, 2007), 132.

38 Dhruv Raina and S. Irfan Habib, *Domesticating Modern Science* (New Delhi: Tulika Books, 2004), 83–147.

39 *The Dawn and Dawn Society's Magazine*, New Series II, no. 4 (March 1906): 213–14.

40 *The Dawn and Dawn Society's Magazine*, New Series III, no. 5 (January 1907): 37.

41 Raina and Habib, *Domesticating Modern Science*, 148.

42 In the final countdown, the institutes imparting pure technical training survived. From the beginning they successfully reduced the dependency of the Bengali entrepreneurs on foreign technical assistance:

> Thus, we find that at Serajgunge, a Hydraulic Jute-Press Engine of Messrs. A. P. Kerr & Co was laying out of order for a long time. It was reported that the pinion of the governor and some other parts of the Engine were missing. Every one of the European firms consulted was of opinion that the missing parts could not be replaced here and advised the Company to write to the manufacturer of the Engine in England, with the numbers of its several parts. However, the Company thought it proper before taking final steps to obtain the opinion of the Bengal Technical Institute in the matter. Now the College Engineer, from what he could gather about the condition of the Engine, was of opinion that it would not be necessary to write to the English manufacturer of the Engine, for

the parts could well be replaced here; and it was after considerable persuasion that the diffidence of the Manager of the Serajgunge firm could be overcome; and it was finally arranged that the work of repairs should be undertaken by the Bengal Technical Institute....

The Dawn and Dawn Society's Magazine, New Series V, no. 10 (October 1909): 332–4. Repair and management of the foreign-made machines were important steps towards technological self-sufficiency of the country. Although the goal, that is, manufacturing, was a long way away, such displays of technical skills, no doubt, enhanced their confidence level.

43 P. C. Ray, *Career Lectures: Organized by the Appointments and Information Board* (Calcutta: University of Calcutta, 1939), 35.

44 Dhruv Raina, *Images and Contexts* (New Delhi: Oxford University Press, paperback 2nd imp., 2011), 57.

45 P. C. Ray, *A History of Hindu Chemistry*, Vol. I (Calcutta: Chuckervertty, Chatterjee & Co. and Kegan Paul, 1902), 195.

46 P. C. Ray, *Life and Experiences of a Bengali Chemist*, Vol. I (Calcutta: Chuckervertty, Chatterjee and Co., 1932), 489–91.

47 Ibid., 361–78.

48 Pratik Chakrabarti uses the terms 'ambivalent' and 'ambidextrous'. What is striking about Prafulla Chandra is that, Chakrabarti argues, he belonged actively to both worlds. Chakrabarti, *Western Science*, 271–2.

49 P. C. Ray, *Essays and Discourses* (Madras: G. A. Natesan, 1918), 66.

50 S. Chattopadhyay, '*Pramatha Nath Bose*', 122.

51 P. N. Bose, 'Notes on the Geology and Mineral Resources of Mayurbhanj', *Records of Geological Survey of India* XXXI, no. III (1904): 167–73.

52 Frank Harris, *Jamsetji Nusserwanji Tata* (Bombay: Blackie & Son, 2nd edn, 1958), 40.

53 *Report of the National Council of Education, Bengal for 1939* (Calcutta: NCE, Bengal, not dated), 11–13.

54 P. N. Bose, *The Illusions of New India* (Calcutta: W. Newman & Co., 1916), 105.

55 Ibid., 137.

56 P. N. Bose, *National Education and Modern Progress* (Calcutta: Kar, Majumder & Co., 1921), 15.

57 P. N. Bose, 'Reminiscences and Reflections of a Septuagenarian', *Amrita Bazar Patrika*, 24 January 1932.

58 Bose, *National Education*, 73.

59 David Hardiman and Projit Bihari Mukharji (eds), *Medical Marginality in South Asia* (London and New York: Routledge), 2012.

60 Ashis Nandy, *A Very Popular Exile* (New Delhi: Oxford University Press, 2007), 85.

61 Ray, *Life and Experiences of a Bengali Chemist*, 502–13.

62 Pramatha Nath Bose, the great geologist, observed in the early twentieth century,

> Among the Hindus, Manu condemned the institution of huge machinery as a sin. Plain living and high thinking, poverty and culture (especially ethical and spiritual culture) have form remote antiquity been the only passports to distinction and veneration among them. Viswakarma, the divine patron of arts in India, receives homage only from artisans, and he is in no way superior to Maya, the architect of the Danavas.

P. N. Bose, *National Education*, 14.

63 Ranajit Guha (ed.), 'On Some Aspects of the Historiography of Colonial India', *Subaltern Studies I* (New Delhi: Oxford University Press, 1982), 1.

64 Jahnavi Phalkey, *Atomic State* (Ranikhet: Permanent Black, 2013); Dhruv Raina, *Needham's Indian Network* (New Delhi: Yoda Press, 2015).

65 Amitabha Ghosh, 'Some Eminent Indian Pioneers in the Field of Technology', *Indian Journal of History of Science* 29, no. 1 (1994): 63–75.

66 The 12 horse-power steam engine of Thwaites Hick & Rothwells imported from England was an object of wonder. One contemporary journal reported: 'Even the Steam Engine although it has been in operation for four years does not cease to draw crowds of natives to inspect it from week to week, who, … quietly inspect it at leisure, and departed convinced that all knowledge was not engrossed by their fore-fathers….' *Calcutta Gazette*, 27 May 1824, quoted in Anil Chandra Das Gupta (ed.), *The Days of the John Company* (Calcutta: West Bengal Government Press, 1959), 13–15.

67 *Calcutta Gazette*, 17 January 1828; quoted in ibid., 272–3.

68 George Smith, *The Life of William Carey* (Calcutta: Everyman's Library, 1885), 231.

69 J. D. Bernal, *Science in History* (London: Watts, 1954), 390.

70 Sidhartha Ghosh, *Karigari Kalpana O Bangali Udyog* (Kolkata: Dey's, 1988), 48.

71 Krishnalal Shridharani, *Story of the Indian Telegraph* (New Delhi: Post and Telegraph Department, 1953), 13.

72 During the construction of the Calcutta–Dacca line, it became necessary to lay 7 miles of underwater cable across the River Padma. With no steamer company willing to lend their vessels for the work at less than 10,000 rupees, a determined Nundy got it done by hiring country fishing boats. Hemendra Prasad Ghosh, 'Shiv Chandra Nundy', *Masik Basumati*, Kartik 1360 B.S. (1953): 107–14.

73 Shridharani, *Story of the Indian Telegraph*, 15.

74 *The Statesman* commented on 25 April 1902: 'A Rai Bahadurship seems to have been a poor reward for his excellent services.'

75 Kalidas Moitra, *Electric Telegraph ba Taritbartabaha Prakaran* (Serampore: J. H. Peters, 1855); see also Kalidas Moitra, *Baspiya Kal O Bharatiya Railway* (Serampore: J. H. Peters, 1855).

76 Kalidas Moitra, *Manabdehotatwa or the Human Frame* (Serampore: J. H. Peters, 1855).

77 These were the leading Bengali journals of the nineteenth and early twentieth centuries.

78 Moitra, *Electric Telegraph*, 120–31.

79 Ibid., 150–3.

80 Moitra, *Baspiya Kal*, 4.

81 Ibid., 48.

82 Deep Kanta Lahiri Choudhury, *Telegraphic Imperialism* (Basingstoke: Palgrave Macmillan, 2010), 26.

83 Jogindra Nath Samaddar, 'Sitanath Ghosh', *Prabasi* 13, no. 2, 1319 B.S. (1912): 237–9.

84 *Sulav Samachar*, 21 February 1871; *Amrita Bazar Patrika*, 2 March 1871.

85 Chittabrata Palit, *Scientific Bengal* (Delhi: Kalpaz, 2006), 75.

86 Jogesh Chandra Bagal, *Jatiyatar Nabamantra O Hindu Melar Itibritta* (Calcutta: Salil Kumar Mitra, 1945), 40.

87 Sitanath Ghosh, 'Tarit bishoyok jnan', *Tattobodhini Patrika* 8, no. 2, issue 352, Pous 1794 Saka (1872): 148.

88 *Sadharani*, 27 February 1876.

89 Bagal, *Jatiyatar Nabamantra*, 55.

90 Samaddar, 'Sitanath Ghosh', 241.

91 Ibid.

92 Sitanath's magnetic healers, one small and one big (2 feet and 4 feet), were composed of 6,000 and 10,000 feet of copper wire passing through a wooden frame cushioned with mat and jute, wax, and leather linings. They had brass hooks at the end of which were attached the wires of the galvanic battery for creating the magnetic field. The patient would be made to lie on this platform so that electric waves passed through the body. Bagal, *Jatiyatar Nabamantra*, 219.

93 Arabinda Chattopadhyay, *Jogesh Chandra Ray Vidyanidhi* (Kolkata: Bangiya Sahitya Parishad, 2009), 18.

94 Professor Jagadish Chnadra Bose once remarked,

> From what I have seen the elements of Physics and Physiography in Bengali by Babu Joges Chandra Ray, M.A., I found them in many respects superior to other books of the same class. The method of treatment is commendable and the explanations clear and concise. The woodcuts are excellent. I trust they would be found of great service to those for whom they are intended.

Quoted in Jogesh Chandra Ray, *Atmajebani* (Bankura: Anandakumar Roy, 2002), 298.

95 A. Chattopadhyay, *Jogesh Chandra Ray Vidyanidhi*, 59.

96 Jogesh Chandra Ray, 'Ranjita O Chritrita Bastra', *Nabyabharat* 10, no. 4, Sraban 1299 B.S. (1892): 177–83.

97 Jogesh Chandra Ray, *Sahitya Parishad Patrika* 21, no. 2, 1321 B.S. (1914): 81–96.

98 Ray, *Atmajebani*, 239.

99 Ibid., 243.

100 Jogesh Chandra Ray Vidyanidhi, 'Kala-Siksha', *Bharati* 26, Kartik 1309 B.S. (1902): 674–87.

101 Ibid., 685.

102 Jogesh Chandra Ray Vidyanidhi, 'Kala-Siksha', *Bharati* 26, Agrahayan 1309 B.S. (1902): 770.

103 Jogesh Chandra Ray, 'Deshe Vijnan-Pratistha', *Prabasi* 15, no. 1, Baisakh 1322 B.S. (1915): 127–41.

104 *Arthik Unnoti* 2, no. 1, Baishak 1334 B.S. (1927): 13.

105 *Calcutta Municipal Gazette* XV, no. 15 (19 March 1932): 698.

106 'The Swadeshi Motor Car', *Calcutta Municipal Gazette* XVI, no. 1 (3 June 1933): 56.

107 *Calcutta Municipal Gazette* XV, no. 24 (21 May 1932): 1078.

108 Ibid.

109 'Swadeshi Motor', *Banik* 7, no. 2, Jaistha 1339 B.S. (1932): 42.

110 Quoted in *Calcutta Municipal Gazette* XVI, no. 6 (18 November 1933): 1105–7.

111 Ghosh, 'Some Eminent Indian Pioneers in the Field of Technology', 72.

112 A routine obituary in the *Calcutta Municipal Gazette* concludes with the comment: 'He was undoubtedly justified in his claim to have been the only Indian manufacturer of a car in this country.' 'Mr. B. B. Das Dead', *Calcutta Municipal Gazette* XIX, no. 7 (9 April 1938): 1107.

113 William Crossgrove, 'The Vernacularization of Science, Medicine, and Technology in Late Medieval Europe: Broadening Our Perspectives', *Early Science and Medicine* 5, no. 1 (2000): 47–63.

114 'Bangalir Abonatir Karan', *Nabyabharat* 12, no. 9, Pous 1301 B.S. (1894): 483 and 491.

115 Pradip Kumar Bose (ed.), 'Introduction', *Health and Society in Bengal* (New Delhi: Sage, 2006), 1.

116 Jawaharlal Dhar, 'Souro-boudyutik Jantra', *Mahajanbandhu* 1, no. 7, Bhadra 1308 B.S. (1901): 261–2.

117 Tarak Nath Mukhopadhyay, 'Bharatiya Shilpa, Krishi O Banijjer Sanrakshan O Unnoti', *Janmabhumi* 14, no. 10, Baishak 1313 B.S. (1906): 365.

118 *Prabasi* 5, no. 10, 1312 B.S. (1905): 608.

119 The journal identified another obstacle – the absence of general scientific temper among the Bengali students. *Prabasi* 6, no. 1, 1313 B.S. (1906): 36–41.

120 Umeshchandra Mitra, 'Engraj Rajatte Bharater Siksha', *Nabyabharat* 21, no. 1, Baishak 1310 B.S. (1903): 45–6.

121 Jogesh Chandra Ray Vidyanidhi, 'Deshiyo Kal', *Prabasi* 11, no. 1, Jaistha 1318 B.S. (1911): 173–5.

122 However, with a note of caution: One Pramathanath Bhattacharya narrated the failure of the *swadeshi* industry. During the time of Swadeshi many people wanted to take the opportunity and launched their own businesses. They did not have any previous experience or training. This newly emerged 'industrialists', without any technological aptitude, became manufacturers. But their dream was distant from reality. Most even failed to manufacture anything and those few who succeeded found it almost impossible to sell their *swadeshi* products in the market. Pramathanath Bhattacharjee, 'Swadeshi Industry', *Bharatbarsha* 2, no. 2, Pous 1321 B.S. (1914): 132.

123 The journal wanted that with those donations the country's leaders should plan to establish commercial museums throughout the country. Industrial products, both foreign and indigenous, along with the relevant technical information could be displayed in those museums. Enterprising Indians could then tally those products and chalk out their future agenda. *Bharatbarsha* 2, no. 1, Bhadra 1321 B.S. (1914): 425.

124 *Bharatbarsha* 9, no. 1, Aswin 1328 B.S. (1921): 465.

125 The journal ridiculed:

> A single laboratory of Germany can incorporate 500 researchers, whereas it is beyond doubt that in the last 50 years Calcutta University produced that many M.A. degree-holders in chemistry! The reason is simple – absence of chemical industry in our country. But the assumption of industry preceding scientific research is also ridiculous.

Ibid., 467.

126 An important dissenting voice came from one of its members, Madan Mohan Malaviya, a leading nationalist. *Report of the Indian Industrial Commission, 1916–18* (Calcutta: Superintendent Government Printing, 1918), 245–300.

127 Srijukta Pashupati Bandopadhyay, 'Iron and Indian Industry', *Janmabhumi* 32, no. 1, Chaitra 1333 B.S. (1926): 29–31.

128 *Bharatbarsha* 6, no. 1, Aswin 1325 B.S. (1918): 477.

129 Ibid., 481.

130 *Bharatbarsha* 6, no. 2, Baishak 1325 B.S. (1918): 657–9.

131 Benoy Kumar Sarkar, 'Coal and Electricity', *Bharatbarsha* 11, no. 1, Agrahayan 1330 B.S. (1923): 886.

132 This was the presidential address of Benoy Kumar Sarkar at the Howrah Teachers' Council Meeting (3 April 1927) and later published in the *Arthik Unnoti* 2, no. 2, Jaistha 1334 B.S. (1927): 108.

133 Benoy Kumar Sarkar, 'Arthik Jeevaner Parer Dhap', *Arthik Unnoti* 2, no. 7, Kartik 1334 B.S. (1927): 545–1.

134 *Arthik Unnoti* 2, no. 12, Chaitra 1334 B.S. (1927): 936–53.

135 *Arthik Unnoti* 3, no. 5, Bhadra 1335 B.S. (1928): 362.

136 Shiv Visvanathan, 'The Dreams of Reason: Rabindranath Tagore and the Invention of Science in India', *Economic and Political Weekly* 48, no. 47 (23 November 2003): 43–9.

137 Rabindranath Thakur, 'Banglar Kal Karkhana', *Banik* 8, no. 9, Pous 1340 B.S. (1933): 277–9.

138 *Bijoli* 1, no. 3 (November 1933): 109.

139 Anupama Debi, 'Nari Jatir Karmadhara', *Bijoli* 1, no. 2 (October 1933): 54. Another similar article was Sucharu Sarkar, 'Bidyutik Shakti O Banglar Nari', *Bijoli* 1, no. 3 (November 1933): 115.

140 *Bijoli* 1, no. 2 (October 1933): 47.

141 Manindra Chandra Basu, 'X-Ray', *Bijoli* 1, no. 4 (December 1933): 169; Manindra Basu in the same issue, 'Telephone' (p. 182); Bankim Chandra Roy in the same issue, 'Bijoli Bati O Rajpathe Tahar Babohar' (p. 190); Surekha Debi, 'Electricity in Agriculture' (p. 151); Bhim Chandra Chattopadhyay, 'Bharate Bidyutik Uniter Uccahar O Tahar Bipod', *Bijoli* 1, no. 7 (March 1934): 272.

142 Aditya Mukherjee, *Imperialism, Nationalism and the Making of the Indian Capitalist Class* (New Delhi: Sage, 2002).

143 Quoted in *BNCCI Annual Report* (Calcutta: BNCC, 1889), 2.

144 Chittabrata Palit, *Growth of Commerce and Industry in Bengal* (Calcutta: BNCCI, 1999).

145 In this context, the then President of the BNCCI, Nalini Ranjan Sarkar, remarked:

> Let us recognise our comparative want of enterprise in commerce and industry; the genius of our people seems to lie in other directions and that is why we may boast of so many distinguished lawyers, doctors, literary men and scientists, and so few first rate commercial men, Sir Rajendra Nath Mookerji for instance....

BNCCI Annual Report, 1931 (Calcutta: BNCC, 1932), 13–16.

146 *BNCCI Annual Report, 1932* (Calcutta: BNCC, 1933), 76.

147 *BNCCI Annual Report, 1933* (Calcutta: BNCC, 1934), 111.

148 *BNCCI Annual Report, 1934* (Calcutta: BNCC, 1935), 86.

149 Ibid., 314–15.

150 *BNCCI Annual Report, 1935* (Calcutta: BNCC, 1936), 135.

151 Ibid., 136.

152 *BNCCI Annual Report*, 1936 (Calcutta: BNCC, 1937), 66–7.

153 *BNCCI Annual Report, 1937* (Calcutta: BNCC, 1938), 78–80 and 524.

154 *BNCCI Annual Report, 1939* (Calcutta: BNCC, 1939), 577–84. When the Government of India set up a Board of Scientific and Industrial Research in early 1940, the BNCCI suggested pursuing rigorous research in the following branches to strengthen the industrial base of India in basic industries: (*a*) essential oils and their derivatives, (*b*) neutral glass, (*c*) oil plastics, (*d*) sulphur, (*e*) dichromate of soda and potash, (*f*) raw materials required by the enamel industry, such as, mild steel, cryolite, fluorspar, and so on, (*g*) manufacture of pipes, (*h*) acetic acid, (*i*) cellulose acetate, and (*j*) industrial carbon, among others. *BNCCI Annual Report, 1940* (Calcutta: BNCC, 1941), 133.

155 *BNCCI Annual Report, 1942* (Calcutta: BNCC, 1943), 93. The problem persisted for another few years. For example, the BNCCI stressed the necessity for supplying diesel oil in large quantities to various electric supply companies, especially in the *mofussil* areas, in order to enable them to generate maximum electrical energy. *BNCCI Annual Report, 1944* (Calcutta: BNCC, 1948), 101.

156 When the Bengal government authorized the electrical undertakings to levy surcharge of up to 25 per cent in the case where diesel oil or steam was used for generation of electricity and up to 15 per cent where hydroelectric power was supplied, the BNCCI supported the move. *BNCCI Annual Report, 1944*, 100.

157 Ibid., 77.

158 *BNCCI Annual Report, 1945* (Calcutta: BNCC, 1949), 83.

159 Ibid., 101.

160 Jagadish N. Sinha, *Science, War and Imperialism* (Leiden and Boston: Brill, 2008), 46.

161 Pratik Chakrabarti, *Western Science in Modern India*, 272.

162 Shiv Visvanathan, *Organizing for Science* (Delhi: Oxford University Press, 1985), 105.

163 Robert S. Anderson, *Nucleus and Nation* (Chicago and London: The University of Chicago Press, 2010), 83.

164 *Science and Culture* IV, no. 3 (September 1938): 137–9.

165 'Electricity – Its Use for the Public and for Industries', *Science and Culture* I, no. 6 (November 1935): 306.

166 'Public Safety of Electricity in India,' *Science and Culture* I, no. 7 (December 1935): 367–71.

167 'Symposium on India's Power Supply', *Science and Culture* III, no. 11 (May 1938): 594–601.

168 'On the National Supply of Electricity', Editorial, *Science and Culture* III, no. 2 (August 1937): 65–8.

169 Time is now past when we should look upon education merely in the abstract or only as a means of imparting culture. The international competition and the struggle for existence have revolutionized our ideas. The educational resources of our country must be harnessed in the cause of its industrial expansion and development.

Science and Culture III, no. 9 (March 1938): 489.

170 'Problem of Industrial Development', *Science and Culture* II, no. 11 (May 1937): 529–31.

171 'Twelve Years of Science and Culture', Editorial, *Science and Culture* XIII, no. 1 (July 1947): 1–2. The journal also announced: '... future belongs to those who know how to use machines as slaves and not ask human and animal muscles to bear the strains which machine can bear.' *Science and Culture* XIII, no. 2 (August 1947): 43.

172 Jagdish N. Sinha, 'Technology for National Reconstruction: The National Planning Committee, 1938–49', in *Technology and the Raj*, ed. Roy Macleod and Deepak Kumar (New Delhi: Sage, 1995), 254.

173 K. T. Shah (ed.), *Power and Fuel* (Bombay: Vora & Co., 1947).

174 K. T. Shah (ed.), *General Education and Technical Education and Development Research* (Bombay: Vora & Co., 1948), 41.

175 Ibid., 141–9.

176 Ibid., 150.

177 Sinha, 'Technology for National Reconstruction', 258.

178 Kumar, *Science and the Raj*, 228–48.

179 *Scientific Education and Research in Relation to National Welfare, Department of Industries and Civil Supplies, Government of India* (New Delhi: The Manager, Government of India Press, 1944), 17–18.

180 Pramod V. Naik, *Meghnad Saha: His Life in Science and Politics* (Dordrecht: Springer, 2017), 121–9.

181 Jayati Bhattacharya, 'Colonial Capital and National Retrieve: Profile of an Entrepreneur', *Indian Historical Review* 35, no. 1 (January 2008): 108–27.

182 Nalini Ranjan Sarkar, *Our Education* (Calcutta: Century Press, 1949), 4.

183 Ibid., 41.

184 Nalini Ranjan Sarkar, *Economic Policy and Programme for Post-War India* (Patna: Patna University, 1945), 64–70.

185 'Mechanised cottage industries using electricity as the source of power and aided by the Government in the technical and marketing sides may lead to mass production by the masses.' Ibid., 72.

186 The Interim Report of the Sarkar Committee submitted in February 1946 said, '... the existing facilities for higher technical education in India are inadequate, both in terms of quantity and quality, to satisfy India's post-war needs of high grade technologists.' *Development of Technical Institutions in India* (Simla: Government of India Press, 1946), 2.

187 The basic undergraduate courses recommended by the Committee for the Eastern or Calcutta Institution: Aeronautical Engineering, Chemical Engineering, Civil and Sanitary Engineering, Electrical Engineering, Mechanical Engineering, Architecture (Building construction and Town Planning), Metallurgy, Botany, Meteorology, Geology or Geophysics, Industrial Administration, Hygiene and Economics, Humanities, Mathematics and Statistics, Chemistry, and Physics. Ibid., 3–7.

188 Benoy Kumar Sarkar, *Education for Industrialization* (Calcutta: Chuckervertty, Chatterjee & Co., 1946), 298–300.

189 *Proceeding of the Second Meeting of the All India Council for Technical Education* (New Delhi: Bureau of Education, 1947), 26.

Conclusion

> We had an interview with Sir R. Mookerjee.... In his opinion the standard of education in mechanical and electrical engineering up to the 'Improver Class' does not need extending, but should be of a very practical nature. He did not think very high training was required as men so trained would not obtain appointments, and he, from a commercial point of view, would much prefer an European to an Indian of similar qualifications when a man with a higher training was wanted.
>
> —E. H. deV. Atkinson and Tom S. Dawson, in a report (1912)[1]

> In engineering colleges, we found that the engineers that the colleges turned out were only operation and maintenance engineers – none of them was an engineer of a higher type who could undertake work of designing except in civil engineering – say of the Damodar Valley or other river valley projects which we are undertaking. We did not find any place where any research work was being done on the production of machinery or other articles which we very badly need for the reconstruction of the country.
>
> —Meghnad Saha during a Lok Sabha debate in 1952[2]

The history of technology in South Asia, as an academic discipline, is witnessing a debate between the significance of 'big' technology (railways, canal irrigation, hydraulic dam, and so on) and 'small everyday technology' (wristwatch, bicycle, sewing machine, and so on) in understanding its appropriation in the Global South. In this methodological deliberation, the former is linked to imperial politics and the latter to everyday life experiences of the people. The narratives of big technologies coincide with subjugation and ultimately the 'tools of empire' thesis, whereas the advocates of 'everyday technology' believe that the small technologies mingled with South Asian culture without much contestation. However, for a better understanding of the subject, we need to accommodate both the extremes. This is relevant to discuss a complex question: What is South Asia in science, technology, and innovation on the one hand, and what are science, technology, and innovation in South Asia on the other?[3] Put another way: Can one see South Asians as intellectuals thinking about and making technology based on intellect?

This book partially aims to unsettle this contrast by presenting a narrative of the technology and industry interface with reference to electricity. Power generation and distribution were organized by big technology and imperial politics, but concurrently infused into and altered several aspects of everyday experiences of ordinary Indians. Eventually, being a crucial factor in the broader developmental discourse, with a larger role in academia and industry linkages, electricity in the early twentieth century cannot be understood as an imperial tool alone. Erudite Indians exercised a good amount of agency over the new knowledge and technology, beyond the command of the state, and expressed a great demand for it, on several occasions even altering the meanings attributed to it by the state.

In recent years, human capital has increasingly been viewed as central to the issues of development. The human capital theory suggests that individuals and society gain significant economic benefits from investments in people: in the sense of the production function, both capital and labour undergo transformation through education and the subsequent skill development.[4] The increase in productivity cannot be explained simply in terms of a rise in effective labour force and capital. Technological change is also crucial. To one scholar, the 'colonial' technical education was 'ad-hoc, half-hearted and incongruent colonial imperatives'.[5] Such an exploitative paradigm is well documented in the literature. It is true that the Raj was not a philanthropic organization – it had definite objectives. Thus, geographical relocation of technology was recurrent on the agenda, not its cultural diffusion. No technological spin-off, in the true sense of the term, was visible at the workshops due to the restricted transfer of technical knowledge. The engineering colleges merely turned out semi-skilled technicians of economical rate to man various government offices. But one interesting feature of the colonial education system, including techno-scientific, was that it did produce political leaders, world-class scientists, entrepreneurs, and technologists, not just clerks or pleaders. No simple model can help us understand why colonial education had the kind of effects it had. Within the limited opportunities created by the Raj, there were several instances where Indian protagonists excelled in the field of technology.

From the beginning, the favourite argument of the British government was that cultural obstacles prevented Indians from learning to operate Western machinery. To colonial administrators, native cultural bias was a useful argument. But despite their cultural ambivalence, many Bengali intellectuals identified Western science and technology as their key to material improvement. Naturally, they sought adequate avenues to master it. Even the so-called conservative peasants were not averse to new techniques and tools. They had no objection to adopting those, provided the new tools brought profits and were within their means. The problem was not cultural stagnation or social conservatism.[6] They rejected only those technologies that were not economically viable for them. This is a question of technological choice. The assumption that the new is clearly superior to what went before, according to David Edgerton, has an important outcome. Failure to move from one to the other is explained by 'conservatism', not by stupidity or straightforward ignorance. The idea of 'resistance' makes sense only if there are no alternatives. To Edgerton, resistance is essential. In selecting one technology, the society or the individual resisted many old and new alternative technologies. In that sense, many technologies failed.[7] This is true for the traditional Indian society as well. Blaming the non-Europeans for their cultural bias against technology was driven by political motives.

The last two decades of the nineteenth century witnessed a sudden demand among the Indian erudite circles for Western techno-scientific knowledge. In Bengal, the only institution that imparted technical education at the collegiate level then was the Bengal Engineering College, Sibpur. To the government, it was enough to cater to the need for technical manpower in eastern India. But their Indian subjects had entirely different arguments. The training in technology at Sibpur was highly elementary in character. The college could admit only 40 students annually and this attracted huge criticism: 'Is that an adequate arrangement for the technical education of a people numbering 70 million?' The impractical stiff system of examinations and stringent rules practised there also attracted widespread condemnation: 'Is the Bengali character or the college rules to blame for the paucity of students in the mining classes?' But race distinction was perhaps the most serious allegation against the Sibpur college – the authorities were soft while handling Eurasian and Anglo-Indian students.[8] Thus, there was no dearth of people to point out the loopholes in the system. Remember the curious case of Bholanath Das (Chapter 5)?

The Sibpur college produced a limited number of industrial entrepreneurs. Most of the graduates preferred government service (employed as subordinates, draughtsmen, or overseers) or private engineering firms. This was the result of faulty curricula. Despite the continuous demand, even from the faculty members, for the introduction of mechanical and electrical engineering, the degree-level course in these two advanced branches was introduced only in the 1930s. Interestingly, one insider linked the tendency to prefer government service over business with the overall degradation in the national character. Lack of entrepreneurship was the most crucial lacuna. The college courses had nothing to do with this. The training was ideal for prospective industrialists. But students only came here when other avenues of employment were already closed to them. The engineering aspirants chose the college for guaranteed employment, mostly in the Public Works Department (PWD); they were not very interested in learning the intricacies of the industry.[9]

The only notable example among the alumni of the Sibpur college who excelled in the field of industry was Sir Rajendra Nath Mookerjee. He believed in friendly cooperation between indigenous and foreign capital, and of an alliance with Western practice in technical matters. He conducted his business at a time when nationalism and *swadeshi* were dominant in Indian minds. But Rajendra Nath had no time for the 'vain prejudices of a narrow-minded *Swadeshi* which mistakenly advocates the exclusion of foreign experts'.[10] Devoid of unnecessary emotions, he wanted to administer Martin & Co. in a practical manner. This is apparent from the report of E. H. deV. Atkinson and Tom S. Dawson (1912) quoted at the beginning of the chapter.

Martin & Co., which emerged from the joint initiative of Rajendra Nath and an Englishman, Acquin Martin, developed into a massive managing agency between 1892 and the mid-1930s. The Bengal Iron & Steel Company (BISCO) and the Indian Iron & Steel Company (IISCO) were under their management. During this period, Martin & Co. had built several feeder railways in India and developed several docks, engineering works, and electric supply companies. Almost all the major waterworks in the country built during the first quarter of the twentieth century were equipped by the firm under the leadership of Rajendra Nath. Several magnificent buildings of Calcutta, including the famous Victoria Memorial, were also built by them. Rajendra Nath opposed the idea of sending young untrained youths to foreign countries for technical training and opined that solutions would come only through the provision of equally good facilities at home. Thus, in 1910, he appealed for the establishment of a Central Technical College in Bengal. To the students of the Sibpur college, he had often given practical advice. Nevertheless, he believed that at that moment, Indians, with their technical capabilities, could handle only the middle and lower levels of engineering work and not the work of the superior cadre.

But everybody was not happy with the rudimentary training in technology. They searched for alternatives. One such instance, Dinanath Sen, Headmaster of the Dacca Normal School, produced a huge plan for an institute of mechanical engineering as early as 1876. He did not want to include civil engineering in the proposed institute because, according to Dinanath, Sibpur then used to provide adequate training on the subject. Despite being a non-specialist, his plan, backed by the Directorate of Public Instruction (DPI), was a unique feat in the list of Indian attainments in modern techno-science. But with the passage of time, Indian intellectuals forgot both Dinanath and his plan.

The search for alternatives grew during the Swadeshi Movement. The intelligentsia came to believe that lack of technical education was a major cause of India's economic backwardness and that the British were deliberately denying technical training to Indians. In 1904, an association was formed at Calcutta for the advancement of techno-scientific education of Indians. It sponsored the scientific training of Indian students in Japan, the United States, and Europe. The very next year, an industrial conference supported by Indian industrialists and the Indian National Congress was held at Banaras. The outcomes of the conference were, among others, the establishment of a national polytechnic institute or at least one technical college in each province.[11] The approach of the educated Bengalis towards modern technology began to change: it became the means to economic emancipation from colonial bondage. The search for substitutes to the colonial policy of governing the empire had to be provided by a different system of education. Thus, the idea of having a system of higher education under a national management and on national lines was spreading. The demand was crystallized in the distressing years following the partition of Bengal, as the National Council of Education (NCE) and subsequently the College of Engineering and Technology (CET) in Jadavpur. While other national schools and colleges, including the Bengal National College and School (BNC) (part of the NCE), collapsed, the technical institute (Bengal Technical Institute, or BTI, and its progeny, the CET) survived. From the beginning at Jadavpur, an advanced level of training was imparted on various latest engineering sciences – mechanical, electrical, and chemical – with an eye on the industry. The graduates of Jadavpur were recognized at the leading universities of the world (Harvard, MIT, and so on) for post-graduate training and research. After the completion of their foreign study, some of them were absorbed by the Jadavpur college itself as faculty members and others started or joined numerous industrial ventures.

Prafulla Chandra Ray was closely associated with the NCE. But he had a different vision of technology and its industrial application altogether. To him, the right place to learn the technical intricacies of an industry was not the classroom, but the industry itself. However, his own industrial initiative seems to have been inspired by his professional training. Having obtained a doctorate degree in chemistry from Edinburgh (1888), he began his career as an assistant professor at the Presidency College, Calcutta. Not content with mere teaching, he decided to manufacture such drugs and pharmaceuticals that required small capital and had a good market. With the help of some friends and associates, he started his venture in 1892 and later developed a small laboratory that transformed within less than a decade into the Bengal Chemical & Pharmaceutical Works Ltd (BCPW). Prafulla Chandra's was one of the successful attempts to develop the chemical industry in India. His BCPW had inaugurated a new trend in the industrial history of the country.

Regardless of social origin and magnitude, the indigenous industrialists had little difference in their approach to technology. They all emulated the Western practices, particularly those prevailing in Great Britain. The 'import-only' tendency not only placed an unnecessary limit on India's choice of technology but also inhibited experimentation and further research. However, on several occasions, the scientists and technologists of the BCPW manufactured intricate machines and tools and tried hard for import substitution. One quick example is the fire extinguisher made by Satishchandra Dasgupta, the factory superintendent (1913). These had great demand during the First World War and the BCPW supplied on an average 500 machines each week to government military stores.

The Bengal Electric Lamp Works (Bengal Lamp), specializing in the production of electric bulbs, was the brainchild of three brothers – Suren, Kiran, and Hemen Roy. Suren was a former student and later professor of electrical engineering at the Jadavpur College. Kiran, also a former student of Jadavpur, earned his graduate degree from the MIT. Returning to India, he joined Bengal Lamp as its Technical Director (1933). Electric bulbs were slowly becoming indispensable to the growing middle class; taking advantage of the situation Kiran Roy and his associates were instrumental in ushering in a new era in the electric-bulb manufacturing industry of the country. Such entrepreneurial ventures required significant insights into the manufacturing process and were launched by professionally trained Bengalis. They were symbolic of how Indians with knowledge of technology and engineering could recognize new opportunities even in unusual fields.

Akhil Gupta argues that, as a latecomer to the development discourse, India can be an example to the rest of the world by experimenting with unlikely ways of using electricity. Since power generation and distribution in India are not controlled by a central grid, and power companies are unable to provide electricity round the clock, there are ample opportunities to take advantage of such disability, by combining wind, solar, biomass, and electric power, to meet society's energy needs. Through better energy management, a high quality of life can be attained using a fraction of the electricity consumed currently, and that can also be India's contribution,

Gupta believes, to the notions of sustainable development.[12] What are the lessons from India's colonial past?

The Government of Bengal constituted a sub-committee under the Bengal Post-War Reconstruction Committee to explore the possibilities of electrical development in Bengal. The following is an extract: '... most of the power supply of the province, whether in industry, in traction, in domestic supply or public illumination, is confined to Calcutta and the neighbouring industrial areas. In the interior of the province, electrical development has been spasmodic and half-hearted....'[13] Hence, the study confines itself within the geographical limit of Calcutta and the adjoining areas. The electrification of Calcutta at the end of the nineteenth century serves as a useful medium for understanding Bengal's quest for modernity. Animesh Chatterjee rightly identifies it as significant to the multifaceted cultural and political manoeuvrings of British colonialism, Indian nationalism, and the emerging identities of the Indian middle class.[14]

Colonel Crompton was one of the pioneers who founded the British electrical industry and hence he was invited by the Government of India to assist them in the electrification process of Calcutta (1896). The Calcutta Electric Supply Corporation (CESC), with headquarters in London, was instrumental in setting up power generation as well as distribution in the city and Crompton was involved in the entire process. The power company intended to use aerial lines (overhead wires) in the streets of Calcutta supported on iron posts. This started off a clamorous debate over electrification among various stakeholders that lasted until the end of the colonial era. Many preferred underground cables due to concerns about citizens' safety. The assumption that a new method is inherently superior to older methods was widespread. Thus, alternating current (AC) was assumed to be superior to direct current (DC) in the so-called power-politics of the city. But the DC system remained in operation in the city along with the new AC system – both had their practical utility.

Although discontent was high among the consumers of the CESC over the rate of electricity, which later became one of the tools in the hands of the Indian nationalists to demand for nationalization of the power sector, this new technology no doubt expanded the industrial sector in Calcutta. One contemporary observed:

> One more advantage which Calcutta possesses in the matter of the leather industry is the fact that electricity can be applied with success and this form of motive power can be generated easily and cheaply. Electric tannage seems to possess a brilliant future before it and will revolutionize the industry to the immense benefit of the public and the nation.[15]

Most of the industrial concerns in and around the city started choosing electricity as their major motive power. To meet the increasing industrial demand for electricity on both sides of the River Hooghly, the CESC built a tunnel under the river to carry cables from one bank to the other. Completed in 1931, this became one of the unique engineering feats colonial Calcutta had ever witnessed. But the general trend with respect to the introduction of electricity and electrical machinery in Indian industries was not so promising. Thus, the promoters of electricity, concerned about creating a constant load, attempted to compensate for the lack of industrial demand through urban (street-lighting) and domestic electrification (fans and light).

A few enterprising Bengalis even tried their hands at the more complex technological systems such as the generation of hydroelectricity. The Shillong Hydro-electric Ltd (Assam) was such an example. Dr Bidhan Chandra Roy, the celebrated Chief Minister of West Bengal, along with his two brothers were associated with the project (1927). Calcutta was the monopoly of the CESC, so several small generation and distribution companies owned and managed by Bengalis started coming up in the *mofussil* towns by the second decade of the twentieth century. The examples of the Chittagong Engineering & Electric Supply Co. Ltd, the Electric Supply Co. of Burdwan, the Shiliguri Electric Supply, and many more establish the fact that there was no dearth of enterprising Indians in the electric power industry. They mostly used oil or steam engine for the generation of electricity.[16]

While the general public initially saw electricity as a mysterious force, a small technical elite emerged that viewed it as an instrument of rationality and economic progress. At the turn of the nineteenth century, this group was drawn from the growing ranks of the new professionals. Several old occupations were being eliminated with the introduction of electricity, and the early twentieth century witnessed several new professions that had scarcely existed during the last two decades of the nineteenth century. While the electrical engineers were central to this group, it also included a considerable number of professors in the applied sciences, as well as entrepreneurs. By the end of our period of study, this newly emerged professional group started establishing organizations and publishing journals, and gradually attained considerable social and economic power and responsibility. Thus, the erudite among the Bengalis started publishing an illustrated monthly journal in Bengali, *Bijoli*, that dealt with electricity (both technical and popular articles), and B. N. Dey, the Chief Engineer of the Calcutta Municipal Corporation, drew up a scheme for the generation of electricity at a much cheaper rate than the CESC. The contemporary journals, particularly *Science and Culture*, continuously advocated for nationalizing the electricity generation and distribution sector during the late years of the Raj. The demand for 'Indianization' germinated with the formation of the National Planning Committee – a joint forum of Indian politicians and specialists. They knew the most about electricity and regarded it as a medium of socio-economic progress. While not a large group, they possessed great prestige based on their practical mastery of the new technologies.

Our study also reveals that Indian attainment in the field of technology was not confined to the so-called educated strata of society alone. Institutional training does not always lead to technological proficiency. So, we have numerous semi-literate or illiterate Viswakarmas with their distinctive accomplishment in techno-science. How many of us know about Goluk Chunder or Shiv Chunder Nundy? Goluk Chunder, a blacksmith of Titagar, built a steam engine as early as 1828. There is every reason to acclaim him as the first Indian engineer. Similarly, the first electrical engineer, Shiv Chunder Nundy, was luckily spotted by W. B. O'Shaughnessy, the then Chemical Examiner of the Calcutta Mint. Nundy became his personal assistant. O'Shaughnessy was instrumental in spreading the electric telegraph network in India. Shiv Chunder was his trusted collaborator in the project. Without any formal training in the science of electricity, Nundy excelled in the field of electric telegraph which was considered high-level technology in those days. One Kalidas Moitra of Serampore wrote in 1855 two separate treatises in Bengali on the electric telegraph and the steam railways, and that too in a technical style. Moitra was the first writer to write in Bengali on the complicated issues of technology.

Another example is that of Sitanath Ghosh of Jessore, who entered the Calcutta Medical College but was unable to complete his study due to illness. He studied electricity privately. Later, he built an air pump and a power loom. But his greatest scientific achievement was the magnetic healer, an instrument for electro-therapy. One Jawaharlal Dhar, a self-made electrician, actively participated in the electric installation project of the Old Howrah Bridge. He was involved in the electrification of the Eden Gardens too. The major invention of this self-styled engineer was the safety-door lock on which he received patent right from the government. He also invented a machine to generate solar electricity. The case of Bepin Behari Das, a self-taught mechanic, was equally interesting. He independently built and designed a motor car for the first time in India (1931) and sold it to the Banaras Hindu University. The Calcutta Corporation entrusted him with the task of building another car. Bepin Behari successfully delivered it to the corporation in 1933 at a much lower price than that of foreign-made cars.

It would be wrong to assume that the few protagonists dealt with here were the only examples of creative talent in the field of technology in Bengal. The 'House of Unknown Fame' is a long list. Each one of them deserves individual attention. But, unfortunately, these 'subaltern technologists' remain hidden and forgotten. Even the contemporary elites of the Bengali society were reluctant to acknowledge them. Except Jogesh Chandra Ray, who himself belonged to that the elite section, others never got their due recognition. In western Europe, the Industrial Revolution saw the rise of the millwright from among the village carpenters, blacksmiths, and wheelwrights. This was the transitional stage from the traditional techniques to modern engineering. How can one forget that James Watt, the inventor of the steam engine, began his career as a self-taught skilled artisan! But technical education did not help Indians as it did their counterparts in western Europe. On the contrary, the system of engineering education created a gulf of difference between the social recognition of the 'subaltern technologists' and the 'trained engineers'. Bepin Behari Das's garage was not very far from Jadavpur. But we do not find any reference of him in the correspondence of the NCE and, subsequently, the CET, Jadavpur. So, there was a delinking of the intellectual cream of society (mind) from the ground-level technicians (hands). The result was obvious – disjunction in knowledge circulation. In the future, India would produce world famous scientists, but not engineer-inventors like James Watt or Thomas Edison. Thus, scholars have been researching on Jagadish Chandra Bose, the great Indian physicist, but they seldom discuss the careers of Putiram, Jamshed, Barik, and Malek, the Indian technicians employed by Bose to build his instruments.

The Indian luminaries did not use the term 'knowledge' very often in the mid-nineteenth century. The term in vogue was 'education'. Education was meant for improvement – both moral and material. Even in the last decade of that century, moral principle was high on the educational agenda. Similarly, they did not use the term 'new' when talking of the techno-scientific knowledge that came as a colonial baggage. On the contrary, they used the term 'Western' or 'European'. When we use such terms, we associate that knowledge with a geo-cultural region. This has a specific implication. But in the twentieth century, 'education' was replaced by 'knowledge', 'improvement' by 'development', and 'Western' by 'new'. The change in nomenclature was visible in the descriptions in the contemporary journals, mostly the vernacular ones. Thus, Benoy Kumar Sarkar asked for a 'new kind of knowledge' for rapid industrialization – knowledge about machine, market, and so on.[17]

The erudite Indian elites identified technological training as the mandatory condition to fulfil their dream – industrialization and the subsequent development of the economy. The new buzzwords in the development discourse were planning, institutionalization, and industrialization. The academia–industry coordination was crucial to Indian intellectuals and planners. Sir Asutosh Mukherjee, Vice-Chancellor of the University of Calcutta, remarked during his convocation address (1922):

> Industry and education will march forward, more and more, hand in hand, for this is pre-eminently a time to awaken industry and education alike. Industry in its many-sided interests will look to education for enlightenment and support, and out of the laboratories of the university will emanate in an ever-increasing measure the influences that make for economic and industrial improvement and contribute to the betterment of human living and to the good of mankind.[18]

A comprehensive initiative was taken by Meghnad Saha and the *Science and Culture* group. Saha was a firm believer in industrial progress through careful and deliberate planning backed by scientific research. The members of the newly emerged scientific community, supported by the political leadership, articulated independent India's industrial research plan. The British model was inadequate; the Indians luminaries drew inspiration from the USSR, the USA, Germany, and Japan. Saha envisaged a project on the lines of the Tennessee Valley Authority (USA) for the Damodar valley in western Bengal and similar 'multi-purpose' developments elsewhere along India's major rivers.[19] Electric power generating stations (hydroelectric) had been planned along with the dams. This ultimately led to the creation of India's first river valley project – the Damodar Valley Corporation (DVC) – in 1949.

To another visionary, Nalini Ranjan Sarkar, industrialization of the country was needed, no doubt, and it was demanded by Indians, too; but in view of India's actual requirements and future goals, the exercise should have focused on promoting modern-type cottage industries run by electricity. So, there were differences of opinion among the Indian intellectuals. Apart from the conventional distinction between pure and applied science, the distinction between big and small technologies, and large-scale and cottage industries also loomed large in the development discourse. But by the middle of the twentieth century a sense of technological modernity had emerged in India. Although inclined to blaming the colonial connection for overall disorders, the Indian men of science and their political allies were ready to believe that modern techno-science, rightly applied, could rapidly transform India's future.

A committee was appointed with Nalini Ranjan Sarkar as chairman (1945) to advise on higher technical education, which ultimately led to the foundation of the four Indian Institutes of Technology (IITs) after independence. Technology did not automatically flow from science. What had to be created was an institutional structure that facilitated this transition. Instead of science and technology being opposites, one confined to the university and the other to the factory, there was the need for a proper dialogue between them. The concept of the IIT was meant to increase the probability of scientific ideas being transformed into technological products. The bottom line was the application of a scientific method to the manufacture of technology. Syama Prasad Mookerjee, son of Sir Asutosh Mookerjee, and the Vice-Chancellor of the University of Calcutta between 1934 and 1938, remarked just after independence:

> The provision of technical education in order to train the necessary technical and managerial personnel is one of the fundamental conditions of economic progress. Even the advanced countries of the world with ample facilities for technical education already in existence are making renewed endeavours to enlarge these facilities. The Sarkar Committee, which was appointed to report on the establishment of technical institutions, tartly pointed out that facilities for education in this country are so meagre and insufficient to meet even the existing demand that the establishment of a few technical institutions even before detailed survey is completed can never be regarded as leading to a surfeit of such facilities.[20]

The future organization of technology and the infrastructure envisaged under the reconstruction programme, such as the IITs (a replica of MIT), were not only inspired by the Western models but were also intrinsically dependent on the West for their realization in practical terms.[21] Import of technology into India did not mean import of both expertise and production capabilities. It was mainly the import of hardware in the form of machines, but not the technical expertise so that Indians could be technologically proficient. The traditional indigenous knowledge and technical skills did not find any place in the reconstruction programme. One of the limitations of the traditional knowledge activities of India was the politics of caste. It affected both the generation and the dissemination of knowledge. Indian luminaries such as Prafulla Chandra Ray and Pramatha Nath Bose bemoaned it. Ordinary people like artisans, blacksmiths, carpenters, and so on, were pushed to the margins of society, while the educated elites started cultivating only contemplative knowledge. This caused a separation between mind and hands, which led to a disjunction between scientific ideas and its technological translations. In the wake of independence, while drawing the future road map, Indians planners committed the same mistake. No significant effort was made to identify and harness indigenous knowledge of technology. Instead, the charm for everything 'Western' restricted our choice of technology. This was not only denying a nation its past achievements but also overlooking its immediate needs. The problem continues even now. Our engineers hardly visit the workshops. Our mechanical or electrical engineers, even from the prestigious IITs, turn up as executives in multinational companies, even banks![22] After receiving world-class engineering education from elite institutes like the IITs at a subsidized rate, our engineers prefer to move away from their disciplines. This is a serious concern, and recently one observer remarked:

> Why are the IITs in trouble? They have been unable to replace the superior quality faculty who were first attracted, as several generations have retired. Inadequate funding, much greater opportunities in the private sector, and some deterioration at the IITs themselves have made them less attractive. At present, a significant percentage of academic posts remain vacant because appropriate candidates could not be found.... India's premier institutes of technology are losing their academic edge because of unplanned expansion and excessive politics.[23]

This is one of the contradictions of our own time. *Let There Be Light* is about understanding our culture – more precisely, the acculturation of modern technology. Its diagnosis and remedy may be found in multiple experiences of technological modernity that surfaced in early twentieth-century Bengal.

Notes

1 E. H. deV. Atkinson and Tom S. Dawson, *Report on the Enquiry to Bring Technical Institutions into Closer Touch and More Practical Relations with the Employers of Labour in India* (Calcutta: Superintendent Government Printing, 1912), 21.

2 Quoted in Santimoy Chatterjee and Jyotirmoy Gupta (eds), *Meghnad Saha in Parliament* (Calcutta: The Asiatic Society, 1993), 8.

3 The concept has been borrowed from Clapperton Mavhunga (ed.), *What Do Science, Technology, and Innovation Mean from Africa* (Cambridge, Massachusetts, and London: The MIT Press, 2017).

4 Saumen Chattopadhyay, *Education and Economics* (New Delhi: Oxford University Press, 2012), 23.

5 Deepak Kumar, 'Technology, Education and Colonialism in British India 1830s–1880s', in *The Transfer of Science and Technology between Europe and Asia*, ed. Y. Keiji (Kyoto: International Research Centre for Japanese Studies, 1993), 184.

6 S. Bhattacharya, 'Cultural Constraints on Technological Innovation and Economic Development: Some Case Studies', *Indian Economic and Social History Review* 3, no. 3 (September 1966): 240–67. A recent example is Deepak Kumar and Bipasha Raha (eds), *Tilling the Land* (New Delhi: Primus, 2016).

7 David Edgerton, *The Shock of the Old* (London: Profile Books, 2008), 9.

8 *Sanjivani*, 22 June 1899; *Report of the Native News Papers Bengal*, January–December 1899, 455–6.

9 *Sibpur College Patrika* 1, no 2, Phalgun 1314 B.S. (1907): 25–9.

10 K. C. Mahindra, *Sir Rajendra Nath Mookerjee* (Calcutta: Martin & Burn Ltd, 1933), 166.

11 *The First Industrial Conference: Full Text of the Papers Held at and Submitted to the Industrial Conference Held at Benaras in December, 1905* (Benaras: Industrial Conference, 1905).

12 Akhil Gupta, 'An Anthropology of Electricity from the Global South', *Cultural Anthropology* 30, no. 4 (November 2015): 555–68.

13 *Plans for a Better Bengal* (Alipore: Superintending Government Press, 1944), 36.

14 Animesh Chatterjee, '"New Wine in New Bottles": Class Politics and the "Uneven Electrification of Colonial India', *History of Retailing and Consumption* 4, no. 1 (2018): 97.

15 B. Ramachandra Rau, *The Economics of Leather Industry* (Calcutta: Calcutta University Press, 1925), 75. Rau was a lecturer in economics and commerce at the University of Calcutta.

16 *Arthik Unnoti* 3, no. 3, Aswar 1335 (1928): 218–21. See also *Calcutta Municipal Gazette* XXIX, no. 20 (15 April 1939): 811.

17 *Arthik Unnoti* 2, no. 2, Jaistha 1334 B.S. (1927): 108.

18 *The Calcutta Review* I, no. 1 (July–September 1969, New Series): 14.

19 M. N. Saha and K. Ray, 'Planning for the Damodar Valley', *Science and Culture* X, no. 1 (July 1944): 17–20.

20 Speech delivered at the annual function of the Science and Technology Association of the Delhi Polytechnic on 2 March 1949; Anirban Ganguly and Avadhesh Kumar Singh (eds), *Syama Prasad Mookerjee: His Vision of Education* (New Delhi: Wisdom Tree, 2017), 146–47.

21 Dhruv Raina, 'Engineering Science Education and the Indian Institutes of Technology: Reframing the Context of the Cold War and Science (1950–1970)', *Contemporary Education Dialogue* 14, no. 1 (January 2017): 49–70.

22 Deepak Kumar has recently criticized them as techno-coolies. Historicizing the context, he argues: In the eighteenth century the highest value-added product was sugar. Indians knew how to grow sugarcane and they were bodily lifted from their villages and brought to distant lands (Fiji, Trinidad, or Mauritius) to work as labourers. Today young Indians have wonderful degrees from IITs. They know how to develop a new commodity – software. In the twenty-first century software replaces sugar! They are modern coolies, 'techno or cyber-coolies'. The only difference between them and their predecessors is that the employers do not have to uproot the young engineers to America or Europe, but sitting in Bangalore, they can serve their masters. Kumar asks: is this knowledge-economy, or knowledge-society? Deepak Kumar, *The Trishanku Nation* (New Delhi: Oxford University Press, 2016), 190.

23 Philip G. Altbach, 'Getting the IITs Back on Top', *The Hindu*, 22 October 2013, 7.

Bibliography

The archival documents preserved at the National Archives of India (NAI), New Delhi, and the West Bengal State Archives (WBSA), Kolkata, are most rewarding. Earlier studies on technical knowledge in the colonial context highlighted mostly its exploitative character, which is, no doubt, true. However, a closer examination of the archival sources helps us to understand the inner contradictions within the colonial bureaucracy. Several among them wanted to raise the standard of teaching at the Sibpur Engineering College without success. I enjoyed working at the IIEST, Sibpur. Although they now have a multi-storeyed library and a rich collection of latest books and journals, I found one room (locked from outside) very fascinating – it was stocked with old documents of the nineteenth and twentieth centuries. This was real treasure, but in a very bad shape. Hari Prasad Sharma, the then Deputy Librarian, kindly arranged my access there. The rare works division of the Main Library, Jadavpur University, is doing very well under the supervision of Debashish Mukherjee. They have preserved the annual reports, calendar, and prospectus of the National Council of Education (NCE) along with several other rare documents. Similarly, when I was probing the history of electrification, Ananda Bhattacharya, Sarmistha De, and Bidisha Chakraborty of the WBSA informed me about the Miscellaneous Public Improvement Branch (MPI) of the Public Works Department (PWD) series. These sources are helpful in reconstructing the early events related to the electrification of Calcutta. Mani Shankar Mukherjee (celebrated Bengali author 'Sankar'), Chief Advisor, Corporate Relations, Calcutta Electric Supply Corporation (CESC), enlightened me on the life and works of Swami Vivekananda, including his fascination with electricity and things electrical, over several cups of excellent Darjeeling tea, at the Victoria House. Pradeep Gooptu (former Head, Corporate Communications, CESC) not only helped but also shared his personal collection with me. Professor Samir Kumar Saha kindly explained the evolution of the Heat Power Laboratory, Mechanical Engineering Department (Jadavpur University), during the 1930s and 1940s, in a popular style to a technologically challenged person like me. Amit Chaudhuri, by profession an engineer and an amateur historian, drew my attention towards the autobiography (published from Bankura) of Jogesh Chandra Ray Vidyanidhi. An octogenarian of Barrackpore, who used to work at Martin & Burn Ltd, shared with me several old documents of the company from his personal collection at a very nominal rate! It was impossible for me to do justice on the entrepreneurial skills of Sir R. N. Mookerjee without this favour.

During the second half of the nineteenth century and the early twentieth century, numerous pamphlets, tracts, periodicals, and journals were published in Bengali. They provide first-hand information about the assimilation of modern technological knowledge in a traditional society. Not only that, to know more about the unnoticed and unsung Viswakarmas, one needs to explore these Indian language sources in great detail. Many characters, without formal training in engineering, appear as what may be considered 'subaltern technologists', as they excelled in the field of technology in some way or the other. However, I could not gather their biographical details, and this remains a lacuna in my study. This is also a homage to Siddhartha Ghosh who originally started the project in early 1990, but was unable to finish it due to his sad demise. I consulted the Bengali sources mostly at the Bangiya Sahitya Parishad library and the Centre for Studies in Social Sciences, Calcutta (Hitesranjan Sanyal Memorial Collection). They deserve more attention than they have received so far from the historians of science and technology.

A short stint in the UK (Summer 2017) was useful. I have tried to supplement official and vernacular documents with private papers that are so well preserved at the British Library, the Institution of Engineering and Technology Archives (both in London), and the Centre of South Asian Studies, University of Cambridge (Cambridge), among others. The private papers and correspondences of the European bureaucrats and engineers who lived and worked in India can provide information from the horse's mouth on various technological projects starting from the telegraph and the railways to electricity. I am grateful to the Charles Wallace (India) Trust (CWIT) and the Indian Council of Historical Research (ICHR), New Delhi, for two separate grants that enabled the visit.

Adopting this framework, similar studies can be done in other parts of India too. For example, one may like to investigate on the theme: electrification in the Bombay Presidency, history of the Victoria Jubilee Technical Institute (1887), and the subsequent industrialization of the province.

Primary Sources

Archival Documents

National Archives of India, New Delhi

Proceedings of the Education and Health Department.
Proceedings of the Education Department.
Proceedings of the Home Department.
Proceedings of the Public Works Department.

West Bengal State Archives, Kolkata

Miscellaneous Public Improvement Branch of the Public Works Department.
Proceedings of the General Department; Education Branch and Medical Branch.
Proceedings of the Municipal Department.

Jadavpur University Library (Rare Division), Kolkata

Annual reports of the National Council of Education, 1907–1947.

College of Engineering and Technology, Bengal, Prospectus Session, 1930–1945.

The National Council of Education, Bengal, Calendar, 1906–1908.

Bengal National Chamber of Commerce and Industry, Kolkata

Annual Reports of the Bengal National Chamber of Commerce and Industry, 1898–1947.

Kolkata Improvement Trust, Kolkata

Annual Reports of the Calcutta Improvement Trust, 1910–1945.

Office of the Registrar of Companies, Kolkata

Declaration of Registration of Company (Bengal Electric Lamp Works), 1932.

Prospectus of the Bengal Electric Lamp Works, for the years 1932, 1934, and 1941.

Institution of Engineering and Technology Archives, London

Colonel REB Crompton and India Collection.

Meares, John Willoughby. 'At the Heels of the Mighty: Being the Autobiography of "Your Obedient Humble Servant"' (typescript).

India Office Records, Asia, Pacific and Africa Collection, British Library, London

Bernard Papers, MSS.Eur.C26111.

Calcutta Electric Supply Corporation Ltd: Proposed New Issue of Sterling Capital, Jul 1948–Apr 1950 (L/E/8/7067).

Minutes of the Governor's London Committee and Other Papers on the Distribution of Essential Civil Services in Burma Including Electricity, MSS Eur F145/22: March–June 1945.

Nationalization of Electricity Undertakings in the Central Provinces, Nov 1949 (L/E/8/7699).

Typescript Copy of the Memoirs of the Major-General Sir George Kenneth Scott-Moncrieff, Royal Engineers (1876–1924), MSS.Eur.C.259.

Centre of South Asian Studies, University of Cambridge, Cambridge

Johnston Papers, *Reminiscences of India*, 1915–46, Box 1.

Uhl River Hydro Electric Undertakings, Hunt, G. H., Box 1.

Official Reports and Publications

American Technical Mission to India, A Survey of India's Industrial Production for War Purposes: Report of the American Technical Mission. Simla: Government of India Publication, 1942.

Atkinson, E. H., and Tom S. Dawson. *Report on the Enquiry to Bring Technical Institutes into Closer Touch and More Practical Relations with the Employers of Labour in India*. Calcutta: Superintendent Government Printing, 1912.

Buck, E. C. *Report on Practical and Technical Education*. Calcutta: Government Printing, 1901.

Calcutta University Commission Report 1917–19, Vol. III. Calcutta: University of Calcutta, 1919.

Collin, E. W. *Report of the Existing Arts and Industries in Bengal*. Calcutta: Bengal Secretariat Press, 1890.

Cumming, J. C. *Review of the Industrial Position and Prospects in Bengal in 1908 with Special Reference to the Industrial Survey of 1890* (Part II of Special Report). Calcutta: Office of the Superintendent Government Printing, 1908.

———. *Technical and Industrial Instruction in Bengal, 1888–1908* (Part I of Special Report). Calcutta: Office of the Superintendent Government Printing, 1908.

Development of Technical Institutions in India (Interim Report of Sarkar Committee). Simla: Government of India Press, February 1946.

First Quinquennial Review of Education in Bengal, 1892–96. Calcutta: Government Printing, 1902.

General Report Public Instruction in Bengal. Calcutta: Bengal Secretariat Press, 1885–1946.

Gupta, G. N. *A Survey of the Industries and Resources of Eastern Bengal and Assam for 1907–08*. Shillong: Government Printing, 1908.

Hill, A. V. *Scientific Research in India*. Simla: Government of India Press, 1944.

India in 1929–30: A Statement for Presentation to Parliament in Accordance with the Requirements of the 26th Section of the Government of India Act (5 & 6 Geo. V, Chapter 61). Calcutta: Government of India Central Publication Branch, 1931.

Indian Industrial Commission, Minutes of Evidence 1916–17, Vol. II. Bengal & Central Provinces. Calcutta: Superintendent Government Printing, 1918.

Indian Industrial Commission: Inspection Notes 1916–18 (Confidential). Calcutta: Superintendent Government Printing, 1918.

Indian Railways Administration Report, 1913–14. New Delhi: Government Publication, 1914.

Indian Tariff Board: Evidence Recorded during an Enquiry on Heavy Chemical Industry, Vol. I. Calcutta: Government of India Central Publication Branch, 1930.

New Bridge between Calcutta and Howrah, Appendix to the Report on the Committee of Engineers, February 1922, Vol. II. Calcutta: Bengal Secretariat Book Depot, 1922.

Papers Relating to Technical Education in India, 1886–1904. Calcutta: Government Printing, 1906.

Plans for a Better Bengal: Progress of Post-War Reconstruction Planning in Bengal from 1st January 1944 till 31st October 1944. Alipore: Superintendent Government Press, 1944.

Post-War Educational Development in India: Report by the Central Advisory Board of Education. Delhi: Manager of Publications, January 1944.

Proceeding of the Second Meeting of the All India Council for Technical Education. New Delhi: Bureau of Education, 1947.

Proceedings and Report of the Committee Approved to Advise on the Creation of a Technical Institute for Calcutta and Allied Subjects. Calcutta: Bengal Secretariat Book Depot, 1912.

Quinquennial Review on the Progress of Education in India, 1897–1902, Vol. I. Calcutta: Government Press, 1904.

Report of the Indian Famine Commission. London: George Edward Eyre and William Spottiswoode, 1880.

Report of the Indian Fiscal Commission, 1921–22. Simla: Superintendent, Government Central Press, 1922.

Report of the Indian Industrial Commission 1916–18. Calcutta: Superintendent Government Printing, 1918.

Report of the Indian Mercantile Marine Committee, 1923–24. Delhi: Government Publication, 1924.

Report of the Indian Statutory Commission, Vol. III. Calcutta: Majesty's Stationary Office, 1930.

Report of the Indian Tariff Board on the Machine Tools Industry. Delhi: Government Central Press, 1947.

Report of the Industrial Research Planning Committee. New Delhi: Council of Scientific and Industrial Research, 1945.

Report on the Bengal Engineering College for the Quinquennium 1917–18 to 1921–22. Calcutta: Bengal Secretariat Book Depot, 1922.

Reports on Native Newspapers in Bengal, 1880–1930. National Archives of India, New Delhi.

Roy, A. K. *A Short History of Calcutta, Census of India, 1901*, Vol. VII, Part I. Calcutta: Bengal Secretariat Press, 1902.

Schwendler, Louis. *Report on the Electric Light at the East India Rly Coys Station*. Howrah (Calcutta), 1881.

Scientific Education and Research in Relation to National Welfare, Department of Industries and Civil Supplies, Government of India. New Delhi: The Manager, Government of India Press, 1944.

Spring, Francis J. *Technical Education in Bengal*. Calcutta: W. Newman and Co., 1886.

———. *Technical Education in India*. Calcutta: W. Newman and Co., 1887.

The Bally–Utterpara Electric License, 1920. Calcutta: The Bengal Secretariat Book Depot, 1920.

The Indian Electricity Act, 1910. Calcutta: Superintendent Government Printing, 1922.

Watson, E. R. *A Monograph on Iron and Steel Work in the Province of Bengal*. Calcutta: Government Publication, 1907.

Newspapers and Periodicals

Bengali

Arthik Unnoti
Anandabazar Patrika
Banik
Bharatbarsha
Bharati
Bijoli
Education Gazette O Saptahik Bartabaho
Janmabhumi
Jugantar Patrika
Mahajan Bandhu
Masik Basumati
Nabyabharat
Prabasi
Sadharani
Sahitya
Sahitya Parishad Patrika
Shibpur College Patrika
Sulav Samachar
Tattobodhini Patrika

English

Advance Therapy
Advance
Amrita Bazar Patrika

Calcutta Municipal Gazette
Calcutta Review
Commercial Gazette
The Dawn and Dawn Society's Magazine
Hindusthan Standard
Hindu Patriot
The Hindu
Industrial India
Journal of the College of Engineering and Technology
Science and Culture
The Statesman

Contemporary Tracts and Publications

All India Industrial and Commercial Directory, 1938–39. Bombay, 1938.

Atkinson, E. H. 'Note on Thomason College'. *Educational Conference in Allahabad in February 1911*.

Bagal, Jogesh Chandra. *Jatiyatar Nabamantra O Hindu Melar Itibritta*. Calcutta: Salil Kumar Mitra, 1945.

BCPW Annual Report, 1939. Calcutta: BCPW, 1939.

BCPW Price List of Printing Ink. Calcutta: BCPW, 1946.

Bengal Engineering College, Calendar for 1940–41. No pub., not dated.

Bose, P. N. *A History of Hindu Civilization during British Rule*, Vol. I: *Religious Condition*. Calcutta: W. Newman & Co., 1894.

———. *A History of Hindu Civilization during British Rule*, Vol. II: *Socio-religious and Industrial Conditions*. Calcutta: W. Newman & Co., 1896.

———. *A History of Hindu Civilization during British Rule*, Vol. III: *Intellectual Condition*. Calcutta: W. Newman & Co., 1896.

———. *Essays and Lectures on the Industrial Development of India*. Calcutta: Newman & Co., 1906.

———. *National Education and Modern Progress*. Calcutta: Kar, Majumder & Co., 1921.

———. 'Notes on the Geology and Mineral Resources of Mayurbhanj'. *Records of Geological Survey of India* XXXI, part III (1904).

———. *The Illusions of New India*. Calcutta: W. Newman & Co., 1916.

Calcutta Exhibition: Official Hand-book & Guide. Calcutta, 1923.

Cooper, A. T. 'Recent Electrical Progress in India', *Journal of the Royal Society of Arts* 77, no. 3994 (June 1929): 739-65.

Cotton, H. E. A. *Calcutta Old and New: Historical and Descriptive Handbook to the City*. Calcutta: W. Newman & Co., 1907.

Crompton, R. E. *Reminiscences*. London: Constable & Co. Ltd, 1928.

Deshiyo Oushad. Calcutta: BCPW, 1934.

Directory of Technical Institutions in India Including Agricultural, Industrial, Technical, Commercial and Science School and Colleges (The Indian Industrial Conference). Allahabad: Standard Press, 1909.

Ghosh, Surendranath. 'The Electrification of the Tata Iron Works at Jamshedpur'. *The Calcutta Review*, (June 1924): 496–518. http://www.southasiaarchive.com/Content/sarf.120137/211256/010 (accessed on 22 January 2018).

Hay, Alfred. 'Industrial Development and Electric Power Transmission'. Paper presented at the 5th Indian Industrial Conference held at Lahore on 30 December 1909. Government of India, 1910.

History of Calcutta Electric Supply Corporation Limited (1897–1912). London: Salisbury House, November 1913.

Home, Amal, ed. *The Imperial Silver Jubilee Commemoration Volume, Souvenir Number of Calcutta Municipal Gazette*. Calcutta: Calcutta Municipal Corporation, 1935.

Mahalanobis, P. C. 'Sir Rajendra Nath Mookerjee: First President of the Indian Statistical Institute 1931–1936'. *Sankhya: The Indian Journal of Statistics* 2, no. 3 (1936): 237–9.

Mahaluxmivala, Pestonji D. *History of the Bombay Electric Supply and Tramway Company Limited, 1905–1935*. Bombay: Electric Supply & Tramway Company, 1936.

Maharajadhiraja Bahadur of Burdwan. *The Indian Horizon*. London: Ernest Benn Ltd, 1932.

Mahindra, K. C. *Sir Rajendra Nath Mookerjee: A Personal Study*. Calcutta: Martin & Burn Ltd., 1933.

Majumdar, Satyabrata. 'Television', *Journal of College of Engineering and Technology* 8, no. 1 (September 1936): 37.

Meares, J. W. *Electric Traction: Six Lectures Delivered in March 1902 at the Civil Engineering College, Sibpur*. Calcutta: Bengal Secretariat Press, 1902.

———. *The Law Relating to Electrical Energy in India and Burma: Being the Indian Electricity Act, 1910, Act IX of 1910*, Sixth Edition. Calcutta: Thacker, Spink & Co., 1941.

———. *Water Power: Its Estimates and Development with Particular Reference to India. Practical Treaties for Civil and Electrical Engineers*. Calcutta: Thacker, Spink & Co., 1935.

Minutes of the Meeting of Directors, Bengal Chemicals and Pharmaceutical Works Ltd, 1939 and 1940.

Moitra, Kalidas. *Baspiya Kal o Bharatiya Railway: The Steam Engine and the East Indian Railway Containing a History of India*. Serampore: J. H. Peters, 1855.

———. *Electric Telegraph ba Taritbartabaha Prakaran*. Serampore: J. H. Peters, 1855.

———. *Manabdehotatwa or the Human Frame: An Easy and Familiar Introduction to the Principles of Anatomy and Physiology*. Serampore: J. H. Peters, 1855.

Mookerjee, Sir Rajendra Nath. 'Presidential Address, Eighth Indian Science Congress, Calcutta, January 1921'. Unpublished monograph, Indian Science Congress Association, Kolkata.

Mukherjee, Radhakumud. 'The Exhibition at the Bengal National College'. *The Dawn and Dawn Society's Magazine* 4, no. 4 (February 1908, New Series): 96–8.

O'Shaughnessy, W. B. *Notes on Natural Philosophy, First Series on Galvanic Electricity*. Calcutta: The Baptist Mission Press, 1841.

Rau, B. Ramachandra. *The Economics of Leather Industry*. Calcutta: Calcutta University Press, 1925.

Ray, P. C. *A History of Hindu Chemistry: From the Earliest Times to the Middle of the 16th Century A.D.*, Vol. I. Calcutta: Chuckervertty, Chatterjee & Co. and Kegan Paul, 1902.

———. 'Bengalis in Commerce and Industry'. *Career Lectures: Organised by the Appointments and Information Board*. Calcutta: University of Calcutta, 1939.

———. *Essays and Discourses*. Madras: G. A. Natesan, 1918.

———. *Life and Experiences of a Bengali Chemist*, Vol. I. Calcutta: Chuckervertty, Chatterjee & Co. Ltd, 1932.

———. 'Presidential Address'. *Proceedings of the Seventh Indian Science Congress, January 12–17, 1920*. Nagpur: Indian Science Congress Association, 1920.

Report of the Committee of the Bengal Chamber of Commerce for the Year 1940. Calcutta: Thomas S. Smith, City Press, 1941.

Saha, M. N., and K. Ray. 'Planning for the Damodar Valley'. *Science and Culture* X, no. 1 (July 1944): 17–20.

Sarkar, Benoy Kumar. *Education for Industrialization: An Analysis of Forty Years of Jadavpur College of Engineering and Technology, 1905–45*. Calcutta: Chuckervertty, Chatterjee & Co., 1946.

———. *India's Advances in Industrialism: During the Period of the Depression*. Calcutta: N. M. Ray-Chowdhury and Co., 1936.

Sarkar, Nalini Ranjan. *Economic Policy and Programme for Post-War India*. Patna: Patna University, 1945.

———. *Our Education*. Calcutta: Century Press, 1949.

Schwendler, Louis. 'Precis of Report on Electric Light Experiments'. *Proceedings of the Journal of the Asiatic Society of Bengal* (March 1879): 80–2.

Sen, Dinanath. *A Scheme for the School of Industry or Practical Science Proposed to Be Established in Calcutta, from Funds Raised by The Indian League, with Government Aid: Drawn Up, by Order of the Director of Public Instruction*. Calcutta: Minerva Press, 1876.

Sengupta, Nirmal K. 'What Is Electricity'. *Journal of the College of Engineering and Technology* 9, no. 2 (December 1937): 121.

Shah, K. T., ed. *General Education and Technical Education & Development Research* (NPC Series). Bombay: Vora & Co., 1948.

———, ed. *Industries Connected with Scientific Instruments & Engineering Industries* (NPC Series). Bombay: Vora & Co., 1947.

———, ed. *Manufacturing Industries* (NPC Series). Bombay: Vora & Co., 1947.

———, ed. *Power and Fuel* (NPC Series). Bombay: Vora & Co., 1947.

———, ed. *Report: National Planning Committee*. Bombay: Vora & Co., 1949.

Smith, George. *The Life of William Carey: Shoe-Maker and Missionary*. Calcutta: Everyman's Library, 1885.

Strange, William. *Indian Engineering: Relating to Irrigation, Water Supply of Towns, Roads and Buildings*. London: George Routledge and Sons, 1923.

Thakur, Khitindranath. *Kolikatar Chala-phera (Sekale Ar Kale)*. Calcutta: Adi Brahma Samaj, 1337 B.S. (1930).

The All-India Manufacturers' Organization: Rapid Development of Indian Industries. Bombay, 1947.

The Calcutta Port Trust: A Brief History of Fifty Years Work, 1870–1920. Calcutta: Thacker, Shink & Co., 1920.

The First Industrial Conference: Full Text of the Papers Held at and Submitted to the Industrial Conference Held at Benaras in December, 1905. Benaras: Industrial Conference, 1905.

Secondary Sources

Articles

Anderson, Warwick. 'Remembering the Spread of Western Science'. *Historical Records of Australian Science* 29, no. 2 (2018): 73–81.

———. 'Where Every Prospect Pleases and Only Man Is Vile: Laboratory Medicine As Colonial Discourse'. *Critical Inquiry* 18, no. 3 (Spring: 1992): 506–29.

Arnold, David. 'Europe, Technology and Colonialism in the 20th Century'. *History and Technology: An International Journal* 21, no. 1 (March 2005): 85–106.

Arnold, David, and Erich Dewald. 'Cycles of Empowerment? The Bicycle and Everyday Technology in Colonial India and Vietnam'. *Comparative Studies in Society and History* 53, no. 4 (2011): 971–96.

———. 'Everyday Technology in South and Southeast Asia: An Introduction'. *Modern Asian Studies* 46, no. 1 (2012): 1–17.

Banerjee, Sumantra. 'Hundred Years of Electricity in Calcutta'. *Indian Journal of Power and River Valley Development* 52, nos 7 and 8 (2002): 119–25.

Basalla, George. 'The Spread of Western Science'. *Science* 156, no. 37 (May 1967): 611–22.

Bassett, Ross. 'Aligning India in the Cold War Era: Indian Technical Elites, the Indian Institute of Technology at Kanpur, and Computing in India and the United States'. *Technology and Culture* 50, no. 4 (2009): 783–810.

———. 'MIT-Trained Swadeshis: MIT and Indian Nationalism, 1880–1947'. *Osiris* 24, no. 1 (2009): 212–30.

Bhattacharya, Jayati. 'Colonial Capital and National Retrieve: Profile of an Entrepreneur'. *Indian Historical Review* 35, no. 1 (January 2008): 108–27.

Bhattacharya, S. 'Cultural Constraints on Technological Innovation and Economic Development: Some Case Studies'. *Indian Economic and Social History Review* 3, no. 3 (September 1966): 240–67.

Black, John. 'The Military Influence on Engineering Education in Britain and India, 1848–1906'. *Indian Economic and Social History Review* 46, no. 2 (April–June 2009): 211–39.

Canaparo, Claudio. 'Science and Empire: The Geo-Epistemic Location of Knowledge'. In *History and Philosophy of Science and Technology*, Vol. 4, edited by Pablo Lorenzano, Hans-Jörg Rheinberger, Eduardo Ortiz, and Carlos Delfino Galles, 21–31. Oxford: EOLSS and UNESCO, 2010.

Chakrabarti, Pratik. 'Science and Swadeshi: The Establishment and Growth of the Bengal Chemical and Pharmaceutical Works, 1938–1947'. In *Science and Modern India: An Institutional History, c. 1784–1947*, edited by Uma Das Gupta, 117–42. New Delhi: Pearson Longman, 2011.

———. 'Science in India in the Twentieth Century'. In *Science, Technology, Imperialism and War*, edited by Jyoti Bhusan Das Gupta, 121–73. New Delhi: Pearson Longman, 2007.

Chakrabarty, Dipesh. 'The Muddle of Modernity'. *The American Historical Review* 116, no. 3 (June 2011): 663–75.

Chambers, David, and Richard Gillespie. 'Locality in the History of Science: Colonial Science, Techno-science, and Indigenous Knowledge'. *Osiris*, 2nd Series 15 (2000): 221–40.

Chandavarkar, Rajnarayan. 'Industrialization in India before 1947: Conventional Approaches and Alternative Perspectives'. *Modern Asian Studies* 19, no. 3 (April 1984): 623–68.

Chatterjee, Animesh. '"New Wine in New Bottles": Class Politics and the "Uneven Electrification of Colonial India"'. *History of Retailing and Consumption* 4, no. 1 (2018): 94–108.

Chatterjee, Elizabeth. 'The Limits of Liberalization: The Power Sector'. In *Political Economy of Contemporary India*, edited by R. Nagraj and Sripad Motiram, 52–74. New Delhi: Cambridge University Press, 2017.

Chatzis, Konstantinos. 'Introduction: The National Identities of Engineers'. *History and Technology* 23, no. 3 (September 2007): 193–6.

Choi, Hyungsub. 'The Social Construction of Imported Technologies: Reflections on the Social History of Technology in Modern Korea'. *Technology and Culture* 58, no. 4 (October 2017): 905–20.

Crossgrove, William. 'The Vernacularization of Science, Medicine, and Technology in Late Medieval Europe: Broadening Our Perspectives'. *Early Science and Medicine* 5, no. 1 (2000): 47–63.

Darbyshire, Ian. 'The Building of India's Railways: The Application of Western Technology in the Colonial Periphery 1850–1920'. In *Technology and the Raj*, edited by Roy Macleod and Deepak Kumar, 177–215. New Delhi: Sage, 1995.

Dhar, Bidisha. 'Technical Education Discourse in India: State and the Artisans, 1880s–1914'. *Studies in History* 33, no. 2 (August 2017): 213–33.

Dionne, Russel, and Roy Macleod. 'Science and Policy in British India, 1858–1914: Perspectives on a Persisting Belief'. *Proceedings of the Sixth European Conference on Modern South Asian Studies* (CNRS, Paris, 1979): 55–68.

Edgerton, David. 'Innovation, Technology and History: What Is the Historiography of Technology About?' *Technology and Culture* 51, no. 3 (July 2010): 680–97.

Ghosh, Amitabha. 'Some Eminent Pioneers in the Field of Technology'. *Indian Journal of History of Science* 29, no. 1 (1994): 63–75.

Goswami, Manu. 'From Swadeshi to Swaraj: Nation, Economy, Territory in Colonial South Asia, 1870–1907'. *Comparative Studies in Society and History* 40, no. 4 (1998): 609–37.

Gupta, Akhil. 'An Anthropology of Electricity from the Global South'. *Cultural Anthropology* 30, no. 4 (November 2015): 555–68.

Harrison, Carol E., and Ann Johnson. 'Introduction: Science and National Identity'. *Osiris* 24, no. 1 (2009): 1–14.

Harrison, Mark. 'Science and the British Empire'. *Isis* 96, no. 1 (March 2005): 56–63.

Hughes, Thomas P. 'Emerging Themes in the History of Technology'. *Technology and Culture* 20, no. 4 (October 1979): 697–711.

Hussain, Nazia. 'The City of Dacca, 1921–1947: Society, Water and Electricity'. In *The City in South Asia*, edited by Kenneth Ballhatchet and John Harrison, 197–223. London and Dublin: Curzon Press, 1980.

Inkster, Ian. 'Prometheus Bound: Technology and Industrialization in Japan, China and India Prior to 1914—A Political Economy Approach'. *Annals of Science* 45, no. 4 (July 1988): 399–426.

———. 'Scientific Enterprise and the Colonial "Model": Observation on Australian Experience in Historical Context'. *Social Studies of Science* 15, no. 4 (November 1985): 677–704.

Jain, Sarandha. 'Oil and the Everyday in Colonial and Independent India (1880–1975)'. Occasional Paper, New Series 61, Nehru Memorial Museum and Library, 2015, 1–17.

Kale, Sunila S. 'Structures of Power: Electrification in Colonial India'. *Comparative Studies of South Asia, Africa and the Middle East* 34, no. 3 (2014): 454–75.

Kapila, Shruti. 'The Enchantment of Science in India'. *Isis* 101, no. 1 (March 2010): 120–32.

Kranzberg, Melvin. 'Technology and History: "Kranzberg's Laws"'. *Presidential Address*, SHOT, Henry Ford Museum, Dearborn, Michigan (19 October 1985): 1–12.

Krishna, V. V. 'Science, Technology, Innovation Policy 2013: High on Goals, Low on Commitment'. *Economic and Political Weekly* 48, no. 16 (20 April 2013): 15–19.

Kumar, Arun. 'Bengal Engineering College (Sibpur): A Study in Historical Perspective'. In *Science and Environment*, edited by Chittabrata Palit and Arun Kumar, 1–23. Delhi: B. R. Publishing Corporation, 2013.

Kumar, Deepak. 'New Knowledge and New India: Lessons from the Colonial Past'. In *Education in Colonial India: Historical Insights*, edited by Deepak Kumar, Joseph Bara, Nandita Khadria, and Ch. Radha Gayathri, 45–61. New Delhi: Manohar, 2013.

———. 'Racial Discrimination and Science in Nineteenth Century India'. *Indian Economic and Social History Review* 19, no. 1 (January 1982): 63–82.

———. 'Tagore's Pedagogy and Rural Reconstruction'. In *Shantiniketan- Hellerau: New Education in the Pedagogic Provinces of India and Germany*, edited by Michael Mann, 309–30. Heidelberg: Draupadi Verlag, 2015.

———. 'Technology, Education and Colonialism in British India 1830s–1880s'. In *The Transfer of Science and Technology between Europe and Asia, 1780–1880*, edited by Y. Keiji, 183–96. Kyoto: International Research Centre for Japanese Studies, 1993.

Lundgreen, Peter. 'Engineering Education in Europe and the USA, 1750–1930: The Rise to Dominance of School Culture and the Engineering Profession'. *Annals of Science* 47, no. 1 (1990): 49–51.

Macleod, Roy. 'On Visiting the "Moving Metropolis": Reflections on the Architecture of Imperial Science'. *Historical Records in Australian Science* 5, no. 3 (1982): 1–16.

Mallick, Sambit. 'Democratizing Scientific Knowledge through Building Scientific Institutions in Nineteenth Century India: The Sociology of Science Perspectives'. *Current Science* 90, no. 8 (April 2006): 1138–45.

Manjapra, Kris. 'Knowledgeable Internationalism and the Swadeshi Movement, 1903–1921'. *Economic and Political Weekly* 47, no. 42 (October, 2012): 53–62.

Marsden, Ben. 'Engineering Science in Glasgow: Economy, Efficiency and Measurement as Prime Movers in the Differentiation of an Academic Discipline'. *British Journal for the History of Science* 25, no. 3 (September 1992): 319–46.

Morris, Morris D. 'The Growth of Large-Scale Industry to 1947'. In *The Cambridge Economic History of India* II, edited by Dharma Kumar, 553–676. Cambridge: Cambridge University Press, 1982.

Muraleedharan, V. R. 'The Electrification of Madras City 1905 to 1914'. Paper presented at the Third World Economic History and Development Conference, University of Manchester, 13–15 September 1991, 1–17.

Nair, P. Thankappan. 'Civic and Public services in Old Calcutta' in *The Living City* I, edited by Sukanta Chaudhury, 230–8. Calcutta: Oxford University Press, 1990.

Nathan, Dev, and Abhishek Kumar. 'Knowledge, Education and Labour Practices in India'. *Economic and Political Weekly* 51, no. 36 (September 2016): 37–45.

Nye, David E. 'How Does One Do the History of Technology?' Plenary Lecture, SHOT, Dearborn, Michigan, 6 November 2014, 1–9.

Okamoto, Takuji. 'Reorganization, Deregulation, and Liberalization: Postwar Development of the Japanese Electric Power Industry and Its Change after 11 March 2011'. *Technology and Culture* 58, no. 1 (January 2017): 182–93.

Palit Chittabrata. 'The National Council of Education and Its Progeny: The College of Engineering and Technology, 1906–47'. In *Science and Modern India: An Institutional History, c. 1784–1947*, edited by Uma Das Gupta, 849–70. New Delhi: Pearson Longman, 2011.

Pannabecker, John R. 'For a History of Technology Education: Contexts, Systems, and Narratives'. *Journal of Technology Education* 7, no. 1 (Fall 1995): 43–56.

Raina, Dhruv, and S. Irfan Habib. 'South and South-East Asia: Introduction'. In *History of Humanity: Scientific and Cultural Development*, Vol. VII, *The Twentieth Century*, edited by Sarvepalli Gopal and Sergei Tikhvinsky, 722–4. UNESCO: Routledge, 2008.

Raina, Dhruv. 'Engineering Science Education and the Indian Institutes of Technology: Reframing the Context of the 'Cold War and Science (1950–1970)'. *Contemporary Education Dialogue* 14, no. 1 (January 2017): 49–70.

———. 'Institutions and Knowledge: Framing the Translation of Science in Colonial South Asia'. *Asiatische Studien Ètudes Asiatiques* 65, no. 4 (2011): 945–68.

———. 'Situating the History of Technology in a Philosophical Triptych: Contours of Future Research'. International Centre for Theoretical Physics, Internal Report, IC/93/88 (May 1993): 1–20.

Raj, Kapil. 'Beyond Postcolonialism and Postpositivism: Circulation and the Global History of Science'. *Isis* 104, no. 2 (June 2013): 337–47.

Rao, Srinivasa, and John Lourdusamy, 'Colonialism and the Development of Electricity: The Case of Madras Presidency, 1900–47'. *Science, Technology and Society* 15, no. 1 (2010): 27–54.

Rao, Y. Srinivasa. 'Electricity, Politics and Regional Economic Imbalance in Madras Presidency, 1900–1947'. *Economic and Political Weekly* 45, no. 23 (June 2010): 59–66.

Roberts, Lissa. 'Situating Science in Global History: Local Exchanges and Networks of Circulation'. *Itinerario* 33, no. 1 (March 2009): 9–30.

Roy, Tirthankar. 'Where is Bengal? Situating an Indian Region in the Early Modern World Economy'. *Past and Present* 213, no. 1 (November 2011): 115–46.

Rurup, Reinhard. 'Historians and Modern Technology: Reflections on the Development and Current Problems of the History of Technology'. *Technology and Culture* 15, no. 2 (April 1974): 187–98.

Russell, Andrew, and Lee Vinsel, 'Hail the Maintainers'. *Aeon* (7 April 2016), https://aeon.co/essays/innovation-is-overvalued-maintenance-often-matters-more (accessed on 12 July 2018).

Sarkar, Smritikumar. 'Social Organization of Artisan Production in India: Changing Role of the Market, Technology, and Merchant-Creditor, 18th to 20th Centuries'. In *Economic History of India from Eighteenth to Twentieth Centuries*, edited by Binay Bhusan Chaudhuri, 107–354. New Delhi: Pearson Longman, 2005.

Sarkar, Suvobrata. 'Domesticating Electric Power: Growth of Industry, Utilities and Research in Colonial Calcutta'. *Indian Economic and Social History Review* 52, no. 3 (July–September 2015): 357–89.

———. 'In Pursuit of *Laxmi*: Entrepreneurship, Industry and Technology'. *Archiv orientální: Journal of African and Asian Studies* 82, no. 2 (2014): 263–95.

———. 'The Electrification of Colonial Calcutta: Role of the Innovators, Bureaucrats and Foreign Business Organization, 1880–1940'. *Studies in History* 34, no. 1 (February 2018): 48–76.

Secord, James A. 'Knowledge in Transit'. *Isis* 95, no. 4 (December 2004): 654–72.

Sen, S. N. 'Technological Education in India: 1884–1914'. In *Technological Education-Technological Style*, edited by Melvin Kranzberg, 91–9. San Francisco: San Francisco Press, 1986.

Shamir, Ronen. 'Electricity and Empire in 1920s Palestine under British Rule'. *NTM Journal of the History of Science, Technology & Medicine* 24, no. 4 (2016): 451–80.

Siddiqi, Asif A. 'Introduction: Technology in the South Asian imaginary'. *History and Technology* 31, no. 4 (2015): 341–9.

Sinha, Jagdish N. 'Science and Globalization: Indian Experience in the Second World War'. *Indian Historical Review* 33, no. 2 (July 2006): 134–60.

Staudenmaier, John M. 'Recent Trends in the History of Technology'. *American Historical Review* 95, no. 3 (June 1990): 715–25.

Subrahmanyam, Sanjay. 'One Asia, or Many? Reflections from Connected History'. *Modern Asian Studies* 50, no. 1 (January 2016): 5–43.

Tirupati, Devanath. 'Role of Technological Innovations for Competitiveness and Entrepreneurship'. *Journal of Entrepreneurship* 17, no. 2 (2008): 103–15.

Tomlinson, B. R. 'Colonial Constructs and Technical Education in India, 1880–1914'. Paper presented at the 20th Conference of International Association of

Historians of Asia, Jawaharlal Nehru University, New Delhi, 14–17 November 2008, 1–24.

Tripathi, Dwijendra. 'Colonialism and Technology Choices in India: A Historical Overview'. *The Developing Economics* 34, no. 1 (March 1996): 80–97.

Visvanathan, Shiv. 'The Dreams of Reason: Rabindranath Tagore and the Invention of Science in India'. *Economic and Political Weekly* 48, no. 47 (23 November, 2003): 43–9.

MPhil. Dissertations/PhD Theses

Alexander, Daniel Edward. 'The Development of Engineering Education in the United States', PhD thesis, Washington State University, 1977.

Bangaru, Saroj. 'Debates in Technical Education: A Prelude to the Foundation of the Indian Institutes of Technology'. MPhil. dissertation, Jawaharlal Nehru University, New Delhi, 2004.

Chattopadhyay, Subhayu. 'Pramatha Nath Bose (1855–1934) and Indian Geology'. PhD thesis, Jadavpur University, Kolkata, 2008.

Majumdar, Madhumita. 'Science and the Nationalist Agenda in Bengal – 1904–1947'. PhD thesis, University of Calcutta, 2004.

Ramnath, Aparajith. 'Engineers in India: Industrialisation, Indianisation and the State, 1900–47'. PhD thesis, Centre for the History of Science, Technology and Medicine, Imperial College, London, 2012.

Rao, Y. Srinivasa. 'Electrification of Madras Presidency, 1900–1947'. PhD thesis, IIT Madras, 2007.

Roy, Anuradha. 'Growth and Development of the Chemical Industry in Bengal 1900–47'. PhD thesis, Jadavpur University, Kolkata, 1994.

Sarkar (née Mitter), Sarmila. 'The Urbanization of Calcutta in the Nineteenth Century: A Case Study of City-Lighting'. MPhil dissertation, Jadavpur University, 1991.

Sarkar, Poulami. 'Towards Swadeshi Technology: A Comprehensive Study between the Bengal Engineering College (Sibpur) and the Bengal Technical Institute (Jadavpur), 1843–1947'. MPhil dissertation, Jadavpur University, 2000.

Books

1899–1999: A Century of Power to Calcutta, the Living City, A CESC Release.

Acharya Prafulla Chandra Ray Birth Centenary Volume. Calcutta: University of Calcutta, 1962.

Adas, Michael. *Machines as the Measure of Men: Science, Technology and Ideologies of Western Dominance*. Ithaca: Cornell University Press, 1989.

Anderson, Robert S. *Nucleus and Nation: Scientists, International Networks and Power in India*. Chicago and London: The University of Chicago Press, 2010.

Armytage, W. H. G. *A Social History of Engineering*. Cambridge and Massachusetts: The MIT Press, 1961.

Arnold, David. *Everyday Technology: Machines and the Making of India's Modernity*. Chicago and London, University of Chicago Press, 2013.

———. *The New Cambridge History of India, Vol. III: 5, Science, Technology and Medicine in Colonial India*. Cambridge: Cambridge University Press, 2000.

Baber, Zaheer. *The Science of Empire: Scientific Knowledge, Civilization and Colonial Rule in India*. Delhi: Oxford University Press, 1998.

Bag, A. K., Arnab Rai Choudhuri, and Deepak Kumar, eds. *Emergence of Modern Science in Colonial India*. New Delhi: INSA, 2018.

Bagal, J. C. *Pramatha Nath Bose*. Calcutta: P. N. Bose Centenary Committee, 1955.

Bagchi, Amiya Kumar. *Private Investment in India 1900–1939*. Cambridge: Cambridge University Press, 1972.

Bandopadhyay, Sekhar. *From Plassey to Partition: A History of Modern India*. New Delhi: Orient Blackswan, reprint, 2010.

Basalla, George. *The Evolution of Technology*. Cambridge: Cambridge University Press, 1988.

Bassett, Ross. *The Technological Indian*. Cambridge, Massachusetts, and London: Harvard University Press, 2016.

Basu, Aparna. *Essays in the History of Indian Education*. New Delhi: Concept, 1982.

———. *The Growth of Education and Political Development in India, 1898–1920*. Delhi: Oxford University Press, 1974.

Bengal Engineering College Centenary Souvenir. Calcutta, 1956.

Bernal, J. D. *Science in History*. London: Watts, 2nd edn, 1957.

Bhargava, K. D., ed. *Selections from Educational Records of the Government of India*, Vol. IV. Delhi: NAI, 1968.

Bharucha, Naushir. *The Indian Electricity Act, 1910*. Bombay: Bombay Presidency Association, 1967.

Bhattacharya, Amit. *Business, Politics and Technology*. Kolkata: Readers Service, 2005.

———. *Swadeshi Enterprise in Bengal 1921–47*. Kolkata: Setu Prakashan, 1995.

———. *Swadeshi Enterprise in Bengal: The First Phase 1880–1920*. Kolkata: Readers Service, Second Edition, 2008.

Bhattacharya, Anil, ed. *Acharya Prafulla Chandra Ray: A Collection of Writings*, Vol. II A. Kolkata: University of Calcutta, 2009.

Bhattacharya, Sabyasachi. *The Defining Moments in Bengal 1920–1947*. New Delhi: Oxford University Press, 2014.

Bhattacharya, Sabyasachi, and Pietro Redondi, eds. *Techniques to Technology: A French Historiography of Technology*. New Delhi: Orient Longman, 1990.

Bijker, Wiebe E., and John Law, eds. *Shaping Technology/ Building Societies: Studies in Socio-technical Change*. Cambridge, MA: MIT Press, 1992.

Bijker, Wiebe E., Thomas P. Hughes, and Trevor J. Pinch, eds. *The Social Construction of Technological Systems: New Directions in the Sociology and History of Technology*. Massachusetts: MIT Press, 1987.

Bloch, Marc. *The Historians Craft*. Manchester: Manchester University Press, 1963.

Boff, Richard B. Du. *Electric Power in American Manufacturing, 1889–1958*. New York: Arno Press, 1979.

Bose, Pradip Kumar, ed. *Health and Society in Bengal: A Selection from the Late 19th Century Bengali Periodicals*. New Delhi: Sage, 2006.

Bose, Sisir Kumar, and Sugata Bose, eds. *Netaji Collected Works: Congress President Speeches, Articles and Letters*, Vol. 9. Delhi: Oxford University Press, 1995.

Bulletin Bengal Engineering College: One Hundred Twenty Fifth Anniversary Issue, 1981.

Cardwell, D. S. L. *Technology, Science and History*. London: Heinemann, 1972.

Chakrabarti, Pratik. *Western Science in Modern India: Metropolitan Methods, Colonial Practices*. Ranikhet: Permanent Black, paperback edn, 2011.

Chakrabarty, Dipesh. *Provincializing Europe: Post-colonial Thought and Historical Difference*. Princeton and Oxford: Princeton University Press, 2000.

Chandra, Bipan. *Essays on Colonialism*. New Delhi: Orient Longman, 1999.

———. *The Rise and Growth of Economic Nationalism in India*. New Delhi: Anamika, rev. and abridged edn, 2004.

Chatterjee, Chhanda, ed. *Literature as History: From Early to Contemporary Times*. New Delhi: Primus, 2014.

Chatterjee, Santimoy, and Jyotirmoy Gupta, eds. *Meghnad Saha in Parliament*. Calcutta: The Asiatic Society, 1993.

Chattopadhyay, Arabinda. *Jogesh Chandra Ray Vidyanidhi*. Kolkata: Bangiya Sahitya Parishad, 2009.

Chattopadhyay, Saumen. *Education and Economics: Disciplinary Evolution and Policy Discourse*. New Delhi: Oxford University Press, 2012.

Chowdhury, Indira. *Growing the Tree of Science: Homi Bhabha and the Tata Institute of Fundamental Science*. New Delhi: Oxford University Press, 2016.

Chronology of Important Events. Calcutta: BCPW, not dated.

Cohn, Julie A. *The Grid: Biography of an American Technology*. Cambridge, MA: MIT Press, 2017.

Coleman, Leo. *Electrification as Political Rituals in New Delhi: A Moral Technology*. New Delhi: Speaking Tiger, 2017.

Coopersmith, Jonathan. *The Electrification of Russia, 1880–1926*. Ithaca and London: Cornell University Press, 1992.

Cowan, Ruth Schwartz. *A Social History of American Technology*. New York and Oxford: Oxford University Press, 1997.

Das Gupta, Anil Chandra, ed. *The Days of the John Company: Selections from Calcutta Gazette 1824–1832*. Calcutta: West Bengal Government Press, 1959.

Dasgupta, Arunabha. *Colonel Crompton's India*. Bombay: Tata Press, 1990.

Dasgupta, Subrata. *Jagadish Chandra Bose and the Indian Response to Western Science*, Ranikhet: Permanent Black, paperback edn, 2009.

———. *The Bengal Renaissance: Identity and Creativity from Rammohun Roy to Rabindranath Tagore*. Ranikhet: Permanent Black, paperback edn, 2010.

Datta, Mahendra Nath. *Londone Swami Bibekananda*, Vol. 2. Kolkata: The Mahendra Publishing Committee, 7th edn, 2013.

Datta, Partho. *Planning the City: Urbanization and Reform in Calcutta c. 1800–c. 1940*. New Delhi: Tulika, 2012.

De Sousa, J. P. *History of the Chemical Industry in India*. Bombay: Technical Press Club, 1961.

Debi, Purnima. *Sri Gaganendranath Thakur*. Kolkata: Sahitya Bharati, 2012.

Deshpande, G. P. *The World of Ideas in Modern Marathi: Phule, Vinoba, Savarkar*. New Delhi: Tulika, 2009.

Dhar, Jawaharlal. *Sachitra Kolikata-Rahasya*. Kolkata: Paraspathar, reprint, 2012 [1896].

Doren, Charles Van. *A History of Knowledge: The Pivotal Events, People, and Achievements of World History*. New York: Ballantine Books, 1992.

Dubash, Navroz K., Sunila S. Kale, and Ranjit Bharvirkar, eds. *Mapping Power: The Political Economy of Electricity in India's States*. New Delhi: Oxford University Press, 2018.

Dunsheath, Percy. *A History of Electrical Engineering*. London: Faber and Faber, 1962.

Edgerton, David. *The Shock of the Old: Technology and Global History since 1900*. London: Profile, 2008.

Etzkowitz, Henry, ed. *The Triple Helix: University-Industry-Government Innovation in Action*. New York and London: Routledge, 2008.

Etzkowitz, Henry, Andrew Webster, and Peter Healey, eds. *Capitalizing Knowledge: New Intersections of Industry and Academia*. Albany: State University of New York Press, 1998.

Fara, Patricia. *An Entertainment for Angels: Electricity in the Enlightenment*. Cambridge: Icon Books, 2003.

Ferguson, Niall. *Empire: The Rise and Demise of the British World Order and the Lessons for Global Power*. New York: Basic Books, 2003.

Fifty Years of Bengal Chemical, 1901–1951. Calcutta: BCPW Ltd, not dated.

Forbes, Geraldine. *Positivism in Bengal: Transmission and Assimilation of an Ideology*. Calcutta: Papyrus, rev. edn, 1999.

Fox, Robert, ed. *Technological Change: Methods and Themes in the History of Technology*. Amsterdam: Harwood Academic Publisher, 1996.

Fox, Robert, and Anne Guagnini, eds. *Education, Technology and Industrial Performance in Europe, 1850–1939*. Cambridge: Cambridge University Press, 1993.

Gadgil, D. R. *The Industrial Evolution of India in Recent Times 1860–1939*. New Delhi: Oxford University Press, reprint, 1979.

Gangopadhyay, Sunil. *Pratham Alo*, Vol. I and II. Kolkata: Ananda, 1997.

Ganguly, Arindam, and Avadhesh Kumar Singh, eds. *Syama Prasad Mookerjee: His Vision of Education*. New Delhi: Wisdom Tree, 2017.

Ghosh, Deb Kumar (compiled). *Sir Rajendra Nath Mookerjee: A Pen Portrayal*. Calcutta: The Institution of Engineers (India), 1984.

Ghosh, Parimal. *Colonialism, Class and a History of the Calcutta Jute Millhands, 1880–1930*. Hyderabad: Orient Longman, 2000.

Ghosh, Sidhartha. *Kaler Sahar Kolkata*. Kolkata: Ananda, 1991.

———. *Karigari Kalpana O Bangali Udyog*. Kolkata: Dey's Publishing, 1988.

Goel, R. C. *Mapping Technovation through Multi-Goal Synthesis*. Calcutta: First Indian Engineering Congress, 1987.

Gooday, Graeme. *Domesticating Electricity: Technology, Uncertainty and Gender, 1880–1914*. London: Pickering and Chatto, 2008.

Goode, S. W. *Municipal Calcutta: Its Institutions in their Origin and Growth*. New Delhi: Macmillan, Reprint Edition, 2005 [1916].

Gunergun, Feza, and Dhruv Raina, eds. *Science between Europe and Asia: Historical Studies on the Transmission, Adoption and Adaptation of Knowledge*. Dordrecht and Heidelberg: Springer, 2011.

Guyol, N. B. *The World Electric Power Industry*. Berkeley and Los Angeles: University of California Press, 1969.

Habib, S. Irfan, and Dhruv Raina, eds. *Social History of Science in Colonial India*. New Delhi: Oxford University Press, 2007.

Hannah, Leslie. *Electricity before Nationalisation: A Study of the Development of Electric Supply Industry in Britain to 1948*. Baltimore: The Johns Hopkins University Press, 1979.

Hardiman, David, and Projit Bihari Mukharji, eds. *Medical Marginality in South Asia: Situating Subaltern Therapeutics*. London and New York: Routledge, 2012.

Harris, Frank. *Jamsetji Nusserwanji Tata: A Chronicle of His Life*. Bombay: Blackie & Son, Second Edition, 1958.

Hausman, J., Peter Hertner, and Mira Wilkins. *Global Electrification: Multinational Enterprise and International Finance in the History of Light and Power, 1878–2007*. Cambridge: Cambridge University Press, 2011.

Headrick, Daniel R. *The Tentacles of Progress: Technology Transfer in the Age of Imperialism, 1850–1940*. New York: Oxford University Press, 1988.

———. *Tools of Empire: Technology and European Imperialism in the Nineteenth Century*. New York: Oxford University Press, 1981.

Hughes, Thomas P. *Networks of Power: Electrification in Western Society, 1880–1930*. Baltimore and London: Johns Hopkins University Press, 1983.

———. *Rescuing Prometheus: Four Monumental Projects That Changed the Modern World*. New York: Vintage Books, 1998.

Iftikhar-ul-Awwal, A. Z. M. *The Industrial Development of Bengal 1900–1939*. New Delhi: Vikas Publishing, 1982.

Inkster, Ian. *Science and Technology in History: An Approach to Industrial Development*. London: Palgrave Macmillan, 1991.

Joshi, Sanjay, ed. *The Middle Class in Colonial India*. New Delhi: Oxford University Press, 2010.

Kale, Sunila. *Electrifying India: Regional Political Economic of Development*. Stanford and California: Stanford University Press, 2014.

Kapila, Shruti, ed. *An Intellectual History for India*. Delhi: Cambridge University Press, 2010.

Kling, Blair B. *Partner in Empire: Dwarkanath Tagore and the Age of Enterprise in Eastern India*. Berkeley: University of California Press, 1976.

Kohli, Atul. *State-directed Development: Political Power and Industrialization in the Global Periphery*. Cambridge: Cambridge University Press, 2004.

Kranzberg, Melvin, ed. *Technological Education—Technological Style*. San Francisco: San Francisco Press, 1986.

Kumar, Deepak, ed. *Science and Empire: Essays in Indian Context*. Delhi: Anamika Prakashan, 1991.

———. *Science and the Raj: A Study of British India*. New Delhi: Oxford University Press, 2nd edn, 2006.

———. *The Trishanku Nation: Memory, Self and Society in Contemporary India*. New Delhi: Oxford University Press, 2016.

Kumar, Deepak, and Bipasha Raha, eds. *Tilling the Land: Agricultural Knowledge and Practices in Colonial India*. New Delhi: Primus, 2016.

Kumar, Deepak, Joseph Bara, Nandita Khadria, and Ch. Radha Gayathri, eds. *Education in Colonial India: Historical Insights*. New Delhi: Manohar, 2013.

Kumar, Prakash. *Indigo Plantations and Science in Colonial India*. New Delhi: Cambridge University Press, 2012.

Lahiri Choudhury, Deep Kanta. *Telegraphic Imperialism: Crisis and Panic in the Indian Empire, c. 1830–1920*. Basingstoke: Palgrave Macmillan, 2010.

Landes, David S. *The Unbound Prometheus: Technological Change and Industrial Development in Western Europe from 1750 to the Present*. Cambridge: Cambridge University Press, Second Edition, 2003.

Lourdusamy, J. *Science and National Consciousness in Bengal: 1870–1930*. New Delhi: Orient Longman, 2004.

Macleod, Roy, and Deepak Kumar, eds. *Technology and the Raj: Western Technology and Technical Transfers to India 1700–1947*. New Delhi: Sage, 1995.

Mann, Michael. *South Asia's Modern History: Thematic Perspectives*. London and New York: Routledge, 2015.

Martin Burn Limited, Calcutta: Company Publication, not dated.

Martin Burn Ltd. Calcutta: Martin Burn House, not dated.

Mavhunga, Clapperton, ed. *What Do Science, Technology, and Innovation Mean from Africa*. Cambridge, Massachusetts, and London: The MIT Press, 2017.

McNeil, Ian, ed. *An Encyclopedia of the History of Technology*. London and New York: Routledge, 1990.

Mital, K. V. *History of the Thomason College of Engineering (1847–1949)*. Roorkee: The University of Roorkee, 1986.

Mukherjee, Aditya. *Imperialism, Nationalism and the Making of the Indian Capitalist Class, 1920–1947*. New Delhi: Sage, 2002.

Mukherjee, Amitabha. *Fifty Years of National Education*. Calcutta: NCE, Bengal, 1992.

Mukherjee, Haridas, and Uma Mukherjee. *The Origins of the National Education Movement*. Calcutta: NCE, Bengal, Second Revised Edition, 2000.

Mukherjee, N. (compiled). *A Collection of Addresses and Speeches by Sir Rajendra Nath Mookerjee*, Calcutta: The Art Press, not dated.

Mukherji, Projit Bihari. *Doctoring Traditions: Ayurveda, Small Technologies, and Braided Sciences*. Chicago and London: The University of Chicago Press, 2016.

Mukhopadhyay, Troilokkyanath. *Damru-Charit*. Kolkata: New Age Publisher Pvt. Ltd, Fifth Edition, 2009 [1923].

Naik, Pramod V. *Meghnad Saha: His Life in Science and Politics*. Dordrecht: Springer, 2017.

Nair, P. Thankappan. *Calcutta Municipal Corporation: At a Glance*. Calcutta: The Calcutta Municipal Corporation, 1989.

Nandy, Ashis. *A Very Popular Exile*. New Delhi: Oxford University Press, 2010.

Nandy, H., ed. *IEI Marches On*. Kolkata: Institution of Engineers (India), 2002.

National Council of Education, Bengal: A History and Homage. Jadavpur: Jadavpur University, 1956.

Nye, David E. *Electrifying America: Social Meanings of a New Technology, 1880–1940*. Cambridge: The MIT Press, 1990.

Otsuka, K., G. Ranis, and G. Saxonhouse. *Comparative Technology Choice in Development: The Indian and Japanese Cotton Textile Industries*. New York: Basil Blackwell, 1988.

Pacey, Arnold. *Technology in World Civilization: A Thousand-Year History*. Cambridge and Massachusetts: The MIT Press, 1990.

Palit, Chittabrata, and Subrata Pahari. *Satis Chandra Mukherjee, the Dawn Society and National Science*. Kolkata: Readers Service, 2002.

Palit, Chittabrata. *Growth of Commerce and Industry in Bengal*. Calcutta: BNCCI, 1999.

———. *Science and Nationalism in Bengal (1876–1947)*. Kolkata: Institute of Historical Studies, 2nd edn, 2016.

———. *Scientific Bengal: Science, Technology, Medicine and Environment under the Raj*. Delhi: Kalpaz, 2006.

Phalkey, Jahnavi. *Atomic State: Big Science in Twentieth Century India*. Ranikhet: Permanent Black, 2013.

Prakash, Gyan. *Another Reason: Science and the Imagination of Modern India*. New Delhi: Oxford University Press, 2000.

Prasad, Ritika. *Tracks of Change: Railways and Everyday Life in Colonial India*. New Delhi: Cambridge University Press, 2015.

Raha, Bipasha. *Living a Dream: Rabindranath Tagore and Rural Resuscitation*. New Delhi: Manohar, 2014.

———. *The Plough and the Pen: Peasantry, Agriculture and the Literati in Colonial Bengal*. New Delhi: Manohar, 2012.

Rahman, Abdur. *Intellectual Colonisation: Science and Technology in West–East Relations*. Delhi: Vikas Publishing, 1983.

Raina, Dhruv. *Images and Contexts: The Historiography of Science and Modernity in India*. New Delhi: Oxford University Press, Second Impression, 2011.

———. *Needham's Indian Network: The Search for a Home for the History of Science in India (1950–1970)*. New Delhi: Yoda Press, 2015.

Raina, Dhruv and S. Irfan Habib. *Domesticating Modern Science: A Social History of Science and Culture in Colonial India*. New Delhi: Tulika, 2004.

Raj, Kapil. *Relocating Modern Science: Circulation and the Construction of Scientific Knowledge in South Asia and Europe Seventeenth to Nineteenth Century*. Delhi: Permanent Black, 2006.

Ramnath, Aparajith. *The Birth of an Indian Profession: Engineers, Industry and the State, 1900–47*. New Delhi: Oxford University Press, 2017.

Ray, Jitendranath. *Banglar Kalkarkhana O Karigari Bidyar Ihihas*. Kolkata: Dey's Publishing, 2005.

Ray, Jogesh Chandra. *Atmajebani*. Bankura: Anandakumar Roy, 2002.

Ray, Rajat K., ed. *Entrepreneurship and Industry in India, 1800–1947*. New Delhi: Oxford University Press, 1992.

———. *Industrialization in India: Growth and Conflict in the Private Corporate Sector 1914–47*. Delhi: Oxford University Press, 1979.

———. *Urban Roots of Indian Nationalism: Pressure Groups and Conflict of Interests in Calcutta City Politics, 1875–1939*. New Delhi: Vikas, 1979.

Raychaudhuri, Tapan. *Europe Reconsidered: Perceptions of the West in Nineteenth Century Bengal*. New Delhi: Oxford University Press, 1988.

———. *Perceptions, Emotions and Sensibilities: Essays on India's Colonial and Post-colonial Experiences*. New Delhi: Oxford University Press, 1999.

Reiser, Stanley. *Technological Medicine: The Changing World of Doctor and Patients*. New York: Cambridge University Press, 2009.

Rieger, Bernhard. *Technology and the Culture of Modernity in Britain and Germany, 1890–1945*. Cambridge: Cambridge University Press, 2005.

Rothermund, Dietmar. *An Economic History of India*. New York and London: Routledge, Second Edition, 2002.

———. *The Indian Economy under British Rule and Other Essays*. New Delhi: Manohar, 1983.

Roy, Biren. *Marshes to Metropolis: Calcutta (1481–1981)*. Calcutta: NCE, 1982.

Roy, Tirthankar. *The Economic History of India, 1857–1947*. New Delhi: Oxford University Press, Third Edition, 2011.

———. *Traditional Industry in the Economy of Colonial India*. Cambridge: Cambridge University Press, 1999.

Russell, Edmund. *War and Nature: Fighting Humans and Insects with Chemicals from World War I to Silent Spring*. New York: Cambridge University Press, 2001.

Samaddar, Subhas. 'Bijoli Bichitra'. In *Kolkata Kalaha-katha*. Kolkata: Sahitya Prakash, 1990.

Sarkar, Smritikumar. *Technology and Rural Change in Eastern India 1830–1980*. New Delhi: Oxford University Press, 2014.

Sarkar, Sumit. *Modern Times: India 1880s–1950s*. Ranikhet: Permanent Black, 2014.

———. *The Swadeshi Movement in Bengal 1903–1908*. Ranikhet: Permanent Black, new edn, 2010.

———. *Writing Social History*. New Delhi: Oxford University Press, 1997.

Sarkar, Suvobrata. *The Quest for Technical Knowledge: Bengal in the Nineteenth Century*. New Delhi: Manohar, 2012.

Sen, S. N. *Scientific and Technical Education in India*. New Delhi: INSA, 1991.

Sen, S. P., ed. *Directory of National Biography*. Vol. III. Calcutta: Institute of Historical Studies, 1974.

Shridharani, Krishnalal. *Story of the Indian Telegraph: A Century of Progress*. New Delhi: Post and Telegraph Department, 1953.

Singer, Charles, E. J. Holmyard, A. R. Hall, and Trevor I. Williams, eds. *A History of Technology*, Vol. V. Oxford: The Clarendon Press, 1958.

Sinha, Jagdish N. *Science, War and Imperialism: India in the Second World War*. Leiden and Boston: Brill, 2008.

Srinivasan, N. R. *History of the Indian Iron and Steel Company*. Burnpur: IISCO, 1983.

Story of Electricity in the City of Calcutta. CESC, 1979.

Summerfield, Penny, and Eric Evans, eds. *Technical Education and the State since 1850: Historical and Contemporary Perspective*. Manchester: Manchester University Press, 1990.

Tendler, Judith. *Electric Power in Brazil: Entrepreneurship in the Public Sector*. Cambridge: Harvard University Press, 1968.

Thakur, Rabindranath. 'Jiban Smriti'. In *Rabindra Rachanabali*, Vol. 11. Kolkata: Government of West Bengal, 1989.

Tomlinson, B. R. *The Economy of Modern India, 1860–1970*. Cambridge: Cambridge University Press, 1993.

Tripathi, Dwijendra. *Historical Roots of Industrial Entrepreneurship in India and Japan: A Comparative Interpretation*, New Delhi: Manohar, 1997.

Tripathi, Dwijendra, and Makranth Mehta. *Business Houses in Western India: A Study in Entrepreneurial Response, 1850–1956*. New Delhi: Manohar, 1989.

Tyabji, Nasir. *Colonialism, Chemical Technology and Industry in Southern India, 1880–1937*. Delhi: Oxford University Press, 1995.

———. *Industrialization and Innovation: The Indian Experience*. New Delhi: Sage, 2000.

Visvanathan, Shiv. *Organizing for Science: The Making of an Industrial Research Laboratory*. Delhi: Oxford University Press, 1985.

Viswakarma. *Laxmir Kripalabh Bangalir Sadhana*. Kolkata: Ananda, 1969.

Wickramasinghe, Nira. *Metallic Modern: Everyday Machines in Colonial Sri Lanka*. Oxford: Berghahn Books, 2014.

Wilkenfeld, George and Peter Spearritt. *Electrifying Sydney: 100 Years of Energy Australia*. Sydney: Energy Australia, 2004.

Zachariah, Benjamin. *Developing India: An Intellectual and Social History*. New Delhi: Oxford University Press, 2005.

Websites

http://www.theiet.org/about/libarc/archives/featured/crompton-india.cfm (accessed on 2 June 2011).

http://archives.theiet.org/detail.aspx?parentpriref=110000274 (accessed on 21 June 2012).

Index

academic engineering 36–46
Adams, R. P. 168
aerial lines 122, 158, 250
All India Council for Technical Education (AICTE) 231
All India Institute of Hygiene & Public Health of Calcutta 221
alternating current (AC) 133–4, 139–40, 250
Anderson, Warwick 7
Apprenticeship Training Scheme 48
appropriation 5, 7, 10, 13, 18–19, 198, 217, 244
Armytage, W. H. G. 11
Arnold, David 4–5, 8, 12, 117, 182
Arthik Unnoti 217
assimilation 6, 36, 198–203, 217
Association for the Advancement of Scientific and Industrial Education 197
Atkinson, E. H. deV. 33, 46, 247
Atmajebani 209
Automatic Starting Chronograph 161

Baber, Zaheer 6
Bagchi, Kishori Mohan 20
Bakshi, M. C. 102
Bally-Utterpara Electric License 138
Bandopadhyay, Pashupati 215–16
Banerjee, Gooroo Das 211
Banerjee, Surendranath 176
Basalla, George 5
Baspiya Kal O Bharatiya Railway 206
Basu, Bhupendranath 56
Basu, Jatindranath 1
Basu, Surendra Kumar 39–40
Basu, Surendra Mohan 20, 84
Behari, Bepin 252–3; manufacturing car by 211–12
Bellis Morcom Compound Steam Engine 175
Belvedere 121, 157; electric installation at 157
Bengal Chamber of Commerce 221
Bengal Chemical and Pharmaceutical Works (BCPW) 94–104, 106, 210, 249; and foreign exploitation 100; quality control in factories of 101; zinc chloride of 102
Bengal Electric Lamp Works (BELW) /Bengal Lamp 20, 84, 169–70, 172, 175, 182, 249
Bengal Engineering College (Civil Engineering College, Sibpur college) 29, 32, 35–9, 45–51, 55, 65, 92, 193, 195–6, 246–7
Bengal Iron & Steel Company (BISCO) 93, 247
Bengal National Chamber of Commerce & Industry (BNCCI) 106, 133, 221–4
Bengal National College and School (BNC) 53–5, 57–8, 248
Bengal Post-War Reconstruction Committee 250
Bengal Technical Institute (BTI) 1, 48, 52–3, 56–61, 172, 198, 202, 248
Bengal: identity of 18; partition of (1905) 51, 53, 97, 248; Swadeshi movement of 51

Bengali patriotism 18
bhadralok 9, 23, 51, 56, 164, 199, 204
Bhaduri, Chandra Bhusan 96
Bharatbarsha 98, 162, 213, 215, 218
Bhatpara Power Co 141
Bhattacharya, H. D. 131
Bhattacharya, Sabyasachi 18
'big technologies' 12–13, 18, 244–5
Bijoli 153, 219–21, 251
Biswas, Charu 63
blacksmith 204, 252
Board of Control for Apprenticeship Training 48
Bose, Amulya Charan 95
Bose, Hemendra Mohan , as H. Bose 20, 78
Bose, Jagadish Chandra 119, 211, 253
Bose, Kartik 95–96
Bose, Pramatha Nath (P. N. Bose) 1, 195, 197, 201, 255
Bose, Satyananda 63
Bose, Subhas Chandra 225–6
British electrical industry 120, 250
Browne, R. J. 135, 161
Bruhl, Paul 55, 173
Buck, E. C. (Sir) 32

caffeine manufacturing 97–8, 101–2
Calcutta Civil Engineering College, Sibpur 195
Calcutta Electric License (1907) 132
Calcutta Electric Lighting Act (1895) 121–2, 125–6, 176
Calcutta Electric Lighting Act (1899) 125
Calcutta Electric Lighting License (1901) 127–8
Calcutta Electric Supply Corporation (CESC): Five Year Plan and 51; profit of 137
Calcutta Electric Supply Corporation Ltd (CESC) 106, 118, 122–5, 127–8, 132–42, 154, 157–61, 167–8, 170, 177–81, 222, 226, 250–1
Calcutta Exhibition (1923) 190
Calcutta Improvement Trust (CIT) 135–6, 140, 160
Calcutta Medical College 32, 163, 194, 252
Calcutta Municipal Corporation 135, 157, 251
Calcutta Technical School 50, 222
Calcutta Tramway Company (CTC) 39, 123, 129–31, 164, 177, 179
Calcutta Tramways (Howrah) Act (1905) 131
Calcutta Tramways 122, 129–30; electrification of 123
Canaparo, Claudio 8
capitalism 5, 153
Cardew, P. (Maj.) 124
Cardwell, D. S. L. 3
Central Technical College in Bengal 247
Chakrabarti, Pratik 102, 199
Chakrabarty, Dipesh 9
Chakravarti, Jitendra Nath 48
Chakravarty, Sailendra Mohan 102
Chambers, David 7
Chandavarkar, Rajnarayan 82
Chandra, Pratap 193
Chatterjee, Animesh 250
Chatterjee, Elizabeth 153

chemical engineering 56, 59, 61–2, 64, 105
chemical industry 97, 99, 104, 201, 249
Chittagong Engineering & Electric Supply Co Ltd. 251
Choi, Hyungsub 18–19
Chowdhury, Surendra Narain Singha 167
Chunder, Goluk 204–5, 252
circulation 5, 7
Civil Disobedience Movement 178
Civil Engineering 20, 37, 40, 44–5, 47, 86, 173, 193, 195, 244, 247
Civil Engineering College, Roorke 30
Cleghorn, James 136–7
Coleman, Leo 16–17
College of Engineering and Technology (CET), Jadavpur (Jadavpur college) 29–30, 52, 61, 65–6, 84, 170, 248
Collin, E. W. 38
colonial Calcutta 17, 117, 142, 181, 251
colonial education system 20, 245; Mitra on 214
colonialism 3, 5, 11, 13–14, 64–5, 116, 154, 161, 206, 250
colonies 1–3, 5–7, 8, 10, 16, 143, 168, 197
Committee for the Development of Higher Engineering and Technical Education 50
consumers 18, 106–7, 125–26, 133, 136–7, 158, 166, 219, 222–3, 250
conventional technologies 12
Cooper, A. T. 115
Coopersmith, Jonathan 14
Corporation of Calcutta 59, 86–7, 124, 129, 131–2, 137–8, 159, 170, 177–9, 211, 252
Cossipore Generating Station 139, 141
cotton textile industries 81–3
Council of Industrial & Scientific Research 224
Cowan, Ruth Schwartz 18
creativity 4, 58. *See also* innovation
Crompton, REB (Col.) 120–5, 127, 250
Crompton and Co., 120, 127, 145n24
cultural nationalism 10, 53
Cumming, J. G. 34
Curzon, Lord 126

Dalhousie, Lord 205
Damodar Valley Corporation (DVC) 254
Darbyshire, Ian 6
Darjeeling, hydroelectric generating station in 121
Das Bahadur, Rai Budree 221
Das Gupta, J. K. 44, 198
Das, Alamohan 83
Das, Amar Nath 40
Das, B. M. 201
Das, Bepin Behari 211–12, 252–3
Das, Bholanath 194–5, 246
Das, C. R. 177
Das, Girish Chandra 40, 90
Das, S. R. 136
Das-Gupta, Jatin 56
Dasgupta, Satishchandra 98, 249
Dass, Banesvar 66
Datta, Narendra Nath (Swami Vivekananda) 14, 16
Datta, Surat 56
Davids, Karel 1
Dawn Magazine (*The Dawn and Dawn Society's Magazine*) 52, 198–9
Dawn Society 52–3, 198–9

Dawson, Tom S. 46, 244
deindustrialization 79, 216
Development of Technical Institutions in India 243n186. *See also* Sarkar Committee
Dewald, Erich 12, 117
Dey, B. N. 178–9, 251
Dey, Sil & Co. 119, 165–6, 176
Dhar, Jawaharlal 176, 214, 252
Dhar, Mohini Mohan 201
diffusion 5, 7–8, 10, 80
direct current (DC) 125, 128, 134–5, 139, 250; generating stations 128, 135
Directorate of Public Instruction (DPI) 39, 248
Du Boff, Richard B. 155
Duckback Process 84
Dunsheath, Percy 21
Dutt, Girindra Nath 44
Dutt, R. 198
Dutt, R. C. 35
Dutta, Jogesh Chandra 217
dynamos 119–20, 125, 158, 176

economic development 155, 195, 225, 231, 253
Eden Gardens 138, 252
Edgerton, David 13, 246
Edison System of Distribution (three wire system of distribution) 124
Edison, Thomas 253
Education Commission (1882) 31
education for industrialization 73n119
electric ceiling fans 127, 161, 177
Electric Company of Bombay 132
electric lighting 59, 119–20, 129–30, 135–6, 140, 158–9, 165; lamps 159, 169–70, 172, 178, 182
Electric Lighting Act 120
electric lights 14, 119, 121–2, 127, 153, 155–6, 158, 160–1, 164–5, 169, 176
electric power industry 154–6
Electric Supply and Traction Federation of India, The 138
Electric Supply Corporation 115, 168
electric telegraph 14, 190, 205–5, 252
Electric Telegraph ba Taritbartabaha Prakaran 236n75
electric tramways 40, 129–31, 164
electrical engineering 14, 39, 44–9, 58–60, 62–3, 65, 154–5, 169–70, 172–6, 197–8, 244, 246, 249; for Royal Air Force 174
electrical industry 133, 137, 141, 155, 165–6, 250
electrical inspector 134, 158, 161, 167
electricity 14–18, 39–41, 61, 93, 105–7, 115–29, 132–8, 140–3, 153–61, 163–70, 172–3, 175–82, 205–8, 214, 217, 219–27, 245, 249–52; in bulk supply 132–3; coal for 17; commercial generation 154; Coopersmith on 14; generating stations 107, 118, 121, 123, 128, 131, 134, 138–39, 143, 158, 164; guarantee of supply 138; and industrial development 165–72; invention in 181; and modern machines 161; private companies of 119; privatization of 16; Tagore on 165; universal acccss to 117; and urbanization 156–60
Electricity Act (1887) 117, 120, 126, 132–3, 160
Electricity Boards 180–1
electric-power plant 39

electrification 1–2, 14–17, 20, 115–18, 121, 123, 125, 142, 153–6, 163–4, 168, 175–6, 250–1; of Calcutta 2; in colonial India 16; of Eden Gardens 176, 252; process 2, 16, 116, 130, 250; rural 16, 117
Emambagh Lane 125, 128; first generating station 135, 154
engineering: education (academic engineering) 11, 30, 36, 51, 58–65, 193, 228, 253, 256; profession 11, 92; schools 6, 56. *See also* education for industrialization
engineers: British 11, 19, 88, 91–2; colonial 11, 174; mechanical 32, 37, 44, 48, 55, 197; native 11, 91
entrepreneurial training 79
entrepreneurs 41, 55, 66, 79, 84–5, 106, 218, 221, 228, 245, 251; Bengali 20–1, 79, 85, 153, 169, 221, 224; Indian 80–1, 92, 105, 174
entrepreneurship 2, 40–1, 44, 65, 79, 86, 105, 200, 219, 246
Everett, W. H. 48, 55
'everyday technologies' 12–13, 244

'factorification' 54
Fairhurst, G. H. 93
Faraday, Michael 120
fire extinguisher 98, 249
First World War 47, 49, 93, 99, 138, 164, 218, 225, 249
Fischer 176
Five-Year Plan for industrial development of Bengal 223
Fraser, Andrew (Sir) 39

Gandhi, Mahatma 203
Ganguli, Purna Chandra 48
Ganguly, Bhupen 220
gas and electricity, conflict between 159
gas-filled lamps 170
Geological Survey of India (GSI) 196
Ghatak Iron Works 190
Ghatak, Jagadishwar 190
Ghatak, Umapati 190
Ghose, Behary Lall 193–4
Ghose, Jogendra Chandra 197, 208–11, 217
Ghose, Rashbehari 198
Ghosh, Amitabha 204
Ghosh, Hemendra Prasad 164
Ghosh, Motilal 192
Ghosh, Pratap Chandra 193
Ghosh, Rashbehari 215
Ghosh, Siddhartha 260
Ghosh, Sisir 192
Ghosh, Sitanath 207–8, 252
Gillespie, Richard 7
Glass, J. W. H. 122
Global South 101, 244
Goel, R. C. 11
Government Commercial Institute 222
Goyal, Piyush 17
Graham, William 124
Guha, Bires Chandra 101
Guha, Ranajit 204
Gupta, Akhil 115, 249–50
Gupta, B. C. 48
Gupta, G. N. 34
Gupta, Hem Chandra Das 57, 60

hand-pulled *punkah* (fan) 127. *See also* electric ceiling fan
Haque, Khan Bahadur M. Azizul 29

Hausman, William J. 116, 142
Heaton, B. 46
Herbert, John (Sir) 141
Hertner, Peter 116
higher educational institutions 29, 52, 79
Hindu Mela 207
Hindu Patrika 207
History of Electricity (Electrification) 14–17, 154
History of Hindu Chemistry, A 200
History of Hindu Civilization during British Rule, A 196
Homan, Eileen 139, 141
Homan, F. T. 139
Hooghly River Electric License (1907) 132
'House of Unknown Fame' 204, 211, 253
Howrah Bridge 121, 131, 176, 252
Howrah Bridge Electrical Lighting Act 121
Howrah–Amta Tramways 90
Hughes, Thomas P. 14, 116, 155, 172
human capital 143, 172, 174, 245
Hussain, Nazia 15
Hydro-Electric Survey of India 169, 181

Imperial Chemicals 102
India Cotton Looms 83–4
Indian Association for the Cultivation of Science (IACS) 52–3, 192, 194
Indian Electric Co. Ltd 122, 154
Indian Electric Light Company 119, 161
Indian Electricity (Amendment) Act (1959) 133
Indian Electricity Act (1903) 132
Indian Electricity Bill (1909) 133
Indian Electricity Act (1910) 132–3, 160
Indian Engineering Congress, Calcutta (1987) 11
Indian Famine Commission (1880) 31
Indian Industrial Association 197
Indian Industrial Commission 47, 65, 91, 104, 168, 174, 215
Indian Industrial Exhibition (1906) 128
Indian Institute of Technology (IIT), Kharagpur 22
Indian Institute of Technology (IITs) 22, 229–30, 255–6
Indian Iron & Steel Company (IISCO) 93, 247
Indian Medical Congress, Calcutta 97
Indian Nationalism 191, 204, 250
Indian School of Mines, Dhanbad 49
Indianization 11, 91, 181, 252
indigenization of electrical technology 143
industrial chemistry 58–9, 65; training in 42
Industrial Commission 47, 65, 91, 104, 168, 174, 215
industrial India 66, 199
Industrial Research Planning Committee (1944) 224
industrial: policy 1, 224; revolution 83, 205, 225, 253; technology 4, 215
industrialization 35, 47, 51–5, 58–66, 78, 80–2, 91–2, 94, 104–5, 153–5, 198–9, 201, 223–7, 230–1, 253–4
industries, trends in 79–81
innovation 14, 78–9, 83, 87, 96, 98, 104, 165, 244; technological 6, 11, 79, 84, 205–7, 217

Institution of Engineers (India) IEI 11, 91
institutionalization 64, 231, 254
intelligentsia 56, 199, 248
International Exposition of Electric Lighting, Paris 120
Irfan Habib, S. 6, 30

Jacob, H. T. D. 162
Jadavpur College 62–4, 175, 230, 248–9
John Fleming & Co., Messrs 132
Johnston, R. H. G. 142
Journal of the College of Engineering and Technology 60–1
jute 133–4, 190
jute industries 83

Kale, Sunila 115, 117
Kar, Radha Gobinda 95
Kar, Upendranath 39
Karigar Darpana 194
Khaitan, D. P. 211
knowledge: generation 8, 13, 30; local 6, 8, 213; modern 3, 5, 199; scientific 19, 52, 208, 210; technical 10, 35, 64, 106, 199, 210, 214, 245; technological 5, 7, 213; techno-scientific 6–9, 12, 14, 19, 51–2, 191–2, 198, 217, 226, 253; traditional 4, 6, 9, 255; Western 9, 13
Krishnaswami Rao, K. 35
Kumar, Deepak 6, 11
Kumar, Prakash 3

Lall, Behary 194
Lansdowne, Lord 88
lanterns 159, 169
Leslie, Bradford 86
liberal education 54–5
Life and Experiences of a Bengali Chemist 111–12n75
Light Railway 89–90
'locality' 7, 153, 218; approach by Gillespie 7–8; and Korean meaning of localizing 19
London Electric Lighting Provisional Order (1890) 124
Luke, P. V. 137

MacDonnell, A. P. 31
Mackenzie, Lady 157
Macleod, Roy 6
Madras 15, 47, 105, 127, 162, 164, 170, 181; Cauvery Falls in 39; colleges at 31; rural electrification in 16
Madras Electric Supply Company 127
Madras Tramway 127
magnetic healer 208, 252
Mahajanbandhu 216
Majumdar, Madhumita 10
Majumdar, P. K. 10
Majumdar, Satyabrata61
Malaviya, Madan Mohan 211
Mallick, Sambit 52
Mallik, S. K. 29
Manjapra, Kris 58
Mann, Michael 80
Maples, J. R. 129
Martin & Co. 20, 40, 49, 89–90, 93, 105, 247
Martin Burn & Co. 105
Martin, Acquin 88, 92, 105, 247
Massachusetts Institute of Technology (MIT) 12, 230
Meares, J. W. 169, 173
Meares, John Willough 145–6n30

mechanical engineering 37, 41, 44–6, 48–49, 55, 57–9, 61, 63, 173, 192–3, 247
Messrs Kilburn & Co. 119, 122, 124–6, 129, 158
Meston, Lord 115
metallurgy 49, 200
mining engineering 20, 33, 38–9, 62, 65, 173, 195
'mistrification' 54, 57, 62
Mitra, Anukul Chandra 40, 90
Mitra, Benimadhab 40
Mitra, Umeshchandra 214
modern: industrialism 202–3; machinery 130; technology 1, 4, 19, 21, 81–2, 143, 181–2, 190–1, 201, 213, 217, 221, 224
modernity 3, 8–9, 11, 18, 117, 131, 153, 181, 199, 206; Arnold and 8–9; Bengali Ayurvedic 9; Chakrabarty on 9; vernacularization of 18–19
modernization 18, 30, 53, 84, 115, 173, 250
Mohan, Jotindra 156
Moitra, Kalidas 206, 252
Moncrieff, Scott 124
Mondy, E. F. 37
Mookerjee Committee 48
Mookerjee, Asutosh (Sir) 57, 254–5
Mookerjee, Bhutnath 87
Mookerjee, R. N. (Sir) 20–21, 40, 48, 56, 65, 85–3, 105, 244, 247
Mookerjee, Syama Prasad 78, 255
Morris, Morris D. 81
Mukherjee, Aditya 221
Mukherjee, Radha Kumud 57
Mukherjee, Satish Chandra 29, 52, 198
Mukherjee, Trailokya Nath 197
Mukherji, Projit 9
Mulajore Generating Station 117, 141

Nandi, K. C. 197
Nath, Jogendra 197
Nath, Mahendra 14
Nath, Pramatha 196–7, 201–3
Nathan, R. 33
National Council of Education (NCE) 52–9, 63–6, 105, 175, 199–200, 248, 253
National Medical College of India 29
National Planning Committee (NPC) 180, 226–8, 252
National Policy on Power 180
National Society 207
National Tannery and Government Tanning Research Institute 201
nationalism 11, 18, 35, 54, 66, 181, 196, 199, 224, 247; economic 84; of middle-class 10; technocratic 84
native knowledge systems 3, 143
Nehru, Jawaharlal 180, 225–6
Nehru, Motilal 211
Networks of Power (1983) 14
Nixon & Co, Messrs 132
'Notes on the Geology and Mineral Resources of Mayurbhanj' 201
Nundy, Shiv Chunder 205, 252
Nye, David E. 155

O'Shaughnessy, W. B. 119, 205–6, 252
Orange, H. W. 33
Oriental Gas Company 135, 157, 159, 176–7
overhead wires, cables 124, 131, 158, 250

Pacey, Arnold 6
Palit, Tarak Nath 56–7
Pandya, A. H. 49
Panihati factory 100, 102
patent system 5
Paul, Bhutnath 95
Pedler, Alexander (Sir) 37
Phalkey, Jahnavi 10
polytechnic 194, 227
power company 122, 124, 132, 134, 137, 158, 160, 167, 249–50
power generation and supply. *See under* electricity; power
power: and fuel 180, 226; industry 14, 142; supply 1, 81, 120, 153, 160, 167, 180–1, 226, 250; theft 133
Prabasi 239n119
Prakash, Gyan 9
Presidency College 32, 36–7, 84, 86, 94, 195, 225, 248
presidency towns 105
privatization 17
Public Works Department (PWD) 32, 86, 247
Purnima Debi 153

Rahman, F. 49
Railway electrification 164
Raina, Dhruv 6, 10, 30, 56, 199–200
Raj, Kapil 7
Rakshit, Nagendra Nath 55
Raman, C. V. 211
Ramnath, Aparajith 11, 91
Ray, Acharya 100, 103–4
Ray, B.C. 102
Ray, Jogesh Chandra 208–10, 214, 253
Ray, Prafulla Chandra (Sir) 20–1, 59, 66, 84–5, 95–106, 172, 200, 211, 225, 248, 255; producing citric acid 94
Ray, Rajat K. 93, 179
Report of the Famine Commission 20
Reynolds, C. H. 124, 158
rice-mill 190
Roberts, Lissa 8
Rontgen X-rays 162–3
Rontgen, Wilhelm 162
Rothermund, Dietmar 80
Roy, A. K. 130
Roy, A. L. 207
Roy, B. C. 101, 169, 251
Roy, H. L. 59, 66, 182
Roy, Hemen 170, 249
Roy, Kiran 20, 84, 170, 249
Roy, P. C. 198
Roy, Ramanath 169
Roy, S. K. 60, 66, 182
Roy, Sadhan Chandra 169
Roy, Subodh Chandra 169
Roy, Suren 20, 59, 84, 170, 249
Roy, Tirthankar 80, 83
Royal Astronomical Society 208
Royal Microscopical Society 208
Rurup, Reinhard 3

Saha, Meghnad 180, 225–8, 244, 254
Saha, Shrish 102
Sarkar Committee 22, 229, 255
Sarkar, Aannada Prosad 40
Sarkar, Benoy Kumar 54–58, 63–4, 175, 217, 230, 253
Sarkar, Chandrasekhar 218
Sarkar, Nalini Ranjan 228–9, 231, 254–5
Sarkar, Nilratan 56, 95
Sarkar, Smritikumar 12

Sarkar, Sumit 51
Schwendler, Carl Louis 119, 176
Science and Culture 180, 225–6, 228, 251, 254
scientific education 34, 56, 61, 192, 195, 197
Second World War 2, 49–50, 62, 102, 141, 223, 227–8
Secord, James 5
self-reliance 83, 215, 228
Sen, Debendra Nath 86
Sen, Dinanath 192–3, 247
Sen, G. C. 197–8
Sen, Gopal 56
Sen, Rajendra Nath 43
Sen, Triguna 63, 6
Sengupta, Nirmal K. 61
Shah, K. T. 226
Shavaksha, Sarabji 37
Shibpur College Patrika 40
Shillong Hydro-electric Ltd 169, 251
Sibpur college. *See* Bengal Engineering College
Siddiqi, Asif A. 13
Sir Prafulla Chandra Research Laboratory 101, 103
Sircar, Baboo Nolin Bihari 129
Sircar, Mahendra Lal 52, 192
Slater, J. S. 39
small-scale industry, Roy on 83
Smith, George 204
Social Construction of Technology (SCOT) 18–19
Society for the History of Technology (SHOT), America 4
Society for the Promotion of Technical Education (SPTE) 53–4, 56, 58
software, Karel Davids on 1
South Asia 3–4, 8, 13–15, 64, 115, 203, 244; electricity in 14–17
South Indian Science Association 92
Southern Generating Station 139–40
Spring, F. J. E. 38
Spring, Francis 32
Srinivasa Rao, Y. 16
Staudenmaier, John M. 4
Street-lighting 135, 140, 157–9, 221, 251
Subaltern Studies 204
subaltern technologists 23, 203–12, 231, 253
sulphuric acid 95–7, 99–100, 105
supply of electricity in bulk 132
Swadeshi Motor Car 212
swadeshi: industrialization 53, 55, 217, 239n122; movement in Bengal 30, 97, 218, 248
Swaraj Party 177
Swaraj, technological 224–30
Swastha Prasanga 102
syllabus Revision Committee 59

Tagore, Jotindra Mohan 136, 156
Tagore, Rabindranath 156, 164–5, 211, 219
Tata Iron and Steel Company (TISCO) 11, 82, 93, 143, 201–2, 222
Tata, J. N. 82, 201–2
Technical Institute of Calcutta 45
Technical School at Kanchrapara 48
technical: education 1–2, 6, 9–12, 20, 29–32, 35–6, 38, 45–7, 50–8, 64, 92, 194–9, 202, 210, 227, 229–31, 245–6, 255; institutions 45–6, 53, 56, 59, 64, 104, 106, 192, 196, 201, 226, 229, 255

techno-coolies 258n22
'technocratization' 57, 62
technological education 20, 31–6, 202; Spring on 32
technological System 138, 182, 251
technology 3, 6, 81–5, 115, 118, 191–8, 212–13, 215; Cardwell on history of 3; history of 1, 3–6, 12–13, 17–18, 29, 154, 190, 196, 212, 244; Prakash Kumar on 3; Rurup on 3; Sarkar on 12–13; social fashioning of 12, 117; transfer of 1, 154
technomodernities 8–9
technoscience 2, 3, 7–8, 19, 23, 30, 47, 49, 52, 193, 196, 198–201, 211, 248, 252, 254; policy on 228; skill development in 54; training in 21, 81, 215
techno-scientific: education 10, 30, 53–4, 58, 191, 196, 199, 201–3, 248; ideas 18, 40
Temple, Richard 192
Tendler, Judith 155
Thakur, Debendranath 207
Thakur, Khitindranath 164
thermal power 120, 122, 127, 135, 142, 154, 168–9
Thomason College, Roorkee 33, 47
Tomlinson, B. R. 80
tramcars 40, 129, 164; as mass transport 131
tramways 115, 129, 164, 173
transmission 8–11, 40, 44, 64, 142, 155, 191
Tripathi, Dwijendra 82

underground cables 122, 136, 158–9, 250
Underground Tunnel, under River Hooghly 139
University of Calcutta 47, 49, 51, 57, 173–4, 194, 211, 215, 254–5
urbanization 15, 156, 177

V. B. System 159
vacuum lamps 170
Victoria House 141, 151n134
Victoria Jubilee Technological Institute (1888) 81
Victoria Memorial 40, 90–1, 127–8, 247
Viswakarma 194, 204
vitamin products 100–1
Vivekananda, Swami. *See* Dutta, Narendra Nath

Watt, James 253
Western industrialism 53, 199, 203
Wilkins, Mira 116
World Wars and electricity Industry 141. *See also as separate entries*
workshop 48, 53, 62–5, 92, 98–9, 167, 177, 192

X-ray photograph, as first in India 162, *see also* Rontgen X-rays

Zakarian, A. K. M. 179
zamindars 56, 192